T0265704

CHILDREN
OF THE
HOUSE OF CLEVES

CHILDREN
OF THE
HOUSE OF CLEVES

ANNA AND HER SIBLINGS

HEATHER R. DARSIE

AMBERLEY

First published 2023

Amberley Publishing
The Hill, Stroud
Gloucestershire, GL5 4EP

www.amberley-books.com

British Library Cataloguing in Publication Data.
A catalogue record for this book is available from the British Library.

ISBN 978 1 4456 9942 4 (hardback)
ISBN 978 1 4456 9943 1 (ebook)

1 2 3 4 5 6 7 8 9 10

Typeset in 10pt on 12.5pt Sabon.
Typesetting by SJmagic DESIGN SERVICES, India.
Printed in the UK.

Back in May 2019, after the release of *Anna, Duchess of Cleves: The King's 'Beloved Sister'*, my only uncle, Hugh Darsie, asked how he could be mentioned in my next book. When I first received word that the proposal for *Children of the House of Cleves* was accepted, I told Uncle Hugh that I would dedicate the book to him. In the interim, we learned on Christmas Eve, 24 December 2019, that my father, Hugh's brother, had advanced oesophageal cancer. My father passed away on Good Friday, 10 April 2020. For the first time in 114 years, there is only one person in my family alive who is named Burns. As I write this, it is a mere twelve days since my father's passing, 22 April 2020. My world has forever changed.

To that end, I dedicate this book to all the Darsie men I have had the pleasure of meeting. Cheers to you Burns 'Buddy' Darsie, Jr.; Hugh Harold Darsie; my much-missed father Burns Darsie III, and my beloved brother Burns Darsie IV.

Contents

Acknowledgements

First and foremost, I would like to thank the reader for granting me and the persons discussed in this book your time and attention. I have spent the last ten or more years of my life dedicated to researching first Anna of Cleves, and now her brother and sisters. I am delighted to bring you *Children of the House of Cleves: Anna and Her Siblings*, and hope that it brings these important historical individuals to life.

I would like to thank the following PhDs whose courses I took during my Master of Arts program through Northern Illinois University. In alphabetical order, thank you to Drs H. Fehrenbach, V. Garver, A. Hanley, B. Hoffman, I. Montana and B. Sandberg. Thank you also to Drs A. Bruno and S. Farrell for their assistance in guiding my academic career during my time in the History Department.

Thank you to Melanie V. Taylor, whose stamina for listening to my musings on Anna of Cleves and her family knows no bounds. Thank you to Rebecca Larson of *Tudors Dynasty*, who has expanded my thinking and pushed me to think more critically in some areas. Thank you to Chris and Kelly Engler, who read drafts of this work and provided valuable feedback.

A special thank you to Shaun Barrington, my patient editor, and the creative team at Amberley Publishing.

As always, thank you to my dear husband Kris Piereth, who learned far more about sixteenth-century Germany than he ever imagined he would.

It is very humbling to realise what an army of people I have behind me, encouraging me along my journey. I couldn't be who I am without you.

Family Trees

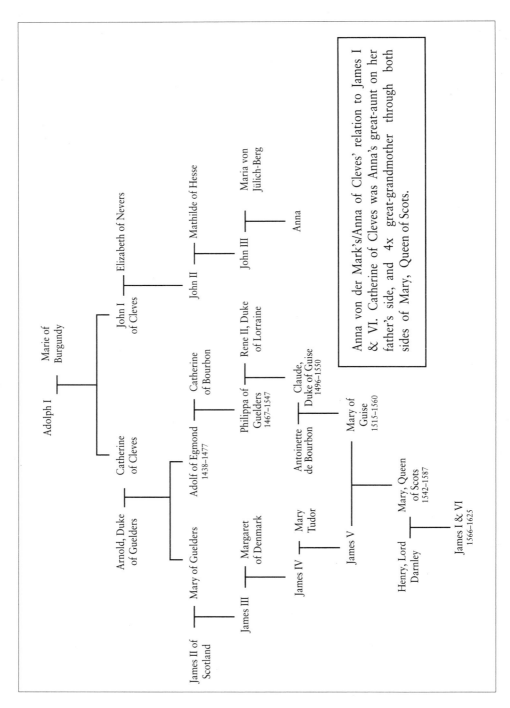

Adolph I — Marie of Burgundy

John I of Cleves — Elizabeth of Nevers

John II — Mathilde of Hesse

John III — Maria von Jülich-Berg

Anna

Catherine of Cleves

Arnold, Duke of Guelders — Catherine of Cleves

Adolf of Egmond 1438–1477 — Catherine of Bourbon

Philippa of Guelders 1467–1547 — Rene II, Duke of Lorraine

Claude, Duke of Guise 1496–1550 — Antoinette de Bourbon

Mary of Guise 1515–1560

Mary of Guelders — James II of Scotland

James III — Margaret of Denmark

James IV — Mary Tudor

James V

Mary, Queen of Scots 1542–1587 — Henry, Lord Darnley

James I & VI 1566–1625

Anna von der Mark's/Anna of Cleves' relation to James I & VI. Catherine of Cleves was Anna's great-aunt on her father's side, and 4x great-grandmother through both sides of Mary, Queen of Scots.

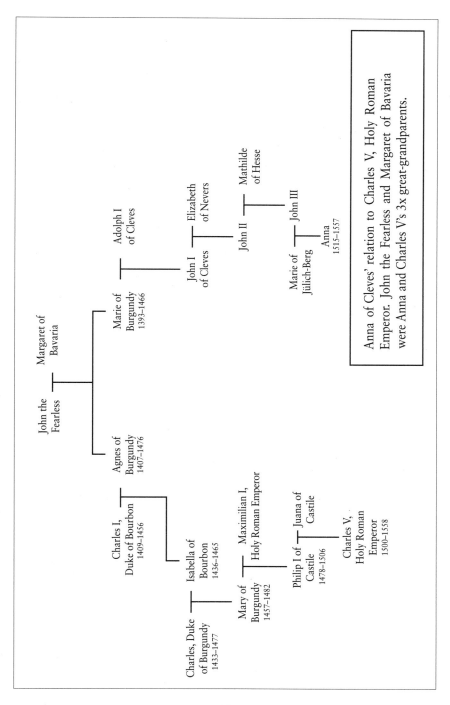

Anna of Cleves' relation to Charles V, Holy Roman Emperor. John the Fearless and Margaret of Bavaria were Anna and Charles V's 3x great-grandparents.

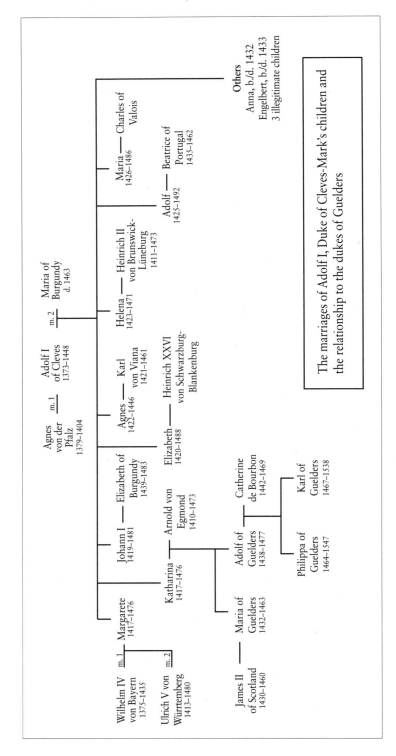

The marriages of Adolf I, Duke of Cleves-Mark's children and the relationship to the dukes of Guelders

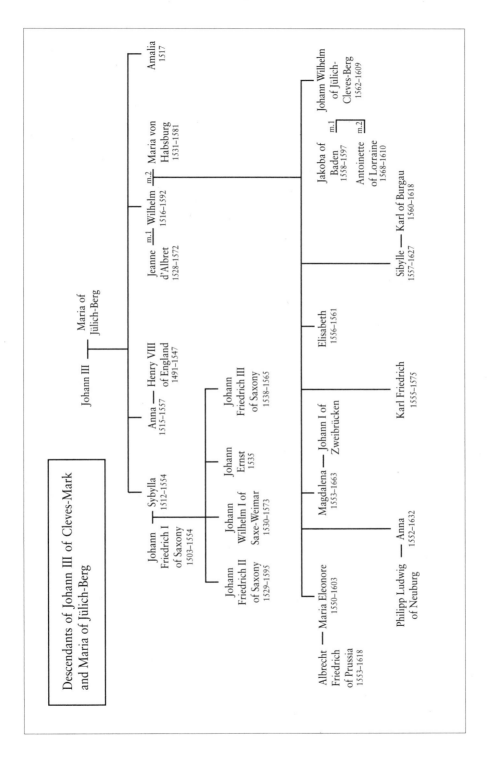

Descendants of Johann III of Cleves-Mark and Maria of Jülich-Berg

Johann III — Maria of Jülich-Berg

Johann Friedrich I of Saxony 1503–1554 — Sybilla 1512–1554

Anna 1515–1557 — Henry VIII of England 1491–1547

Jeanne d'Albret 1528–1572 — m.1 Wilhelm 1516–1592 m.2 — Maria von Habsburg 1531–1581

Amalia 1517

Johann Friedrich II of Saxony 1529–1595

Johann Wilhelm I of Saxe-Weimar 1530–1573

Johann Ernst 1535

Johann Friedrich III of Saxony 1538–1565

Magdalena 1553–1663 — Johann I of Zweibrücken

Elisabeth 1556–1561

Johann Wilhelm of Jülich-Cleves-Berg 1562–1609

Jakoba of Baden 1558–1597 — m.1 | m.2 — Antoinette of Lorraine 1568–1610

Albrecht Friedrich of Prussia 1553–1618 — Maria Eleonore 1550–1603

Philipp Ludwig of Neuburg — Anna 1552–1632

Karl Friedrich 1555–1575

Sibylle 1557–1627 — Karl of Burgau 1560–1618

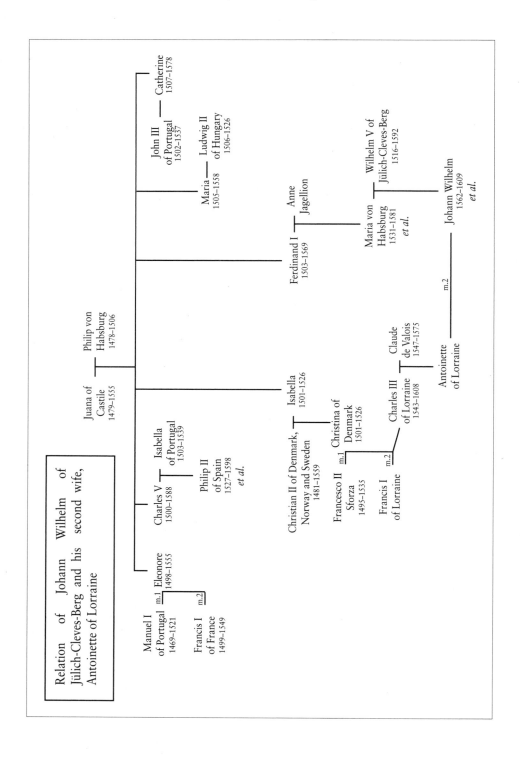

Relation of Johann Wilhelm of Jülich-Cleves-Berg and his second wife, Antoinette of Lorraine

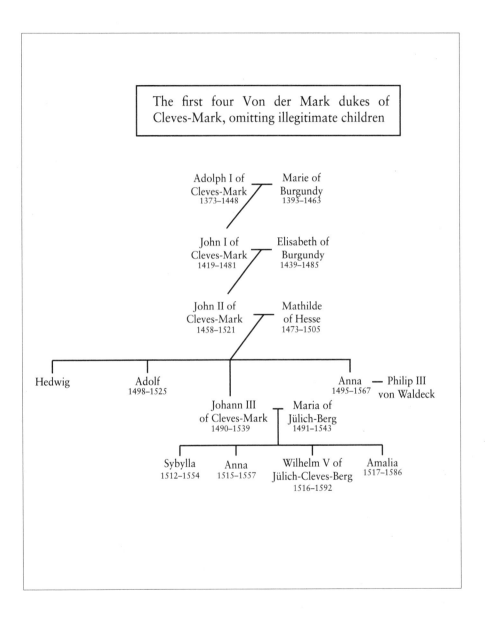

The first four Von der Mark dukes of Cleves-Mark, omitting illegitimate children

Adolph I of Cleves-Mark 1373–1448 — Marie of Burgundy 1393–1463

John I of Cleves-Mark 1419–1481 — Elisabeth of Burgundy 1439–1485

John II of Cleves-Mark 1458–1521 — Mathilde of Hesse 1473–1505

Hedwig

Adolf 1498–1525

Anna 1495–1567 — Philip III von Waldeck

Johann III of Cleves-Mark 1490–1539 — Maria of Jülich-Berg 1491–1543

Sybylla 1512–1554

Anna 1515–1557

Wilhelm V of Jülich-Cleves-Berg 1516–1592

Amalia 1517–1586

Note on Names of Persons and Places

For this work, I have used the special German character of 'ü' in place names where appropriate, such as in 'Düsseldorf'. For the most part, I use the German names of places with a few exceptions, such as Brunswick/Braunschweig, Nuremberg/Nürnberg, and Munich/München.

For Anna of Cleves, her parents, her siblings, and their spouses, I have used their proper German names. I use a mixture of proper German and anglicized names for Anna's nephews because she had two pairs of nephews with the same name. Several Tables of Important Persons follow this note to aid the reader in keeping them separate. The tables are specific to the United Duchies of Jülich-Cleves-Berg, the Holy Roman Empire, Saxony and England. Anna and her family are mostly known to English speakers because of Anna's time in England. I thought it would be helpful to have a basic description of the persons encountered in this book to which the reader could refer, especially because of my penchant for using the person's true, German name. As a *nota bene*, the Von der Marks had a habit of naming their children after their relatives, too, which can be confusing regardless of how familiar one is with their family history.

The Tables of Important Persons are listed alphabetically.

Table of Important Persons: Jülich-Cleves-Berg

Amalia von der Mark (b. 1517, d. 1586) – Known as Amalia of Cleves, fourth child, third daughter and youngest of the Von der Mark children, Hereditary Duchess of Jülich-Cleves-Berg, was considered along with her sister Anna of Cleves as a possible bride for Henry VIII of England

Anna von der Mark (b. 1515, d. 1557) – Known as Anna of Cleves, second child and second daughter of the Von der Mark children, Hereditary Duchess of Jülich-Cleves-Berg, Queen Consort of England from January 1540 to July 1540, known to English speakers as Anne of Cleves

Anne of Jülich-Cleves-Berg (b. 1552, d. 1632) – Second child and second daughter of Wilhelm von der Mark and Maria von Habsburg of Austria, her descendants would later struggle over the fate of Jülich-Cleves-Berg during the Thirty Years War

Antoinette of Lorraine (b. 1568, d. 1610) – Second wife of Johann Wilhelm of Jülich-Cleves-Berg, granddaughter of Christina of Denmark, great-granddaughter of Isabella von Habsburg

Elisabeth of Cleves (b.?, d.?) – Known illegitimate daughter of John II or Johann III von der Mark

Elisabeth of Jülich-Cleves-Berg (b. 1556, d. 1561) – Fifth child and fourth daughter of Wilhelm von der Mark and Maria von Habsburg of Austria, died in childhood

Ernst of Bavaria (b. 1554, d. 1612) – Elector-Archbishop of Cologne beginning in the 1580s, his election was supported by Wilhelm V von der Mark

Children of the House of Cleves

Francis I of France (b. 1494, d. 1547) – King of France, usually an enemy of the Holy Roman Empire, sometimes friendly with England, had short alliance with the United Duchies of Jülich-Cleves-Berg, uncle of Jeanne d'Albret

Franz von Waldeck (b. 1526, d. 1574) – Cousin of Anna of Cleves through her paternal aunt, also named Anna; accompanied Anna to England, later married a relative of Johann Ghogreff

Gerhard von Jülich – Personal secretary to Wilhelm V von der Mark and possible maternal cousin of unknown parentage

Heinrich Barr (b. before 1500, d. 1575) – Known as Oligschläger and anglicized to Olisleger; Vice Chancellor of Cleves from 1534 to 1546 or 1547, Chancellor of Cleves from 1546 or 1547 to his death; married Elisabeth of Cleves's granddaughter

Jakoba von Baden (b. 1558, d. 1597) – First wife of Johann Wilhelm of Jülich-Cleves-Berg, died under suspicious circumstances

Jeanne d'Albret (b. 1528, d. 1572) – Niece of Francis I of France, first wife of Wilhelm von der Mark

John, the Bastard of Cleves – Illegitimate son of John II of Cleves-Mark, made military career for himself

John of Berg – Illegitimate son of Duke Wilhelm V von der Mark

Johann Ghogreff (b. 1499, d. 1554) – Chancellor of Cleves and Jülich-Berg from 1530 to 1546/7

John of Jülich – Illegitimate son of William III of Jülich-Berg; Anna of Cleves' maternal half-uncle

Johann of Jülich – Son of John of Jülich, accompanied Anna of Cleves to England

John I von der Mark (b. 1419, d. 1481) – Duke of Cleves-Mark, paternal great-grandfather of the Von der Mark siblings

John II von der Mark (b. 1458, d. 1521) – Duke of Cleves-Mark, paternal grandfather of the Von der Mark siblings

Johann III von der Mark (b. 1490, d. 1539) – Duke of Jülich-Cleves-Berg, father of the Von der Mark siblings

Johann Wilhelm of Jülich-Cleves-Berg (b. 1562, d. 1609) – Second son of Duke Wilhelm V von der Mark and Maria von Habsburg of Austria; later Bishop of Münster, then Duke Johann Wilhelm I of Jülich-Cleves-Berg, last of the Von der Mark dukes

Karl Friedrich of Jülich-Cleves-Berg (b. 1555, d. 1575) – First son of Duke Wilhelm V von der Mark and Maria von Habsburg of Austria, heir at birth to the United Duchies of Jülich-Cleves-Berg

Karl Harst (b. 1492, d. 1563) – Ambassador to the English court during Anna of Cleves' marriage and afterward

Konrad Heresbach (b. 1496, d. 1576) – Wilhelm V's tutor, and later tutor for Wilhelm's sons; humanist and politician

Maarten van Rossum (b. 1478, d. 1555) – Military leader from Guelders, led Wilhelm V's armies during the Cleves War; personal motto was, 'Smoking and burning are the ornaments of war'

Magdalena of Jülich-Cleves-Berg (b. 1553, d. 1633) – Third child and third daughter of Wilhelm von der Mark and Maria von Habsburg of Austria; her descendants would later struggle over the fate of Jülich-Cleves-Berg during the Thirty Years War

Marguerite d'Angoulême (b. 1492, d. 1549) – Sister of Francis I of France, Queen Consort of Navarre, mother of Jeanne d'Albret

Maria of Burgundy (b. 1393, d. 1463) – Daughter of John the Fearless, wife of Duke Adolf of Cleves-Mark, credited with founding religious houses in Cleves-Mark and bringing Burgundian culture to Cleves-Mark

Maria von Jülich-Berg (b. 1491, d. 1543)– Hereditary Duchess of Jülich-Berg, mother of the Von der Mark siblings

Maria von Habsburg of Austria (b. 1531, d. 1581) – Daughter of Holy Roman Emperor Ferdinand I, hereditary Archduchess of Austria, second wife of Wilhelm V, and mother of his legitimate children

Maria Eleonore of Jülich-Cleves-Berg (b. 1550, d. 1608) – First child and first daughter of Wilhelm von der Mark and Maria von Habsburg of Austria; her descendants struggled with those of her sisters over the fate of Jülich-Cleves-Berg during the Thirty Years War

Phillip Eberhard of Cleves-Mark, Lord of Ravenstein (b. 1456, d. 1528) – Served Charles the Bold, Maria of Burgundy, and Holy Roman Emperor Maximilian I

Sibylle of Brandenburg (b. 1467, d. 1524) – Second wife of William von Jülich, mother of Maria von Jülich-Berg; daughter of the powerful Elector Albrecht Achilles of Brandenburg

Sibylle of Jülich-Cleves-Berg (b. 1557, d. 1627/1628) – Youngest daughter and youngest child of Wilhelm von der Mark and Maria von Habsburg of Austria, stayed on at court in Jülich-Cleves-Berg until her marriage in 1601

Sybylla von der Mark (b. 1512, d. 1554) – Known as Sybylla of Cleves, first child of the Von der Mark children; Hereditary Duchess of Jülich-Cleves-Berg; Electress Consort of Saxony, wife of Johann Friedrich von Wettin

Stephanus Pighius (b. 1520, d. 1604) – Tutor for Karl Friedrich of Jülich-Cleves-Berg; accompanied him to Rome, wrote *Hercules Prodicius* about how he tutored Karl Friedrich, dedicated the work to Johann Wilhelm when it was printed in 1587

Werner von Gymnich (b. ?, d. 1582) – Court Master of Cleves, accompanied Karl Friedrich to Rome

Wilhelm V von der Mark (b. 1517, d. 1592) – Known as Wilhelm of Cleves, third child and only boy of the Von der Mark children, later Duke Wilhelm V of Jülich-Cleves-Berg; known as Wilhelm the Rich

William von Jülich-Berg (b. 1455, d. 1511) – Duke of Jülich-Berg, father of Maria von Jülich-Berg, and father of the illegitimate John of Jülich; Anna of Cleves' maternal grandfather

Table of Important Persons: Holy Roman Empire

Anne of Bohemia and Hungary (b. 1503, d. 1547) – Daughter of Vladislaus II of Hungary, wife of Ferdinand von Habsburg; the couple had fifteen children, of which ten girls and three boys survived to adulthood

Catherine von Habsburg (b. 1507, d. 1578) – Sixth child and fourth daughter of Juana of Castile and Philip von Habsburg of Burgundy, married her cousin John III of Portugal

Charles von Habsburg (b. 1500, d. 1558) – Second child and first son of Juana of Castile and Philip von Habsburg of Burgundy, known as the Handsome; Holy Roman Emperor as Charles V, King Charles I of Spain, Archduke of Austria

Eleonore von Habsburg (b. 1498, d. 1558) – First child and first daughter of Juana of Castile and Philip von Habsburg, known as the Handsome; Queen Consort of Portugal to Manuel I, then Queen Consort of France to Francis I, Hereditary Archduchess of Austria

Ferdinand von Habsburg (b. 1503, d. 1564) – Fourth child and second son of Juana of Castile and Philip von Habsburg of Burgundy, known as the Handsome; King of the Bohemians, King of the Romans/Germans, Holy Roman Emperor as Ferdinand I, Archduke of Austria

Isabella von Habsburg (b. 1501, d. 1526) – Third child and second daughter of Philip von Habsburg and Juana of Castile. Wife of Christian II of Denmark, mother of Christina of Denmark and Dorothea of Denmark

Isabella of Portugal (b. 1503, d. 1539) – Daughter of Manuel I of Portugal and Maria of Aragon, wife of her cousin Charles von Habsburg; mother of Philip II of Spain, Holy Roman Empress Maria, and Joanna, Princess of Portugal; Charles was devastated by her early death

Ludwig II of Bohemia and Hungary (b. 1506, d. 1526) – Husband of Maria von Habsburg, died young at the Battle of Mohacs in 1526, was adopted by Holy Roman Emperor Maximilian I after the death of Ludwig's father

Maria von Habsburg, Queen of Hungary (b. 1505, d. 1558) – Fifth child and third daughter of Juana of Castile and Philip von Habsburg of Burgundy, known as the Handsome; Regent of the Netherlands for her brother Charles von Habsburg; married Ludwig II of Bohemia and Hungary, sister-in-law to Anne of Bohemia and Hungary

Mary of Burgundy (b. 1457, d. 1582) – Hereditary Duchess of Burgundy, married Maximilian von Habsburg, future Holy Roman Emperor Maximilian I, mother of Philip von Habsburg and Margaret von Habsburg; had hereditary claim to Duchy of Guelders, Maximilian greatly expanded his family's territory *jure uxoris*, by right of his marriage to Maria

Margaret von Habsburg, Duchess of Savoy (b. 1480, d. 1530) – Daughter of Maria of Burgundy and Maximilian von Habsburg; married and widowed twice by the age of twenty-four, she became the Regent of the Low Countries for her father in 1507 until her death in 1530

Maximilian I von Habsburg (b. 1459, d. 1519) – Holy Roman Emperor Maximilian I, father of Philip von Habsburg, grandfather of Charles V

Maximilian II von Habsburg (b. 1527, d. 1576) – Son of Ferdinand I; became Holy Roman Emperor after Ferdinand's death

Philip von Habsburg – Husband of Juana of Castile, son of Maximilian I, father of Charles V, King Philip I of Castile and Leon

Rudolf II von Habsburg – Grandson of Ferdinand I through Maximilian II; Holy Roman Emperor, died without legitimate issue, invited Karl Friedrich to the Imperial court

Table of Important Persons: Saxony

Frederick von Wettin (b. 1463, d. 1525) – Elector of Saxony and Landgrave of Thuringia, known as the Wise, uncle of Johann Friedrich, protector of Martin Luther

George von Wettin (b. 1471, d. 1539) – Duke of Albertine Saxony, Margrave of Meissen, known as the Bearded; a Catholic

Heinrich von Wettin (b. 1473, d. 1541) – Brother of George the Bearded, known as the Pious; a Catholic; father of Moritz von Wettin

Johann Friedrich von Wettin (b. 1503, d. 1554) – Elector of Saxony, known as the Magnanimous, husband of Sybylla von der Mark, founder of the Schmalkaldic League, supporter of Martin Luther

John von Wettin (b. 1468, d. 1532) – Elector of Saxony, known as the Constant; father of Johann Friedrich von Wettin, supporter of Martin Luther

John Ernest von Wettin (b. and d. 1535) – Third son of Johann Friedrich von Wettin and Sybylla von der Mark, died in infancy

John Frederick von Wettin II (b. 1529, d. 1595) – Eldest son of Johann Friedrich von Wettin and Sybylla von der Mark, later Duke of Saxony, known as the Middle

John Frederick von Wettin III (b. 1538, d. 1565) – Fourth son of Johann Friedrich von Wettin and Sybylla von der Mark, later Duke of Saxony, known as the Younger

John William von Wettin (b.1530, d. 1573) – Second son of Johann Friedrich von Wettin and Sybylla von der Mark, later Duke of Saxe-Weimar

Martin Luther (b. 1483, d. 1546) – Reformist preacher, instructor at the University of Wittenberg, and mainstay at the Saxon court

Moritz von Wettin (b. 1521, d. 1553) – Son of Heinrich the Pious, Catholic, Margrave of Meissen and Duke of Saxony, became Elector of Saxony in 1547 after his cousin Johann Friedrich's fall

Philip of Hesse (b. 1504, d. 1567) – Friend of Johann Friedrich, Landgrave of Hesse, co-founder of the Schmalkaldic League

Philipus Melanchthon (b. 1497, d. 1560) – Pupil of Martin Luther's, Reformist preacher, instructor at the University of Wittenberg, mainstay at the Saxon court

Table of Important Persons: England

Anne Boleyn (b. 1501/1507, d. 1536) – Second wife of Henry VIII of England, mother of Elizabeth I, supporter of religious reform, executed for treason

Catherine Parr (b. 1512, d. 1548) – Sixth and final wife of Henry VIII, outlived him by twenty months, died of puerperal fever

Catherine Willoughby (b. 1519, d. 1580) – Fourth wife of Charles Brandon, friend of Anna of Cleves

Charles Brandon (b. 1484, d. 1545) – Duke of Suffolk, husband of Catherine Willoughby, close friend of Henry VIII

Edmund Bonner (b. 1500, d. 1569) – Bishop of London between 1539 and 1549 and 1553 to 1559, ambassador to Holy Roman Emperor Charles V during the Cleves War of 1542 to 1543

Edward Seymour (b. 1550, d. 1552) – Duke of Somerset, uncle of Edward VI, became Lord Protector of England after the death of Henry VIII

Edward Tudor (b. 1537, d. 1553) – Henry VIII's legitimate son, only child of Jane Seymour, later Edward VI of England; stepson of Anna of Cleves

Elizabeth Tudor (b. 1533, d. 1603) – Henry VIII's youngest legitimate daughter and middle child, stepdaughter of Anna of Cleves, later Elizabeth I of England

Henry VIII (b. 1491, d. 1547) – King of England, second Tudor monarch, father of Edward VI, Mary I, and Elizabeth I; Anna of Cleves' only husband

Jane Grey (b. 1537, d. 1554) – The '9 Days Queen', great-niece of Henry VIII, alleged Queen of England for nine days between the death of Edward VI and the reign of Mary I

Jane Seymour (b. 1508, d. 1537) – Henry VIII's third wife, died after giving birth to Edward Tudor; Anna of Cleves' predecessor

Katharine of Aragon (b. 1485, d. 1536) – First wife of Henry VIII, mother of Mary Tudor

Katheryn Howard (b. 1521, d. 1542) – Young woman, possibly a teenager, who became Henry VIII's fifth wife, niece of Thomas Howard, 3d Duke of Norfolk; Anna of Cleves' maidservant initially

Mary Tudor (b. 1516, d. 1558) – Henry VIII's oldest legitimate child and daughter, only surviving child of Katharine of Aragon, future Mary I; eldest stepdaughter of Anna of Cleves, roughly eight months younger than Anna of Cleves

Nicholas Wotton (b. 1497, d. 1567) – Instrumental in arranging the marriage between Henry VIII and Anna of Cleves; was in the Low Countries during the height of the Cleves War in 1543

Thomas Cromwell (b. 1485, d. 1540) – Chief minister of Henry VIII from 1534 to 1540, and chief orchestrator of the marriage between Henry VIII and Anna of Cleves, also provided statements in support of the annulment of Anna's marriage

Thomas Howard (b. 1473, d. 1554) – Duke of Norfolk, uncle of both Anne Boleyn and Katheryn Howard, politician

Thomas Seymour (b. 1508, d. 1549) – Brother of Jane Seymour, served as ambassador to Ferdinand von Habsburg, King of the Romans-Germans, and Maria von Habsburg, Regent of the Netherlands in the early 1540s and during the Cleves War

Thomas Wriothesley (b. 1505, d. 1550) – Earl of Southampton, tasked with securing Henry VIII's annulments from both Katharine of Aragon and Anna of Cleves; was main minister involved with the Secret Council which created the bases for Anna's annulment

Thomas Wyatt (b. 1503, d. 1542) – Poet and politician, served as ambassador to the Holy Roman Empire from 1539 to 1540; consistently updated Henry VIII during this time as to Wilhelm von der Mark's rising tensions with Holy Roman Emperor Charles V

Timeline

9 January 1455	William IV, Duke of Jülich-Berg is born
13 April 1458	John II, Duke of Cleves-Mark, is born
3 November 1489	John II of Cleves-Mark marries Mechthild of Hesse
10 November 1490	Johann III, Duke of Jülich-Cleves-Berg, is born
3 August 1491	Maria of Jülich-Berg is born
Circa **1495**	John of Jülich, illegitimate son of Duke William of Jülich-Berg, is born
25 November 1496	Johann III of Cleves-Mark and Maria of Jülich-Berg are betrothed at Burg Castle
30 June 1503	Johann Friedrich I, Elector of Saxony, is born
6 September 1511	William IV of Jülich-Berg dies
17 July 1512	Sybylla of Cleves is born to Johann III of Cleves-Mark and Maria of Jülich-Berg
28 June 1515	Anna of Cleves is born to Johann III of Cleves-Mark and Maria of Jülich-Berg
28 July 1516	Wilhelm V of Cleves is born to Johann III of Cleves-Mark and Maria of Jülich-Berg
17 October 1517	Amalia of Cleves is born to Johann III of Cleves-Mark and Maria of Jülich-Berg
15 March 1521	John II, Duke of Cleves-Mark, dies
10 May 1521	Johann Friedrich's younger half-brother Johann Ernst is born
1526	Marriage negotiations are completed for Sybylla, Anna, and Wilhelm of Cleves, and John of Jülich

8 January 1529	John Frederick II is born to Johann Friedrich of Saxony and Sybylla of Cleves
11 March 1530	John William is born to Johann Friedrich of Saxony and Sybylla of Cleves
16 August 1532	Johann Friedrich becomes Elector of Saxony
1535	Anna of Cleves' betrothal to Francis of Lorraine is cancelled
5 January 1535	John Ernest is born to Johann Friedrich of Saxony and Sybylla of Cleves
11 January 1535	John Ernest of Saxony dies days after birth
16 January 1538	John Frederick III is born to Johann Friedrich of Saxony and Sybylla of Cleves
30 June 1538	Wilhelm of Cleves becomes Duke of Guelders
1539	Marriage between Henry VIII of England and Anna of Cleves is negotiated
6 February 1539	Johann III, Duke of Jülich-Cleves-Berg, dies, Wilhelm of Cleves becomes Duke of Jülich-Cleves-Berg
11 December 1539	Anna of Cleves arrives in Calais
6 January 1540	Anna of Cleves marries Henry VIII of England
9 July 1540	Anna of Cleves' marriage to Henry VIII is annulled
14 June 1541	Wilhelm V marries his first wife, Jeanne d'Albret
12 October 1545	Wilhelm V's marriage to Jeanne d'Albret is annulled via papal dispensation
18 July 1546	Wilhelm of Cleves marries his second wife, Archduchess Maria of Austria
24 April 1547	Johann Friedrich loses the Electorate of Saxony
1550	John of Jülich dies
25 June 1550	Maria Eleonore is born to Wilhelm of Cleves and Maria of Austria
1 March 1552	Anne of Jülich-Cleves-Berg is born to Wilhelm of Cleves and Maria of Austria
2 November 1553	Magdalena of Jülich-Cleves-Berg is born to Wilhelm of Cleves and Maria of Austria
8 February 1553	Johann Ernst of Saxony dies
21 February 1554	Sybylla of Cleves dies

Timeline

3 March 1554	Johann Friedrich of Saxony dies
28 April 1555	Karl Friedrich of Jülich-Cleves-Berg is born to Wilhelm of Cleves and Maria of Austria
1556	Elisabeth of Jülich-Cleves-Berg is born to Wilhelm of Cleves and Maria of Austria
16 July 1557	Anna of Cleves dies
26 August 1557	Sibylle of Jülich-Cleves-Berg is born to Wilhelm of Cleves and Maria of Austria
1561	Elisabeth of Jülich-Cleves-Berg dies aged roughly 5 years
28 May 1562	Johann Wilhelm of Jülich-Cleves-Berg is born to Wilhelm of Cleves and Maria of Austria
21 October 1565	John Frederick III of Saxony dies
14 October 1573	Maria Eleonore of Jülich-Cleves-Berg marries Albert Frederick, Duke of Prussia
2 March 1573	John William of Saxony dies
27 September 1574	Anne of Jülich-Cleves-Berg marries Count Palatine Philip Louis of Neuburg
9 February 1575	Karl Friedrich of Jülich-Cleves-Berg dies
1579	Magdalena of Jülich-Cleves-Berg marries Count Palatine John I of Zweibrücken
11 December 1581	Maria of Austria, Duchess Consort of Jülich-Cleves-Berg dies
16 June 1585	Johann Wilhelm of Jülich-Cleves-Berg marries Jakoba of Baden
1 March 1586	Amalia of Cleves dies
5 January 1592	Wilhelm of Cleves dies
19 May 1595	John Frederick II dies
3 September 1597	Jakoba of Baden dies under mysterious circumstances
1601	Sibylle of Jülich-Cleves-Berg marries Charles, Margrave of Burgau
1 June 1608	Maria Eleonore of Jülich-Cleves-Berg dies
25 March 1609	Johann Wilhelm of Jülich-Cleves-Berg dies
1628	Sibylle of Jülich-Cleves-Berg dies
6 October 1632	Anne of Jülich-Cleves-Berg dies
30 August 1633	Magdalena of Jülich-Cleves-Berg dies

Introduction

Many books have been written in the English language about Anna von der Mark, Hereditary Duchess of Jülich-Cleves-Berg. She is usually simply called Anne of Cleves, and is known to posterity as Henry VIII of England's fourth wife. Not very many pages have been written in English about Anna's grandparents, parents, siblings, nieces or nephews, despite their important positions within the Holy Roman Empire, and ongoing contact with England. In this work, I hope to bring a better understanding of Anne of Cleves' culture and family, from their rise in the mid-fifteenth century to their fall in the early seventeenth.

Writing this book predominantly during 2020 and early 2021 presented a unique set of challenges. The ongoing pandemic and its attendant private and public challenges made it difficult to secure as many sources as one would hope for. Archives were sporadically either completely closed to the public, or otherwise more difficult than usual to meaningfully explore. Additionally, travel to Germany was out of the question – a highly disappointing turn of events. Despite the constantly shifting landscape of available research, this work was eventually completed. I respectfully ask that those who read it bear in mind the challenges of researching during a pandemic in which North America and Europe effectively shut down for swaths of time.

Structure of this Work

The lives of the Von der Mark dynasty are spread out over four main areas beyond Jülich-Cleves-Berg. In the early fifteenth century, the family had strong ties to Burgundy. The first three dukes of Cleves spent time at the Burgundian court, especially John I and John II. In the early sixteenth century, the family became intertwined through marriage in the politics of the Electorate of Saxony, which was at the heart of the German Reformation. By the mid-sixteenth century, the family gained a modicum of influence in England. The family's marriage into the powerful Habsburg dynasty shaped its politics for over sixty years, or roughly a third of the time that Cleves-Mark, and later Jülich-Cleves-Berg, was governed by the Von der Marks.

Given that the Von der Marks were rather spread out, this book approaches their family history from different geographical regions during the first portion. After the deaths of Sybylla of Cleves and Anna of Cleves, the histories of Saxony and England, respectively, are mostly not mentioned because they are no longer pertinent. The sphere of influence became much more centralised.

The Prologue in this work was written with a mind to helping the reader understand what the Holy Roman Empire was and some of the finer points of late medieval to early modern German culture. Additionally, it gives background history about the Von der Marks before the reign of John I of Cleves-Mark. Thereafter, the main narrative begins with John I. He was the son of Maria of Burgundy and Duke Adolf of Cleves, and the heir to the duchies of Cleves-Mark. John I is discussed in greater detail in Chapter 1, which explores the lives of John I, John II and Johann III up to Johann's marriage to Maria of Jülich-Berg in 1510. Chapter 2 chronicles the Saxon electoral court from the early fifteenth century until the marriage of Sybylla of Cleves and Johann Friedrich of Saxony in the mid-1520s.

Chapter 3 looks at the many changes Johann III of Cleves instituted within his territory. Sybylla of Cleves' marriage is the main subject of Chapter 4. Chapters 5, 6 and 7 concern the international politics in which the United Duchies of Jülich-Cleves-Berg became entangled.

Chapter 8 is concerned exclusively with the Cleves War, and the lasting impact it had on Duke Wilhelm V's rule of the United Duchies. Chapter 9 provides the finer details of how the United Duchies interacted with its former political allies, after coming heavily under the influence of the Holy Roman Empire. Chapter 10 looks at the downfall of the Ernestine branch of the House of Wettin. Chapter 11 primarily discusses the births of Duke Wilhelm's children and the deaths of Sybylla and Anna. Chapters 12 through 16 concentrate on the middle period of Duke Wilhelm's rule. Chapters 17 through 19 look at the various issues which led to the end of the United Duchies. The Epilogue covers in broad strokes how the United Duchies were redistributed after the Thirty Years War.

Two appendices at the end of the book consider curious happenings during the time period that proved difficult to assign to any part of the structure as described.

The Early Von der Mark Dynasty and the Holy Roman Empire

The Von der Mark dynasty, rulers of the United Duchies of Jülich-Cleves-Berg, had a profound impact on the area that is now the German federal state of North Rhine-Westphalia. The children of the House of Cleves – Sybylla, Anna, Wilhelm and Amalia – grew up within Germany at a time when this collection of scattered principalities and Imperial possessions was gaining its national identity. Though it was still centuries away from being its own country, the changes seen within the area in the sixteenth century developed the German identity. The Von der Mark children were direct witnesses, victors and losers during the sixteenth century. Their actions shaped and were impacted by the rapidly changing political landscape of sixteenth-century Germany.

Who were the Von der Marks? Why were they important? Why did the United Duchies of Jülich-Cleves-Berg matter?

Family Origin, and the First Counts of Cleves

The noble Von der Mark family traces its lineage from a princess named Beatrix and her hero, the mythical Swan Knight Elias Gral.[1] It was Gral who gave the Duchy of Cleves its distinctive heraldry of a red shield bearing eight *fleur-de-lis*-capped sceptres. Before the arrival of the Swan Knight, Cleves used a red rose on a gold shield. This latter device, according to the fifteenth-century chronicle by Gert van der Schuren, was taken from the Orsini

---

1 Also spelled Helias, Elyas or Helyas.

family of Rome. Family lore held that the particular branch of the Orsini who arrived in Cleves were descended from the Trojans. Such tales of noble classical heritage were common in the medieval to early modern period. The ancient origins of the Von der Mark family are unknown.

The tale of a Swan Knight is recounted in French literature as early as 1192. In *Le Chevalier au Cigne*, a mysterious knight named Helias comes to the rescue of Beatrice in a swan-drawn boat. The couple go on to have several children, before Helias disappears due to Beatrice breaking a covenant between the two. The tale of a Swan Knight being the ancestor to illustrious noble families on the Continent is not uncommon.

A family origin tale specific to the Von der Marks involves the young, beleaguered Beatrix, heiress of Nijmegen and Cleves, who married the legendary Swan Knight after he floated down the Rhine in his boat, pulled by a swan wearing a golden collar. At the time, according to legend, Beatrix was being aggressively pursued by her suitors. The Swan Knight, named Elias Gral, came to her rescue. He agreed to be Beatrix's husband on the condition that she never ask about his origin. The couple were happily wed for some time and had three sons together, but Beatrix eventually convinced one of her sons to ask Elias about his background. Elias understood what was going on, and instantly disappeared. Beatrix died shortly afterwards.

The Beatrix detailed in the *Stammbuch der Grafen und Herzöge von Kleve* (*Stammbuch*) resided mainly at a castle on the Waal River in Nijmegen, the name of which has been lost to the sands of time. She had the Schwanenburg, or Swan Castle, rebuilt during her reign. Legend has it that the surrounding area was named Cleves because the Swan Castle was built on a cliff overlooking the Rhine River.

The Elias Gral detailed in the *Stammbuch* lived in the eighth century, if he lived at all, and served the Frankish leader Charles Martel. Martel is best known for being the grandfather of Charlemagne (and as the victor at the Battle of Tours in 732 fought against the invading Muslim forces of the Umayyad Caliphate). Martel was imprisoned in Cologne around 714 by his stepmother Plectrude because his father had died and Plectrude wished for her grandson Theudoald to be heir. Gral helped free Martel from prison in Cologne. In return, Martel raised the bailiwick of Cleves to the status of county, creating Gral the first Count of Cleves. Gral's direct male line lasted until Count Johann II of Cleves, who died in 1368 without issue.

The Von der Marks Come to Power

The Von der Mark dynasty, thought to have arisen from servants of the Grals, was established when Margaretha, Count Johann II's niece, married Count Adolf von der Mark. Through the right of Margaretha, Adolf and Margaretha's children became counts and countesses of the combined county of Cleves and County of Mark, simply called Cleves-Mark. Margaretha's father and Count Johann II's brother, Count Dietrich IX, assisted Edward III of England during Edward's invasion of France in 1346.

The First Duke of Cleves

Margaretha's and Count Adolf von der Mark's son, also named Adolf, greatly expanded the territories under Cleves-Mark's control. Adolf of Cleves-Mark[2] had his own son, whom he also named Adolf. This second Adolf of Cleves-Mark was the last Count of Mark and first Duke of Cleves. Cleves was elevated from the status of county to that of duchy due to Adolf's loyal service to the Holy Roman Empire. He first married Agnes in 1400. Agnes was the daughter of Rupert, King of the Romans-Germans. Sadly, Agnes died in 1404. Duke Adolf next married Maria of Burgundy in 1406. Maria was a daughter of John the Fearless, and sister of Philip the Good. She was only about thirteen years old when she married Adolf, and did not move to Cleves until 1415, when she was around twenty-two years old.

Duke Adolf and Maria of Burgundy had a lasting impact on the court culture in Cleves. Maria popularised the concept of the *Frauenzimmer*, which is directly translated as 'women's room' but was more like a women's shadow court of the main masculine court. Women occupied the offices necessary to administering the *Frauenzimmer*. When considering this aspect of German culture and tradition, it is important to remember that the courts of England and France were rather debauched by standards of the time. German culture was very different than what one would encounter in England or France, but not oppressively so.

Maria of Burgundy and Duke Adolf of Cleves-Mark had eight children together, all of whom lived to adulthood and married well. It is through these children that Mary, Queen of Scots and Louis XII of France were related to Anna of Cleves and her siblings.

Cultural Context: The German Nobility's Marriage System

German culture and marital practices were rigid, as was antenatal culture. The marital arrangements were controlled by the local government. Having an idea of how the government of Jülich-Cleves-Berg was organised gives further insight into the court culture of the United Duchies. The dukes of Cleves were masters at making good marriage matches, increasing their power. The culmination of this power is found in Johann III, who overhauled the system of government in his territories.

Social mobility via marriage was rule-bound during the early modern period in Germany. The German dowry system was strict, with specified amounts needed for a daughter to marry into a certain noble rank. If there were multiple daughters in a noble family, then the family would have to produce sufficient funds for each daughter to marry. The result of this system was that daughters would marry laterally, such as a *Gräfin* or countess marrying a *Graf* or count,

---

2 The family last name remained 'Von der Mark' until the death of Johann Wilhelm in 1609. A cousin branch, known as the La Marcks, began in roughly the late fourteenth to early fifteenth century.

but not a higher-ranking *Herzog* or duke. If there were multiple daughters in one family, then a daughter might marry down or be placed in a convent, or the daughter may not otherwise marry at all. The opposite was true for sons. Sons would frequently marry women of higher social rank because the family would not have to produce as large a dowry for the bride than they would if she were to marry laterally or upward.

So social mobility in early modern Germany occurred mainly through wedding a lower-ranking man to a higher-ranking woman. This was mainly due to the German dowry system being oriented toward male social mobility and against the mobility of German women with unusual amounts of wealth. Additionally, if a nobleman married a common woman, then their children could not inherit land or titles despite the rank of their father.

Inheritance Rights in Early Modern Germany
Primogeniture – the right of the eldest male to inherit – had been slowly adopted throughout the previous centuries and this process went on into the sixteenth. The result was a narrow way of determining who was able to inherit property, as opposed to partible inheritance. A family was defined by the male line's descent from a common ancestor. Female children were excluded from the inheriting landed property. This meant the property descended along the male line.

During the early medieval period, descent was traced along both the female and male lines. Inheritances were divided more or less equally among all the siblings in a group, not just the males. Over time, the idea of tracing lineage through male descent gained prominence. Eventually, the system evolved such that women were given dowries at marriage instead of inheriting property.

Beliefs Surrounding Pregnancy
A great amount of significance, both symbolic and spiritual, was tied to procreation in sixteenth-century Germany. This included the mother's role in praying for the soul of her unborn child and the actions an expecting mother should take while pregnant to protect the baby's developing body and its soul. During pregnancy a woman held the most power within a family unit. Effectively, because a pregnant woman was growing not just a small body but also a soul, it was important that she be cared for and nurtured lest the baby come out deformed or spiritually defective.

Containing maternal imagination was of utmost importance. If not properly protected, that could lead to deformities and other issues with the child growing within the mother. Refusing the mother her food cravings could also lead to deformities of the body, mind or spirit of a child.

The most important family within the Holy Roman Empire, who surely followed at least some of these ideas, was that descending from Maximilian von Habsburg and his wife Mary of Burgundy.

The Structure and Origin of the Holy Roman Empire of the German Nation

The world of sixteenth-century western Europe feels vaguely familiar, and yet in some ways entirely foreign. The rise in literacy and the volume of records surviving from this period make it feel like it was not that long ago. On the other hand, the wide gulf in culture – not to mention geography for some – makes the customs, governance and behaviours of the people from the sixteenth century seem somehow other.

It can be difficult to imagine what people from the past were like. How did they live? What was their social structure like? What was their government like? How did their ruler behave? To understand how Sybylla, Anna, Wilhelm and Amalia lived their lives, it is important to understand under whose governance they lived. During their lifetimes, the Holy Roman Emperors were Maximilian I, Maximilian's grandson Charles V, Charles' brother Ferdinand I, and Ferdinand's son Maximilian II. Maximilian II's son Rudolf reigned during the later lives of Wilhelm and Amalia. Charles V, who reigned from 1519 to 1556, had the most profound impact.

The origin of the Holy Roman Empire of the German nation, its social structure and court life, and the changes in technology and economy, will each be considered here. By looking at what society was like and how Holy Roman Emperor Charles V conducted his court and affairs, a lot can be understood about the lives of the Von der Marks.

Beginning and Development of the Holy Roman Empire

The area which lies within the borders of modern-day Germany was a burgeoning concept in the sixteenth century. The different political regions, made up of ecclesiastical Imperial Estates like the electorate-archbishoprics of Cologne, Trier and Mainz; prince-bishoprics like Münster, Regensburg[3] and Speyer; plus Imperial Free Cities like Augsburg, Cologne[4] and Bremen. By the time Charles V became the Holy Roman Emperor in 1519, there were over fifty ecclesiastical principalities spread throughout what is now modern Germany, the Netherlands, Italy, Switzerland and France.

In addition to the ecclesiastical principalities and free cities, there existed secular Imperial Estates like Saxony and Brandenburg. The leaders of the secular Imperial Estates were styled as prince-electors (*Kurfürsten*), electors (*Erzherzogen*), archdukes or dukes (*Herzöge*), counts palatine (*Pfalzgraf*), margraves (*Markgrafen*), landgraves (*Landgrafen*) or counts (*Grafen*). The electoral leaders of both the ecclesiastical and secular Imperial Estates had the power to elect the next Holy Roman Emperor. The Holy Roman

3 Regensburg is sometimes called Ratisbon.
4 Cologne, much like Cleves and Jülich, was the name of both a city and of a larger territory. For example, the City of Cleves was within the Duchy of Cleves. The Imperial Free City of Cologne was within the Electorate-Archbishopric of Cologne.

Emperor was also called the King of Italy and King of the Germans until the sixteenth century. Thereafter, once it became clear that the position of Holy Roman Emperor would be hereditary, the emperor-elect was called the King of the Germans or King of the Romans.

Throughout the sixteenth century, there were seven electorates. The ecclesiastical electorates were Cologne, Mainz and Trier. The secular electorates were Bohemia, Brandenburg, Rhine Palatinate and Saxony. Leaders of the electorates were the Archbishop of Cologne, the Archbishop of Mainz, the Archbishop of Trier, the King of Bohemia, the Margrave of Brandenburg, the Count of the Palatinate and the Duke of Saxony. Particular to Saxony, there was a portion which fell under the control of the Elector-Duke of Saxony, and a portion which fell under the control of the cadet branch Duke of Saxony.

The electors, princes, and free cities in Germany comprised three branches or councils of the Imperial Diet. The official term for these branches was the *collegia*. One individual could hold a position in more than one council, such as the *Kurfürst* or Elector Johann Friedrich of Saxony. Johann Friedrich was a member of both the Council of Electors and Council of Princes. Other persons, such as Duke Wilhelm of Jülich-Cleves-Berg, were members of only one council.

The structure of the Holy Roman Empire's electoral college was established by the Golden Bull of 1356. Charles IV of the House of Luxembourg, Holy Roman Emperor at the time, sought to politically exclude the Austrian House of Habsburg and Bavarian House of Wittelsbach as much as possible from obtaining voting rights within the electoral college. Charles IV was originally the King of Bohemia. The House of Habsburg did not obtain voting rights until 1526, when Charles V's brother Ferdinand became King of Bohemia. The House of Wittelsbach was excluded until 1623.

The Rise of the Habsburgs

The Habsburg family had obscure beginnings in the late tenth century. Count Radbot von Klettau was born at the very end of the tenth century. He built Habsburg Castle in Habsburg, County Aargau, Switzerland, early in the eleventh century. The precise source for the name 'Habsburg' is unknown. It seems to have come from the German word for ford, because the castle was near the Aar River. The more romantic version is that Radbot of Klettau saw a hawk perched on one of the castle walls, and therefore decided to name it 'hawk palace', or *habsburg* in German.

Radbot von Klettau's grandson Otto, born a century after Habsburg Castle was built, decided to adopt the last name 'von Habsburg' instead of 'von Klettau'. Although more research is needed, it is generally believed that Otto is the first person to be titled 'Count of Habsburg'. The family was still based at Habsburg Castle at the time. It should be noted that this part of Switzerland was considered part of the German Duchy of Swabia until the early fifteenth century.

The first Habsburg to achieve meaningful power within the Holy Roman Empire was Count Rudolf I, who was later elected King of the Romans-Germans. Remember that there is no distinction between King of the Romans and King of the Germans. The titles are used interchangeably, and eventually came to mean the Holy Roman Emperor-elect. Born in 1218, Rudolf gained control of the duchies of Styria and Austria over his lifetime by defeating King Ottokar II of Bohemia in 1278. Despite initial rejection of his rule by the Austrian and Styrian princes, Rudolf was able to maintain control of the duchies. His family held power over Austria and Styria for more than 600 years.

Upon Rudolf's death in 1291, Adolf of Nassau became King of the Germans. The German electors were afraid of Rudolf trying to establish the title King of the Germans as a hereditary one. Rudolf's eldest son Albrecht was eventually elected King of Germany in 1298, anyway. Albrecht also shared the duchies of Styria and Austria with his younger brother Rudolf II until 1283, when Rudolf II was required to give Styria and Austria to Albrecht in exchange for Rudolf II becoming Albrecht's successor to the title King of the Germans.

Rudolf II married in 1289, and had one son, Johann. Rudolf died either shortly before or shortly after Johann's birth. Johann was insultingly nicknamed 'Johann, Duke Lackland' due to his father Rudolf's failure to secure any sort of meaningful inheritance for any of his future heirs back in 1283. Johann, very displeased with this unfair situation, set upon his uncle Albrecht, King of the Germans, on 1 May 1308. He cleaved Albrecht's head in two before fleeing to Italy. The title King of the Germans then passed out of Habsburg hands until 1438, when Albrecht the Magnanimous, a Knight of the Garter, regained the title.

The first Habsburg emperor, Albrecht ruled for two years. After his death, Frederick, Duke of Styria and from the cadet line, became Holy Roman Emperor. Frederick III reigned for most of the second half of the fifteenth century, but had little meaningful impact. His son, Maximilian I, had an immense power base through his marriage to Mary of Burgundy that brought strength to the Holy Roman Empire. Maximilian's full title indicates how much territory he controlled:

Maximilian I, by the grace of God elected Holy Roman Emperor, forever August, King of Germany, of Hungary, Dalmatia, Croatia, etc. Archduke of Austria, Duke of Burgundy, Brabant, Lorraine, Styria, Carinthia, Carniola, Limburg, Luxembourg, Gelderland, Landgrave of Alsace, Prince of Swabia, Count Palatine of Burgundy, Princely Count of Habsburg, Hainaut, Flanders, Tyrol, Gorizia, Artois, Holland, Seeland, Ferrette, Kyburg, Namur, Zutphen, Margrave of the Holy Roman Empire, the Enns, Burgau, Lord of Frisia, the Wendish March, Pordenone, Salins, Mechelen, etc. etc.

Developments under Maximilian I

When Maximilian became Emperor Elect after the death of his father in 1493, the printing press was fully functional, and the Renaissance reached northward from Italy into other areas of Europe. Henry Tudor, now Henry VII of England, was on the throne for around eight years. France was stable enough under the reign of Charles VIII of France. Spain was still under the strong guidance of Isabella of Castile and Ferdinand of Aragon. Military technology was changing, and it became more and more common to have professional soldiers rather than a feudal military. Humanism was making its way north, too. All these components influenced the Holy Roman Empire of the German Nation in the late fifteenth century.

The German identity was not fully formed during the sixteenth century. The *Deutsche* or *Teutsche* people, as is and were the German words to describe the Germans, began claiming their identity in the mid-fifteenth century as the text of Tacitus's *Germania* became increasingly important to the German people. Before the fifteenth century, the people living in what is now Germany were unified in the ninth and tenth centuries under the *Deutsch* Empire.[5] Martin Luther harked back to this time, comparing the Twelve Tribes of Israel with the founding ethnic groups of Bavarians, Franks, Saxons and Swabians.

In the eleventh century, Pope Gregory VII recognised the *rex Teutonicorum*, or King of the *Deutschen*. The word to describe the head of these ethnic groups evolved during the eleventh through thirteenth centuries, from titles such as the *Imperator Alamannorum* or Emperor of the Alemans, *Imperator Teutonicorum* or Emperor of the Teutons, governing over the territory which was named the *Sacrum Imperium* or Holy Empire in 1157, *Sacrum Romanum Imperium* or Holy Roman Empire.

In the late medieval period and on into the early modern, the Holy Roman Empire was made up of mostly German territories, but included parts in Italy, Burgundy and Lorraine. Emperor Frederick III was the first to recognise the predominantly Germanic character of the Holy Roman Empire. In 1486, after the election of Frederick's son Maximilian as King of the Germans, a ten-year peace was instituted. It was in these documents that the German identity of the Holy Roman Empire was established. It was not until 1512, however, at the Diet of Cologne that this concept became closely related to the German people as the *Heiligen Römischen Reich der deutsche Nation*, or Holy Roman Empire of the German Nation.

The word 'nation' in the context of the Holy Roman Empire of the German Nation did not have the same implications as it does today. Within the Empire, a person could be from the Burgundian nation or Saxon nation, for example. There were multiple areas within the Holy Roman Empire that inhabitants referred to as their nation. The rediscovery of Tacitus's *Germania* by humanists lent itself to further solidifying the identity of the German people.

The burgeoning German identity in 1512 and attempts of secular German leaders within the Holy Roman Empire during the German Reformation led

---

5 *Deutschen Reich*, which means German Empire.

to sweeping religious and political changes, which often went hand in hand. It was during this time of serious change that the Von der Mark children were born. Each child's life was affected by the Reformation, with some experiencing a more international impact and others struggling within their own household.

The Seven Estates of Early Modern Germany

The feudal system was still alive, but not well, in early sixteenth-century Germany. As the rest of western Europe, especially England, moved toward commercialised farming, German peasants were expected to work the land of a wealthy landowner for very little in exchange. Peasants paid taxes, laboured and produced for everyone else in German society. A German peasant was the property of the local lord, and did not have much opportunity to move to a different area.

The plebeians were effectively the working class. Some had skills, like the journeymen counted among their ranks. These individuals had opportunities to move up a social notch and become burghers. Plebeians did not own land, which was a source of security for peasants and wealth for the upper estates. A plebeian in society was *persona non grata*, and had almost no rights. They were vagabonds and drifters.

The burghers were the comparatively wealthy middle class. City and local leaders came from burgher families, albeit not without pushback from the patriciate class. The burghers did not believe that the patriciates should be the only ones to control local government. Guilds, which were dominated by burghers, slowly developed into corporate entities which protected the rights of their members. The burghers opposed the clergy's right to not pay taxes, especially because the clergy appeared to be failing in their spiritual duties.

The genuinely wealthy patriciate class was under increasing threat of losing prominence and control to the burghers. City councils were long dominated by patriciate families, and simony was a common practice. Patricians squeezed as much money as they could from the peasant class, with new taxes frequently devised to their detriment. Taxes collected by the patricians, whether from peasants or guilds, were not formally counted. The lack of proper bookkeeping allowed the already wealthy patrician families to steal money from the city's coffers with impunity.

The prelates had lost a lot of their intellectual influence by the early sixteenth century. Originally looked to as bastions of intelligence and higher learning, their stature was reduced by the advent of the printing press. They were not educated or interested in the new humanist teachings which sprung up during the Renaissance. On top of that, they were perceived as corrupt and lazy. The heads of the prelate class, such as bishops or the local abbots, extracted money from their flocks whenever they could. The sale of indulgences became popular. Archbishops held dominion over their archbishoprics in a way similar to the German princes, but having even more power.

The lesser nobility was more or less comprised of knights. The war tactics of knights rapidly became obsolete during the early sixteenth century.

Gunpowder, mercenaries and the reduced value of heavy calvary undermined the wealth of the knights. To maintain the appearance of their status, knights had to borrow more and more money. Their financial situation became increasingly unstable during the early sixteenth century.

At the very top of society were the German princes. Depending on the area, a German prince could be a duke, an archbishop or an elector. The princely class could enact taxes whenever the situation, in princely eyes, merited it. The princely system of taxation was slanted greatly in favour of the clerical class and cities. Cities usual had some sort of agreement with the local prince which exempted them from paying most of the prince's taxes. In effect, the lowest classes in German society paid the most taxes.

The German princes taxed the peasantry so much that it virtually forced them into serfdom. In addition, the princes made use of the vestiges of ancient Roman law to claim property and land from the lower classes. This caused a gaping divide between the poorest and richest in early modern German society.

Above everyone was the Holy Roman Emperor.

Holy Roman Emperor Charles V's Court Structure by 1551

Charles V's main court was based in the Low Countries and served as an example to others within the Holy Roman Empire. The Venetian ambassador wrote a detailed report about Charles V's court in roughly 1551, describing how many people were in which offices, how the people were able to reach higher stations, and how much money they made. The ambassador described Charles' personality, character and behaviour in depth, contrasting him with his withdrawn Spanish son Philip II.

Charles V's court followed the Burgundian model, and his court of personal attendants was impressive. Charles V had 'from thirty to forty pages, sons of counts and lords who are his vassals … for the support of whom his Majesty pays every day one-sixth of a crown apiece to the one in charge, and moreover clothes them every year … abundantly'. The young men learn valuable courtly skills and are refined during their time at Charles' court, such skills as fencing, dancing and horsemanship. If the pages stay with Charles long enough – usually fifteen to twenty years – they are promoted, becoming gentlemen. A gentleman is given one-third of a crown as daily allowance.

Eventually, gentlemen who have earned their rank within the emperor's walls can join other gentlemen from the emperor's territories in becoming Gentlemen of the Household. They earn two-thirds of a crown per day. The duties of a Gentleman of the Household are varied but include providing horses and armies for the emperor as befitting each gentleman's rank. The Gentlemen of the Household usually numbered around 300.

From the Gentlemen of the Household, fifty are chosen to be the 'gentlemen of the mouth', as described by the Venetian ambassador. These fifty gentlemen have more duties than the others. They act as stewards, carvers, cupbearers, butlers and so on, and assist in bringing food to and from the kitchens. They are each paid one crown per day.

In addition to the gentlemen already mentioned, the emperor employed thirty-six as gentlemen of the chamber. This title was an honorific. The thirty-six gentlemen were usually princes from one of the emperor's vast territories, and they had their own servants as well. They had no true responsibility, but were there to socialise with Charles. They were each paid one crown per day.

The two most important positions within the emperor's court were the Steward of the Body and the Great Chamberlain. The Great Chamberlain oversaw everyone within the emperor's chambers. The Steward of the Body, a Knight of the Golden Fleece, slept in Charles' bedchamber. Of them, the Steward of the Body was the highest earner, with a staggering wage of 1,000 crowns per month. A portion of this income was used to provide food for all the emperor's personal servants.

The Master of the Court had the largest income of everyone, and was the overall head of Charles' court. He procured meals for the emperor's soldiers, too, including the 300-strong Imperial bodyguard. This unit comprised 100 each of Burgundian mounted archers, German halberdiers and Spanish infantrymen.

Other courts in continental Europe, like Cleves, were modelled on the Habsburg-Burgundian court of Charles V.

A Day at Court in Western-central Germany

The lifestyle of a person living at court during the German Renaissance was different in detail from that of an English courtier. Councillors began working between six and seven in the morning, with the rest of the workers arriving to start the day sometime later. A duke in the Holy Roman Empire expected court officials to attend a minimum of one religious service each morning. Next came *Morgensuppe*, 'Morning Soup', which was a drink of either beer or wine depending on a person's station at court. The first meal of the day came at ten o'clock in the morning, and lasted for around two hours. Work was usually completed by midday. However, high-ranking officials occasionally had to attend meetings in the afternoon.

The court would come alive in the afternoon, with gentlemen calling on the well-supervised and chaperoned ladies. The Von der Mark sisters came out of the *Frauenzimmer* to socialise. Around two o'clock, snacks and refreshments were served. Four or five hours later, supper would begin. This was at times a lengthy affair, with the cellars and kitchens closing as late as nine o'clock. Those who did not live at court would leave at that time. It was typical for a courtier to maintain a residence in the city and close to court; they would be bound to that apartment and could only give it up with the permission of the Great Chamberlain.

Roughly 300 to 400 people could enjoy as many as nine courses of an evening at a German prince's table. At a supper that large, one can be sure that there would be minstrels for entertainment and high-ranking nobles for networking. The feast itself could occupy several rooms. Dishes of venison and fish were accompanied by wines made from the grapes of the Neckar or Rhine valleys. It was not uncommon for poor folk to be at such feasts, hoping to receive leftover food. The German princes were ostensibly concerned for poor and sick people, and were willing to give out food to those in need.

Some German courts enjoyed hunting, which was a great passion of the age. Burg Castle, where the Von der Mark sisters and their maternal family spent a lot of time, was originally a hunting lodge. Hunts were often lavish. Unfortunately, a hunting party could wreak havoc on the labour of the peasants: it was not uncommon for crops to be trampled by passing bands of nobles.

Change in Military Tactics and Strategies

General warfare changed rapidly during the sixteenth century. It became more expensive, stretching the budgets of some areas in western Europe and bankrupting others by the middle of the century. Armies and navies for hire were the norm on continental Europe, and proved to be easier and less expensive to administer in some cases.

Part of this rise is attributable to the unprecedented inheritance of Charles von Habsburg. By 1519, the nineteen-year-old was Holy Roman Emperor Charles V, King Charles I of Spain and Lord of the Netherlands, among other dignities. His territory covered the majority of the Iberian Peninsula, roughly all of what is now Germany, and portions of modern France, the Netherlands, Belgium, Italy, Hungary, the Czech Republic and Austria; of course, there was also his empire in the New World. Maintaining a grasp on this much physical space and the people living within it was an awesome task.

Charles V, born to Juana of Castile and Philip von Habsburg (known as the Handsome), spent his first years being educated in the Low Countries. He was blessed with five capable siblings, two of whom helped him maintain a presence in his territories. Maria von Habsburg, sometimes called Maria of Austria or Maria of Hungary, served as Regent of the Low Countries during most of his reign. She was widowed in the early 1520s, and when she refused to remarry Charles saw fit to have her installed as his representative. In Bohemia and Hungary, Charles' younger brother Ferdinand was elected king after Maria's husband died. Another sister, Isabella, married the King of Denmark; Eleonore married first the King of Portugal and then Francis I of France; and Catherine married the next King of Portugal. His aunt Katharine of Aragon was of course married to King Henry VIII of England early in his reign.

This vast structure of influence and control was always at risk of collapsing. By the early sixteenth century, bands of professional mercenaries had sprung up in Switzerland and Germany. The Swiss Guard was – and to this day is – employed by the papacy. *Landsknechte* in Germany, sometimes called Lance Knights[6] in English, were highly effective. If one had the money, then many mercenary companies could be hired. However, disaster beckoned if the soldiers were left unpaid. Unlike local military units, they frequently had no ties to the lands they invaded. If they were not paid on time, they were likely to pillage the subjugated enemy. An excellent example of this was the 1527 Sack of Rome.

In May 1527, when Charles V failed to pay his troops after a campaign in Italy, they decided to march on Rome. Growing restless, they attacked the city, including the Vatican. All manner of atrocities were committed, including the slaying of many members of the Swiss Guard tasked with protecting Pope Clement VII, who narrowly escaped St Peter's. Clement VII made it to Castel Sant'Angelo, where Charles V was able to keep him captive. The Pope surely heard the cries of the people outside over the next eight days, while the emperor's rogue troops murdered, raped and looted their way through the city.

To give an idea of the increase in numbers of soldiers from the 1490s to the 1520s and beyond, Charles VIII of France had about 20,000 to 30,000 soldiers during his Italian campaign in 1494. Twenty-five years later, France's military boasted roughly 50,000 soldiers. England's army went from numbering around 14,000 during the reign of Henry VII in 1492 to the staggering 48,000 Henry VIII took across the Channel to invade France. Charles V had about 28,000 soldiers fighting Francis I's army in 1525, which increased to 50,000 by 1552. Charles V's son Philip II of Spain maintained an army of 45,000 in 1558, and it had grown to 85,000 by 1574.

When Wilhelm became Duke of Jülich-Cleves-Berg in 1539, he was surely conscious of the massive size of Charles V's army when compared to his own. Wilhelm needed allies, and enjoyed a modicum of diplomatic success in securing such allies from 1539 to 1543. Wilhelm and Amalia, the longest lived of the Von der Mark children, died in a very different world than the one into which they were born.

Money
Within the Holy Roman Empire there existed a plethora of currencies. The Imperial taler (from which the term 'dollar' is derived), guilders, Rhenish florins, Dutch florins and others were all in use and had varying values.

During the sixteenth century, clever individuals employed myriad methods to either counterfeit money or gain added value from it. Coins were sometimes clipped and new, unauthorised copies created. At other times, the coins were placed into a sack and shaken until precious metal dust fell off,

---

6 *Landsknecht* means servant of the land; however, Lance Knight has a similar-sounding pronunciation and look, and describes the pike warfare used by the *Landsknechte*.

which was collected to make more coins. One approach taken by Henry VIII of England was to debase the coinage by adding a less valuable metal.

As we will see later, Wilhelm, due to the overwhelming costs of war during the 1540s, had to engage in metal-conserving techniques with his currency. He is known to history as the Rich, but he had to earn that epithet. The value of the guilder, much like the Saxon thaler used by his brother-in-law, went up and down during the tumultuous mid-sixteenth century.

The complicated politics of the Holy Roman Empire, the rise of a German national identity, changes in warfare and endless economic fluctuations were some of the subtle but important factors which guided the lives of Sybylla, Anna, Wilhelm and Amalia.

1

In the Beginning, before the United Duchies

Background

Sybylla, Anna, Wilhelm and Amalia von der Mark played an important yet overlooked role in western European history during the sixteenth century. Born as Hereditary Duchesses and Duke of Jülich-Cleves-Berg, the children frequently went by their territorial title, 'of Cleves'. English speakers are most familiar with Anna, known as Anne of Cleves, due to her marriage to Henry VIII. Thanks to the popular TV show *The Tudors*, there is a vague awareness that Anna had a brother, Wilhelm, and a sister, Amalia. Sybylla is rarely mentioned.

The problems that would dog the Von der Mark children during their lives began in the fifteenth century, long before they were born. Their father's side was fairly stable, but lingering dynastic issues on their mother's side were of serious concern.

Sybylla von der Mark, the eldest child of the House of Cleves, married into the Saxon House of Wettin, which also experienced difficulties in the fifteenth century. Anna's marriage to the King of England was swiftly annulled for political reasons, as was the first marriage of Wilhelm von der Mark. Amalia, the youngest, never married. Despite all these challenges, the Von der Mark children left their imprint on the histories of Germany and England, and are still much talked about today. Although their story, like any child's story, begins with their parents, the shape of their lives was set before anyone had given a thought to their existence.

On 25 November 1496, an engagement ceremony took place between a five-year-old blonde girl and a six-year-old dark-haired boy. The children were Maria von Jülich-Berg, Hereditary Duchess of Jülich-Berg, and Johann von der Mark, future Duke Johann III of Cleves-Mark. Maria's illegitimate baby brother, John of Jülich, was around a year old. It was vital for Maria's marriage to be determined before her half-brother had a chance to grow up and cause trouble by making his own claim.

The marriage between Maria and Johann would unify the slightly weaker territory of Cleves-Mark with the much stronger territory of Jülich-Berg. It would consolidate the fractured territories into a contiguous geographical region, with the territories covering a combined 5,500 square miles. Most importantly to Cleves-Mark, uniting with Jülich-Berg would bring more money.

The Cleves-Mark Line

Johann von der Mark's family was closely tied to the Burgundian royal family. His great-grandfather Adolf I of Cleves-Mark married Maria of Burgundy, who lived from 1393 to 1466. Their eldest son, John I of Cleves, was raised at the court in Burgundy. Maria brought Burgundian traditions to the Cleves-Mark court, including the aforementioned tradition of the *Frauenzimmer*, a separate women's court. John I was one of at least ten children, eight of whom lived to adulthood.

John I of Cleves-Mark

John I, born in 1419, was raised at the court of his uncle Philip 'the Good', Duke of Burgundy. He grew up alongside the future duke, Charles. During his time there, his uncle captured Joan of Arc at Compiègne. Burgundy's alliances shifted away from being pro-English to pro-French in 1435 with the Treaty of Arras. Philip the Good later laid siege to Calais in 1439. John I would have known about all these developments, perhaps even participating in them. Over this period, his uncle considerably expanded the Burgundian territory.

John was recalled to Cleves in 1444, when his father Adolph was at war with Dietrich, Archbishop of Cologne. The conflict concerned the city of Soest, which wished to leave the archbishop's control and become part of Cleves-Mark. Dietrich would not give up the city so easily, and also attempted to seize control over the Cleves city of Xanten. Upon his return it was remarked that John I's manners were very different from what was common at the court of Cleves-Mark. As a result, he was nicknamed 'the Child from Flanders'.

In 1450, John went on a tour to the Holy Land and was awarded a knighthood. On his return, he passed through Rome and Venice before heading home. Along the way, he plundered the City of Doesburg,[7] part of the Duchy of Guelders and now in the Netherlands. He brought to Cleves valuables he had pilfered from Doesburg.

Aside from John, Adolf of Cleves and Maria of Burgundy had seven other children who survived to adulthood. Margaret was born in 1416, and was quickly followed by Catherine in 1417. As mentioned, John was born in 1419. His sisters Elisabeth, Agnes and Helena were born in 1420, 1422

---

7 Not to be confused with Duisburg, Germany

and 1423 respectively. John's only brother, Adolf, was born in 1425, and his sister Mary arrived in 1426. John and his siblings all went on to marry into power and status, albeit to varying degrees.

John I's oldest sister, Margaret, married twice. First she married William III of Bavaria, with whom she had two sons. After his death, she married Ulrich V of Württemberg in 1441. They had one daughter, named Katharina, before Margaret's death in 1444.

John I's second-oldest sister, Catherine, married Arnold of Egmond, Duke of Guelders, in 1430. The couple had three sons and three daughters, but only one son and two daughters survived to adulthood. Their eldest, Maria, married James II of Scotland in 1449. Their only son, Adolf, married his cousin Catherine of Burgundy in 1463. Adolf was rumoured to be Katharina's favourite child. The couple's youngest surviving child secretly married the Bishop of Liège, with whom she had three sons.

Of John I's five younger siblings, all made good matches. Elisabeth, the closest to John in age, married Henry XXVI of Shwarzburg-Blankenburg in 1434. Agnes married into the Iberian ruling family of the Trastámara when she wed Charles IV of Navarre in 1439. This marriage was childless. Helena married Henry II of Brunswick-Lüneburg in 1436, and the couple shared one daughter. Adolf, John's only surviving brother, married Beatrice of Portugal in 1453. Their children were Philip of Ravenstein and a daughter named Louise.

John I's youngest surviving sibling, Mary, married Charles de Valois, Duke of Orléans, in 1440. The couple had three children. Their oldest, Marie, married Jean de Foix. Their youngest, Anna, became Abbess of Fontevrault. Their only son went on to become Louis XII of France. Louis XII had three wives, the last of whom was Mary Tudor in 1514.

Needless to say, John I, who married his cousin Elisabeth of Burgundy in 1455, was a very well-connected duke. His wife was the daughter of Count John of Étampes-Nevers, a territory stretching roughly from just south of Paris through the centre of what is now France. John went on to have six children of his own, with four of his sons and one daughter surviving to adulthood.

John II of Cleves-Mark

The eldest son of John I and Elisabeth became John II, Duke of Cleves. Born in 1458, he was raised at the Burgundian court like his father. The second son, Adolf, became Lord of Liège. Next was Engelbert, who became Count of Nevers and Eu, and married Charlotte of Bourbon. John I's only daughter, Marie, lived from 1465 to 1513. She was engaged to Duke Adolf of Jülich-Berg, but the marriage never came to pass; she never made another match. The youngest, Philip, became the Bishop of Nevers, then Amiens, then Autun. All in all, John I's children led successful lives. John I continued as Duke of Cleves until his death on 5 September 1481.

John II fought alongside Duke Charles of Burgundy during the Battle of Nancy in 1477. Reported to be of bellicose and heroic character, John II's councillors wished to discourage his warlike behaviour and make him more peaceable so they allowed him free rein in the *Frauenzimmer*. The thought was that time spent in the more peaceful environment would rub off on him. This did not turn out to be the case. Almost unfettered access to the women at court saw John II extend his family's circle of influence even further by fathering an alleged sixty-three illegitimate children, earning him the nickname 'Childmaker'.

After assuming the rule of Cleves-Mark in 1481, one of John II's first actions was to go to war against the illegitimate David of Burgundy, Bishop of Utrecht, his distant relative through Philip the Good. The civil war from 1481 to 1483 was part of a larger series of wars known as the Hook and Cod Wars, which took place between 1350 and 1490. John II's Burgundian relations were involved because of Philip the Good trying to expand his territories into Utrecht. The appointment of David as Bishop of Utrecht in 1456 had not been well received by the locality, but peace was maintained while his half-brother Charles the Bold ruled Burgundy. After Charles's death in 1477, however, things came to a head. The Burgundian side was able to put down the opposition.

In 1482 John II sent his brother Engelbert of Cleves to Burgundy to fight in favour of the anti-Burgundian, or Hook, side. This risked alienating Maximilian von Habsburg, whose wife was Mary of Burgundy, Hereditary Duchess of Burgundy. The young woman was thrown from her horse in March 1482, dying on the 27th; Philip of Cleves, Lord of Ravenstein, witnessed Mary's fall. Through the marriage of Mary of Burgundy to Maximilian von Habsburg, allying with the Burgundians also meant joining the pro-Habsburg, or Cod, side. Mary was the only surviving heir of Charles the Bold, and Maximilian von Habsburg ruled Burgundy by right of his marriage to her.

Engelbert of Cleves and his large army were initially successful in ejecting David of Burgundy from Utrecht. However, as soon as Maximilian was able to free up his troops in 1482, he turned his attention to them. The Siege of Utrecht in 1483 saw the victory of Maximilian, the reinstatement of David and the capture of Engelbert, who was later released.

Not harbouring any hard feelings for John II, Maximilian officially settled the territories of Cleves-Mark and the cities of Xanten and Soest upon John II. The ceremony took place in Aachen at the behest of Maximilian, the future Holy Roman Emperor.

Maximilian Becomes King of the Romans

On 9 April 1486 at Frankfurt am Main, Maximilian was crowned King of the Romans. Many important persons from Cleves, Jülich and Saxony attended. Adolf of Cleves, Lord of Ravenstein until his death in 1492, was there, as were Duke William of Jülich and Elector Ernst of Saxony. An anonymous eyewitness account records their encounter:

Elector Ernest of Saxony, Duke Adolph of Cleves, Duke Albert of Saxony, and Duke William of Jülich came to the Roman king. There the two electors dressed themselves as befitted their electoral rank, and then they marched to church in the following order: the nobles in front, followed by the bishops, and after them Duke Albert of Saxony, the Duke of Jülich, and the Lord of Cleves, the last of whom wore very expensive armbands adorned with pearls and a hat decorated with a brooch of pearls and precious stones. Last came His Imperial Majesty [Frederick III] in a golden garment with a very valuable sculpted chain that bore an expensive cross. On the emperor's right walked his son, Maximilian, the Roman king, in a golden, ermine-fringed mantle that covered the shoulders of his highness down to the elbows and whose front closure was decorated with pearls and precious gems; on his head he wore a golden hat, cut in the Italian style and trimmed in ermine. On the emperor's left trod Elector Ernest of Saxony in a similar coat and tunic made from red satin and a large, tall scarlet hat, likewise trimmed in ermine. Elector Palatine Philip walked on Maximilian's right; he was similarly dressed and wore a red satin hat. Thus, they entered the church.

The positioning of the Elector of Saxony, and representatives from Cleves and Jülich, shows the prestige which the territories held not only by right, but also in the eyes of Maximilian.

John II of Cleves-Mark Settles Down
Three years later, on 3 November 1489, John II of Cleves married Mechthild of Hesse in Soest. The couple welcomed three legitimate children. The oldest, Johann III, was born on 10 November 1490. Johann III eventually became Duke of the United Duchies of Jülich-Cleves-Berg. The second child, a daughter named Anna, was born in 1495. The last legitimate child, Adolf, was born in 1498. He was destined to become Lord of Ravenstein upon the death of John's cousin Philip of Ravenstein, but sadly predeceased him. Adolf, who lived a military life and never married, died in Spain in 1525. Philip died three years later.

From 1514 to 1518, a marriage between Anna and Duke Karl of Guelders was negotiated. One advantage of the match was that any children it produced would settle Duke Karl's claims to Cleves without disinheriting the family. Duke Karl was the grandson of Anna's great-aunt Catherine of Cleves. However, Anna went behind the backs of her father and brother, secretly marrying Philip III, Count of Waldeck in 1517. For this transgression Anna was imprisoned from 1517 to early 1519. Maximilian I, who was not in favour of a match between Anna and Duke Karl, interceded for the newlyweds. Their marriage was recognised on 20 November 1518, but as a condition Anna had to give up any inheritance rights to Cleves-Mark for herself and her heirs.

The Jülich-Berg Line
The neighbouring ducal family, in Jülich-Berg, were much less well connected due to fewer children being born into the family during the fifteenth century.

Gerhard, Count of Ravensburg, became Duke of Jülich-Berg in 1437 after his uncle Adolf died. Gerhard fought in the Second War of Guelderian Succession against Count Arnold of Egmond, the brother-in-law to John I of Cleves. Gerhard gave up his hereditary claim to Guelders in 1473, selling his rights to Charles, Duke of Burgundy. Charles' daughter Mary inherited the right, which was then assumed by Mary's husband, Holy Roman Emperor Maximilian I. Of interest is that Gerhard founded the chivalric Order of St Hubertus, sometimes called the Order of the Horn, in 1444, after the Battle of Linnich.

William of Jülich-Berg

Gerhard's first son, William, was born in 1455. William's life would be marked by personal, dynastic and marital struggle. By 1460, Gerhard's mental health had declined to the point where his wife, Sophia of Saxony-Lauenburg, took over the regency of Jülich-Berg, waiting for William to come of age. Gerhard fell in and out of madness, beginning when William was still an infant, leading to a regency which lasted until Gerhard's death in 1475. Gerhard nonetheless managed to father a second son, Adolf, but the boy died in 1473 during an epidemic, possibly the Black Plague. William's mother Sophia also died during the epidemic, just before Adolf. William took over Jülich-Berg in 1475 when he was roughly twenty years old.

William of Jülich-Berg's Marriages

William of Jülich-Berg married twice, first to Countess Elisabeth of Nassau-Saarbrücken in 1472. This was an excellent match for William, bringing honour to the duchies of Jülich-Berg, as well as wealth. The couple anticipated the birth of a child in 1479, but sadly the child was stillborn, and Elisabeth died shortly after the delivery. It is very possible her death was a result of puerperal fever, sometimes called childbed fever.

Negotiations for a marriage between William and Philippa of Guelders began shortly after Elisabeth's death. This match would strength William's claim to Guelders, despite the contract for the duchy being sold to Charles of Burgundy back in 1473. France, often at odds with Burgundy, was in favour of the match. However, a marriage between William and Philippa would almost certainly lead to war between Burgundy and Jülich-Berg, which William wanted to avoid, and so he abandoned the negotiations.

William married his second wife, Sibylle of Brandenburg, in 1481. Their wedding was a grand affair. Born 31 May 1467, Sibylle was the daughter of Elector Albrecht III Achilles of Brandenburg and Anna of Saxony. She was the sixth of thirteen children, and this fact made up for the lack of direct relatives in William's family. This was another prestigious match for William, bolstering Jülich-Berg's support of the Holy Roman Empire. The Elector of Brandenburg had a staunch relationship with the Holy Roman Emperor Maximilian I, as well.

Interestingly, Sibylle was descended from both William I and Henry II of England.

Ten years after their marriage, William and Sibylle finally had a surviving child together, Maria of Jülich-Berg, born 3 August 1491. William fathered at least one illegitimate son, John of Jülich, born around 1495. Besides his legitimate daughter Maria and illegitimate, or natural, son John, William did not have any other known children.

William's marriage to Sibylle was supposed to bring an immense amount of much-needed money to Jülich-Berg, but the money came at a trickle. William repeatedly petitioned the Elector of Brandenburg for funds, which were intended to support the military stability of Jülich-Berg during the tumultuous 1480s and 1490s.

Territorial Conflicts during William of Jülich-Berg's Youth

When William was coming of age in the 1470s, Burgundy and Cologne struggled over control of the Archdiocese of Cologne. By the end of 1474, William had followed in his father Gerhard's footsteps by allying himself with Burgundy. His international policies remained in favour of Burgundy until 1498, from which point he slowly abandoned political relations with Burgundy in favour of France. This was likely because he had no bone to pick with France over his succession rights come spring 1498.

Charles VIII of France died on 7 April 1498. Charles, William and Duke Karl of Guelders all had a claim to Jülich through a common ancestor. With the death of Charles, Jülich was a little more secure. Unfortunately, William only had a daughter and an illegitimate son, so the succession still was not clear-cut.

An Imperial Diet, or Reichstag, had begun at Freiburg[8] on 28 September 1497. Charles VIII's passing during this diet was fortuitous in that loose political ends could be tied up more easily. Holy Roman Emperor-Elect Maximilian I initially wanted the diet to take place in Worms the previous spring but had changed his mind and directed everyone to Freiburg. With reservations, the assembled notables from within Germany agreed on 7 August 1497 to move it to the Habsburg-controlled Freiburg. The original purpose of the diet was to finish ironing out the details outstanding from Imperial reforms established back in 1495.

One of the chief concerns of those assembled in the small, overburdened city was to sort out inheritance rights. Within Germany, urban estate holders managed to gain title to more property by purchasing or seizing privileges from the Imperial powers. This threatened the strength of the local ruling families and undermined the efficacy of Germany's feudal system. A German noble's main property went to his eldest son, and any spiritual territories were used to benefit second and subsequent sons, or an unmarried daughter. By chipping away at a nobleman's property, the urban estate holders increased their wealth at the expense of that of the nobleman and his future generations.

---

8 Freiburg-im-Breisgau, in modern Baden-Württemberg.

The Imperial Diet at Freiburg accomplished very little. Maximilian did not attend until late June 1498, almost nine months after it began. The idea of a unified legal code was broached, but nothing meaningful happened with it. In the end, the diet succeeded in cementing the German princes against Maximilian and spreading a new disease, the French pox. This was an early name for syphilis, which emerged in the fifteenth century.

Cooperation between Maximilian, William of Jülich-Berg, and John II of Cleves-Mark

The diet also brought Maximilian closer to William of Jülich-Berg and John II of Cleves-Mark. On 19 June, a few days before Maximilian showed up, William and John secured the Freiburg Agreement. Back in December 1497, the dukes had entered into an agreement with Maximilian's son Philip the Handsome, the terms of which were not entirely favourable to Jülich and Cleves. Maximilian smoothed out the terms of this agreement with William and John II. The parties entered into the Treaty of Freiburg on 19 June 1498, which in part clarified who owned what in the Low Countries. Cleves, Guelders and parts of Jülich were all very close to the Low Countries; indeed, the majority of Guelders and a portion of Cleves are now part of the modern-day Netherlands.

Additionally, Duke William and Duke John II promised 3,000 soldiers each to support Philip and Maximillian in their efforts against Duke Karl of Guelders. None of the parties were allowed to enter into agreements without the consent of the other signatories of the Treaty of Freiburg.

Duke William Secures Treaties for the Safety of Jülich-Berg

During the same period, unrest in the Lower Rhine region of Germany led to William securing various treaties for the security of Jülich-Berg. Most of the treaties were successfully agreed upon in the 1470s, including the initial treaty with Cleves-Mark and a treaty with Cologne.

William supported the efforts of Maximilian, Duke of Burgundy *jure uxoris* through his marriage to Mary of Burgundy. He assisted Maximilian in putting down a rebellion in the Netherlands in 1483, as discussed above. After Maximilian became King of the Romans in 1486, he was destined to become Holy Roman Emperor. William was largely pro-Imperial throughout the 1490s, even for a time after Karl of Egmond was made Duke of Guelders. Karl had a possible claim to Jülich, causing William some anxiety.

The Second War of Guelderian Succession

William's father Gerhard of Jülich-Berg was the nephew of Adolph of Jülich-Berg, who had become Duke of Berg in 1408. In 1423, Adolf's distant relative Rainald of Jülich-Guelders died without issue. The son of William II of Jülich and Maria of Guelders, Rainald had agreed with his councillors in 1418 that, should he die without children, his successor would have to be jointly accepted by both Jülich and Guelders.

The Second War of Guelderian Succession was the result, fought from 1423 to 1444 between Adolf of Jülich-Berg's forces and Arnold of Egmond's forces. The latter was elected sovereign of Guelders on 8 July 1423, and was officially enfeoffed with the territory by the future Holy Roman Emperor Sigismund on 15 August 1424. As part of the enfeoffment, he had to pay 14,000 guilders, which he did not do. Sigismund reacted by destroying the feudal deeds and placing Guelders under Adolf of Berg's control on 24 May 1425.

The parties reached a temporary cessation of war in July 1429, and there was relative peace until 1436. By this time, Adolf of Jülich-Berg had died childless, and his own nephew Gerhard continued the fight for Guelders. Gerhard, Duke William of Jülich-Berg's father, eventually stopped pursuing the claim. The dispute would resurface in very dramatic fashion between 1538 and 1543, this time between Duke William's grandson Wilhelm of Cleves and Holy Roman Emperor Charles V.

Marital Negotiations between Cleves-Mark and Jülich-Berg

In 1493, Duke John II of Cleves and Duke William of Jülich decided to meet in a field between the areas of Angerort and Wanheim. Now that William and John II both had children, they wished to formalize discussions that William had with John I in 1482. A castle existed in Angerort, perched where the Anger Creek meets the Rhine River. The crumbled foundations of the castle are still visible today, slowly tumbling into the creek.

The dukes travelled to the field by boat. Their aim was to discuss the future of their houses, and what concords they could reach to unify their respective duchies. At the time of the initial discussions between William and John I around 1482, William did not have children. The negotiations continued over the years, with Duke John II and Duke William eventually able to strike an agreement.

William wanted to avoid a succession crisis in Jülich-Berg and consolidate power in the Lower Rhine region. He and John II of Cleves-Mark agreed to the Cleves Union, one of the conditions of which was the marriage of their children. John gave William 10,000 guilders to help seal the deal. The money was not paid until many years later, when the marriage between Maria of Jülich-Berg and Johann III of Cleves-Mark was consummated.

The engagement *de praesenti* of Maria of Jülich-Berg and Johann III of Cleves-Mark took place on 25 November 1496 when Maria was five and Johann was six. However, Louis XII of France vacillated between supporting the match and wanting to wed Maria to the much-older Karl of Guelders to settle the dynastic disputes over Jülich and Guelders.

Maximilian I was in support of this marriage, as the only other potential union at the time was one between Cleves and Saxony. Maximilian feared that would cause too powerful a conglomeration of territories within the Holy Roman Empire. A union between Jülich-Berg and Cleves-Mark presented its own possible issues for a Holy Roman Emperor, but the landmasses were more consolidated rather than being spread out, as would be the case for a Cleves–Saxony union.

In early 1497, John II sent word to the clerical community throughout the duchies of Jülich and Berg about the future marriage of Johann and Maria. Pastors were directed to announce the marriage to their congregations. John requested that prayers be given for the happiness of Johann and Maria's marriage, and for peace in the Cleves-Mark and Jülich-Berg lands.

Louis XII of France Mediates for the Lower Rhine

Louis XII was further involved in the politics of the Lower Rhine region by agreeing to mediate any disputes between William of Jülich-Berg, John II of Cleves-Mark and Karl of Guelders. William, still worried about Duke Karl's claims to Jülich, travelled to France in the 1490s to work out diplomatic specifics concerning Guelders. Karl appeared in France as well, but John II chose to remain behind in the Cleves-Mark territories.

The Treaty of Orléans between Jülich and Guelders was ratified on 29 December 1499. By its terms Louis XII was given the final say in any disputes between Jülich and Guelders. Although this likely assuaged William's fears, it entirely excluded the input of Holy Roman Emperor Frederick III and his son, the future Maximilian I, under whose jurisdiction both Jülich and Guelders fell. This caused an almost immediate cooling of the relationship with Maximilian, still only King of the Romans. He struck back by trying to position Jülich-Berg and Cleves-Mark overtly against Guelders at the cost of Jülich-Berg and Cleves-Mark.

In 1500, as part of the ongoing efforts to bring peace to Jülich-Berg and Cleves-Mark, Duke John II put down a 1,500-strong army from Nijmegen. The army attacked the city of Cleves but was easily defeated. This small insurrection further illustrates the domestic concerns underlying the Cleves Union.

Despite Maximilian's posturing, William successfully maintained a diplomatic relationship with him. He was a guest of Maximilian's in Innsbruck for a long period in 1501 to determine reparations for Jülich-Berg's involvement with the struggle over Guelders. For the rest of his life, William visited with Maximilian roughly once a year.

Duke Karl of Guelders Stirs up Trouble

Peace did not last for long, and there was cause for concern in Cleves when Duke Karl of Guelders decided to attack. In 1502, the cessation of arms between Guelders, France and Cleves was agreed upon. Duke Karl of Guelders broke it on 25 May, even though he had declared a Sunday or two before that no one from Guelders should harm any person from Cleves or Jülich-Berg for any reason.

Karl and his army invaded and burned villages and towns within the Cleves territories on 25 May 1500. They took over the city of Huissen on 28 May, managing to hold the area for a month. Early in the morning of

26 June 1502, Duke Karl and around 1,500 *Landsknechte* advanced on the town of Westervoort. The Cleves army engaged them there and won an easy victory, taking captive 500 *Landsknechte*. The remainder of Karl's army fled to Arnhem.

The Guelderian force that was still situated at Huissen abandoned the city so quickly that they left behind valuable cannon. They also left their provisions, including beer and wine. According to the chronicler Johann Wassenberch, 'Four heavy cannons were captured, named Vernenborch, Pluckroisken, Breckmuren and Plump. Four beautiful howitzers and eleven light guns, long-barrelled cannons and muskets were also captured during the assault by Cleves.' Duke Karl's horse was seized, and his banner torn down. Remarking about the event, Johann Wassenberch wrote in his chronicle that 'the colourful cow (of Cleves) succeeded in cornering the Guelderian bull.'[9] The attack launched by Duke Karl was considered baseless and shameful, given that the ruling Egmond family of Guelders and Von der Mark family of Cleves were related.

The year 1503 was difficult to bear in Cleves-Mark. The plague raged through the archdiocese of Cologne, and there was an outbreak of war. Duke Karl of Guelders was at it again, harrying John II. After John II defeated him, Karl fled to France. A rumour spread that he was dead, but, unfortunately for the Von der Marks, he was alive and would continue to annoy them. Maximilian I had no interest in interceding at this point, either.

In late January, English ambassadors present in Cologne remarked on Maximilian's behaviour. He was still known as King of the Romans at this time, having not been invested as Holy Roman Emperor yet. Their remarks were reported in the English-held Venetian Papers:

The English ambassadors ... were surprised at the departure of [Maximilian] who was gone to the frontiers of the territory of the Duke of Guelders. The baggage-carts had on that day proceeded thither with an escort of 200 cavalry, so that his Majesty will have 600 men at arms, including those of the Marquis of Brandenburg, and as many more are being sent to him by the Duke of Cleves, who is the enemy of the Duke of Guelders ... The Duke of Guelders is gone to the King of France, having lost two battles in the territory of the Duke of Cleves, who was assisted by the neighbouring barons; others say that the Duke of Guelders is dead.

The English embassy, including Sir Thomas Brandon,[10] were after Richard de la Pole. Known as the White Rose, Henry VII perceived him as a serious

---

9 The crest in Cleves's heraldic achievement is a red cow with gold horns, and Duke Karl is considered the Bull of Guelders due to his constant warring.
10 Uncle of Charles Brandon, Duke of Suffolk, who was a close friend and brother-in-law to Henry VIII of England.

threat. Apparently, Richard de la Pole was in Aachen, roughly two days' journey from Cologne. The English wanted help capturing him. Whatever the outcome of the negotiations, he did not die until 1516.

Supporting Burgundy

A set of curious incidences occurred in the years 1503 and 1504, causing some in both Jülich-Berg and Cleves-Mark to fear that the Apocalypse was drawing near. In 1503, crosses and other signs relating to Jesus Christ fell from the sky onto people's naked bodies, burning and injuring them. Priests standing before their altars saw the signs fall onto the altar cloths. What really happened here can only be pondered. An earthquake in Cologne occurred in 1504, again causing anxiety in Jülich-Berg and Cleves-Mark. Wassenberch records that the earthquake was easily felt, and 'caused the pots hung on the wall near each other to clink together'.

On 19 May 1505, Maximilian held an Imperial diet in Cologne. Many princes, lords and abbots attended, likely including Duke William of Jülich-Berg and at least a representative from Cleves-Mark, if not Duke John II himself. Maximilian, who was declared Holy Roman Emperor by the Pope in 1503, visited the territories of Jülich-Berg and Cleves-Mark on at least three occasions that year. Maximilian's son Philip the Handsome attacked Arnhem, an important city in the Duchy of Guelders, roughly a month later 22 June. As the son of Mary of Burgundy, Philip had a claim to the duchy.

Duke John II joined his army with Philip's, amassing a huge force of infantry and cavalry. The joint armies of Cleves-Mark and Burgundy assailed Arnhem until 6 July, when the city finally surrendered. A peace agreement between Philip the Handsome and Duke Karl of Guelders was swiftly concluded. Among the terms it was stipulated that whatever Philip seized would stay in his possession and that people could move throughout the territory unmolested. The treaty would be revisited in two years. However, Duke Karl, who never saw a chance for battle he didn't like, could not maintain his end of the bargain.

Mechthild of Hesse, Duchess Consort of Cleves, passed away in 1505 after being treated for illness by doctors in Cologne. After a funeral procession through Cologne befitting her station, Mechthild's body was brought by ship to Cleves, where she was buried.

Maximilian, still on very good terms with Duke William of Jülich-Berg, commissioned William for a peacekeeping mission in 1506. That same year, from 28 July to 23 August, a comet hung in the sky, leaving the people to contemplate its meaning. Not long after, in 1507, it was rumoured that Maximilian wanted to install William as Regent of the Low Countries. However, in the event he entrusted the position to his widowed daughter Margaret of Savoy.

More Aggression from Duke Karl

In February of 1507, Duke Karl decided to seize the property which Philip the Handsome had taken back in 1505. Philip had died the year before on 25 September 1506, leaving his young son Charles, then being raised by his paternal aunt Margaret in the Low Countries, virtually powerless to assert his rights either through the 1505 treaty or his inheritance as the grandson of Mary of Burgundy.

After this most recent round of aggression exhibited by Duke Karl, representatives of the various Cleves knighthoods and cities approached Duke William of Jülich-Berg to ask when his daughter Maria would wed Johann III. The Cleves knights were tired of fighting against Duke Karl unaided. They demanded that a date certain be set, but William felt he was not able to do so because Maria's status as Duke William's official heir had not been established at the Imperial level. Anxieties were increased due to an outbreak of the plague in the Duchy of Cleves, too.

A Stable Future for Jülich-Berg

Finally, Maximilian agreed to support Duke William's daughter Maria's claim to Jülich-Berg. On 4 May 1509, Maximilian signed a patent in his capacity as Holy Roman Emperor, securing Maria of Jülich-Berg's rights as William's sole heir. This secured Johann III's position and his right *jure uxoris* to the lands of Jülich-Berg. Maximilian's patent in favour of Maria precluded her illegitimate brother John of Jülich and any of his future children from laying claim to the territories of Jülich-Berg, bringing further stability.

With Maria's claim to Jülich-Berg cleared up, her planned marriage to Johann III of Cleves could take place. The couple were wed on 12 March 1510 in Düsseldorf after Johann arrived to a fabulous reception. Maria's parents, Sibylle of Brandenburg and Duke William, along with the nobles from Jülich-Berg and Cleves-Mark, attended the wedding. Johann and Maria officially consummated their marriage on 6 October 1510, after which three days of joyous feasting and revelries followed. Johann returned to his friends in Cleves for another celebration, which went on from the night of 16 October into the next day.

All looked well for the new ducal couple. With the heir of Cleves-Mark wed to the heiress of Jülich-Berg, Johann and Maria's children would not have many concerns about territorial squabbles. The family was on good terms with the Holy Roman Emperor, and the blending of interests could only help them at court. The future was bright for the Von der Marks.

2

Saxony, the Powerful Electorate to the East

Saxon Succession

The Electorate of Saxony had its own succession crisis brewing in the early fifteenth century. Elector Frederick II von Wettin, who reigned from 1428 to 1464, had six children who survived to adulthood: three girls and three boys. The second eldest, a daughter named Anna, married Elector Albrecht-Achilles III of Brandenburg. Anna of Saxony was the grandmother of Maria of Jülich-Berg. The eldest son, Frederick, died in 1451 at the age of twenty-two. When Frederick II passed away in 1464, his son Ernst von Wettin became Elector of Saxony. The youngest brother, Albrecht, remained as a Duke of Saxony. A dispute between Elector Ernst's children and Duke Albrecht's children would rear its ugly head in the 1540s.

Duke Albrecht, known as the Brave, was born 31 July 1443. He had four children, a girl and three boys, who all survived to adulthood and made excellent matches. Katharina, the eldest, married Archduke Sigmund of Austria; George the Bearded married a Polish princess; and Heinrich the Pious wed Katharina of Mecklenburg. Finally, the youngest, Friedrich, became Grandmaster of the German Order. Heinrich's oldest son Moritz, born in 1521, came to value his personal ambition over the security of his cousins.

Elector Ernst of Saxony

Ernst became Elector of Saxony, Landgrave of Thuringia and Margrave of Meissen during his tenure, which began in 1464. Ernst and his brother Albrecht succeeded in expanding the lands under their control, in part due to excellent administration. The cities of Meissen and Dresden grew their circles of influence during Ernst's reign. He purchased the Vogtland in 1466, and forced Quedlinburg to come under his control in 1477. His youngest sister, Hedwig, was Abbess of Quedlinburg at the time. Ernst also went to Rome in 1480 so he could receive control of Mainz and Magdeburg.

Upon the death of the Landgrave of Thuringia in 1480, Ernst seized control of Leipzig. Ernst then decided to divide up the Saxon territories with his brother Albert, which weakened the power of Saxony overall. Each brother minted his own coins in his own territory, marking a major development in the Saxon monetary system. The first big changes came in the 1470s, when the brothers agreed to use a silver alloy coin as currency before changing it to a fine silver coin because the citizenry did not trust the value of alloys.

Ernst invested his political energies in being on good terms with the Bohemians. He had a cordial relationship with Holy Roman Emperor Frederick III as well. As an Elector, Ernst was one of the few charged with electing the new Holy Roman Emperor once the incumbent passed away or stepped down. Ernst outlived Frederick III, and spent his last days trying to secure support for Frederick's son Maximilian as the next Holy Roman Emperor. Ernst died on 26 August 1486 after falling from his horse.

The Ernestine Electors

Ernst had seven children, five of whom were boys, but only the eldest four sons survived to adulthood. The eldest brother, Frederick the Wise, and the youngest surviving brother, John the Steadfast, each became Elector of Saxony in their own turn. The middle brothers were destined for the ecclesiastical life.

Holy Roman Emperor Maximilian I was tenuously an uncle by marriage to Frederick the Wise and John the Steadfast. Their mother was Elisabeth of Bavaria. Elisabeth's brother Albrecht IV of Bavaria married Kunigunde of Austria, Maximilian's sister. It was a distant relation, and a relation by marriage, but Maximilian was still regarded as an uncle.

Elector Frederick the Wise

Frederick III, known as both the Cheap and the Wise, was born at Torgau on 17 January 1463. He never had legitimate children of his own, but maintained a long-term affair with Anna Weller which produced two illegitimate sons and an illegitimate daughter. Frederick and his four younger brothers, including Ernst and John, were educated through the monastic school in Grimma. Frederick developed a higher degree of intellectual refinement and was better educated than had been the custom. He gained a good command of both Latin and French, and favoured the study of history and theology. Despite understanding Latin, however, he rarely spoke it.

Frederick was very intellectually engaged, and invited famous humanists, theologians and artists to his court. These included the philosopher Erasmus of Rotterdam and the artists Albrecht Dürer and Lucas Cranach the Elder. Frederick was quite learned in the sciences and encouraged classicist teachings. He once fought to acquire a collection of thousands of Greek books from Venice.

Frederick's personality could not be more different than his vibrant uncle Maximilian's. Despite enjoying intellectual discourse and the exchange of ideas, he was not known for possessing the same ingenuity and problem-solving skills as Maximilian. He was an awesome collector of intellectually stimulating items, such as the books mentioned above, and holy relics. In addition, he was enamoured with knightly and court protocol, and immersed himself in its intricacies to great effect.

As a ruler, Frederick often dithered. More often than not, he was confident that Providence would lead to the right solution. His temperament had a devastating effect on Imperial–Saxon politics in the early sixteenth century and was a direct cause of Saxony stopping its expansion. Despite his failures, Frederick did his best to seek autonomy for the German princes as a whole.

Elector John of Saxony
John was born on 30 June 1468 in Meissen, and spent time at the Holy Roman Emperor Frederick III's court in Grosseheim. In his youth, he campaigned with Maximilian I against the Hungarians and Venetians as well. John married twice; with his first wife he had one child, a boy named Johann Friedrich. From his second marriage he had two daughters and two sons, but only the eldest and youngest children survived. He also had at least two illegitimate sons.

Elector Frederick's Reign
Frederick the Wise took over the princely responsibilities of Elector in 1486, after his father Ernst died. Frederick and John ruled the territory jointly, excluding their brother Archbishop Ernst of Magdeburg. The two brothers ruled the Electorate of Saxony in harmony. John ruled the Kurland alone, however. During his lifetime, only Frederick was called Elector of Saxony.

In 1488, to raise funds, the brothers mortgaged off a portion of Saxon-held Bohemian fiefs. In 1490, Frederick and his brother John travelled to the court of Maximilian I. The brothers stayed there for a time.

Three years later, in 1493, Frederick went on pilgrimage to the Holy Land. In preparation, Frederick issued a decree at Torgau on 19 March 1493 which served as his last will and testament. The document was signed and sealed by the three brothers: Elector Frederick, Archbishop Ernst and Duke John. Frederick left his main inheritance to John, with the remnants going to Archbishop Ernst and their Albertine cousins. Frederick brought back upwards of 5,000 relics from the Holy Land. He deposited them in the All-Saints monastery at Wittenberg.

The brothers inherited territorial disputes from their father, who was still trying to hammer out the division of Saxon territory between the Ernestine and Albertine branches as late as 1485. The relationship between Frederick and his cousin George was tense throughout Frederick's time as Elector.

Frederick returned from the Holy Land in 1493 and was invited to join Maximilian's Royal Council the following year.

Changing the Government in Saxony

On 2 March 1499, Frederick and John agreed upon a modified form of governance for the Electorate of Saxony. The goal of the brothers was to reform and streamline the current legal system and hearing of court cases. Among the issues tackled were methods to create legally binding documents and bring cases to court, concerns over enforcing confidentiality, and the permanent appointment of four men to the council. Frederick took a keen interest in Saxony's legal system and its administration throughout his time as Elector. He also encouraged the use of the German language in the legal system.

Early 1500s for John and Frederick

John married Sophie von Mecklenburg in 1500. The couple welcomed one child, a boy named Johann Friedrich, on 30 June 1503, John's thirty-fifth birthday. The baby was born in Torgau, and possibly named after his father and his uncle, whose names in German were Johann and Friedrich, respectively. Sadly, Sophie von Mecklenburg died days later from complications related to Johann Friedrich's birth.

In 1502, Frederick officially founded the University of Wittenberg. He funded the endeavour by using the money originally collected for papal indulgences. Frederick, who was very pious, was not comfortable with the use of indulgences.

Frederick sought the guardianship of Philip, Landgrave of Hesse, after the death of Philip's father from syphilis in 1509. However, Frederick's cousin George of Saxony was firmly against this and wanted the guardianship for himself. Frederick managed to keep control over the young Philip until 1514, when Philip's mother seized control. She convinced Maximilian I to have Philip declared of age in 1518, despite Philip being only thirteen years old.

Fate moved rapidly in the 1510s. Frederick invited the not-yet-radicalised Martin Luther to teach at Wittenberg University in 1512. The next year, Frederick and John's brother Archbishop Ernst of Magdeburg died. With his death, John became next in line to the Electorate of Saxony. The various Saxon territories were divided up as well.

Saxony and Martin Luther's Influence

In October 1517, Martin Luther posted his Ninety-Five Theses on Wittenberg Castle's chapel door. The act of posting the theses in and of itself was not odd or rebellious; matters of debate were frequently posted there so that others who wished to join the discussion could understand the premises. It was what followed from Luther's action that was different, and increasingly powerful. Frederick supported Martin Luther initially more out of duty to the Saxon legal system than because Frederick agreed with Luther's position on theology. Additionally, Luther became a major attraction for potential students to Frederick's new university in Wittenberg.

Throughout the late fifteenth and early sixteenth century, various disputes over territory sprung up across the German-speaking portions of the Holy

Roman Empire. In 1517, a new facet of rebellion against the empire was introduced in Saxony when Martin Luther's Ninety-Five Theses became known. Maximilian I was still the Holy Roman Emperor in 1517. He could not know what the changing attitudes toward the Catholic Church would do to the fabric of the empire.

In 1518, an Imperial diet was held at Augsburg to discuss who would become the next Holy Roman Emperor. Maximilian had serious concerns for his health, and with good reason. Maximilian put forward his eighteen-year-old Burgundian-Spanish grandson Charles. By this time, Charles was recognised as Charles I of Spain. Frederick was against the idea.

At the same diet, the topic of Martin Luther's teachings arose. Frederick secured a meeting with the papal legate, who promised that Luther would only be interrogated. This satisfied Frederick for the time being. Frederick made sure to provide Luther with good legal counsel in Augsburg, just in case. It slowly dawned on him that keeping Luther in Saxony was dangerous for the Electorate. Frederick's Catholic cousin George disapproved of Martin Luther, causing a larger division between Electoral and Ducal Saxony.

Frederick's health began to decline in 1518. He was passive in both personality and body, and developed an issue with gall or kidney stones. Complications from the disorder eventually killed him. Frederick avoided war at all costs, particularly in his later years.

By December 1518, Frederick threw caution to the wind and asked Luther to stay on at Wittenberg University. Frederick managed to maintain a neutral stance toward the theologian, never formally declaring in favour of Luther's burgeoning religion. He chose to protect Luther because he felt it was his duty, as a Christian prince, to allow for the cautious exploration of Luther's teachings just in case Luther was correct.

Frederick no doubt realised there were serious issues within the Catholic Church. He corresponded with Luther directly in 1518, and continued the correspondence until his death a few years later. He continued to celebrate the Catholic Mass on his deathbed.

Death of Maximilian I and Rise of Charles V

Holy Roman Emperor Maximilian I passed away on 12 January 1519. Between Maximilian's death and the election of the next Holy Roman Emperor, Frederick acted as Regent of the Holy Roman Emperor. He became widely respected for his refusal to accept bribes, and treated any monies paid to him by the Habsburg faction as repayment of debts owed by Maximilian to Saxony. Additionally, the Habsburgs proposed Catherine of Castile, Maximilian's youngest granddaughter, as a bride for Frederick's nephew Johann Friedrich. Frederick entertained the match, but insisted that it had nothing to do with his position on who should be the next emperor. Frederick and the Electorate of Saxony were considered the most influential figures in Imperial Germany. Frederick was offered the Imperial throne at one point, but turned it down.

The threat of Turkish invasion into German lands was quite real in 1518. Frederick, despite being a powerful Elector, simply did not have access to the sheer number of troops Maximilian's grandson Charles did. For the safety of Christendom, Frederick threw his weight behind electing Charles V. This did nothing to impress Henry VIII of England and Francis I of France, who also hoped to become Holy Roman Emperor. Charles' first coronation, in Germany, took place in 1520. At the time, the marriage negotiations between Johann Friedrich and Catherine had not been completed, much to Frederick's annoyance.

Charles V's Enthronement as King of the Romans-Germans
Twenty-year-old Charles V was crowned in October 1520 as the King of the Romans-Germans at a grand ceremony in Aachen. By being crowned King of the Romans-Germans, Charles V was the Holy Roman Emperor Elect. Pope Leo X gave Charles V permission to style himself as the Holy Roman Emperor until Charles' 1530 coronation at Bologna by Pope Clement VII.

Charles V's train was massive. It had at least 2,000 horses. The various electors, including Elector Frederick of Saxony, made up part of Charles V's company.

Curiously, Frederick had a run-in with Duke Johann III of Jülich-Cleves-Berg, then still only recognised as Duke of Jülich and Berg. Though the details are unclear, it is recorded in an account of Charles V's coronation printed around 1520 that the Elector of Saxony and 'Duke of Gülch' – an archaic spelling of 'Jülich' – squabbled for a long time over precedence during the procession to Aachen Cathedral.

Frederick of Saxony believed that Johann III of Cleves should have been included with the Saxon contingent rather than Johann being independent of Saxony. This went back to the ongoing debate over whether Johann III had the stronger claim to Jülich, or if Frederick did. In effect, if Frederick had the stronger claim, then Johann III was a vassal of Frederick's. Johann's rights to Jülich and Berg, as mentioned in Chapter 1, were secured by Maximilian I. In the end, Johann III entered the city before Elector Frederick of Saxony. Frederick likely took exception to this snub.

Frederick's relationship with Charles V was friendly up until the latter's appointment as King of the Romans-Germans. Thereafter, things quickly cooled between the two. Francis I of France took advantage of the situation, quietly allying himself with Frederick of Saxony. To maintain harmony, Charles V revived the suggestion that his youngest sister Catherine be wed to Frederick's nephew Johann Friedrich. The arrangement stood in place for the first part of the 1520s.

On 2 February 1521, Thomas Spinelly, a representative of Henry VIII, wrote to Cardinal Thomas Wolsey in England about the opening of the Imperial diet at Worms. Spinelly noted the ongoing discord between the German electors, on full display during the opening celebration of the Mass:

Please it your grace [Cardinal Wolsey] to understand that the 24th day of January I wrote my last letters unto the same, and the Sunday following, the 27th, in the cathedral church... was celebr[at]ed the mass of the Holy Ghost, there being the Emperor [Charles V] arrayed with a rich gown of cloth of gold furred with sables, with five Electors and many spiritual lords, the which after the accustomed order kept their rooms... And as to the other temporal princes, because they could not agree together of their places, none of them all sat; signifying unto your grace that divers councils hath been kept for to concord them, and after found no means that I know of, and seeing no remedy in the matter it was said ever of them should stand to all assemblies on their feet unto they agree. At the which solemnity, the elector [Frederick] of Saxon[y] to and fro did bear the naked sword before the Emperor; and the [same] day at the afternoon all the said Electors and Princes went to the court, and in the great hall appointed for the same the Emperor sat upon a seat of three degrees, under a rich cloth of state, the Electors being of both sides with other as before.

Charles V then spoke to the assembled princes in slightly broken German, confirming that he wished for the princes to act together. The fracturing of the German empire had begun.

Frederick was still in favour of the match between his nephew and Charles' sister Catherine, and it was further reported that:

He showed me likewise that the elector of Saxon[y] is well assured and pleased of the alliance of marriage between his nephew and heir and the Emperor his sister; and thereby I suppose by procurations of both parties the matrimony hath been contracted *per verba de præsenti*.

Effectively, seventeen-year-old Johann Friedrich and thirteen-year-old Catherine were married.

The 1521 Imperial Diet of Worms

A couple months later, the Diet of Worms still sitting, Martin Luther was ordered to appear on 17 April at four o'clock in the afternoon. Frederick did not agree with Luther being put on trial at the Imperial diet, and believed that the proper legal protocol was for Luther to be interrogated in Saxony before the issue was put before the Empire. Nevertheless, Luther was questioned, and his answers displeased Charles V.

In May 1521, the Edict of Worms was issued. It read in part,

For this reason we forbid anyone from this time forward to dare, either by words or by deeds, to receive, defend, sustain, or favour the said Martin Luther. On the contrary, we want him to be apprehended and punished as a notorious heretic, as he deserves, to be brought personally before us, or to be securely guarded until those who have captured him inform us, whereupon we will order the appropriate manner of proceeding against the said Luther. Those who will help in his capture will be rewarded generously for their good work.

Luther was allowed to return home. Frederick, fearing for Luther's safety, intercepted him at Wittenberg and took him into custody. He then hid Luther in Wartburg Castle in Eisenach. Luther took up the disguise of 'Junker Jörg' or 'Young Lord George'.

The Lutheran Church grew in Electoral Saxony in part because Frederick looked the other way. His unwillingness to either remove Luther from Wittenberg University or quash the preaching and circulation of Luther's teachings angered Charles V. As a result, Charles terminated the engagement of Catherine and Johann Friedrich, coincidentally shortly before Frederick's death.

The Prophets of Zwickau

Later that year, in December 1521, three individuals appeared in the Saxon town of Zwickau. The town sprang up at the base of the Erzgebirge mountains, where a large silver deposit was discovered in the Schneeberg[11] in 1470. The mining of iron was well established before the silver lode was discovered. Miners exploited the land for silver throughout the late fifteenth century and on into the sixteenth.

The influx of money from mining further widened the gap between rich and poor. Larger mining operations either absorbed or bankrupted the smaller ones.

A man named Thomas Müntzer had the pleasure of meeting Martin Luther in Wittenberg in 1517. He was very supportive of Luther's ideas to reform religion. By May 1520, Müntzer was installed at St Mary's Church in Zwickau upon the recommendation of Luther. In the years between 1517 and 1520, Müntzer grew increasingly radical in his beliefs. He studied not only theology, but also mysticism.

Once installed at St Mary's, Müntzer preached Luther's teachings with a heavy dose of radicalism. Müntzer's sermons unsettled the local officials, but he was not removed because he was still teaching Lutheranism overall. Müntzer was permanently established at St Katharine's, visited in high numbers by the local weavers, as resident pastor after a town council vote in September 1520.

Placement at St Katharine's brought Müntzer into contact with another radical, the weaver Nikolaus Storch. Both men believed in the idea that spiritual enlightenment could be obtained through dreams. Müntzer's sermons and beliefs became more radicalised. The local Catholic clergy were concerned about the sermons coming out of St Katharine's. Things came

---

11 Translated as 'Snow Mountain'.

to a head in April 1521, at which point Müntzer was dismissed from St Katharine's.

Seven months later, in December 1521, Nikolaus Storch joined with Markus Stübner and Thomas Dreschel to form a new religious movement.[12] The Zwickau Prophets, as they became known, had two outstanding features which were central to their religious movement. First, they did not believe that infants should be baptised. Second, they believed in spiritual revelations through dreams. This meant that, rather than studying established theology, the Zwickau Prophets interpreted their dreams as their theological basis. The Zwickau Prophets also believed that the Apocalypse was coming, although this was not too radical of an idea for early sixteenth-century western Europe.

The Zwickau Prophets were forced out of Zwickau by the town council. The trio made their way to Wittenberg, stopping there for a few days. Around the same time, there were disturbances in Wittenberg. The disturbances are traditionally blamed on the Zwickau Prophets, although recent scholarship shows it might have been more of a coincidence.

A letter sent to Duke John of Saxony[13] arrived shortly before the Zwickau Prophets. In the letter, Duke John was warned about them:

> Some men doubted whether the belief of the godfather can be of use in the baptism. And some think that they can be blessed without being baptised. And some state that the Holy Bible is not useful in the education of men, but that men can only be taught by the Spirit, for if God had wanted to teach men with the Bible, then He would have sent us a Bible down from heaven. And some say that one should not pray for the dead. And suchlike horrible abominations which are giving your Lordship's town an unchristian and *Picardish* name.

The Prophets had eight articles which they agreed upon for their religious movement. A couple of these centred upon Christian marriage. The Prophets believed that marriage was a Christian institution, and not divinely recommended. Additionally, they claimed that men could take multiple women and be as promiscuous as desired. As mentioned before, infant baptism was discouraged. Adult baptism was not encouraged, meaning that the Prophets did not believe in baptism. They believed that all property should be held communally. Secular authorities were to reform or be abolished, especially because everyone enjoyed free will when it came to their individual faiths. Church ceremonies were unnecessary, as well.

---

12 The identification of Markus Stübner and Thomas Dreschel as the other two persons is disputed by historians. The important fact is that there were three of them, including Nikolaus Storch.

13 This particular Duke John was the son of George the Bearded of the Albertine line, making him a cousin of Electors Frederick and John.

Philipus Melanchthon, a student and then colleague of Martin Luther, did his best to bring peace to Wittenberg. He was unsuccessful, and asked Luther to come out of hiding at Wartburg Castle to put down the unrest. Luther acquiesced, but not before the universities were temporarily shut down in response to the Prophets' preaching.

Luther's Return, with More Unrest

Luther came back to Wittenberg in March 1522. When he publicly returned to the pulpit, he gave eight sermons against religious fanatics. It is thought that this series of sermons was in response to the Zwickau Prophets, whom Luther suggested should be banned from Zwickau, Erfurt and other Saxon territories. The Prophets and Müntzer were expelled and roamed throughout Germanic lands over the coming years. Their preaching rapidly gained support among the lower German estates.

Moving forward to 1524, an uprising began during the harvest season in south-western Germany. It would be the largest peasant uprising for centuries. In Stühlingen, the harvest was poor and there was little work so the local peasantry was ordered to collect snail shells instead. Incensed, over 1,000 peasants gathered to petition the local lord, the Countess of Lupfen, for various benefits and rights. They were organised, having appointed officers and created their own standard.

The uprising swept across the south and up into Bavaria. By February, another well-organised group of peasants in Memmingen, Bavaria, presented a list of twelve articles to the city council for consideration. They promoted Luther's idea of a plain reading of the Bible, from which the articles were drawn. Their purpose was to do away with tithes, unlearned clergy and other perceived wrongs. The articles represented a significant break from the Catholic Church and the Holy Roman Empire.

Martin Luther did not support the revolt. He published a polemic, 'Against the Murderous, Thieving Hordes of Peasants'. The peasants used Luther as a rallying cry, nevertheless. Luther published the work to disassociate himself from the rebels' violent actions. His protest was against the Church – 'Render unto Caesar...' Luther sided firmly with the authority of the German princes.

The uprising became a revolt in Thuringia, threatening the Landgrave of Hesse and Saxon territory. On 29 April 1525, the peasants started gathering and terrorizing nobles in the countryside. On 11 May, the radical preacher Thomas Müntzer brought 300 troops to the city of Mühlhausen to fight the princes. Thousands of peasants flocked to him. Duke George the Bearded of Saxony and Landgrave Philip of Hesse brought their mercenaries, German *Landsknechte*, to put down the force of roughly 6,000 peasants.

The force of *Landsknechte* was roughly the same size as that of the peasants, but these were professional soldiers who knew how to fight. The peasants managed to obtain a truce with Duke George and Landgrave Philip on 14 May. The very next day, the princes turned on the peasants and slaughtered them at the Battle of Frankenhausen.

The peasants had been camped outside Frankenhausen and made a wagon fort, which did nothing to stave off the princes' attack. The battle lasted less than an hour. Anywhere from 3,000 to 10,000 peasants were slaughtered, but fewer than ten *Landsknechte* died. It was reported that streams of blood ran down the hills.

Müntzer retreated into Frankenhausen. He was quickly given up to the authorities, and imprisoned. He was tortured before being executed on 27 May 1525.

Subsequent battles took place in Würzburg in May and June. Another battle occurred in Habsburg-controlled Freiburg. The revolt ended in September 1525, having led to the deaths of roughly 100,000 peasants.

Death of Elector Frederick and Rise of Elector John

Elector Frederick of Saxony died at Lochau on 15 May 1525, the same day as the Battle of Frankenhausen. As a slap in the face to Charles V, Frederick took both the Catholic and the Lutheran forms of the last rites. With Frederick's death, the rebellious peasants felt they lost their beacon of hope among the princes.

Per the 1513 agreement, Frederick's younger brother John became the next Elector of Saxony. John firmly embraced Luther's teachings. He did not care one whit for Charles V's sensibilities, and grew openly hostile toward Charles over time.

John the Constant was born 30 June 1468, the fourth of Ernst's five sons. In his youth, John spent time at Emperor Frederick III's Imperial court. Later, after Frederick III's son Maximilian became Holy Roman Emperor, John campaigned with Maximilian against the Venetians and Hungarians.

As co-ruler of Electoral Saxony with his elder brother Frederick, John supported Frederick's attempts at reforming the Saxon government and legal system. John governed the Saxon territory of Weimar by himself; it was partitioned off for him in 1513, and he moved his court there shortly after.

John was very different from Frederick. Where Frederick was passive, John was active. Where Frederick was peaceful, John, though shrewd, was aggressive. Most dangerously, where Frederick respected the Emperor, John could not care less. He would frequently clash with Charles V, fuelling a breakdown between the Holy Roman Emperor and John's son and successor, Johann Friedrich.

3

The Young Family of Jülich-Cleves-Berg, 1511–1527

The New Ducal Family

The newlyweds took on increasing responsibilities soon after their marriage. In mid-July 1511, Maria's mother Sibylle of Brandenburg went to the city of Duisburg for religious purposes, donating money to the religious community there. That same year, their fathers entered into an agreement about the minting of money. The values of money in the region were inconsistent, and the two patriarchs wished to correct the situation. Duke William of Jülich-Berg died on 6 September 1511.

Johann became Duke of Jülich-Berg *jure uxoris* after the death of his father-in-law. Maria, being a woman, was not able to hold property in her own right. As a hereditary duchess, a status recognised within the Holy Roman Empire, anyone who married Maria (and the heirs they had with her) would maintain title to Jülich-Berg.

The Von der Mark dukes had great success in improving their family's standing through marriage, extending back to John I and forward to Wilhelm V. They were able to bring wealth and international connections to Cleves-Mark.

Their diplomatic involvements helped the Von der Mark dukes garner respect on the international scene, too. The dukes of Cleves were regularly included in international treaties, such as the Treaty of Paris from March 1515. The Treaty of Paris was between the new French king, Francis I, and Charles V (then only the Count of Flanders and Duke of Burgundy). England, under Henry VIII, was also part of the treaty.

The Relationship between Johann III and Maria of Jülich-Berg

The couple had a successful marriage overall. Johann III, known as either the Peacemaker or the Simple, took Maria's concerns about Jülich-Berg into consideration when making policy. The blonde Maria was described as late as 1535 as being energetic, intelligent and attractive, if a little bit heavier than when she had married Johann twenty-five years earlier. Johann was slim, with brown hair and a strong jaw.

The couple spoke two different dialects of German. Johann spoke a form of German that was heavily influenced by Dutch, whereas Maria's dialect was prevalent in Düsseldorf and Jülich, and more like modern German. Likely all three of the Von der Mark girls spoke German that was closer to their mother's dialect than their father's. It is certain that at least Sybylla spoke a Rhenish dialect like Maria's. Sybylla's prayer book, in the collection of the State Library of Munich, is undated, but reflects her linguistic preference. This would have been a result of the girls being raised in the *Frauenzimmer* by their mother. From Anna's letters, it appears that her dialect was a mixture of how her parents spoke, with her spellings and words favouring neither.

The First Child of Cleves

Maria of Jülich-Berg enjoyed the affection of her husband Johann III and admiration of the court in early 1512, leading up to the birth of her first child. On a warm summer morning in 1512, a much-anticipated baby entered the world:

[In the year 1512] on St. Alexius' Day [of 17 July], at around 7:00 in the morning, the first child of Duke Johann III of Cleves, Jülich, and Berg was born. It was a daughter, who was named after the Duchess' mother Sibylle. The godparents were the Count of Waldeck, the old Duchess of Jülich [Sibylle of Brandenburg], and the wife of the old governor of Nesselrode, from Berg.

The infant Sybylla von der Mark was dubbed as being 'of Cleves', as would her younger sisters and brother.

Earlier that year, in late February, one of Johann's better-known illegitimate brothers fought at the Siege of Brescia. Known as John,[14] the Bastard of Cleves, or simply the Bastard, he helped give Cleves a reputation for producing fierce soldiers, seemingly without morals. A report from the battle says,

The Germans ... put all they can find in the city to the sword, break into the nunneries and monasteries, spare neither women or children. The whole city was given up to plunder and the licentiousness of the soldiers; every

---

14 The dukes of Cleves-Mark and Jülich-Berg had a habit of naming their illegitimate sons 'Johann', or 'John' in English. John of Jülich was born to Duke William of Jülich-Berg in the 1490s. John, the Bastard of Cleves, was born in the 1470s or so to John II of Cleves, and John of Berg was born to Wilhelm V of Jülich-Cleves-Berg in roughly the 1540s.

house they entered they abused as they pleased ... The writer saw infinite number of corpses in all the streets and lanes in the city, so thick in some places it was impossible to pass through on horseback without trampling on them. Mothers and husbands were put to the torture; their children were violated; the shrieks were incessant.

At the same time, Maximilian I was on the verge of settling disputes with Duke Karl of Guelders.

Maximilian had help from the Albertine Duke George of Saxony, and was moving heavy Imperial artillery through Cleves into Guelders, according to a report from Thomas Spinelly to Henry VIII of England from 27 July 1512, when Sybylla of Cleves was ten days old:

The Emperor has ordered 12 great pieces of artillery to proceed to Cleves, thence to Guelders... [The] Duke of Guelders, by means of Duke George of Saxony, has proposed a truce with the Emperor. They intend to accept it, as they can manage Guelders better when France is chastised.

The wily Duke Karl never saw a fight he didn't fancy.

A Little Sister for Sybylla

Sybylla was joined three years later by a sister. Born on 28 June 1515, the new baby was named Anna after her father's only legitimate sister. In stark contrast to her namesake, the elder Anna possessed a rebellious character, but she was also pious. She married Count Philip III of Waldeck for love, which resulted in her spending a period of time under house arrest. The illicit couple had to pay a large fine and agree to give up any claims to the duchies of Cleves-Mark. Later in life, the elder Anna published a religious tract. The text itself is lost, but we know of its publication through secondary sources.

Anna's name was familiar on her mother Maria's side, too. Maria's grandmother was Anna of Saxony, making the name pleasing to both parents. Though it is up for debate after whom Anna of Cleves, the future bride of Henry VIII of England, was named, the existing primary source explicitly states she was named after her paternal aunt:

This year [of 1515], on [28 June], the day before St. Peter and Paul, a second daughter was born to the eldest son of Duke John II of Cleves, Duke Johann III from Jülich and Berg. The godfathers were John von Waldeck, the abbess of Neuss, Petrissa von Oberstein, and Anna of Cleves, a sister of the Duke [Johann III]. The child was baptised in the name of Anna.

Anna possessed a gentler spirit than her elder sister Sybylla, which served Anna well during her life in England.

The Final Two Children of Cleves Enter the World

It is possible that Maria of Jülich-Berg experienced at least one miscarriage given the gap between the births of Sybylla and Anna. Whatever fertility woes there may have been, Maria and Johann quickly welcomed two more children. The first, the ever-important male heir,

> …[in 1516] on St Pantaleon's day [of 27/28 July] the first son of Duke Johann III of Cleves, Jülich, and Berg was born around 4:00 in the afternoon in Cleves. On 1 September [1516], he was baptised by the honourable clergyman Anton Grymhold, the Abbot of Werden, and was named Wilhelm.

Wilhelm was likely named after his maternal grandfather, William of Jülich and Berg.[15] Wilhelm's baptism was a grand affair, and he had none other than the Archbishop-Elector of Cologne as a godfather:

> His godparents were … the Archbishop of Cologne, Hermann von Weid, the old Duke Johann II of Cleves, and the wife of Friedrich of Egmont, from the Neuenahr branch. Particularly precious gems were given as gifts for this occasion.

Wilhelm went on to enjoy a meticulous education befitting his future as Duke of Jülich-Cleves-Berg.

A final child was born to Maria and Johann in October 1517. She was named Amalia, possibly after Maria's maternal aunt Amalie of Brandenburg who had married Kaspar, Duke and Count Palatine of Zweibrücken on 19 April 1478 at the age of sixteen. Her husband displayed signs of instability, which Amalie termed going into a 'frenzy', and so she decided to leave him. Not long after, Amalie was stricken with a serious illness and died in 1481, a month before her twentieth birthday. Fortunately, Amalia of Cleves would enjoy a very long life, even by modern standards.

Somewhere along the way, two illegitimate sisters were born. It is not known whether these girls were born before or after Johann and Maria's marriage. A descendant of the illegitimate Elisabeth of Cleves went on to marry an important official at the Cleves court. The other became a nun. Beyond slight mentions during the reign of their half-brother Duke Wilhelm, not much is known about the girls.

Growing up German: The Cleves Girls Enter the *Frauenzimmer*

Sybylla, Anna and Amalia were raised in the *Frauenzimmer*. The *Frauenzimmer* was almost a mirror of the main court, but comprised almost entirely of women. A young noblewoman in Germany was taught practical

---

15 'Wilhelm' is the German form of William.

skills, such as how to administer a household, how to cook and how to sew. Skills in sewing were used to mend clothing and embroider. Some women learned to spin and weave, as well. Sybylla was known to enjoy spinning, and even had her spinning wheel brought with her to Saxony. The Von der Mark girls were introduced to the realities of pregnancy in the *Frauenzimmer*, and may have been witnesses to childbirth.

The idea of the *Frauenzimmer* was imported to Cleves from Burgundy in the fifteenth century. The *Frauenzimmer* was part of the overall noble household, but was separate from that of the master. The term encompassed the people who comprised daily life in the *Frauenzimmer*, such as the lady of the house, her daughters, a *Hofmeisterin* or governess, cousins, wards and attendants. The *Frauenzimmer* was not unique to Cleves or the Lower Rhine area, and spread eastward into Poland.

The purpose of the *Frauenzimmer* was to provide training to young noblewomen on how to run a household, cook for the household, mend clothes and embroider, among other practical tasks. Visits from men to the *Frauenzimmer* were limited. No male over the age of twelve was allowed to be a member, and men were expressly forbidden from visiting at night. Exceptions were made for the physician.

A woman's life at court was subject to ordinances surrounding the administration of the *Frauenzimmer*. The ordinances, or written laws, gave instructions regarding the moral behaviour of the women in the *Frauenzimmer*. This included when and how the women and girls were allowed to interact with men, and construction of the hierarchy within the *Frauenzimmer*. Only certain individuals were allowed to have keys to the *Frauenzimmer*. The types of dances the ladies could enjoy were restricted.

No detail was spared in regulating a court's *Frauenzimmer*. There were contractual arrangements, saying who did what for whom, and how they were compensated for the work. A person could receive anything from food or clothing to shelter or horses. Money was an option, too. Mealtime was very strict, with specific instructions for where each lady sat, who was allowed to eat what, when and how the dishes were presented, and so on. A *Frauenzimmer* had its own kitchen staff, but it was much smaller than that for the general household.

Despite the description of a strict household, ladies in the *Frauenzimmer* certainly had their fun. Far from being cloistered, the presence of the *Frauenzimmer*, occasionally used as a collective noun referring to the members of the women's household, was a meaningful source of increased merriment. For example, the chronicler Hans von Schweinichen remarked upon the daily pattern of living at court in Liegnitz, now part of Poland. The Duchess of Liegnitz put on a banquet every night, followed by dancing, which sometimes lasted all night. Of the dances Schweinichen commented, 'The music was lovely, the wine good, the *Frauenzimmer* (here used as a collective noun) beautiful and the company discreet.' Schweinichen goes on to describe the fun had by the *Frauenzimmer*, which included 'riding, ring-races, music, and dancing'.

Sybylla, Anna and Amalia's exact activities within the *Frauenzimmer* as girls and young women are not known. However, there is evidence that hunting was a pastime enjoyed greatly by both the courts of Jülich-Berg and Cleves-Mark, and that the closely watched *Frauenzimmer* occasionally partook in these festivities. Sybylla was recorded as enjoying chess, and Anna was known to play cards.

Burgundian Influence on the Cleves Court

The court structure was slowly adopted by Johann III during the 1510s, and echoed that found in Burgundy. Some elements of the court's structure, such as the *Frauenzimmer*, were adopted in the mid-fifteenth century. Johann III continued to adapt the Cleves-Burgundian system during the 1520s and 1530s. Young Wilhelm chose to keep virtually the same structure when he became duke. There existed three main positions at court. First, there was the court master, who oversaw the administration of Cleves-Mark and later the United Duchies of Jülich-Cleves-Berg. Second, the marshal was in control of all things related to the military and the business of war. Finally, the legal arm was led by the chancellor for each duchy and oversaw governmental affairs at all levels, internal and external.

To properly administer each of these court offices, several secretaries and other officials provided support services. Two sets of offices were established for the administration of the United Duchies, one for Cleves-Mark and a duplicate set for Jülich-Berg. There were two chancellors as well, with one chancellor for Cleves-Mark and one chancellor for Jülich-Berg. Each chancellor had three court masters, three marshals, two chamberlains, a stablemaster and councillors.

In addition to these offices, each chancellor employed a caretaker, four door attendants, two kitchen masters, a servant in charge of the wine cellar, two persons appointed to supervise and guard the storage areas at court, two tailors, cutters and cupbearers. The rest of the ducal court contained around eight noblemen per court, at least twenty *Junkers* or young male servants, a marksman, two men trained in the law, three secretaries, one personal physician, two surgeons, two kitchen clerks whose job it was to procure goods for the ducal and court tables, and then numerous lower-level servants. For the *Frauenzimmer*, there was one court official who, by law, kept the keys. The *Frauenzimmer* was locked at night, and no one was allowed to enter unless there was a genuine emergency.

Such an extensive system was necessary to administer one of the largest territories in the Holy Roman Empire of the German Nation. The United Duchies had a lot of political potential, which Johann III likely realised, but did not exploit. Johann was interested in maintaining stability, improving the region's legal system, and following Godly principles.

Johann III as Duke

As a ruler, Johann did not indulge in radicalism of any sort. For him, peace was the only way to go. He preferred maintaining an alliance with the Spanish-Burgundian forces of Charles V and his powerful siblings. Johann did not support Lutheranism or its being taught, and initially tried to prevent its spread in the first years after 1517.

In May 1519, Henry VIII of England sent his secretary, Richard Pace, to Germany in advance of Charles V's election. During his journey, Johann hosted Pace in Düsseldorf before having Pace safely conducted to Cologne. At the time, relations were uneasy between France and Cleves. After proving he was not a Frenchman, Johann's officials agreed to help Pace on his journey to Cologne from Düsseldorf. In a letter from Pace to Cardinal Thomas Wolsey, who was firmly entrenched in Henry's government, Pace recalled

> ...affirming that I was [the Englis]h ambassador ... and showed them, in confirmation, one of the English nobles he had given them for his safe conduct hither. On this evidence, they said [the Duke of Cleves] might have the whole town to accompany [Pace] to Cologne; for, considering the old amity between the houses of England and Burgundy, Pace must be sent to the election of the Emperor for the King of Aragon's [future Holy Roman Emperor Charles V] claim, and not for the king of France...

Johann III still identified heavily with his Burgundian heritage, not just in the structure and administration of his court but also with his political leanings. Johann would rely on the 'old amity' between Burgundy and England in the 1530s, when he first proposed a marriage between the Tudors and the Von der Marks.

Johann III Becomes Duke and Ally to the New Emperor

On 15 March 1521, John II of Cleves-Mark died. With his passing, Johann III took his father's place. Now he was Duke of Cleves-Mark in his own right and *jure uxoris* Jülich-Berg. This paved the way for Johann III to unify these three duchies of Jülich, Cleves and Berg, along with the other territories to which he had a right. The United Duchies of Jülich-Cleves-Berg was born.

The unification of these three territories was seen by some as a fulfilment of Cleves' destiny. Remembering that one of the heraldic symbols used for Cleves was a red shield with three gold clovers on it, each duchy was seen as representing a leaf of the clover. As John II of Cleves-Mark and William of Jülich-Berg hoped, power was finally consolidated in the Lower Rhine region.

Johann III chose to maintain a good relationship with the Holy Roman Emperor. An amity was already established because of the actions of both his father and father-in-law, and Johann did not wish to upset things. Johann was quite friendly with the youthful Holy Roman Emperor Charles V, and Charles valued Johann's support. In 1522, Johann was part of Charles' entourage to England. At the time, Charles was at war with Francis I of France in what became known as the Italian War of 1521–26, which was another in the series of wars called either the Italian Wars or the Habsburg–Valois Wars. The Emperor and his Imperial entourage agreed to meet with Henry VIII and finalise mutual support between the Empire and England. This meeting produced the Treaty of Windsor.

The Treaty of Windsor allied England with the Holy Roman Empire against France. Henry VIII was uncle to Charles V, by virtue of Henry's marriage to Katharine of Aragon. Katharine of Aragon was Charles' maternal aunt. The Treaty of Windsor was ratified by Henry VIII and Charles V on 16 June 1522. One of the terms of the treaty was that Charles V would marry Henry VIII's daughter Mary, who was all of six years old at the time the Treaty of Windsor was created. Along with other important persons from the Empire, Johann's presence at the signing of the Treaty of Windsor was noted.

The Von der Mark Children and the Marriage Market

The first round of marital arrangements for the Von der Mark children happened in 1518, when little Sybylla was initially promised as a bride to the electoral prince Johann Friedrich of Saxony. Johann Friedrich was promised to Catherine of Castile, sister of Charles I of Castile, later Holy Roman Emperor Charles V, during negotiations in 1519–20. When Catherine married the King of Portugal in 1524, the idea of a Saxony and Jülich-Cleves-Berg marriage became concrete.

By early 1525, Sybylla of Cleves was therefore destined to marry Johann Friedrich of Electoral Saxony. Part of the marital negotiations included that Electoral Saxony would give up its claims to the Duchy of Jülich. However, if there were no surviving male heirs from Johann III and Maria, then the claim to Jülich would revert to Sybylla and her heirs. The terms agreed upon, all that was left was to await Sybylla's majority.

In 1526, a betrothal *de futuro* was negotiated between Anna and Francis of Lorraine. As part of the negotiations, Anna's father Johann was to pay her dowry in instalments, among other requirements. By 1535, Johann had failed to fulfil his part of the marriage contract. Duke Karl notified Johann that the marriage between Anna and Francis was over. Anna was only about eleven years old when the marriage was originally negotiated, and her groom around the same age. The tender ages of Anna and Francis were taken into consideration when terminating the marriage contract. Neither child really knew what was going on or what a marriage contract meant for them.

There was talk of marrying Wilhelm to Francis' sister Anne of Lorraine, too. The possible double Cleves–Lorraine marriages would shore up succession rights of the Von der Marks to the Duchy of Guelders. The grandmother of Francis and Anne was Philippa of Guelders. She was the only sibling of Duke Karl of Guelders, who remained childless. When he died, his rights to Guelders would, in theory, transfer to the ruling family of

Lorraine. Unfortunately, as Wilhelm would learn in 1538, there was much more intricacy behind who could lay claim to the Duchy of Guelders.

The year 1526 set the Von der Mark children on each of their separate paths. Sybylla, Anna and Wilhelm were betrothed, as was their illegitimate maternal half-uncle John of Jülich. Amalia, who was only eight years old when the various marital arrangements were made, was an afterthought. John of Jülich married Maria Durffendal in 1526 or 1527, and it is possible that one of his sons accompanied or joined Anna of Cleves in England.

The Von der Mark children were subject to a rigid social scheme that did not support much mobility via marriage. As touched upon earlier, the German dowry system was strict, with specified amounts needed for a daughter to marry into a certain noble rank. If there were multiple daughters in a noble family, such as that of the Von der Marks, then the family would have to produce sufficient funds for each daughter to marry. The result of this system was that daughters would marry laterally, such as a *Gräfin* or countess marrying a *Graf* or count, but not a higher-ranking *Herzog* or duke. With multiple daughters, then one might marry down or be placed in a convent, or a daughter might otherwise not marry at all. Such was the case with Amalia of Cleves. The opposite was true for sons. They would frequently marry women of higher social rank because the family would not have to produce as large a dowry.

The choice of spouse was extraordinarily important, and served as much to limit the upward mobility of wealthy women as to promote the upward mobility of men. There was no meaningful difference during the German Reformation of marriage strategies between Lutherans and Catholics. The controlling factor when finding a spouse for a child, or conversely leaving the child unmarried, was the dowry system.

The dowry system also excluded daughters born to common merchant families from scaling the social ladder. If a nobleman married a common woman, then their children could not inherit land or titles despite the rank of their father. That seems to be the case with John of Jülich, who was safely married off to Maria Durffendal.

Early on during the medieval period, Germany's kinship system was bilateral. The bilateral system recognised that all children, whether male or female, were of equal standing in inheritance matters. By the end of the period, the dowry system was increasingly dominant. Descent shifted from being shared among all children to passing only down the male line.

Primogeniture was slowly adopted, making inheritance practices even more strict. Women were forced to give up their inheritances and accept dowries instead. By defining the family line in terms of heirs male, then property could only pass along the male line. In instances of a lack of male heirs, such as Duke Karl being childless or Maria of Jülich-Berg being the only legitimate child, the property would pass to the next male heir. In Duke Karl's case, this was Francis of Lorraine. This practice changed slightly in pro-Lutheran states because the noble children who normally would have been destined for ecclesiastical life effectively did not have that avenue open to them. By placing children in religious institutions to become monks and nuns, the children were removed from the family inheritance. As a result, partible inheritance was introduced in the Lutheran states. This prevented the children from effectively being disinherited.

By allying the ruling families of Lorraine, Guelders and Jülich-Cleves-Berg, Johann III could better protect his borders. Having a double marriage between Johann's children Anna and Wilhelm with the Duke of Lorraine's children Francis and Anne would settle any dynastic disputes and ideally guard against more invasions from Duke Karl. Karl and his predecessors had been involved in various battles throughout the years, some of them against Cleves. If Johann's children inherited Guelders from the heirless Duke Karl, the chances of that behaviour continuing were almost non-existent.

Anna's marriage contract with Francis of Lorraine followed the inheritance rights as spelled out in Sybylla's contract of marriage with Johann Friedrich. If Johann died without heirs, first Sybylla's heirs male would inherit the United Duchies, then Anna's. The contract called for the payment of 20,000 gold guilders and for each party to retain their inheritance rights. Duke Karl later unilaterally changed the contract, escalating the payment to 30,000 gold guilders plus an additional annual tribute from the small city of Lobith, across the Rhine from Cleves. Lobith is now part of Rijnwaarden in the Netherlands.

Similar arrangements were made for Wilhelm's betrothal to Anne of Lorraine.

Religion in Saxony and Cleves

In August 1525 at Weimar, Johann Friedrich's father John showed his devotion to Lutheranism by ordering the preachers there to preach only the Gospel, without any additions. He also invited Luther to give his official opinion on matters of public importance, something which Frederick would not do. John virtually ignored threats from Charles V. Some months later, to help secure his position John met with Philip of Hesse in Gotha during February 1526 to align their territories. This led to an alliance in Torgau between the North German leaders, who were predominantly evangelical.

Over in Cleves, Johann III was against the spread of Lutheranism within the United Duchies. To try and stop it, an edict was issued in March 1525. This strategy worked for the most part, and Lutheranism was put down within Jülich-Cleves-Berg. Johann followed up with an ordinance in July 1525, demonstrating his desire for reform of the Catholic Church within his lands. Although Johann wished to remain on Charles V's good side, he did not wish to aggressively eradicate Lutheranism. This strategy might be evidence of Desiderius Erasmus's influence. It was not that the Catholic Church was perfect, but rather that Luther and his followers were dangerous. The decrees were issued during and after the Peasants' War, when the multitude in rebellion clung to Luther's teachings as justification for their actions.

The influence of Erasmus led to Konrad Heresbach being retained to educate the young Wilhelm. Heresbach finished his legal education in both Cologne and Orléans in 1520, before travelling to Basel with Erasmus and staying there. In 1523, Heresbach returned to Germany. He was appointed Wilhelm's tutor in late 1523 to early 1524. Heresbach stayed on at the Cleves court long enough to become one of the principal politicians there. Heresbach believed in religious tolerance, and he likely passed this on to Wilhelm.

At around the same time that Heresbach joined the Jülich-Cleves-Berg court, so did Johann Ghogreff. He was allegedly related to the Von der Marks, although the relationship is not clear. It is thought he was somehow related to Duke Johann's sister Anna, who married into the Waldeck family a few years before. Ghogreff was frequently sent on diplomatic missions by Johann. He and Heresbach shared a respect for each other, if not a friendship. Heresbach dedicated his edition of Herodotus to Ghogreff in 1526.

Wilhelm's education was practical and humanist. He was instructed in languages by Heresbach, and mastered German, Latin and French.

Over in Saxony, at around the same time as John the Constant was negotiating with Johann for Sybylla's marriage to Johann Friedrich, John was preparing for the next Imperial diet. The Evangelicals, now a genuine party, attended the 1526 Diet of Speyer. John was their leader, and he was openly treated as such. Charles V was not a fan of this behaviour once he learned of it, and sent his brother Ferdinand as his representative.

The main purpose of the Diet of Speyer was to drum up support for the war against the Turks. John of Saxony and Philip of Hesse were more concerned with the religious issues, particularly the Edict of Worms issued years before. The diet, which ran from late July to late August 1526, was successful for both sides. The Imperial Estates pledged around 25,000 troops to defend against the Turks, and Ferdinand agreed to let each area implement the Edict of Worms as its leader saw fit.

The same year as her marriage, 1527, Sybylla's father-in-law John the Steadfast established the Evangelical-Lutheran State Church of Saxony after the Diet of Speyer. John was extremely active in establishing the principles of the Reformation within Saxony, much to the chagrin of Charles V.

Charles V and Guelders

Charles V grew bored with Duke Karl of Guelders avoiding the issue of officially handing over the duchy on his death. In 1528, when he was roughly fifty-nine years old and without any heir, Duke Karl was forced into the Treaty of Gorkum by Charles V. Charles, as the heir to Charles the Bold through his daughter and Charles V's grandmother Mary of Burgundy, had a strong legal claim to Guelders. Aside from Guelders being part of his rightful inheritance, various contracts went back and forth in the late fifteenth century which strengthened Charles V's claim. Duke Karl finally agreed to allow Guelders and the County of Zutphen to become Imperial property if he died childless. Other provisions of the treaty meant that, effectively, Duke Karl stopped fighting everyone.

The Rosenkranzbruderschaft Altarpiece

In the year of the Treaty of Gorkum, 1528, an altarpiece depicting the ducal family of Jülich-Cleves-Berg was completed. It shows Johann III and Wilhelm on the left wing, and Maria, Anna and Amalia on the right. Sybylla is not in the portrait because she was already living in Saxony. Wilhelm was roughly twelve years old when the altarpiece was created. Anna and Amalia were probably thirteen and eleven, respectively.

Anna, wearing a red dress, kneels directly behind her mother. Amalia, in a gold dress, is above and behind her mother and sister, looking at them with her face mostly turned toward the viewer. It is the only confirmed portrait of Amalia and Maria that still exists. Painted in 1528, it was first restored in the late seventeenth century. Further restoration and the attendant report of the altarpiece in 2013 by Börries Brakebusch shows that the images of the ducal family were still in great condition, and did not need much attention.

4

Sybylla of Cleves Weds Johann Friedrich of Saxony

Johann Friedrich's Habsburg Fiancée

Johann Friedrich was first intended to marry Infanta Catherine of Spain, sister of Holy Roman Emperor Charles V. Shortly after Charles V ascended to the Imperial throne, the idea of Johann Friedrich marrying Charles' youngest sister was looked at with seriousness.

Johann Friedrich and Catherine exchanged their espousals in late 1519 to early 1520. Johann Friedrich turned sixteen years old in June 1519, and Catherine turned thirteen years old in January 1520. The negotiations were completed by Johann Friedrich's uncle, Frederick the Wise. Queen Juana of Castile and Aragon supposedly negotiated on behalf of her daughter Catherine. In reality, Juana was sent to the Royal Monastery of Santa Clara in Tordesillas, Castile in 1509, allegedly because she was mad. Juana was banished by her own son, Charles V. Although she held title to Castile and Aragon, she had no meaningful power.

Charles V's reasoning behind the marriage between Johann Friedrich and Catherine was that it would secure the support of the powerful Electorate of Saxony, and with it the territory's important Imperial electoral vote. Martin Luther and his teachings were trickling throughout Saxony by 1520, and political winds were changing. To keep the Holy Roman Empire secure, Charles needed to affirm the support of all his electors.

Shifting religious views in Saxony and political needs in Spain led to the engagement being abandoned by 1524. Catherine went on to marry her uncle, and through this match became Queen Consort of Portugal.

A Von der Mark Bride for Johann Friedrich

As mentioned before, Johann Friedrich's uncle Frederick the Wise died on 5 May 1525 during the Peasants' War. John the Steadfast, Johann Friedrich's father, became the next Elector of Saxony. Johann Friedrich was in his early twenties by this point, and his marital eligibility came to the fore. In 1526, John the Constant of Saxony and Johann III of Cleves decided that Sybylla, born in 1512, would marry Johann Friedrich. The negotiations were not without difficulty.

During the reign of Holy Roman Emperor Frederick III, who reigned from 1452 to 1493, Saxony obtained feudal claims to Jülich-Berg, the territory of Sybylla's mother. Sybylla's father Johann III wished for the Electorate of Saxony to renounce its claims to Jülich-Berg. The marriage of Sybylla von der Mark of Cleves to Johann Friedrich von Wettin of Saxony provided another way for Saxony to lay claim to Jülich-Berg and, by this time, Cleves-Mark: if Sybylla's brother Wilhelm died without heirs, claim to the United Duchies would fall to Sybylla's heirs.

As will be discussed in further detail, the negotiations were completed and the engagement declared in Johann Friedrich's city of Mainz on 8 August 1526. On 8 September, the marriage was finalised at Sybylla's home of Burg Castle in Solingen, the very same building where Johann III and Maria completed their marriage negotiations in the 1490s.

Maria of Jülich-Berg, already in the mid-1520s being referred to as the 'old duchess from Jülich', may have suggested Sybylla as a bride for Johann Friedrich.[16] Duchess Maria certainly was present for all of her daughter's important events when it came to Johann Friedrich. Sybylla, accompanied by her mother, first met Johann Friedrich, who was chaperoned by the Saxon court preacher Frederick Myconius, in Cologne on 13 April 1526. Sybylla was not quite fourteen, and Johann Friedrich was just shy of twenty-three. It is not known whether Sybylla spoke directly to Johann Friedrich or if Duchess Maria spoke on Sybylla's behalf.

Sybylla, already blossoming in her beauty, did make a good initial impression. Johann Friedrich appeared to take a liking to his future bride, accompanying Sybylla and Duchess Maria as far as Bensberg during their journey back to the United Duchies. The purpose of this meeting, aside from seeing whether Sybylla pleased Johann Friedrich, was to determine whether she was amenable to the German Reformation. Johann Friedrich left for Saxony on 5 May 1526.

Negotiations concerning the inheritance rights of Sybylla, Anna, Amalia and any other possible children born to Johann III and Duchess Maria were discussed in Frankfurt that summer. Part of the negotiations included that Sybylla be treated as a princess of a higher station than her sisters after the marriage pact was formalised. Surely, eleven-year-old Anna and nine-year-old Amalia were not terribly impressed with Sybylla's new treatment. The

---

16 Maria's mother and Sybylla's maternal grandmother, Sibylle of Brandenburg, died on 9 July 1524. Conceivably, she could have been the 'old duchess from Jülich', but it seems unlikely that she would have participated in the marital negotiations for her granddaughter.

marriage pact was formalised on 8 August 1526 in Düsseldorf. It appears that Duchess Maria had a strong presence during the negotiations with Saxony because it impacted rights to her hereditary lands of Jülich-Berg.

After the marriage pact was finalised in Düsseldorf, Johann III and Duchess Maria invited John of Saxony and Johann Friedrich for a small celebratory feast. Unfortunately, John was tied up in Speyer so he could not attend. Johann Friedrich and his keeper, the preacher Myconius, arrived around 24 August to take up the offer.

On 8 September 1526, the Cleves court gathered at Burg Castle in Solingen. This was customarily a hunting castle, but Sybylla, Anna and Amalia spent a lot of their childhood there. Johann Friedrich came for the religious formalities, which were performed by Myconius. The Saxon court was anxious for the marriage between Sybylla and Johann Friedrich to be concluded, even if the official wedding celebration and reception of Sybylla in Electoral Saxony had to wait. Johann Friedrich remained in the United Duchies until 11 October before going home.

Delighted with the match, Sybylla's parents wanted to mark the day. The bride-to-be enjoyed a happy but solemn celebration at Burg Castle. The *Frauenzimmer* likely joined the main court, meaning that Sybylla's sisters Anna and Amalia were there to celebrate. There was likely a small church service, feasting and perhaps even a bit of dancing under the watchful eye of a governess.

Wedding Portraits of the Young Electoral Couple

As part of his train, Johann Friedrich brought with him the Saxon court painter Lucas Cranach the Elder. Cranach painted two different portraits of Sybylla, inspired by the celebration of Sybylla's engagement to Johann Friedrich. The more famous of these portraits shows a mature-looking Sybylla wearing a cross pendant and a red dress. Red was symbolic of Cleves, and this particular portrait was kept at Weimar with the companion portrait of Johann Friedrich. Sybylla's dress has slit sleeves to show the gold silk underneath. On her head, Sybylla wears a wreath of the flower bittersweet with a feather. Johann Friedrich wears a similar outfit.

The lesser-known portrait shows a younger-looking Sybylla wearing a green dress and a diamond gem around her neck. The gem, bearing the letters, 'I B C S', is symbolic of the four territories coming together. Remembering that the letter 'I' was interchangeable for 'J' in the sixteenth century, and that the sixteenth-century German spelling of Cleves began with a C (modern spelling begins with K), the pendant stands for 'Iülich-Berg Cleves Saxony'. Additionally, gold fabric in the dress is reminiscent of the arms of Saxony, and green was commonly worn as one of Saxony's colours. It is thought that this second portrait of a younger-looking Sybylla in green was painted for the Cleves court.

The green portrait might be truer to Sybylla's appearance in 1526 if it were painted for her family to keep. The portrait of her in the red dress, because it shows her as being much more mature, may have been so simply because she was getting married and there was a desire for her to appear older.

Johann Friedrich's Winter Visit to the United Duchies

Johann Friedrich returned to Weimar on 11 October 1526, but then went back to Cleves in January 1527. In the interim, the two lovebirds sent a bevy of letters back and forth. Johann Friedrich stayed in Düsseldorf until the middle of March under the pretence that he was securing permission for the marriage from Charles V. Around this time, Johann Friedrich's cousin Elisabeth of Saxony sent him a teasing letter, inquiring whether Sybylla was growing a little thick around the middle.

As part of the marriage pact, the lands of Jülich-Berg and Cleves-Mark had to reaffirm their prior agreement that created the United Duchies. This was done in Düsseldorf on 17 March and 15 May 1527, respectively. Duchess Maria wished to bring a certificate bearing the renewed unification to Saxony.

John of Saxony sent a proposed route and documentation for Sybylla's safe conduct to her parents. He suggested that she travel from the United Duchies through Hildesheim, Brunswick and Magdeburg before arriving in Torgau. At least part of this plan was abandoned because it took the bridal party rather far from their destination of Torgau. Wishing to take a more leisurely route, the bridal train would cut through Thuringia.

Sybylla's Journey to Saxony

Sybylla remained in the United Duchies until late spring 1527, when she and her train finally set off for Torgau in the north-west of what is now Saxony. Sybylla, Duchess Maria, the noblewomen at court, and possibly Anna and Amalia set out from Düsseldorf on 7 May 1527 for Torgau, Sybylla's new home.

Sybylla's train was massive. She was escorted by four gold carriages of state, four red wagons bearing her *Frauenzimmer*, a closed-top wagon for her silver plate, and an additional seventeen wagons carrying the clothes, jewels and other luggage for the women and young male servants. In addition, there were roughly 140 horses used to pull the twenty-six carriages and wagons, and a stableboy for each horse. There were another 200 horsemen making up the train.

Sybylla's gold carriage had gold velvet pillows for her comfort, a gold roof and gold decorations. Her mother Maria rode in the same carriage. If Anna and Amalia accompanied their sister and mother, they were not mentioned. Johann III escorted Sybylla for the first two days of her journey before returning home on 9 May.

On her way to Torgau, Sybylla stopped at Creuzberg, Gotha and Erfurt. At each location she was gifted venison, oats, beer and wine. Her train was put up overnight by the local nobility. The Bailiff of Creuzberg took over escort duties, leading the party to Gotha. Originally, Saxon horsemen were supposed to meet Sybylla once she crossed into Saxon territory, but the changes to her route were not communicated in time.

Nearing Erfurt, the city officials came to meet her and escort her into the city. There, Sybylla was showered with even more gifts, including sweets, liquor and wine. She was lauded by the local university officials and clergy. She and her entourage spent a Thursday and Friday in Erfurt, fêted by the local counts and resting before carrying on with her journey.

The honour guard sent by Sybylla's father-in-law finally caught up with her outside Erfurt. City officials escorted her part of the way out of Erfurt to this honour guard. Roughly forty riders, including several counts and knights, then led Sybylla toward her next stop in Weimar, collecting an additional 100 knights and riders on the way. She arrived in Weimar on Saturday and stayed on through Sunday. Weimar would become a very important city for Sybylla during the last years of her life.

After Weimar, Sybylla and her train moved to Jena. They overnighted there, too. Next she stopped in Altenburg, then Grimma. In Grimma, the train replenished supplies. Johann Friedrich set out for Torgau as soon as he heard that Sybylla had made it to Grimma.

After Grimma, the bridal party headed toward Eilenburg, passing Leipzig on the way. Eilenburg was close to the border of Electoral Saxony. Sybylla spent almost a week there gathering her strength before continuing toward Johann Friedrich in Torgau.

Johann Friedrich, eager to see Sybylla again, wanted to leave Torgau with a large force to intercept her train on their way from Eilenburg. It was 2 June 1527. To the blasting of trumpets, Johann Friedrich and his company rode out to find his bride. She was about a half-mile away. Her train was broken into eight different segments, probably for security, all on their way to Torgau.

Sybylla's groom met her in the woods just outside Torgau. He brought with him the noblemen and noblewomen of Electoral Saxony and other officials with their servants. In total, a party of 200 persons astride their horses, caparisoned in black, came to greet Sybylla and Duchess Maria. Prince Wolfgang von Anhalt, Count Albrecht von Mansfeld and others were present to greet Sybylla as she came to her new land. The large company escorted the party from Jülich-Cleves-Berg.

Duke George of Saxony, his wife Barbara, and two of their sons boarded a boat on the Elbe River to make their way toward the impending wedding festivities. Duke George's son John of Saxony escorted his wife Elizabeth of Hesse and her *Frauenzimmer* by boat, too.

Other important nobles, including Landgrave Philip of Hesse, Palgrave Wolfgang of Pfalz-Zweibrücken and Duke Henry of Mecklenburg, came to Electoral Saxony for the wedding. Duke Henry was Johann Friedrich's maternal uncle, and he brought two of his sons with him. Duke Ernst of Brunswick and Lüneburg came for the festivities, too. This large host of nobility gathered in Wittenberg to await news of Sybylla's arrival.

Sybylla and company arrived in the city of Torgau on 2 June, almost four weeks after they left the United Duchies. The train from the United Duchies entered Torgau, although it took a little while for the portion that concluded Sybylla's *Frauenzimmer* to arrive. Duchess Maria and Sybylla assembled with the *Frauenzimmer* inside Hartenfels Castle, which would become Sybylla's first home in Saxony.

Elector John of Saxony posted a placard outside the gates to Torgau, directed at miscreants and exiles. In German tradition, during large celebrations like weddings, people in exile could follow a lord into the local prince's city, and have the ban of exile lifted. In Cleves, a special rope was tied to the duke's saddle. A person in exile had to grab hold of the rope and maintain a grip until arriving at the duke's lodgings, where they could plead their case to a judge, who would then welcome them back to society. Anyone in Cleves who was welcomed back from exile kept a piece of the rope on them as proof of their forgiveness. Presumably, using a rope limited the number of exiles who could regain favour. In any case, John of Saxony's placards clearly stated that no one would have the ban of exile lifted from them if they followed Sybylla of Cleves or any nobles into Torgau; if they did so anyway, they could expect due punishment. John of Saxony remained unhappy with the events of the Peasants' War from two years earlier.

Sybylla's Arrival in Torgau

Many Saxon noblewomen were ready to officially welcome Duchess Maria and Sybylla at Hartenfels Castle. Once somewhat settled into Hartenfels Castle, Duchess Maria assembled the *Frauenzimmer*. They helped Sybylla prepare to see her groom. One can imagine the excitement young Sybylla felt, finally in Saxony to prepare for her big day. She may have felt slightly out of place with the clothing she brought; Saxon fashion was quite distinct from that of the Lower Rhine region. Women's dress seemed to use as much fabric as possible, particularly on the sleeves, while still maintaining the skirt's bell shape. Heavy gold chains were very fashionable, as were ostentatious hats.

Johann Friedrich was in another set of apartments with the other Saxon dukes, making his own preparations. He too would have wished to make a good impression on Sybylla, Duchess Maria, and the people of the United Duchies. He had to represent Electoral Saxony to his own people, too. Whether or not any of that was weighing on his mind is unknown, although his thoughts likely wandered to Sybylla's comfort and happiness.

Elizabeth of Hesse, Duchess Consort of Ducal Saxony, prepared with her *Frauenzimmer*, as well. It is possible that Elizabeth, in favour of the Reformation, took on some of the maternal duties for the groom's side during the wedding. Johann Friedrich's father was twice widowed by 1527. Johann Friedrich's cousin Duke George, Elizabeth's father-in-law, was still in favour of Catholicism. The adherence to Catholicism might have precluded George's wife Barbara from standing in as a maternal figure for Johann

Friedrich. Elizabeth's brother, Landgrave Philip of Hesse, was good friends with Johann Friedrich.

The Festivities Begin

Once all the noble ladies and their respective *Frauenzimmern* were collected, the Saxon women escorted Sybylla and her *Frauenzimmer* to the castle chapel. It was just past noon. Organ music was played, and a *Te Deum* sung, along with other holy music appropriate for this stage in Sybylla's life. After the small church service, Duchess Maria led Sybylla and the gathered *Frauenzimmern* back to the women's apartments, also called the *Frauenzimmer*. (Remember that *Frauenzimmer* is both the name for the apartments where the ladies of court reside and spend their day, and also the collective noun for the noblewomen who lived in it.)

The women next readied themselves for the start of celebrations. At around five o'clock in the evening, it was time for everything to begin. The noblemen and their entourages entered the *Frauenzimmer*, where a feast was held to celebrate Sybylla's arrival. After eating together, the massive party enjoyed dancing into the night.

At around nine o'clock that evening, Sybylla became determined to enjoy a dance with her groom. Sybylla and the court ladies left Hartenfels to seek out Johann Friedrich within Torgau. She reportedly was offered local pastries and sweets during her excursion outside of the castle. Sybylla could not find Johann Friedrich, so they went back to the castle. It is possible that this excursion was planned, in the sense that it gave the people of Torgau a chance to see the new bride and welcome her.

Sybylla and her party returned to Hartenfels Castle after a while, and conveniently found Johann Friedrich in the room where the dancing was held. Sybylla danced with Johann Friedrich until after midnight.

Unfortunately, given the large number of guests who descended upon Torgau, not everyone was able to stay within the walls of Hartenfels. The *Frauenzimmern* belonging to the countesses and lower stations had to find lodgings within Torgau and still be present on-time in the mornings to attend Sybylla. The same was true for lower-ranking noblemen and their servants. Over 30,000 people entered Torgau specifically for the wedding.

The next morning, Monday 3 June, the visiting dukes, duchesses, other nobles and their parties made their way to the meeting room. Once at court, everyone assembled in what was likely the great hall, bedecked with costly tapestries and carpets. There were at least thirty-five tables laden with food and drink for everyone, individuals being seated by rank. The women of the *Frauenzimmer* had their own tables so that they could dine separately from the men.

After breakfast that morning, the marriage pact was solemnized in Hartenfels. It is not known what Sybylla, or really anyone, wore. She may have chosen to wear a red dress similar to the dress in her engagement portrait from the year before. The Von der Mark girls appeared to favour red for their engagements, given that both Sybylla in 1526 and Anna in 1539 wore red dresses for their official portraits. Sybylla may have chosen to wear yellow and black, the colours of Saxony, or possibly even white, as Anna did thirteen years later for her own wedding.

With the marriage now officially agreed in both the United Duchies and Saxony, special care was taken to tell Sybylla all about her new land. The people, industries, and geography were carefully explained to her. Expensive gifts were presented by the assembled nobles, including Johann Friedrich. The act of giving gifts to the new bride strictly followed Saxon tradition. Johann Friedrich, a robust man who was fond of wine and the hunt, gave Sybylla a thick gold chain bearing a pendant that had the word 'Jesus' written in diamonds. Philip of Hesse gave Sybylla a bonnet with a costly jewel on it. Sybylla received more silver and gold plate from the lesser nobility. Duchess Maria presented Johann Friedrich with expensive silver plate as part of Sybylla's dowry. This done, the jousting tournament could begin.

The Tourney of Torgau

Celebrations for the marriage of Sybylla and Johann Friedrich were grand, and are known as the Tourney of Torgau. Many celebrated persons attended, including Martin Luther and Philipus Melanchthon, not to mention innumerable nobles and officials such as the Cleves court official Johann Ghogreff. Torgau being the seat of his power, John the Steadfast hosted the celebration and paid for it out of Saxony's coffers. Tournaments such as this were a regular part of Saxon life, and were traditionally done in a more medieval style with few allegorical or mythological elements.

After Sybylla was presented to the people of Saxony as Johann Friedrich's bride, the festivities began in earnest. Johann Friedrich competed during the tournament, impressing his new wife and her entourage. His two illegitimate cousins through his uncle Elector Frederick the Wise, named Balthasar and Frederick von Jessen, also participated in the tourney. All three of the young men showed off their skills in sport and arms to the delight of the crowd.

The next several days were like the first, albeit with men and women separated as per German custom. Each morning, the nobility and their servants would flood Hartenfels to dine, then the tournament would start. After the tournament, the evening meal was served, followed by dancing. The various duchesses divided their time between the *Frauenzimmer* in Hartenfels and the tourney, according to the German custom of not being unsupervised around men.

The *Frauenzimmer* within Hartenfels was specially decorated for Sybylla, Duchess Maria and the other noblewomen who were guests. The rooms were hung with gorgeous tapestries to promote the festive mood. After enjoying a lighter breakfast than the wedding feast, the women attended Mass. After this, they were met by knights from their various lands to escort them to the day's tournament. Duchess Maria and Sybylla occupied two of the rooms themselves, and were led by a host of twenty counts and knights each day.

At the tournament, Sybylla and Duchess Maria sat with John of Saxony, Johann Friedrich, Duke George of Saxony and his son John, and Elizabeth of Hesse. There were upwards of 350 people staying in Hartenfels, everyone finely dressed. This included the customary thick, heavy, long gold chains fashionable in Saxony.

On Wednesday night, during the dancing, twenty people in costume entered the dance hall. These performers wore masks which completely covered their heads, utterly disguising their identities. The guests were delighted, and even more so when the performers were revealed to be members of the nobility.

The next day, Thursday, a hunting excursion was arranged in the forest around Torgau. Sybylla and Johann Friedrich delighted in hunting together throughout their lives, and there are several paintings by Lucas Cranach the Elder depicting the couple and their entourage enjoying the hunt.

That day the new couple was after deer. The hunting party managed to kill eight of them, then headed back into Torgau. The tourney was still going on, continuing to provide entertainment for the enormous number of wedding guests and their servants.

Throughout her marriage, Sybylla took it upon herself to promote Luther's teachings in Jülich-Cleves-Berg, managing to secure Heresbach's help. Her attempts seem not to have gotten any farther than her youngest sister, Amalia. Anna, Wilhelm and their parents all remained Catholic to their deaths.

Duchess Maria paid Johann Friedrich Sybylla's dowry on 9 June, before returning home to the United Duchies. The dowry was roughly 25,000 guilders. For comparison, the wedding festival itself cost over 19,000 guilders. On 12 June, John of Saxony, Duchess Maria and the newlyweds went to Lochau for another hunt. Maria ordered most of her servants and nobles to press on to Wittenberg, meeting them there the next day. Duchess Maria left Saxony on 14 June, arriving back in Düsseldorf around 9 July. Sybylla never saw her parents or siblings again.

Sybylla's Life in Saxony

Sybylla experienced an immediate difference in culture when it came to religion in Saxony. In the United Duchies, the concept of the Reformation was not to utterly upend religion as it was known, but to take a more moderate approach and perfect what was already in place. Not so in Saxony, the home of Martin Luther and his teachings. Sybylla converted to Lutheranism in 1528.

Johann Friedrich had a similar education to Wilhelm of Jülich-Cleves-Berg, in the sense that both young leaders were introduced to the Bible, the classics, French and Latin. Johann Friedrich's religious instruction was given by George Spalatin, and heavily influenced by Lutheranism. He was very serious as a young man and remained so into adulthood, being logical and frank. He was not considered terribly attractive, and was already overweight at the time of his marriage to Sybylla. Possessed of great physical and mental strength, he was a fearsome opponent in any context. At the time of his marriage, Johann Friedrich felt loyalty to Holy Roman Emperor Charles V. Above all, he was interested in preserving and elevating the achievements of the House of Wettin.

The regulation of Sybylla's *Frauenzimmer* in Saxony was very strict, and likened to a convent. Whether it was actually strict or just strict for Saxony is a matter for debate. The ladies were expected to pray, read the Bible and attend a church service daily. Sybylla grew to be a very pious woman, who loved her husband and was devoted to Lutheranism.

5

Cleves and Saxony, 1529–1539: A Time of Change

Saxony and the Reformation

Sybylla and Johann Friedrich welcomed their first son in Torgau on 8 January 1529. Sybylla was sixteen years old, turning seventeen that summer. The couple named their first son John Frederick, after his father. John Frederick came to be known as 'the Middle'.

Two months later, in March, another Imperial diet was held. This one, in the Imperial Free City of Speyer,[17] was called to discuss the Ottoman threat from the east. John of Saxony attended the diet in person. On his way there, his train was overtaken by that of Holy Roman Emperor Charles V's brother Ferdinand. John brazenly had his motto, '*Verbum Dei Manet in Aeternum*' ('The Word of God Lives Forever'), the motto of the Lutheran revolution, on his servants' livery, to the displeasure of Ferdinand.

Once in Speyer, John displayed his motto over the entrance to his chambers, too. In response, John was forbidden from having his Lutheran preacher give

---

17 The *Reichskammergericht*, or Imperial Chamber Court, was kept in Speyer from 1527 to almost the end of the 1600s. It was one of the highest courts in the Holy Roman Empire. The other, the Aulic Council, sat in Vienna and held jurisdiction over feudal and Imperial governmental issues, which were not typically heard by the *Reichskammergericht*. Charles V's brother Ferdinand attended this diet on his behalf, which was fairly common practice throughout Charles' reign. Ferdinand did not receive Charles' instructions about religious differences before the diet, and made a rather harsh statement about there not being any religious divisions within the Empire.

sermons inside a church during the diet. It was customary for a Latin Mass to be held at the opening of a diet. In defiance of Ferdinand and the Emperor, John went ahead and skipped the Mass. Instead, he attended a service in the courtyard outside his lodgings with a Lutheran preacher from Saxony. A quite noticeable portion of the German princes and their entourages skipped the Mass and instead went to John's Lutheran sermon. The Catholic princes present were astounded by John's behaviour, and turned their backs on him.

Attempts were made to convince John that moderation in religion was key. Indeed, this notion was part of the 1526 Edict of Speyer. The Catholic princes used it to stop John from making any further changes to religion in Saxony. Initially, John gave signs of capitulating. By the end of the diet, however, he had concluded an alliance with the Evangelical princes and refused to follow the Edict of Speyer. Ferdinand and Charles were furious. John arrived back in Saxony to rumours that Charles was going to take away his position as Elector.

Religion and the Albertine Dukes of Saxony

John and his cousin Duke George were on opposite ends of the religious spectrum. John was blatantly Lutheran, whereas George was devoutly Catholic. George remained loyal to the Habsburgs, which made him and his children a threat to John, Johann Friedrich and the children Johann Friedrich shared with Sybylla. George entered into the League of Dessau back in 1525 with the electors of Brandenburg and Mainz and the Duke of Brunswick in response to John's dealings with Philip of Hesse. Where John was the leader of the Evangelicals, George was the leader of the Catholics.

George took an active stance against the spread of Lutheranism. In the areas which he controlled in the electoral lands of Saxony, he persecuted any Lutherans he could find. However, in the mining towns which were controlled by both John and George, Lutheranism became more vigorous with each persecution. George spoke against Luther whenever he could, which led to Luther calling him the 'Assassin in Dresden'.

The issues between John of the Ernestine, Lutheran line and George of the Albertine, Catholic line were temporarily settled by an agreement reached by the men in Grimma in July 1529.

The Turks Frighten the West

Later that year, 21 September 1529, the West was shaken to its core when Vienna was attacked by Turkish forces. Vienna was the traditional seat of the Habsburg Holy Roman Emperors, so an attack on the Imperial city had serious implications for the Empire. About 400,000 troops moved on Vienna. One of the Ottoman tactics was to dig tunnels under the walls with the goal of placing about 16 tons of gunpowder under the Hofburg, the main Imperial palace. Strong storms in mid-October foiled the Ottoman plan, but they did manage to blow apart some of the city wall. When the Ottomans retreated, one could hear the gruesome shrieks and cries of Imperial prisoners in the Ottoman camps.

Of Children and Diets
Sybylla's second child, John William, was born on 11 March 1530 in Torgau. John William was raised and educated alongside his elder brother John Frederick. John William grew to have strong Lutheran beliefs. He pursued a military career from the late 1540s to mid-1550s.

Three months later, Sybylla's husband and father-in-law headed off to the next Imperial diet.

In June 1530, an Imperial diet at Augsburg took place. It is out of this diet that the Augsburg Confession was born, authored largely by Philipus Melanchthon. Emperor Charles V requested John to attend this diet in person. John could not defy Charles V, but he could bring other important members of the Electoral Saxon court with him. He brought Johann Friedrich, George Spalatin, Philipus Melanchthon and others. Charles was not there when John arrived. After waiting in Augsburg, John sent a small embassy to the Emperor. In response, Charles invited John to meet with him in Innsbruck.

Many important matters were raised at the diet. The Ottoman Empire and the widening religious divide were serious threats to Christendom. Charles V sought the election of his brother Ferdinand as King of the Romans-Germans, which would effectively declare Ferdinand the Emperor Elect. Both John and Johann Friedrich opposed the election of Ferdinand. Charles V had his criminal constitution, or *Constitution Criminalis Carolina*, introduced at the diet, hoping to create a more unified legal system in the Holy Roman Empire. One effect of the *Constitutio* was the increase in witch burnings. Even before the *Constitutio* the prosecution of witches in Jülich-Cleves-Berg was fairly frequent, although the dukes of Cleves grew to have a curious relationship with witches in the 1590s. Most importantly for the future of Sybylla and her sons, the Augsburg Confession was presented.

Formation of the Schmalkaldic League
Not at all impressed with the young Emperor, John of Saxony and Philip of Hesse decided to form an alliance with other Lutheran estates in Germany. The adherents to the new Lutheran religion rejected the articles enumerated in the Recess of the Diet of Augsburg. In February 1531, three months away from the Emperor's deadline, the Elector of Saxony met with Landgrave Philip of Hesse in the town hall of Schmalkalden and the two officially formed the League of Schmalkalden, or the Schmalkaldic League. The building in which the league was formed still stands in Schmalkalden.

The Schmalkaldic League started as a defensive coalition against Charles V, but it eventually developed into more of a diplomatic organisation. Francis I of France, himself a Catholic who was persecuting the Protestants in his own territory, supported the league because it was inimical to Charles V. Members agreed to contribute infantry and cavalry for the mutual protection of each. They never took serious military action against Emperor Charles V. Instead, members reclaimed property from the Catholic Church and removed religious leaders. It is fair to compare this type of activity to England's dissolution of the monasteries. In 1537, the league drew up the Schmalkald Articles (*Schmalkaldische Artikel*). The articles were another proclamation of Protestant faith. Martin Luther was involved in drafting these new articles but could not fully participate as he was suffering from kidney stones. The league met at his private home when drafting the articles to facilitate his input. They were to be incorporated into the Lutheran Book of Concord in 1580.

Johann Friedrich Becomes Elector of Saxony

John the Constant was overcome with weakness in his limbs in mid-August 1532. On 16 August, he recovered briefly and went boar hunting around Torgau. A chill overtook him, and he died on 18 August shortly before noon in Schweinitz. He was buried in the chapel of Wittenberg Castle, and Martin Luther gave a sermon at his funeral.

At his death, John left behind four surviving legitimate children. Both of John's wives predeceased him. Sophia of Mecklenburg died shortly after the birth of Johann Friedrich in 1503, her only child with John. John's second wife Margarete von Anhalt bore him two daughters, Maria in 1515 and Margarete in 1518. A boy named John was born in 1519, but he died shortly after his birth. Margarete's final child, Johann Ernst, was born 10 May 1521. Margarete died in October of 1521. Johann Ernst was created Duke of Saxe-Coburg in 1541.

After the death of his father John the Constant, Johann Friedrich became Elector of Saxony. A pair of portraits executed around this time by Lucas Cranach the Elder show Sybylla of Cleves and Johann Friedrich at the very beginning of Johann Friedrich's reign. Sybylla had just turned twenty years old, and her husband was twenty-nine. Johann Friedrich was the new leader of the Lutherans, and had to be vigilant against any challenges to his power. He, and the rest of Germany and the Low Countries, did not have to wait long for a threat to arrive. Within eighteen months of Johann Friedrich and Sybylla becoming Elector and Electress of Saxony, the Anabaptists arrived in Münster.

The Beginnings of an Anglo-Cleves Alliance

By 1530, Johann III of Cleves had two children who were eligible for marriage: Wilhelm and Amalia. Possibly remembering his time in England back in 1522 at Henry VIII's court, Johann sent a letter to Henry suggesting a marital alliance:

[Johann]
1. Recommends the King to strengthen himself by a matrimonial alliance with some prince of these parts in case of war with France, Spain, or Burgundy.

2. Urges especially an alliance with the duke of Cleves, who possesses three most powerful duchies and two earldoms, and many towns not only strong but populous. If England were in danger he could alone raise an army sufficient to defend it; and he is descended from the same stock as the kings of England, as will be shown by a genealogy.

3. The Duke has but one son, though he has three daughters. His son is fifteen years old, of middle height, brown complexion, sound in body and limbs, well learned, and speaks Latin and French. His name is William, undoubted heir of the duchies of Cleves, Juliers, and Berg..., the earldoms of March and Ravensburg. By the death of Philip de Cleve, who died in Brabant without children, he came into possession of the lordship of Ravenstein, and lands to the value of 20,000 florins. The rest of the duchy, though partly mortgaged, produces ample rents. If freed from incumbrance, which could be easily done, it would yield 340,000 g.fl.

4. The eldest sister, Maria [sic: Sybylla], is married to John Frederic, only son of John duke of Saxony, who, in wealth and power, has scarce an equal among the German princes. Allied with him are the principality of Hesse, the dukes of Pomerania, Mecklenburg, Lunenburg, Prussia, and Holstein, who is now elected king of Denmark, with the Hanseatic Towns of the Northern Ocean. The second sister [Anna] is affianced (*desponsata*) to a son of Anthony duke of Lorraine, Calabria and Bari. He will be heir of these duchies and of the marquisates of ... Pont-à-Mouson, of the earldom of Vaidemont, and of the province of Narbonne. There is said to be an article in the marriage treaty, that on the death of the duke of Guelders that duchy should devolve upon the aforesaid son of Lorraine, notwithstanding the opposition of the house of Burgundy. A third sister [Amalia] is in her minority, and not yet affianced. A table follows showing how a son of the duke of Cleves is sprung of royal and imperial blood, on the father's side and on the mother's, with some remarks on their genealogies.

Johann was hoping to plant the seed for an Anglo-Cleves alliance, which could be achieved through the marriage of Henry's daughter Mary and Johann's son Wilhelm. Alternatively, once Amalia was old enough, she could be married to a high-ranking English noble. The very Catholic Johann could not foresee that Henry would break from the Church a mere couple of years later.

By 1532, Eustace Chapuys, the Imperial Ambassador to England, reported to Charles V that there was a rumour regarding Princess Mary and Wilhelm. The rumour came mostly out of Cleves, but was concerning to Charles V. Given the marital difficulties between Charles' maternal aunt Katharine of Aragon, Queen Consort of England and Henry VIII, he might not have been too keen on an Anglo-Cleves alliance.

Johann of Cleves introduced more religious reforms within the United Duchies in January 1532 and April 1533. These new reforms were greatly influenced by the collection of humanists present at the Cleves court or, like Erasmus, in close contact with Johann. Heresbach, Karl Harst, Jülich Chancellor Johann von Blatten, Berg Chancellor John Ghogreff and Cleves Vice Chancellor (later Chancellor) Olisleger all contributed. As part of the reforms, Johann ordered church visits, which took place between 1533 and 1534. However, progress was stalled when a dangerous religious sect took hold in Münster.

The Anabaptist Threat

Anabaptism was preached by Melchior Hoffman beginning in the 1520s, springing out of the failed Peasants' War. Among other beliefs, the Anabaptists held that a person had to be baptised as an adult. Hoffman predicted the Second Coming of Christ, claiming that it would occur in 1535. He was eventually imprisoned in Strasbourg in 1533 after preaching all over the Low Countries and Switzerland. After this, two distinct sects of Anabaptists split off. The first sect adhered to the concepts of living a Christian life in anticipation of Christ's return in 1535. The second sect, led by Jan Matthys, was far more dangerous. Effectively, the members of this second sect wanted to speed up Christ's return. They believed that if they prepared a New Jerusalem, Christ would return to earth sooner than predicted.

Matthys determined that Münster would be the New Jerusalem sought by the Anabaptists. On 5 January 1534, a handful of men who fancied themselves disciples were baptised in the Archbishopric of Münster. Within a week or so, the new Anabaptist disciples managed to baptise upwards of 1,400 people within Münster into the new faith. Over the course of January, the Anabaptist movement grew in size and strength. In February 1534, calls by Anabaptist leaders for the citizens of Münster to repent their sins caused hysteria within the city. A supernatural temperament took over the citizenry. Some of the women in Münster experienced violent visions of the apocalypse, so violent that they writhed on the ground and foamed at the mouth. This mass hysteria allowed the Anabaptists to arm themselves and take over the city. Anabaptists from nearby areas were then invited to settle immediately within Münster.

On 23 February 1534, Anabaptist officials were elected to the city council. Matthys hurriedly came to Münster to take over leadership. Two days later, on 25 February, he ordered executed anyone within the city who refused the Anabaptist doctrine. Matthys was persuaded to give non-Anabaptists a deadline of 2 March to either accept Anabaptism or leave Münster, but Matthys' followers took matters into their own hands. On 27 February, non-Anabaptists were driven out of Münster. Those who wished to convert to Anabaptism were publicly baptised in the marketplace, resulting in the entire city of Münster consisting of only Anabaptists. This was a tremendous coup, to say the least.

Franz von Waldeck, Prince-Bishop of Münster and Osnabrück, was the brother-in-law of the elder Anna of Cleves. This elder Anna of Cleves' youngest child, another Franz von Waldeck, would eventually join her niece and namesake Anna of Cleves after she made her way to England in 1539. The location of Münster, not to mention the family ties, posed a threat to the United Duchies not seen since the Peasants' War a decade before. From March 1534 onwards, things only got worse within Münster. A form of communism was established, and those unwilling to give up their money for the commune were executed. Matthys appointed deacons to confiscate and redistribute property.

In April 1534, Prince-Bishop Franz von Waldeck's army attacked Münster to try and take back control of the city. Matthys, declaring that he had received a divine communication from God, exited Münster with a small group of men to face Waldeck's army. Predictably, he was cut down. After Matthys' demise, Jan Beukels, who also went by Jan of Leiden, became the next Anabaptist leader of New Jerusalem. Under Beukels' leadership, things within Münster went from bad to worse.

In May 1534, Beukels reportedly stripped off his clothes and ran around Münster in the nude. After his naked exertion, Beukels entered a three-day trance. This was the first hint that something was not quite right with Beukels.

Next, Beukels did away with Matthys' city council. Beukels' government was formed of twelve elders, and he placed himself at the head. Beukels and the elders instituted a new set of laws to govern New Jerusalem. The most insidious and hideous effect of the new laws was that even minor offences were punishable by death.

Polygamy was implemented by Beukels in July 1534. He claimed a divine vision in which God ordered him to be fruitful and multiply, which was enough justification for the leaders of New Jerusalem. The citizens and some of the preachers did not agree, so Beukels threatened violence. This led to Beukels and his supporters being overthrown and imprisoned on 29 July.

Beukels' imprisonment did not last long. He and his imprisoned comrades were quickly freed when the would-be usurpers were busy contemplating other matters. Beukels had the primary actors in his imprisonment, roughly fifty people, executed immediately, and continued to order the execution of those in New Jerusalem who opposed polygamy.

In August 1534, the unwed women of New Jerusalem were ordered to marry. There were roughly three marriageable women for every one man in New Jerusalem, which gave each polygamist husband three wives on average. Girls as young as twelve were deemed old enough to marry. A husband would lay with one wife until she became pregnant, then move to the next wife. Any woman who did not comply was executed.

On 31 August, Waldeck's troops again tried to besiege Münster. His bands of *Landsknechte* were severely beaten. They retreated, and several left

Waldeck's employ. Giving up on a direct assault, he next chose to starve the Anabaptists into submission.

A report contained within the Letter Book of Francesco Contarini, held in St Mark's Library in Venice, details what happened next. The anonymous report was written in December 1534, after Johann Friedrich of Saxony and Johann III of Jülich-Cleves-Berg met to discuss how to tackle the Anabaptist threat in Münster.

Eight days after the failure of the assault on Munster, the Prophet of Munster, by name John of Leyden, a tailor, convoked all the people, telling them he was commissioned by God to be King of Israel and of justice, and to govern throughout like King David. Another prophet immediately appeared, a goldsmith, by name John of Warendorf, saying that God had charged him to be the prophet in the stead of the aforesaid King, who has commission from God, to be king of justice, which has to prevail over the whole world, and that he is to march with a large army to destroy kings, princes, and all superiors, spiritual and temporal, without any mercy, and in this manner the humble and compassionate are to govern the whole world.

The King (John of Leiden) immediately commenced ruling, and appointed his Court, with all such officers as becoming a great prince, such as maggiordomo, marshal, counsellor, servants for his table, &c, and from amongst seven women he has elected a queen, a gentlewoman of Holland, very handsome, the widow of another prophet who was killed under Munster. The Queen has a separate Court. The King has thirty-one horses with gold trappings, and some golden saddles, and costly habits of brocade and of other sorts, made with the ornaments of the churches, which have also served to array his gentlemen, and finally the Queen and her maids of honour.

Beukels' throne, which he sat upon three times a week to dole out judgement, was set up in the market square of Münster. The Venetian report described Beukels' behaviour when travelling through Münster:

When the King cavalcades through the town he wears a gown of cloth of silver, slashed and lined with crimson, fastened with gold thread, and on his right hand is a well-clad page carrying the Bible, there being another on the other side with a naked sword. One of these pages, who was captured in the town by force, is the son of the Bishop of Munster.[18]

The King wears a triple crown of refined gold, very richly set, and a gold chain with a costly jeweled ornament in the form of an orb, with

---

18 Franz von Waldeck Jr, born in 1524; he is not the same Franz von Waldeck who went to England for a time.

two swords, one of gold and the other of silver, which traverse the orb, on whose summit is a gold cross surmounted by the words 'King of justice for the whole world'.

The Queen also wears a similar ornament. The King ascends a lofty, well-decorated platform on the market-place, together with his lieutenant … the lieutenant always places himself two steps below the King, at whose feet stand his councillors. Whosoever has any demand to make for justice or favour is obliged to kneel three times; at the fourth obeisance he prostrates himself, and then begins to plead.

The Anabaptist leaders were certainly taking themselves seriously.

In October 1534, one of Beukels' prophets of God stated that the Lord's trumpet would give forth three blasts in the coming days, after which the citizens of New Jerusalem had to meet at the cathedral. After assembling, according to the prophet, the citizens were to face Waldeck's armies and allies outside the city walls. The citizens of New Jerusalem, the prophet declared, would be imbued with divine strength and thus able to defeat Waldeck.

Not long after this, the prophet duly blew a trumpet thrice. The citizens of New Jerusalem assembled in front of the cathedral, but Beukels decided against attacking Waldeck. Instead, he held a banquet for his subjects after which he capped off the banquet by executing one of Waldeck's captured mercenaries.

The ongoing occupation of Münster unsettled Johann of Cleves and Johann Friedrich of Saxony. It no doubt unsettled Sybylla, Anna, Wilhelm and Amalia, too. Duke Karl of Guelders, the perpetually bellicose, would not put up with the Anabaptists. He intercepted an Anabaptist force of 1,000 in January 1535, preventing them from attacking Waldeck or providing relief to the Anabaptists in Münster.

By April 1535, Waldeck and his remaining army were still camped outside Münster. The Anabaptists within were starving. Beukels allowed people to start leaving the city in May, with the promise that those who abandoned New Jerusalem would be damned to Hell. For those who did leave Münster, the brief life they had outside the walls may have seemed like Hell.

Waldeck's troops swiftly captured and killed any men of fighting age upon their exit. The starving women and children were not killed, but also were not fed by Waldeck. They were not allowed to leave the area directly outside Münster. For over a month they ate whatever they could find, reportedly eating grass like cattle. Many of them died. The ground between Münster's walls and Waldeck's camp was soon piled with corpses.

Within New Jerusalem, Beukels went back on his word to allow people to leave. Instead, he ramped up policing of the few remaining inhabitants, with several being beheaded by Beukels himself for trying to leave.

In June 1535, in concert with a former resident of Anabaptist Münster, Waldeck's army was able to take back control. They attacked the night of 24 June, and were met by the roughly 300 remaining residents of New Jerusalem. After a couple hours, the defenders gave up. Initially, the Anabaptists were allowed to go to their homes in Münster. However, within days, Waldeck reversed course and killed the remaining Anabaptists. It is thought that, from February 1534 to early July 1535, around 8,000 people were killed either because of the conflict between Waldeck and the Anabaptists or because they were violating laws put in place by Beukels.

Six months later, in January 1536, Beukels and two of his main supporters were publicly executed in Münster after being fiendishly tortured. The bodies of the three men were moved to cages, which were then hung from the steeple of St Lambertus Church. Even in the twenty-first century, almost 500 years later, one can still see the cages hanging from the steeple of St Lambertus.

Anabaptist Münster, a wild tale to us in the twenty-first century, was a terror in sixteenth-century Germany and beyond.

Meanwhile, in Saxony

In Saxony, while the Anabaptist takeover of Münster went on, Sybylla became pregnant with her third child. The child, another son, was born on 5 January 1535. They named him John Ernest, possibly after his young half-uncle Johann Ernst. Sadly, the baby died only six days after his birth.

A Venetian report from November 1535 described Sybylla and Johann Friedrich:

[The] Duke of Saxony is 32 years old, and has to wife the daughter of the Duke of Cleves and Juliers, who bore him two (*sic*) sons. Besides all his other titles of Elector, Lord Marshal, &c., he is now head of the whole Lutheran sect. Every morning as soon as he is dressed he hears the sermon in his public eating room; he does not hear Mass, save when he communicates, and the Mass is ordained after the manner of his own doctors of divinity, who are Martin [Luther], Melanchthon, and his companions, who however are not here, but there are here five others, Agricola (and he is the one who preaches at present), Spalatin (*sic*), [and] others... The motto of the Duke of Saxony ... and of other lords who have accompanied him, is still 'Verbum Domini manet in sternum,' and round his coins ... are the words, 'Spes mea in Deo est.'

It seems that Sybylla's *Frauenzimmer* truly reflected the court of her husband. On top of that, Sybylla and Johann Friedrich were the Lutheran political power couple.

Over in Cleves

The well-known fickleness of Duke Karl was evident when he angrily demanded an ambassador announce the cancellation of the match between Anna and Francis of Lorraine. Johann III of Cleves never paid the full monies due Karl, and he was tired of waiting. Besides, Anna was eleven and Francis nine when the *de futuro* terms of the contract were drawn, and nothing meaningful had been done toward securing the marriage. Being fully acquainted with Duke Karl's temperament, Johann was willing to keep hope of a Cleves–Lorraine marriage alive.

By late 1537, Duke Karl was feeling his age. He had no heirs of his body, and the engagement arrangements between Anna and Wilhelm of Cleves with Karl's Lorraine relations had fallen through. Twenty years before, Karl's own attempt to marry Anna of Cleves the Elder never came to fruition because the young woman married Philip of Waldeck instead. Despite these dynastic setbacks, Duke Karl still wished for control of Guelders to pass to his next closest male relation, the young Wilhelm of Cleves.

A marriage between Wilhelm and Christina of Denmark, niece of Emperor Charles V, was pursued by Johann III beginning in September 1537. '[Four] commissioners from the duke of Cleves [came] to conclude the marriage [of the princess of Denmark with his son and heir.' By January 1538, Henry VIII of England began pursuing Christina himself: 'As the proposed marriage of the duchess of Milan and the duke of Cleve and Juliers is stayed, the King might honour the said duchess by marriage, considering the reports of her.' Despite the cooling of Wilhelm's suit for Christina, he had other reasons to be happy.

Wilhelm Receives his First Dukedom

The month of January 1538 was a joyful one for both Sybylla and Wilhelm. On 16 January, Sybylla and Johann Friedrich's final child, another boy, was born. They named him after his father, too. The little boy is known to history as John Frederick the Younger.

On 27 January, Wilhelm's status as heir to Guelders was ratified. Johann was not in favour of the move, knowing the serious threat which the United Duchies would face if Wilhelm became the next Duke of Guelders. Wilhelm was twenty-one years old and, like so many his age, disregarded the wisdom of his parents.

Duke Karl did not have the authority to give away Guelders, or so Holy Roman Emperor Charles V believed. Charles V had multiple different legal claims to Guelders, including his descent from his grandmother Maria of Burgundy and that his grandfather Maximilian I had effectively bought the duchy. There were a couple more nuanced avenues to ownership which Charles V could claim, too, such as the Treaty of Gorkum from 1528. Duke Karl did try to give rights to Guelders to Francis I of France in 1534 through the secret Treaty of Grunsvoort, but Charles caught wind of it and forced Duke Karl to sign another treaty in 1536 to reinforce Gorkum.

On 30 June 1538, Duke Karl died. The young Wilhelm became Duke of Guelders a month before his twenty-second birthday in July. Later that year, Johann's health began failing. It looked like Wilhelm was going to control the might of Guelders, Cleves, Jülich, Mark, Berg, Ravensberg and Zutphen in short order.

Trouble with Guelders Begins

Johann was against Wilhelm's desire to grab power and magnify the might of the United Duchies. Johann's family had always been friendly with Holy Roman Emperors Maximilian I and Charles V, and the same was true for Maria. However, in 1538 the young Wilhelm accepted the title after Duke Karl's death in June. This gave Johann a glimpse into his only son's nature as a ruler.

The people of Guelders were in favour of having the young Duke Wilhelm as their new leader. They did not want a Spanish-Burgundian overlord, and in any case Wilhelm arguably had a stronger hereditary claim to Guelders through his mother than did Emperor Charles V. To strengthen Wilhelm's claim to Guelders, Anton of Lorraine suggested that his daughter Anne marry Wilhelm. The idea of Anna marrying Francis of Lorraine had been initially cancelled by Duke Karl of Guelders in 1535, then partially revived in 1536 and 1537. By the time Wilhelm was given title to Guelders, the point of a marriage between Anna and Francis of Lorraine was moot, and the *de futuro* conditions of the contract were never fulfilled.

Johann was extremely worried over Wilhelm's assumption of Guelders. He notified Charles V immediately, hoping that the situation could be mediated peacefully. Charles V, due to the old amity between them, agreed to maintain a peaceful stance during Johann's lifetime. Once Johann shuffled off his mortal coil, however, all bets were off.

The idea of a marriage between Christina of Denmark and Wilhelm became urgent. Depending on how long Johann, who turned forty-seven in 1538, would survive, Charles V needed another way to claim Guelders for the Holy Roman Empire. Marrying his niece to Wilhelm seemed a viable option. Inheritance and general rights to Guelders could be hammered out through a marital agreement.

The Death of Johann III

On 6 February 1539, Anna of Cleves' father Johann III von der Mark, Duke of the United Duchies of Jülich-Cleves-Berg, died after suffering a stroke. He was forty-eight. It was erroneously reported at Henry VIII's court that it was Wilhelm, still only twenty-two, who died. This is likely due to a rumour in Brussels that Wilhelm had been poisoned, and not because of any news directly out of Germany. Johann's death allowed Wilhelm to pursue his clever but reckless political agenda, which included wedding one of his sisters to the King of England.

Johann III was known as the Simple during his lifetime, and the Peaceful after his death. He did his best throughout his reign to stay away from military entanglements unless necessary. He smoothed out the administrative and bureaucratic issues which came to the fore during the reign of his father, and overhauled the tax system. He created new governmental organisations to administer his plans and expanded territories of Jülich-Cleves-Berg. Johann reformed the legal system in his territory as well, with positive results.

There are conflicting reports as to whether Johann was agile in mind or whether it was his wife Maria who had a keen sense of politics. Either way, the reforms introduced during their marriage made the United Duchies a successful, stable place to live despite the occasionally violent issues brought on by the German Reformation.

Johann maintained a close relationship with Desiderius Erasmus, even offering the humanist a stipend and place at the Cleves court. Like his wife and their four children, he was raised Catholic.[19] He adopted a stance of religious tolerance in the United Duchies, but did not outright allow Lutheran texts or teachings to be circulated within his territories. He remained a Catholic throughout his life.

Possibly recognising that he was weakening, Johann had portraits made of Anna, Wilhelm and Amalia in 1538, shortly before his death the following year. The portraits of Anna and Amalia were requested by Henry VIII, who later sent his own court painter, Hans Holbein, to make a portrait of Anna.

One likeness, known as the Rosenbach portrait, could be from this set. Held by the Rosenbach Museum in Philadelphia, it is painted on vellum. Initially, Barthel Bruyn the Elder was suspected to be the artist. However, it now appears that none other than Hans Holbein might have been behind it. Although further research is needed, the fact that the portrait was painted on vellum and not wood makes it an outlier at least and decidedly not by Barthel Bruyn. The latter typically painted on wooden panels, while Holbein was known to paint on vellum. If it is a work by Holbein, then it was possibly painted in 1540. Hopefully, a more thorough examination of the Rosenbach portrait will be carried out by experts to determine the portrait's true provenance.

Johann left behind at least two illegitimate daughters as well. One became a nun, and the other, named Elisabeth of Cleves, was grandmother to the second wife of Olisleger, ultimately Chancellor of Cleves.

Swiftly after the burial of Johann in Cleves, Wilhelm jumped at the chance to wed one of his sisters to Henry VIII of England. Exactly eleven months after Johann's death, his middle daughter, Anna, married Henry on 6 January 1540. Within six months of the marriage, Wilhelm's political plans began to unravel.

---

19 As mentioned, Sybylla became a Lutheran within a year of her marriage to Saxon Elector Johann Friedrich. Amalia became a Lutheran, too. Wilhelm never could quite make up his mind when it came to religion. Anna, for all intents and purposes, remained a Catholic until her death.

6

Political and Marital Intertwinement with England

Charles V Goes into Mourning

On 1 May 1539, the Holy Roman Empire witnessed the death of Isabella of Portugal, Empress Consort to Charles V. Ten days earlier, a sickly Isabella had suffered a miscarriage while pregnant with her seventh child. It is possible that she suffered from tuberculosis, because she was terribly thin shortly before her miscarriage. She was thirty-five years old.

Charles V was devastated by the death of his wife. He shut himself away in a monastery for the summer of 1539, refusing to escort Isabella's body to its burial place. Charles was so profoundly sad about her death that he wore black for the rest of his life, and never remarried.

For Wilhelm, Charles V's extended absence was the perfect opportunity for him to arrange a marriage for one of his sisters without Imperial oversight. Remember that the Von der Marks were subjects of the Emperor, and thus would have to obey his will if he were against any such arrangement. However, Wilhelm was bent on keeping the Duchy of Guelders, and sought powerful allies who could provide military support. Possibly remembering his father Johann's suggestion of matching him with Mary of England, Wilhelm saw an excellent opportunity when Mary's father Henry VIII came calling for Wilhelm's sisters.

The Anglo-Cleves Alliance Moves Forward

Throughout the summer of 1539, Wilhelm's representatives worked hard with Thomas Cromwell and the English ambassadors to the United Duchies to strike up a marital pact. The widowed Duchess Maria, for her part, was not in favour of the match. She might have been aware of Anne Boleyn's death, and the dubious circumstances of her trial and execution. On the other hand, given that Maria was a Catholic, she may have seen Anne Boleyn's reputation as a Protestant as a good enough reason for the woman to not be Queen of England. Additionally, Maria may have preferred to keep her daughters closer to the United Duchies where any bonds of marriage would be more readily beneficial to their territories. Given that Maria was an astute politician, she may not have agreed with her son's reasons for marrying off one of his sisters to an English king.

After receiving portraits of Anna and Amalia, Henry chose Wilhelm's elder sister Anna as the future Queen Consort of England. He then sent Holbein, who painted at least three portraits of Anna: two miniatures and a three-quarter-length. The first miniature, which is effectively a smaller version of the three-quarter-length portrait in the Louvre, is held by the Victoria and Albert Museum in London. Contained within an ivory box carved to look like a rose, it shows a simplified, though still lovely, portrait of Anna and her distinctive eyes. The second work, the Louvre portrait, is large, detailed and painted on vellum. An ornament in Anna's headdress on the left side bears miniature portraits of Henry and Anna, a charming detail added by the talented Holbein. It is possible that, during this visit to Germany, Holbein could have created enough sketches or indeed started the Rosenbach portrait, if he is the artist. The second miniature of Anna was likely painted after her arrival in England.

Once the terms of the Anglo-Cleves marriage were settled, Henry began making plans to bring his new bride from Germany to England. Initially, he assembled a fleet of ten ships for the purpose. As the French ambassador Charles de Marillac reported to Francis I of France on 3 October 1539,

> It is to be presumed that the marriage of this King with the sister of the duke of Cleves is agreed upon and will shortly be consummated, and, although the ministers still say only that they have good hope of it, appearances indicate that it is settled, especially the equipment of 10 ships, in which the Admiral and other lords of this Court go to conduct the said lady hither in all solemnity and triumph. To this may be added the great caresses made to the ambassadors who came about the matter... Moreover, repairs and ornaments have been renewed in the King's principal house, and especially in the quarter where queens are lodged, and some of the principal lords of this Court have bought much cloth of gold and silk, a thing unusual for them except for some great solemnity.

While not openly advertised to the English court, Anna was about to start a new life there.

Eventually, it was decided that it would be safer and better for Anna's complexion if she travelled to England over land. Safe conducts had to be secured from the Emperor, through whose territories she would travel.

Charles V, who wished to stay friendly with Henry and Wilhelm for the time being, was obliging. Maria of Hungary, Regent of the Netherlands, arranged for an escort for Anna.

On 4 October 1539, the marriage treaty relating to Anna and Henry was ratified by the English king's commissioners in London. Things continued moving forward for Anna throughout October 1539, particularly her new husband forgiving Wilhelm's debt of 100,000 florins, which normally would have been provided as part of Anna's dowry to Henry.

Marillac was finally informed of the pending marriage around 14 October, and he duly reported it to duly reported it to Anne de Montmorency, French soldier and diplomat: 'This King has announced to him his marriage with Anne of Cleves, concluded with the ambassadors of the duke of Cleves, who left eight days ago to conduct the lady to Calais by land ... who is expected in a month.' Unfortunately, Anna would face several delays on the journey to her new home.

The manor house in Calais called the Exchequer was ordered to be prepared for Anna's arrival. The city itself was supposed to be spruced up, and presumably made festive in advance of Anna resting there before sailing across the English Channel.

Marillac, writing directly to Francis I, spelled out Henry's hopes for the marriage. Henry was glad to now have a tangential alliance with Elector Johann Friedrich of Saxony, given the latter's marriage to Sybylla. This new friendship would ideally provide a counterbalance should England be attacked. Given that the United Duchies and Saxony were to the east of France, Spain and other areas which could potentially become hostile, the Germans were poised to intercede on England's behalf. Additionally, given the recent enactment of the Catholic-leaning Six Articles in England, Marillac explained to Francis that the 'third advantage is in religion; as he hopes by the intercession of Cleves to soften many innovations in Germany, which are too harsh, and to find some middle way to compose difficulties'. Of course, there was also Henry's desire for a spare male child, given that he had but one son.

Henry believed Anna to be an ideal candidate in the realm of creating more children, 'which he could not better have than with the said lady, who is of convenient age, healthy temperament, elegant stature, and endowed with other graces, as the said King affirms'. However, her arrival so close to Christmastide was expected to delay the opportunity for consummation, given the strict ecclesiastical rules observed surrounding copulation and the Church calendar. Either way, it was quite obvious in London that the people were delighted by the Anglo-Cleves marriage and could not wait for Anna to come to her new country.

Anna's Journey to England

The original plan was for Anna to travel to Calais with an escort of 400 horsemen, cross to Dover and then celebrate her marriage and its consummation in Canterbury. It was believed that Anna would arrive in England sometime between 25 and 30 November. However, in a letter from Vice Chancellor Olisleger to Lord Lisle dated 10 November it was suggested that Anna would not arrive at Calais until 7 or 8 December. She finally arrived on 11 December, not too much later than Olisleger predicted. The two highest-ranking persons in her train were Prefect Wenherus von Hoghestein and Vice Chancellor Olisleger.

Anna enjoyed a grand entrance into Calais. One description of her arrival, although not written in an overtly sixteenth-century hand, provides detail:

Setting forth the stages between Düsseldorf and Antwerp, where she was met by the English merchants four miles outside the town, in 50 velvet coats with chains of gold, and received inside the town, with 80 torches burning in the daylight, and brought to the English lodging, where they kept open household one day for her and her train. Next day, the English merchants brought her on her way to Stekyn (the first stage on the way to Gravelines) and gave her a gift.

The stages from Antwerp to Gravelines, where she was received by the captain with a shot of guns. Next morning, 11 Dec. [1539], she arrived within the English pale at Calais between 7 and 8 a.m., and was received by the lord Deputy, the lieutenant of the Castle, the Knight Porter, and the marshal of Calais, Sir George Carow, captain of Resbanke, and the captain of the Spears, well-appointed with great horses, and with them the men of arms, in velvet coats and gold chains, and all the archers in the King's livery well appointed; and so brought her towards Calais, a gentleman of arms of the King's and another of hers riding together. Within a mile of Calais she was received by the earl of Southampton, lord Admiral, with the lord W[ilia]m Howard, Sir Fra[nci]s Brian, the lord Grey of Wilton, the lord Hastings, lord Clifford, lord Herbert, lord Tailbush, Sir Tho[ma]s Seymour, Sir Henry Knyvett, Mr. Gregory Cromwell, with...gentlemen in coats of satin damask and velvet, besides the said lords, who wore three collars of cloth of gold and purple velvet and chains of gold, and 200 yeomen...in the King's colours, red and blue cloth.

Then the King's ships [off] Newland as she came by them let 200 shots of guns, after which the town of Calais shot 300 pieces of ordnance. When she came to the Lantern Gate she stayed and viewed the King's ships, the *Lion* and the *Sweepstake*, decked with 100 banners of silk and gold, wherein were 200 master gunners and mariners and 31 trumpets, and a double drum that was never seen in England before; and so her Grace entered into Calais. At her entry, 150 pieces of ordnance let out of the said two ships made such a smoke that one of her train could not see another. Where stood in order on both sides the streets, like a lane, with 500 soldiers in the King's livery of the retinue of Calais, and the mayor of Calais with his brethren, and the commons of Calais, and the merchants of the Staple, stood in like manner in array, and made a lane wherethrough she passed to her lodging. There the mayor and his brethren came to her and gave her 50 sovereigns of gold, and the mayor of the Staple, 60. Next morning she had a gun shot, j[o]usting and all other royalty that could be devised in the King's garrison; and kept open household there for the 15 days that she remained.

Anna's escort to Calais and her reception there were more ostentatious than her elder sister Sybylla's experience in Torgau. If nothing else, Anna could delight in the fact that she was elevated above both Sybylla and Wilhelm.

Due to delays with her lengthy travel from the United Duchies to Calais, plus a long stretch of inclement whether impacting the English Chanel, Anna did not arrive in England until 27 December 1539.[20] She disembarked at the Downs, moving on to Deal Castle and then Dover. Anna next stayed at Canterbury, where she was originally supposed to celebrate her marriage to Henry. She finally arrived at Rochester on 31 December 1539, where she had her first meeting with her new husband.

Anna's Time as Queen

On 1 January 1540, per a report from Olisleger, which is sadly only preserved in an edition of the *Zeitschrift des Bergischen Geschichtsvereins*, Henry arrived at Rochester in the afternoon. Anna was watching bull baiting when he entered in disguise. The incognito king presented Anna with a crystal goblet that had a gold lid and foot, beset with diamonds and rubies, and a gold jewel and necklace similarly beset with diamonds and rubies.

At some point, either Anna did recognise Henry, or his identity was revealed. There could not have been too many six-foot-tall, portly men with red beards and in their late forties who accompanied Henry. If Anna was given any description of her new husband when she was in Calais, it's conceivable that she recognised him. Either way, the two went on to enjoy dinner together that evening. Henry spent the night at a location far enough away to preserve her dignity, then enjoyed breakfast with Anna the next morning. According to Olisleger, the two got along just fine.

Anna's official meeting with Henry, at which she wore a hat embroidered with pearls and a cloak bearing the lion of Jülich and escarbuncle of Cleves, went off without a hitch. The new royal couple formally met at Black Heath on 3 January 1540, before riding through the gate to Greenwich.

It is possible that the hat Anna is shown wearing in the Rosenbach portrait is the same one.

The wedding at Greenwich on 6 January 1540 was a standard ceremony, although Anna came a bit late. During her time as Queen of England, Anna adopted the French style of dress that was still popular at the English court, although she brought a touch of modesty to the low-cut bodice by pairing a German-style high-collared shirt with the plunging French neckline.

Anna and Henry appeared to get along well. There were no rumblings of discontent between the two. The only hiccup appeared to come around 26 February 1540:

---

20 Vanessa Cain-Tait of Secret London Runs, Ltd did an excellent job showing just how long a trip from Düsseldorf to Rochester would take on foot in the Anna of Cleves segment of her Six Queens virtual race.

Copy of notarial certificate of the production, on Thursday, 26 Feb. 1540, before [Wenherus von Hoghestein, Prefect] and [Cleves Vice Chancellor Heinrich] Olisleger, councillors of W[ilhelm] duke of Cleves, of the precontract ... of Anne of Cleves with [Francis of Lorraine,] the son of Anthony, duke of Lorraine, which appears to have been made on the 15 Feb. 1535.

This was a belated attempt by Wilhelm and his government to prove definitively that Duke Karl of Egmond had formally ended the *de futuro* marriage contract made between Anna and Francis of Lorraine. Whether Henry or his councillors were aware that Anna's father briefly tried to revive the Lorraine match in 1536 and 1537 is unclear. As far as the officials in the United Duchies were concerned, the marriage contract was never completed, and Duke Karl's fickle hissy fit in 1535 had ended things. Anna was free to marry whomever she wished.

Holbein painted his second miniature of Anna, this time as queen consort, at some point in early 1540. Thanks to research by Franny Moyle, whose recent biography on Hans Holbein is quite comprehensive, it is now known that a miniature sometimes identified as Katheryn Howard, Henry's fifth wife, is more likely to be of Anna. The miniature is mounted on a four-of-diamonds playing card, a nod to Anna being Henry's fourth wife. Beyond this less than subtle element, using the evidence of our eyes, one can see that Anna of Cleves is the individual in the 1540 Holbein miniature.

The sitter wears the Consort's Necklace, with its combination of ruby, diamond and pearl in the jewel standing for hope, faith and charity. The hair colour of the sitter in this miniature matches Anna's braids in the Rosenkranzbruderschaft altarpiece from 1528. There are the physical features of the sitter as well, in particular her hooded eyelids. The very same eyelids are seen in the Louvre and Rosenbach portraits and the Holbein 1539 miniature of Anna. When specifically comparing the 1539 and 1540 miniatures, the eyebrows are the same and the nose, chin and mouth bear striking similarities.

The sitter's style of dress matches contemporary descriptions of Anna in that the woman is wearing the French fashion. As mentioned above, the sitter is wearing a high-collared shirt, which was popular in German fashion in the 1540s. Katharine of Aragon wore high-collared shirts as well, perhaps showing that both women sought to instil a sense of modesty in their dress. It has been hinted at that there are even stylized escarbuncles on the sitter's green sleeve, although it is hard to tell with any certainty. The portrait shows an adult woman, and Anna was twenty-four years old when she became queen. This is very different from Katheryn Howard, who was still a teenager when she married Henry. Given the fate of Katheryn Howard, it is possible that Henry had all images of her destroyed, much as he did for Anne Boleyn. For these reasons and more, the 1540 Holbein miniature should be recognised as depicting Anna of Cleves, not Katheryn Howard.

Ambassador Karl Harst's Dispatches

Karl Harst, Ambassador of Cleves to England, arrived in London on 15 March 1540. In his letter written that day to Chancellor Ghogreff, a close relationship between Anna and Thomas Cromwell is revealed: the German princess called Cromwell 'Father', likely because Cromwell was appointed Henry's 'vicegerent of spirituals', which furthered the Dissolution of the Monasteries by allowing Cromwell to investigate religious properties and holdings, and seize them. Alternatively, Anna may truly have seen him as a sort of father figure, and so nicknamed Cromwell 'father'.

Cromwell was very pleased with Anna's presence at court. On the other hand, Harst mentions some months later that it would be a shame for Anna to lose a 'father' like Cromwell, who acted as Anna's friend. Harst mentioned that he was aware of the difficult sentiments between Wilhelm and Charles V, and that the only way to ensure a modicum of peace would be if Charles V's niece Christina of Denmark wed Wilhelm.

Eight days later, on 23 March, Harst wrote to Ghogreff again, informing him of how happy Anna and Henry were together. Harst and Anna held a private audience, where some of Wilhelm's dissimulation was shown in the form of an antedated letter. Anna was concerned about the letter, but ultimately accepted it and its contents. Harst revealed that Henry VIII was aware of the political situation between Wilhelm and Charles V, and that Charles' brother Ferdinand, King of the Germans, was trying to mediate between the two. Harst's letters show that Henry had full knowledge of any issues brewing between the United Duchies and the Holy Roman Empire. Anna's command of English was imperfect at this point, with Henry asking Harst to translate for her. It might have simply been more comfortable for Anna to hear information in German rather than the headache of English.

Most importantly, Harst gave Cromwell the documents reflecting that Anna's marriage contract with Francis of Lorraine was cancelled. Henry was overall very pleased with Anna as a wife, too. There was no foreseen issue for Anna's and Henry's marriage as late as Lady Day 1540, it would seem.

By the end of March 1540, Harst came into direct contact with Lady Mary. He did not realise it was her. She revealed her interest in Wilhelm as a husband, but also may have revealed some trepidation about his religious leanings. Duke Henry of Saxony, the very Catholic Albertine duke, proposed marriage to Amalia of Cleves. Wilhelm rejected the idea outright. It seems there was some confusion on the part of either Mary or Harst because Duke Henry was already married. It is likely that they meant Duke Henry's son, Moritz of Saxony, who went on to marry Agnes of Hesse in January 1541.

The tide began to turn against Anna's marriage by mid-April 1540. Harst reported Anna being very shaken about a letter Henry received from her brother. Anna was so distraught that she demanded to speak with Harst twice in one day. Harst thought that perhaps Anna was pregnant, which added to her agitation. She revealed to him some days later that she did not think she was pregnant. Cromwell endlessly praised Anna, believing her to be prudent. Cromwell broached the issue of whether Guelders was in favour of having Anna's brother as their duke, which Harst believed was the case.

Anna, for her part, was preoccupied with three things in April 1540. First, that Henry had not fully settled upon her possessions as queen, because he was waiting for Parliament to finalise it. Secondly, that her coronation probably would not take place in 1540, which displeased Anna and might have made her sad, fearful, or both. Finally, despite her exertions, Anna was not pregnant.

Harst reported that Henry, for his part, was growing increasingly agitated that Wilhelm was not seeking or taking Henry's advice.

A glimmer of hope was revealed in late May 1540, when not only were Anna's queenly possessions confirmed by Parliament but she received more than anticipated. Despite her melancholy over Wilhelm's obnoxious behaviour, things were going positively for Anna. She even revealed to Harst that she liked Lady Mary, and said it was a shame that Lady Mary was demoted after her parents' annulment. Anna, who certainly missed her homeland, even asked that she be sent dachshunds. Anna had several cousins, legitimate and illegitimate, with her. First, the young Count Franz von Waldeck, a legitimate cousin through her paternal aunt, was there. Additionally, a maternal cousin through her illegitimate uncle John of Jülich, and two ladies from the United Duchies who were appointed to serve her by virtue of their relation to Anna, although they were from illegitimate stock. It is possible that they were granddaughters of Anna's paternal grandfather John II of Cleves, the Childmaker.

The rest of Harst's letters from late May 1540 through early June echo what Sir Thomas Wyatt reported to Cromwell and Henry in his capacity as English ambassador at the Imperial court. Namely, Wilhelm was nowhere near sorting things with Holy Roman Emperor Charles V, and was flirting with danger. Most tellingly, Cromwell revealed to Henry that, because Henry and his heirs through Anna were not heirs of any sort to Wilhelm or the United Duchies, Henry offered Wilhelm support only as a courtesy.

Harst duly reported Cromwell's downfall in June 1540. He voiced his own concern for Anna now that Cromwell was gone, because he had been a champion for her and friendly toward Anna and Wilhelm. Anna was not at court on 10 June 1540 because she was visiting with Edward and one of Henry's daughters, likely Lady Elizabeth.

Anna remained as positive as circumstances allowed, requiring Harst to share a meal with her and her ladies. During this meal, the Countess of Rutland declared Harst to be her brother, which utterly confused Harst when Anna translated for him. Harst updated Chancellor Ghogreff on Cromwell's tribulations. It seems that Harst suspected things were not going to go well for Anna in the coming days. To that end, he suggested to Ghogreff that marriages be secured for Amalia and Wilhelm as soon as possible.

By mid-June, Harst told Anna that he thought Charles V would be amused by Cromwell's downfall over the accusation of treachery. Anna astutely pointed out that, if it were true, then Charles V would relax his stance against Wilhelm over the Guelders issue. Anna made a misstep in June by telling Henry that she was worried over Charles V going to war against Wilhelm. Harst bemoaned the loss of Cromwell, whom Anna viewed as a father figure of sorts.

Harst's worry over Anna being cast aside by Henry continued to increase throughout June. He worried that, because Anna was not pregnant, Henry would treat her like Katharine of Aragon. Anna, for her part, did not outwardly appear to share these concerns.

Things took a turn by 26 June 1540, such that Harst wrote to Duke Wilhelm directly. Anna had been in high spirits and Henry treated her well up until 24 June, when Anna was sent to Richmond Palace. This upset Anna, but a friendly bishop counselled her and suggested that she remain cheery. Harst began worrying that Anna was being pushed away because she still had not conceived a child with Henry, and Harst was even more worried that Anna would be labelled as infertile.

For his part, Henry kept up appearances by sending Anna valuable trinkets every day. Anna seems to have been aware of Henry giving Katheryn Howard romantic attention. She adamantly did not want her mother Duchess Maria to find out what was happening, especially because Duchess Maria was not in favour of Anna's marriage to the English king in the first place.

Harst was notified by 8 July 1540 over the alleged concerns of Anna's precontract to Francis of Lorraine, and that any children Anna conceived with Henry could be deemed illegitimate. Harst balked at the accusation, especially after so much proof was provided to show the contract was cancelled. Harst protested that Anna and Francis of Lorraine were mere children when the marriage was contracted, but Henry's counsellors countered that Anna was supposed to go to live at the court in Lorraine when she was seventeen. That did not happen, and the contract was cancelled in 1535, when Anna was roughly twenty years old. However, Henry's counsellors stated that the proof Harst brought and Anna's oath before notaries in England were insufficient.

On 10 July, Harst expressed outrage at learning that Anna was presented with a set of documents which were virtually incomprehensible to her and that she had been 'hoodwinked' by Henry and his officials. Henry duly informed Anna that if she complied with his wishes, she would be treated well. If not, then Henry could not make her any promises. Anna shed bitter tears and told Henry that he was the only husband she had ever had. Henry was unmoved.

Anna did express some resistance to the annulment, namely when Henry wanted her to agree that he never touched her. Anna told Harst that Henry, 'has lived with her like husband and wife ought to live together'. Anna further reiterated her position by stating she would rather be decapitated than agree to such a falsehood. Unfortunately for Anna, Henry swore on a Bible that the two never consummated their marriage.

After this series of heavy blows, Anna consented to the annulment, albeit expressing her fear that if she did not agree. she would be beheaded. This was an unreasonable fear, but such is the nature of fear itself. Harst described Henry as a tyrant and poor Katheryn Howard as a whore, and pleaded for a delegation from Cleves and Saxony to come to Anna's aid. Harst was possessed of the fears, again unreasonable, that Anna would be poisoned or that Henry would try to conceive a child with Anna despite their marriage being annulled. This shows two things: first, Harst's nihilist attitude; and second, the unfettered wildness of Henry's actions.

In his letters throughout the rest of 1540, Harst reported on Anna's emotional state and her whereabouts. He also reports Henry's actions with Charles V, which Harst suspected might have been part of the basis for the annulment. Harst reported that Anna was first at Richmond, but then moved to a castle 20 miles outside of London. The castle was owned by the father of the 'beheaded queen', Anne Boleyn. He was, of course, describing Hever Castle.

Anna, for her part, remained ever hopeful that Henry would take her back.

The Beginning of the End for Queen Anna

On 24 June 1540, Anna was sent to Richmond Palace. Henry, ever afraid of diseases, told her that she was moved to protect her health. The dreaded English sweating sickness had first surged in the summer of 1528, almost killing Anne Boleyn and making it as far as the United Duchies the following year. The disease typically appeared in the summer. If Anna remembered the 1528–29 outbreak, she would have understood Henry's desire to move her to safety. She had no reason to suspect that anything was amiss. She may even have been looking forward to celebrating her and Henry's shared birthday on 28 June.

Behind Anna's back, however, Henry was desperately trying to annul the marriage. He had learned from his ambassador to the Imperial court, Sir Thomas Wyatt, that Wilhelm was dangerously close to war with Emperor Charles V over ownership of the Duchy of Guelders. On top of that, Wilhelm was sneaking behind Henry's back and secretly making deals with Francis I of France. Henry had no interest in a tacit alliance with France by way of his youthful brother-in-law, nor was he interested in being dragged into a war with the Empire over a piece of land that had no meaning to him. Whatever his true feelings about Anna, politically he could not afford to stay in the marriage.

Anna was sent away so that Parliament and a special convocation could review the marriage documents between Anna and Henry and look over evidence of the cancellation of the Lorraine match, along with collecting depositions supporting the idea that Henry never consummated the marriage. If the marriage were consummated, Henry would then have to pursue a divorce. That was trickier.

On 29 June, Thomas Cromwell was arrested and taken to the Tower. The next day, he was presented with an attestation detailing all the times Henry complained of Anna and their lack of consummation. Cromwell, knowing he was in danger of execution, willingly signed the attestation. He dashed off a letter in his own hand that had almost identical information in it, begging Henry for 'mercy, mercy, mercy'.

The collection of depositions continued through early July. The entire purpose of these depositions, the attestation, and Cromwell's letter, regardless of the truth, was to annul the marriage. On 6 July 1540, a commission of archbishops and bishops in England was asked to review all evidence of the lawfulness of Anna's marriage to Henry. This convocation could surely come to only one conclusion: Anna's marriage to Henry was void. Anna was aware of the convocation but had no reason to worry about the validity of her marriage. She rightly knew that there were no impediments. Anna's trusting nature was her downfall.

The convocation continued on 7 July with a review of the depositions. Finally, after more proceedings on 8 July, the marriage between Anna and Henry was officially annulled.[21] Anna was absolutely devastated when she was told of the annulment. After some pressure from Henry's representatives, Anna consented to the findings:

> Though the case must needs be hard and sorrowful, for the great love she bears to his most noble person; yet, having more regard to God and his truth than to any worldly affection, she accepts the judgment. Asks the King to take her as one of his most humble servants, and so to determine of her as she may sometimes have the fruition of his presence. The Lords and others of his Council now with her have put her in comfort thereof, and that the King will take her as his sister. Richmond, 11 July [1540].

Anna signed this letter under what would become her identity in England for the rest of her life: Anne, the Daughter of Cleves. Pleased with her response, Henry sent Charles Brandon, Duke of Suffolk, and others instrumental in securing the annulment to speak with Anna on 12 July. Their purpose was fourfold. First, they were to determine whether Anna truly was submitting herself to Henry's will. Second, if she was so submitting herself, they were to give her tokens from Henry. Third, a notarised document showing Anna's consent to the annulment was to be solemnised. Fourth, Anna was to be encouraged to write to her brother Wilhelm to tell him what happened.

An Act Declaring the Dissolution of the King's Pretensed Marriage with the Lady Anne of Cleves

Parliament was immediately ready to pass an Act that echoed the convocation's findings. Anna's signed, notarised letter was presented to Parliament as well, showing her supposed agreement with the situation. The Act declared both Henry and Anna free to marry anyone 'not prohibited by the law of God'. Additionally, 'all letters patent made by his Highness unto the said Lady Anne, in consideration of the said pretense marriage for her

---

21 For a full analysis of Anna's marriage and its subsequent annulment, the curious may wish to read *Anna, Duchess of Cleves: The King's 'Beloved Sister'* (Amberley, 2019).

dower and jointure, or otherwise, be void and of none effect'. Beyond that, mention of Anna being queen was strictly and harshly outlawed.

This might have been another instance wherein Henry learned from his past. Years before, during the annulment from Katharine of Aragon and marriage with Anne Boleyn, Henry was constantly dealing with individuals stating Katharine was still the lawful queen. He did not want any propaganda or mention of Anna being the rightful queen, so the Act included the following proviso:

> And be it also enacted by the authority above said, that if any person or persons ... after the first day of September next coming, by writing or imprinting or by any other exterior act, word, or deed, directly or indirectly, accept or take, judge or believe the said pretensed marriage, had between his Majesty and the said Lady Anne of Cleves, to be good, lawful or of any effect: Or by words, writing, printing, deed or act procure or do, or cause to be procured or done, anything or things, to or for the interruption, repeal, or adnullation of this act, or of anything therein contained: That then every such person ... and the aiders, counselors, maintainers and abettors: and every of them, for every such offence before specified, shall be adjudged high traitors, and every such offense shall be adjudged high treason, and the offenders therein, their aiders, counselors, maintainers and abettors, and every of them, being lawfully convict of any such offense by presentment, verdict, confession or process, according to the customs and laws of this realm, shall suffer pains of death, as in cases of high treason.

Effectively, anyone who tried to put forward Anna as the rightful Queen of England on or after 1 September 1540 was guilty of high treason and would be executed for the offence. Additionally,

> ... every such offender, being convict as is aforesaid, shall lose and forsake to his Highness, and his heirs and successors kings of this realm, all such manors, lands, tenements, rents, reversions, annuities and hereditaments, which they had in possession as owners, or were sole seized of by or in any right, title, or means or any other person or persons had to their use of any estate of inheritance at the day of such treasons and offenses by them committed and done.

Any property owned by the guilty would be forfeit to the Crown forever. The Act goes on to specify other forms or property, such as the right to collect a debt, which would be forfeited. On top of this, it was made clear that pamphleteers were free to print or distribute the view that Anna had never been queen.

The Act ends:

> And be it also enacted by authority of this present Parliament, that all and singular the King's loving subjects, which have spoken ... or attempted

directly or indirectly, by words, writings, printings, or any exterior act or acts ... against the marriage solemnized between the King's Majesty and the said Lady Anne, or for the letting forth or preferment of the dissolution thereof, or against the person of the said Lady Anne, or her estate or dignity which she pretendeth by reason of the said marriage or have done anything or things, act or acts, or spoken, written, or imprinted any words, or procured to be done anything ... or any words ... contrary or against the said marriage, or any dependences thereof which might be taken, deemed on interpreted for treason or misprision of treason by any construction ... shall be freely and clearly pardoned ... And that none of his said loving subjects for any of the said treasons or misprision of treason above mentioned, and specified, shall hereafter at any time by any manner of means be impeached, vexed, or troubled, but utterly discharged thereof forever.

Henry was not taking any chances.

Katheryn Howard

Henry married his fifth wife, the very young and unprotected Katheryn Howard, on 28 July 1540. Katheryn, who had served in Anna's household, was a prime candidate for Henry's hand. Her uncle was the powerful Thomas Howard, Duke of Norfolk, who already placed two of his female relatives in front of Henry as marriage prospects. The first, Anne Boleyn, had been dangled in front of Henry beginning in the mid-1520s. As mentioned before, Anne's marriage ended with her execution in May 1536. The second female relative was the Norfolk's own daughter, Mary Howard. She wed Henry's recognised illegitimate son Henry Fitzroy in 1533. At a certain point, Mary was encouraged to become Henry's official mistress after Henry Fitzroy died in 1536. The conveniently orphaned Katheryn Howard was simply the third in a long line of Howard women to be thrust upon Henry.

Legally speaking, it would be very difficult for Wilhelm or anyone else to force Henry to take back Anna if he had already remarried. To do so, Henry's marriage to the young Katheryn would itself have to be annulled. After that, he would have to formally recognise his marriage to Anna. That simply was not going to happen.

Henry adopted Anna as his 'beloved sister' for the rest of his life. She was the highest-ranking woman in England behind Henry's wife and daughters, and was gifted several properties for her grace in dealing with such a terrible situation. The amount of wealth Henry bestowed upon Anna might offer the only true glimpse into his feelings for her. During the rest of Henry's life, Anna lived in relative comfort and security.

On the other hand, Anna had no private communications with her brother, sisters or mother. Her receiver-general Sir Wymond Carew was appointed to this post in 1537 in the service of Jane Seymour. Carew spoke German, making him a valuable source of information. His task was to read and copy any letters between Anna, her mother, her siblings or her countrymen. Anna was furious when she discovered the fact. To her, Carew and his wife were inferior in rank to Anna's German steward. Anna detested this treatment, and initially refused to be subject to such examination. In Germany she might have had a point, but not in England. Carew explained:

> I pray you learn of my lord Privy Seal whether I and my wife shall have the same allowance as Mr. Horssey and his wife have, for I think myself no meaner than he. If his lordship seem not so to esteem me, get my brother … to despatch me hence, for the lady Anne of Clevelond (*sic*) is bent to do me displeasure. I think she has heard how I procured the knowledge of such letters as were sent to her, 'which of truth at the beginning she denied.' She esteems my wife two degrees under Mrs. Horssey. 20 Aug.
>
> P.S.—She had a letter three days past from her Grace's brother [Wilhelm], and because she did not seem minded to send it to the King, I asked her brother's ambassador whether she had had any, and he said they were letters of congratulation from her brother. I further told him he should advise her to send them to the King. I was commanded by my lord of Suffolk to show the King's Council what letters were sent to her, and 'I have moved her chamberlain so to do, who has so moved her.'

Anna was not interested in fully complying if she could help it.

Despite the indignities and Anna's displeasure, she was recorded as 'far from appearing disconsolate, is unusually joyous and takes all the recreation she can in diversity of dress and pastime'. If Anna was depressed over her new circumstances, she certainly did a good job of hiding it in public.

The Fall of Katheryn Howard

Anna stayed away from court until New Year's Day 1541. She brought Henry and Katheryn gifts, showing her good will and slightly flaunting her personal wealth to Katheryn. Henry's new wife was nothing without him, whereas Anna was a Hereditary Duchess of the United Duchies and his adopted sister.

Anna remained away from court for most of 1541, too. Henry paid at least one visit to her in August that year. Roughly three months later, in early November, Queen Katheryn was accused of having extramarital affairs and not being forthright with Henry about her premarital chastity or her freedom from precontract. She was removed, questioned and stripped of her title. Already on 10 November 1541 it was suspected that Anna would be restored to her former position as queen.

Wilhelm wasted no time in trying to reconcile his sister with the King of England. Vice Chancellor Olisleger himself was sent to England with letters from Wilhelm. These were the usual letters of credence required for ambassadors, plus missives from Wilhelm hoping to encourage the remarriage of Anna and Henry. Olisleger managed to meet with Thomas

Cranmer, Archbishop of Canterbury, who quickly shut down Olisleger's attempt at reasoning.

In January 1542, a French tract was brought to Henry's attention. Called 'The Repudiation of Queen Maria (*sic*) of England, Sister of the Duke of Cleves', it is written as a long-form letter allegedly from Anna to Henry. The lengthy letter includes the writer's opinion:

... because I know how difficult it is to persuade those who are already firm and convinced in their judgment, especially when it is born of the great Princes, and Kings; of which there are some who think most of the time that everything they want is lawful and permitted to them; I have no hope of winning or winning my cause, if by chance his goodness, or great equity does not speak for me, without my own giving points of my reasons...

This writing was certainly in violation of the 1540 Act, which outlawed any words in print supporting the validity of Anna's marriage to Henry.

Another Bite at the Cherry

Anna visited Henry at Greenwich for New Year's gift-giving in 1542, where she surprised Henry with expensive cloth. Early in the year she was often absent, reportedly suffering from tertian fever. Illness may have been a convenient excuse for Anna to stay away, although rumours abounded at the time that Henry would take her back.

At some point after the annulment, possibly during Katheryn Howard's trials and tribulations, Henry VIII crafted a recipe to help Anna with her illness, recorded as 'A plaster for my Lady Anne of Cleves, to mollify, and resolve, comfort, and cease pain of cold and windy causes'. The expensive ingredients for the plaster included fenugreek, radicchio, myrrh and chamomile. Once pulverised, the plaster could be applied to the skin in hopes of relieving the ailment. If Henry devised this plaster around the time of Katheryn Howard's downfall, it could have fuelled rumours that Henry and Anna would remarry. Anna's fever was gone by April.

Rumours that Henry would take back Anna were still rife at this time. Eustace Chapuys, Emperor Charles V's ambassador to England, told his master that there was no indication it was true and promised to do everything he could to prevent such a reunion.

Beginning that summer, the struggle for Guelders finally came to a head. Wilhelm began his military offensive. Anna, who was unable to return home, was seldom seen at court. In mid-January 1543, it was reported that 'lady Anne of Cleves ... although she is three or four miles from the Court; nevertheless, I do not hear that she has been summoned thither or that she has been there.' Anna was keeping her distance.

Anna was finally seen at court in March, arriving around the 13th. Chapuys reported this to Charles V, saying, 'Lady Anne of Cleves has been three days at Court. Knows not whether she was called thither or not, but ...

this King made not much of her.' Henry may have been giving Anna the cold shoulder, or at least he was not being overtly friendly with her. On the other hand, Henry did give Anna permission to visit with his daughter Lady Mary. One must wonder how Anna and Mary got on during 1542 and 1543, when Anna's brother was using his military force against Mary's cousins Charles V and Maria, Regent of the Low Countries.

Wilhelm's ambassador was a constant presence at the English court throughout the first part of 1543, although he did not do much. In England, the man was simply regarded as one of Anna's servants.

On 12 July 1543, Henry VIII of England married his sixth and final wife, Catherine Parr. This made it impossible for Anna to remarry Henry. The news must have been devastating to poor Anna, now twenty-eight years old. Chapuys reported to Charles V:

> Reason would that the King should also have sent away the agent of Cleves, but …, the Council answered that they did not take him for ambassador, but as servant of the lady Anne of Cleves. Certainly the good man would like well to be gone, for he does nothing; and … the said lady would like to be in her shirt (so to speak) with her mother, having especially taken great grief and despair at the King's espousal of this last wife, who is not nearly so beautiful as she, besides that there is no hope of issue, seeing that she had none with her two former husbands.

Her hopes dashed, Anna had no reason to tarry any longer in England.

Anna is not mentioned again until January 1544, when Henry VIII wrote to Duke Albert of Prussia and mentioned a white osprey which Anna received as a New Year's gift. Beyond that, Anna seems to have lived relatively quietly away from court for the remainder of 1544 and all of 1545. Anna was mentioned in March 1546, noting, 'Lady Anne of Cleves has been for some time at Court, well treated.' In August 1546, she was summoned to Hampton Court. Whatever frustrations Anna or Henry had about the way things ended, they seemed willing to put it behind them.

Edward VI

Henry VIII died on 28 January 1547. His young son, Edward, was the new king, and did not care much for Anna. He took away several of her properties, beginning with Bletchingley Castle in March 1547. Anna was accustomed to living at Bletchingley, and was not terribly keen on moving to Penshurst Palace. Another property, Bisham Manor, was taken from Anna in 1552.

Anna's life in England is most obscure in the late 1540s to early 1550s, during the reign of Edward VI. The young woman, now in her thirties, was cast aside by the new king and constantly fretted about money. Although she still had a great deal of independence, her life became much harder.

7

Wilhelm's Political Ambitions Come to a Head

Duke Wilhelm's Early Successes

Wilhelm turned twenty-three years old in July 1539. He was the Duke of Guelders, by virtue of Duke Karl of Egmond and the submission of the various localities within Guelders. After the death of Johann III in February 1539, Wilhelm was now also the Duke of the United Duchies. He had two sisters, and himself, to marry off in hopes of forming powerful alliances. Duke Wilhelm already had the benefit of his elder sister Sybylla being wed to the Elector of Saxony, another powerful presence within the Holy Roman Empire. His fortunes were waxing.

Wilhelm's major coup over the summer of 1539 was arranging the marriage between his sister Anna and Henry VIII of England. Even as the negotiations continued into September 1539, Duke Wilhelm was spreading rumours to the English court over Charles V trying to steal his property. Elector Palatine Frederick II, husband to Charles V's niece Dorothea of Denmark and Norway, did what he could to persuade Henry VIII against an Anglo-Cleves marriage. Charles V was still interested in marrying Duke Wilhelm to Dorothea's widowed younger sister Christina of Denmark, but Wilhelm preferred an English alliance and English money.

In late October 1539, it was reported by French ambassador Marillac that Duke Wilhelm 'attempted something against the Emperor'. He was certainly up to something, but in fact he had yet to make a move.

In 1539, Sir Thomas Wyatt the Elder was an English ambassador to the Holy Roman Empire. He wrote reports directly to Henry VIII. In one such report from 12 December, written from Amboise, east of Tours, he chronicled an interaction with Charles V. Apparently, after Charles V's return from hunting with the French princes,

It seemed as though [Charles V] would have dismissed Wyatt, who, however, began again, and said he was commissioned to certify that Henry thanked him for the assurance ... that he would keep all his treaties, and had in this alliance now made done nothing in derogation of them. [Charles V] said he trusted Henry would rather counsel Mons. de Juliac[22] by example of his own subjects than aid him against his sovereign, adding,

'What hath Mons. de Juliac to do with Guelders? I assure you, Mons. Lembassadeur, I shall show him that he hath played but the young man.' Wyatt said he had no further commission in that, but was sure Mons. De Cleves would be reasonable. 'Yea! Mons. Lembassadeur, quoth he, he shall so.' Replied that no doubt Henry would show himself both a good and loving brother to Mons. De Cleves and a friend to the Emperor... The Emperor said, no doubt Henry would advise him to obey his sovereign; 'for,' he added 'I assure you, Mons. de Juliac shall do me reason... I say he shall, he shall (laying his hand on his breast), and he hath, of me, a sovereign, a neighbour, and a cousin; and otherwise he shall lose all three.'

Marked his earnest fashion in speaking of Guelders. ... [It] confirms Wyatt's constant opinion that Guelders is more to [the Emperor] than Milan or all Italy. His coming out of Spain has been upon the news of Henry's alliance with Cleves, and, if that be so, the difficulty of the journey declares his desire ... The duke of Lorraine and his son are come to Court. Supposes he pursues his demand of Guelders.

The Duke of Lorraine had a claim for the Duchy of Guelders through his grandmother Philippa of Guelders, twin sister of Duke Karl. Things were not looking terribly solid for Duke Wilhelm's tenure as Duke of Guelders.

Preparing for the Worst

Chancellor Ghogreff of Cleves was likely in the train which accompanied Anna to England, and he witnessed her marriage to Henry VIII on 6 January. Mere days later, Wilhelm was rumoured to have gathered an army of 5,000 in preparation for an attack on Ghent. Ghogreff left England later that month, and it was rumoured around 17 January that things were becoming dangerous in Imperial territory for those loyal to Wilhelm:

Upon a report that the Emperor was bringing down from Italy into France certain Italians and Spaniards of his garrison there, and because the Landgrave [of Hesse's] ambassador brought news that the Lutherans on the one side, and the bishops and church party of Germany on the other were in arms against each other, the German lords decided to leave [England] at once, under pretext that the safe conduct they have from the Emperor would expire in a few days and they might be shut in here if war broke out...

22 Another spelling of Jülich.

Olisleger left around this time, too.

Wyatt continued to report to Henry VIII from the Imperial court in February 1540. Duke Wilhelm had hoped the matter of Guelders could be submitted to a legal court, but the Emperor

> ... desire[d] Henry not to interfere between [Emperor Charles V] and his subject ... As to the duke of Cleves, [the Emperor] would not hear of putting the matter in justice, he having possession; and [Wyatt] having spoken of the good will borne by Henry to the Duke, the Emperor said the best favour he could show him would be to advise him to submit to his Sovereign.

Unfortunately for Thomas Cromwell, it appears that he was oblivious to the serious struggle between Duke Wilhelm and Charles V over Guelders. Henry, for his part, refused to support Duke Wilhelm in his pursuit of Guelders:

> Wyatt requested that the difference with [Monsieur] de Cleves might be settled by justice. The Emperor answered that, on taking the alliance of Cleves, Henry declared he would not meddle in the matter of Guelders, and that Cleves was his vassal with whom he knew what he had to do.

At the same time, Duke Wilhelm was stirring the pot by having letters sent throughout Guelders. He wished to continue asserting his right to the territory, and this aggravated Charles V. 'The Emperor has arrested a messenger whom the duke of Cleves had sent to all the principal towns here, notifying his right to Guelders and desiring them not to be against him.' Duke Wilhelm seems to have had more courage than wit at this point in his life. Still, the Emperor was interested in settling the matter, as was Henry. The English king had no interest in assisting his new brother-in-law in a battle over Guelders.

Ghogreff accompanied Wilhelm to Paderborn in February 1540, where they met with Johann Friedrich to discuss things concerning the Schmalkaldic League. Harst and Heresbach were there, too. On Ghogreff's return from Paderborn, he was intercepted by Henry VIII's man Dr Wotton, who handed over letters for Wilhelm in the hopes that Ghogreff would deliver them. Wotton had been trying to catch up with Olisleger, the Vice Chancellor of Cleves. Better yet, Wotton hoped to encounter Duke Wilhelm. Sadly, he was out of luck.

More Polite Debate over Guelders

Charles V tried to gently negotiate with Wilhelm for the possession of Guelders, but the latter maintained that he had the best claim. The idea of placing the issue in court was appealing to both Duke Wilhelm and Charles V, but they had very different ideas about the details. Duke Wilhelm wanted the issue presented to a court of law administered by the German princes, whereas Charles V would only agree if his brother Ferdinand oversaw the proceedings. Charles and Duke Wilhelm's impasse over Guelders continued.

Wotton finally managed to speak with Duke Wilhelm in March 1540. He reported to Henry on the 7th:

> The Duke of Cleves, having taken possession of his counties of [Ravensburg] and [Mark], came to [Düsseldorf] on Monday, 24 Feb., and Wotton, while he waited there for the promised answer, received, on the 28th, the King's letter to the Duke, with the part of the treaty sent to him by the Duke ratified under the King's Great Seal. Next morning delivered them to the Duke, who said he would consider the matters. On the 5th he sent for Wotton, and gave him a letter for the King, saying it was in answer to Henry's last, and that he had also written in cipher to his ambassador in England things to be declared to his Highness. Desired a further answer by mouth to his overtures at Lippe, and the Duke, after consultation, caused the Chancellor Ghogreff to tell him that the article last sent to him might be taken by the Emperor and the German princes 'to sowne sumwhat agayne them,' and he had written to his ambassador to feel if you would allow it to be modified, so that the words might be of like effect, but could not be mistaken. He therefore could make Wotton no answer till he heard from the ambassador. After this he very soon took horse, and rode to the Duchess [Maria] at Hambach. In five or six days he will be at Cleves, where he wished Wotton to follow him. He will remain about Cleves, [Nijmegen], and Arnhem till after Easter.

Effectively, Wilhelm was trying to tie up loose ends with Henry in hopes of furthering his interests in Guelders and against Charles V.

Sir Thomas Wyatt spelled out the situation for Henry rather well when he wrote,

> Surely no man wins at the Emperor's hands by tract of time; if the Emperor can assure himself in France better than Henry and make accord with the Almains, it must be to the prejudice of England and the duke of Cleves; and doubtless Guelders … will make the Emperor go as near the brink as he may to please the Almains.

In other words, things were not going to go well for either Henry or Wilhelm.

Troubled by the situation, Henry warned Wilhelm against continuing to agitate Charles V. Wilhelm, meanwhile, was busying himself with trying to negotiate another advantageous marriage for his final unmarried sister, Amalia. Wotton wrote to Cromwell in late March 1540:

> Received on the 18th both Cromwell's letters of the 12th. Had audience next day of the Duke, who said like offers had been made him long ago, but he would not forego Guelders. He thanked the King for his friendly warning … No talk of the Emperor's going into [Germany] and it is hoped he will begin no war against any prince of the Empire … Reports

what was told him by Ghogreff and Olisleger of the causes of the meeting of Paderborn and proposed marriages for my lady [Amalia] ... Cornelius Scepperus of late advised the Emperor to make truces with the Protestants, and meanwhile recover Guelders. Dr. Score, of the Emperor's Council, has said that the Emperor should not try the matter of Guelders by law, for none of the German princes wished him to have it. The king of Hungary[23] wishes some good way taken between the Emperor and the duke of Cleves. The Protestants will make no truce with the Emperor without including the Duke.

One must wonder if Cromwell was beginning to see the collapse of the alliance he had negotiated between England and Cleves. Until now he had firmly believed that Wilhelm and Charles V would come to an agreement, and thus there would be no need for England to aid Cleves.

Wotton, who followed Duke Wilhelm to Nijmegen in Guelders, had lengthy dispatches for both Henry and Cromwell. To Henry, Wotton wrote on 9 April:

Yesterday the 8th, the duke of Cleves being at Nijmegen, in Guelders, sent me word to come to him to-day betimes. I accordingly came at seven in the morning, and was sent for at eleven to dinner, when, having tarried awhile in the chamber, the [vice] chancellor Olisleger told me he was commanded to explain why the Duke had sent for him, viz., that, hearing that Ferdinand, king of the Romans, should come down to the Emperor, he had caused certain princes of Germany by whom he would pass to desire him to mediate between the Emperor and himself about Guelders; that the princes did so, and Ferdinand promised to do his best, and has apparently got the Emperor's leave to labour in it, and that Ferdinand had sent duke Henry of Brunswick to Ravenstein, where the duke of Cleves met him on Tuesday last, to show the duke of Cleves what Ferdinand had done and advise him to come personally to the Emperor, as Ferdinand also wrote to him to do; that duke Henry, although he did not mistrust Ferdinand, took an opportunity, when the Emperor and Ferdinand were together, of saying to the former that his brother would send him to the duke of Cleves to show him that he might come freely to the Emperor and freely return home, and therefore he desired to know if the Emperor agreed. The Emperor consented, and said if the duke of Cleves came to him, he should return when he pleased.

Duke Henry, therefore, earnestly exhorted the duke of Cleves to follow Ferdinand's counsel; which the Duke, though at first he thought it strange, at last consented to do, and promised to go to-morrow from Ravenstein towards the Emperor. He hoped the King would not distrust him in consequence. Wotton replied that these things were very strange,

---

23 Ferdinand, Charles V's brother, and King of the Romans-Germans.

especially considering the communication that was between the Duke and Crucerus, his ambassador in France, and Wotton himself, on Easter Day, after dinner, when the Duke said he would never be so mad as to trust the Emperor's promises. Olisleger, besides, had told Wotton on Wednesday, 31 March ... that duke Henry had written already of this matter to his master, who, with his Council, had determined he should not go to the Emperor. He wondered that Olisleger had not advised the Duke to consult with his friends the King and the Elector of Saxony. He had no doubt Henry would maintain his friendship, but yet that he must suspect something in the matter.

Olisleger said that the Duke's Council had fully represented to him the danger of trusting promises, and some had this very day, with tears running down their cheeks, prayed him not to risk them; but it was the Duke's own mind, and he was fully resolved, as he has faith in the king of the Romans and the duke of Brunswick. That he was sorry that he had no time to give notice to England or the Elector of Saxony, for the king of the Romans and the duke of Brunswick would have left the Emperor before an answer could have arrived. The Duke had given Wotton the option of following him to Brabant or remaining at Cleves till his return, which would be within 14 or 15 days, but he suggested rather to follow him to the Emperor's Court. Wotton was surprised that the Duke would not listen to his Council, and said he would write to the King 'of his request concerning your ambassador by the Emperor.' He was willing to follow the Duke, who departs to-day for Ravenstein and thence, to-morrow, towards Antwerp.

Had a similar conversation with the Duke himself, who owned that he was not acting on his Council's advice, and that he trusted greatly to king Ferdinand's words. The Duke writes of this to Henry and the Queen, and also to the Elector and Duchess of Saxony...

Effectively, Wilhelm had made up his mind. He was going to personally communicate his intentions to Anna, Sybylla and their husbands.

Wotton filled in the details in his separate letter to Cromwell:

On Wednesday, 31 March, hearing that the duke of Cleves would remove from Cleves, sent to Dr. Olisleger to ascertain whither he was going, and whether Wotton should follow him. Olisleger sent word that the Duke would remove that day, but that he himself would remain and come to supper with Wotton, and show him the Duke's mind. He accordingly after supper said the Duke had commanded him to say he was gone to Arnhem, where he would tarry four or five days, and return to Cleves, and thought I might as well remain till he came back. Remained accordingly, but the Duke, hearing that duke Henry of Brunswick would come to Ravenstein to speak with him, left Arnhem on Monday and went thither, where he met duke Henry next day. Duke Henry, as he wrote, had before sent to advise the duke of Cleves to go personally to the Emperor, and, though he was at first not disposed to do so, the duke of Brunswick persuaded him at this meeting to be at Ravenstein again this day, and tomorrow to enter Brabant on his journey to the Emperor's court.

Last night while at supper, received a letter from the Duke's Council to come to him this day at Nijmegen, which he accordingly did about 7 o'clock a.m., but could not speak either with the Duke or his Council till the Duke sent for him to dine with him. There Dr. Olisleger first, by the Duke's commandment, and afterwards the Duke himself, showed him that King Ferdinand has so laboured to the Emperor that he was willing some overture should be made to pacify the controversy for Guelders between the Emperor and the duke of Cleves, and that the duke of Brunswick had been with him at Ravenstein and brought such a message that the duke of Cleves was determined to go straight to the Emperor, believing that a satisfactory arrangement could be made.

This tale, so contrary to his previous conversations with the Duke and Olisleger, surprised Wotton much, but, the matter being already concluded, and a promise made to duke Henry, it was in vain that he spake against it. Yet the Council says he has done this without their advice, and the Duke confirms it, saying he trusts in God and his honesty, and has much confidence in Ferdinand's sincerity. He excuses himself for not asking the King's advice or that of the Elector of Saxony for want of time, as King Ferdinand and the duke of Brunswick would have departed from the Emperor before an answer could have been received, and a good occasion would have been lost.

The country, and especially Guelders, marvels much at this matter, and fears the end of it. The magistrates of the Duchy, with weeping eyes, yesterday, begged the Duke not to put himself in such hazard, but the Duke seems fully resolved. If Ferdinand mean well, cannot tell what to think of it unless he means to make one of his daughters duchess of Cleves. It were a great marriage for his daughter, he having so many children and so little to bestow them with.

Correspondence to both Henry and Cromwell continues like this throughout the rest of spring 1540. The Emperor quietly threatens violence, and Wilhelm asserts his belief that things will come to a peaceful conclusion. Wilhelm consistently failed to talk to either Henry VIII of England or Johann Friedrich of Saxony about his plans.

All the while, Wilhelm was secretly negotiating for a French marriage.

Johann Ghogreff, with assistants, was in France in the second half of June to complete a treaty between Duke Wilhelm and Francis I. From Wilhelm's youthful point of view, there was no better way of sealing an alliance than with a marriage. Henry, knowing what his brother-in-law was doing, informed his ambassador in France, John Wallop. On 22 June, Henry wrote Wallop. A brief of the letter survives:

Has seen his letter of the 16th inst. to the Council, showing the 'friendly rejoyse' of the French king, the Constable, and others, at the discovery of the treasons of the late Privy Seal [Thomas Cromwell], which has been further testified by his own letters to his ambassador here. ...The ambassador of Cleves has informed us that the Duke, his master, finding the Emperor has only practised with him for his own advantage by overtures of marriage, intends to provide marriage for himself elsewhere, and that Cruzerus, his ambassador with the French king, has lately repaired to him from Francis, to advise him not to conclude too hastily; that the Duke desired the King's advice in the matter before despatching Cruzerus back to France, and wished Henry to write to Wallop to help them with his counsel. Desires Wallop therefore, when Cruzerus returns, to inform him that Henry intends sending over some other member of his Council learned in the laws, to join with Wallop, and meanwhile Wallop shall grope and fish out all their purposes and commission, both with the King and other personages of honour there, without laying himself open to suspicion; so that Henry may know what he is seeking, and how he is disposed to all parties, whether the French favour his suit, and whether he has that confidence in Henry which he pretends.

Two days later, Henry sent Wilhelm's sister Anna to Richmond.

A Marriage for Wilhelm

Rumours of a match for Duke Wilhelm were plentiful in early 1540. First, it was possible he would marry the Duke of Brunswick's daughter. Wilhelm might have been destined to marry Charles V's own daughter Maria, who was twelve years old at the time. The strongest rumour was that Charles was keen to have Wilhelm marry Charles' niece Christina of Denmark. If Wilhelm wed Christina, then Charles would make Wilhelm King of Denmark after the current, childless king died. The king who sat on the Danish throne was the same usurper who overthrew Christina of Denmark's father years before. Wilhelm stood to gain an entire kingdom if only he would give up Guelders. But he would not, and had other plans, besides.

Wilhelm sent to the French court his envoy, Hermann Crüser, along with Landmarschal Wachtendonk and Chancellor Ghogreff. Crüser specialised in laws concerning marriage. It was July 1540, and Wilhelm was very interested in concluding a treaty with France and Cleves against the Emperor. If Henry VIII of England had not figured out what Wilhelm was doing in time, Wilhelm would have achieved his goal of being allied with England, France and Saxony against Charles V. Unfortunately, Wilhelm's plan was undone when Henry had his marriage to Anna annulled, leaving the poor woman a political refugee in England.

Before Wilhelm's arrival, Henry VIII sent an ambassador to France to tell Francis I of the annulment. Upon meeting the French king, Henry's ambassador opened the conversation by expressing his hope that Duke

Wilhelm was completely free from any betrothal to Christina of Denmark as he had failed to fully clear Anna from the Lorraine union. This, of course, was untrue, but it quietly implied the alleged reason for Henry and Anna's annulment. Francis was astonished by how swiftly the annulment came to pass.

Incredulous, Francis wished to confirm that the convocation truly was about Anna's marriage. After the ambassador reaffirmed that things were decided regarding Anna's annulment, Francis heaved a great sigh, shaking his head. He was silent for a moment before giving the diplomatic answer that he would not turn away from his friendship with Henry. However, Henry must live with his conscience, he said. Francis would continue to call Henry friend, but he would make up his own mind about the English king's treatment of Anna.

Francis's reaction can be explained by the fact that he was expecting the same political arrangement as Wilhelm. The marriages between Cleves and England, and Cleves and Navarre, would strengthen Francis's position against Holy Roman Emperor Charles V. Unfortunately, Francis now found himself without the connection to England, and with a young niece about to be promised to a German duke instead of a more advantageous match. Would Francis have betrothed his niece to Wilhelm if he knew of Henry's plans to annul the marriage to Anna?

Wilhelm went forward with the French marriage. He was not at all perturbed over losing England as an ally. The French contract was drawn up on 16 July 1540 and included the proviso that if the King of Navarre did not have any sons, the kingdom would go to Jeanne d'Albret. If Wilhelm and Jeanne had a son, the son would become King of Navarre. The contract was ratified by Henri II of Navarre and his wife Marguerite of Angoulême on 17 July 1540. Francis I ratified it on 8 September.

In early October 1540, Charles V was on his way to Ghent. He set in motion improvements to the castle there that cost more than 500,000 ducats. The issue over Guelders was to be heard at the coming Imperial Colloquy at Regensburg (sometimes called Ratisbon). This diet, following so closely after the one at Hagenau, irritated the Pope and his legate. Henry VIII tried his best to send someone to the colloquy so that Anna of Cleves' annulment could be better explained. At this point, though, it seems that Charles V and likely Duke Wilhelm had other things on their minds.

Wilhelm returned to Düsseldorf after staying at Hambach, possibly visiting his mother Duchess Maria there. Henry VIII's ambassador Wotton was still hanging around the Cleves court. His mission was to rehabilitate Henry's image with the German princes, particularly Duke Wilhelm. In theory, Wilhelm was the gateway to the much more powerful Johann Friedrich of Saxony. However, one can imagine that Sybylla, Johann Friedrich's wife, was terribly unimpressed with Henry VIII.

Rumours about Henry's malice and poor disposition toward Anna of Cleves spread like wildfire around the United Duchies. Wilhelm did not make an earnest attempt to stop them. He had no problem giving Wotton lip service over the situation.

Wotton told Henry that the Cleves council deemed Henry's actions to be based on an 'abominable and devilishly invented lie ... also it did tend to the derogation of [Henry's] honour'. Wilhelm promised to try to 'extinguish the rumour'. Wilhelm could not be bothered with soothing Henry. He had more pressing concerns than England, particularly the negotiations for his marriage to Jeanne d'Albret. Wotton was aware that Wilhelm was negotiating, but he was kept in the dark about the specifics of the marriage plans.

By December 1540, friction between the Emperor, Francis and Wilhelm had reduced.

Early 1541

The Colloquy of Regensburg was set to meet in early 1541 in Bavaria. Nuremberg was on the route to Regensburg, lying about 62 miles to the north-west. Several of the electors and dukes gathered in Nuremberg before heading to Regensburg. Emperor Charles V, eager to remind the assembled princes of his military might, entered Nuremberg with his army.

Wilhelm made it known around 25 March that he would personally show up at the colloquy, prompting an Imperial response:

> [Charles] warned the Duke to bring titles and documents of his claim to Guelders in order that the dispute might be examined and decided by the Imperial Chamber. Whereupon the Duke dispatched certain lords of his court and representatives of his chief towns to go to the Diet and obtain that their master might not appear personally...

Ever duplicitous, Wilhelm had a difficult time attending in person. He was busy preparing to leave for France. Adding insult to injury for Charles V, neither Wilhelm nor the Elector of Saxony appeared. This frustrated the whole purpose, and showed the Emperor that many of the German princes were not willing to negotiate with him.

While Wilhelm prepared to leave for France, over 4,000 *Landsknechte* were seen in the area around Cleves. Fearing that these mercenary soldiers were sent by Charles V, Wilhelm had his representatives order the *Landsknechte* to disperse immediately. They left without trouble, and may have only been passing through in hopes of being hired by a local lord. Even better, if the princes at the Colloquy of Regensburg could not sort their differences, then the *Landsknechte* were ready to enter the employ of the highest bidder. Wilhelm decided to send out 500 horsemen in case the *Landsknechte* intended to make trouble.

Duke Wilhelm and his mother were supposed to spend the Easter holiday together in the area around Düsseldorf. It was rumoured that Wilhelm intended to meet with their cousin, the Bishop of Münster. Instead, Wilhelm rode to Castle Hambach, not far from Düren, on Sunday 9 April.

The French Marriage is Concluded

Henry VIII of England was formally notified of the Navarre–Cleves match around 9 April 1541, per Marillac's report back to Francis I of France. On 11 April 1541, Wilhelm and a small group of companions, presumably Wachtendonk, Ghogreff and the Guelders Marshal Maarten van Rossum, set off for Paris from Düsseldorf. Van Rossum, 'who, both in Duke [Karl]'s time and now, has chief authority in Guelders, and is the best man of war in these parts and very popular with everyone … speaks good French and serves the Duke in affairs of Guelders', was an important part of the group.

From Paris, Wilhelm went to Orléans. He met with Jeanne d'Albret and her parents there on 14 June, gifting her a costly ring. After meeting in Paris, Wilhelm and his company moved on toward Blois. He was to marry Jeanne, then twelve years old, in France. She would remain in Navarre until she came of age.

Per a report from Henry VIII's ambassador,

> The Duke of Cleves arrived on the 6th. [The King of Navarre] met him ten miles off and brought him to Court very honourably…The following Sunday there was a great triumph made, with the assaulting of a 'bastillion.' … Describes how the defenders were driven into their bastillion, how scaling ladders were brought to the walls by poor unarmed countrymen who knew not what the matter meant, but who, when they got their heads broken, left the ladders in the ditch and ran away apace, and how finally the bastillion was taken. The King and Queen and Duke of Cleves, and all the ladies stood upon scaffolds, and afterwards supped at Howard's lodging. The King spoke to him. The Duke of Cleves embraced him and asked how Henry did, but asked no question of his sister [Anna of Cleves], and afterwards fell to dancing the Almain dance with Madame de Temps. There is some doubt whether he will marry the Queen of Navarre's daughter or the King's.

The marriage of twelve-year-old Jeanne d'Albret and Duke Wilhelm of Jülich-Cleves-Berg took place on 14 June 1541.[24] The young girl heavily protested the match. Wilhelm left on 28 June, arriving in Düsseldorf on 16 July. Jeanne stayed with her parents.

Back in Germany

The Colloquy of Regensburg came to an end in May 1541, by which time Charles V was even more incensed over Wilhelm's behaviour. Several officials from Guelders attended the colloquy expecting a resolution. They left disappointed.

---

24 For a full description of the wedding, see *Anna, Duchess of Cleves: The King's 'Beloved Sister'* (Amberley 2019).

Duke Wilhelm's journey home was not without possible danger from capture or attack by Charles V or his sister Maria, Queen of Hungary and Regent of the Low Countries. In early July, Wotton informed Henry VIII,

> There is much rejoicing here for the marriage of the Duke, who is much made of in France. The Duke would fain be home again, and has obtained passports of the bishops of Trier and [Liège] ... The Queen Regent could not answer his request for a passport, because, as she said, the number, time, and country must first be known. The Duke has written again that he has such confidence in the Emperor and her that he trusts he needs no passport, but, as the custom of the princes of Germany is to ask such passports, he would have it for 80 horse and through Luxembourg, and supposes that the men of the French king who accompany him will, by the treaties between the Emperor and France, need no passport. ... [Officials of the United Duchies] expect him in his own country within this sevennight. The French king sends 1,000 horse with him; and the old Duchess here has gathered 800, because the Queen has assembled all the bands of the Low Countries at Namur,[25] giving out that it is to receive the Duke of Lorraine's son. Here they reckon the French king so powerful that the Emperor will fear to offend him.

Wilhelm was being cheeky with both Charles V and Charles's sister Maria, and he knew it. It was almost as if he were daring the Emperor to move against him.

The rest of 1541 passed relatively quietly for Duke Wilhelm, although there was a firm rumour in mid-October that he and Francis I would attack the Low Countries in 1542. Chapuys wrote,

> The ambassador's man informs me that he has seen letters from a Secretary of State in France to this French ambassador in England (Marillac), dated 7 Oct., assuring him that unless the King their master thoroughly changes his opinion, there will be war next spring, for the King fully intends invading the Low Countries, now that he has the Duke of Cleves under his orders, the latter having promised to do wonders and obey his command implicitly.

Imagine Wilhelm's delight when, a few weeks later, Henry VIII's wife Katheryn Howard was imprisoned. If Wilhelm could convince Henry to take back his sister Anna, then Wilhelm's plan of allying himself with Saxony, France and England against the Empire could come to fruition. Unfortunately, the only ruler keen on attacking Charles V with Duke Wilhelm was Francis I.

---

25 Namur is between France and the United Duchies, and just outside Liège.

1542

Wilhelm's attempts to convince Henry to remarry Anna during late 1541 and early 1542 came to nothing. Even Francis I tried to convince Henry to take back the repudiated Anna, but to no avail. Eventually seeing that it was going nowhere, Wilhelm turned his attentions to strengthening fortifications and sorting his troops for battle. In April, Charles V asked Wilhelm for support against the Turkish threat, but Wilhelm refused to provide any help unless Charles agreed not to attack or harry him for at least twenty years. Charles V would make no such guarantee. One can imagine he was displeased at his vassal's petulance.

Henry VIII offered his support to Charles V in late June 1542. Per a report from Chapuys to Charles's sister Maria,

> The King said, before determining about the alliance he must know what the Emperor intended about the duchies of Milan and Guelders. Said, as to Milan, he had no idea; as to Guelders, the Emperor could not act otherwise than he had done, or abandon the pursuit, his right being evident. ... As to Guelders its conquest would be difficult, owing to the hatred of the people to the inhabitants of Brabant, and, considering his relations with Germany and France, the Duke might be a dangerous enemy if the marriage so much talked of should take place; also while using his forces against Guelders the Emperor would be prevented from driving the French out of Piedmont.
>
> The King thought it would be better to gain over the Duke [of Cleves], who must now be dissatisfied with the French for not having given him a wife. Were Henry called to settle the matter he would offer him one of his own daughters. In that way the Emperor's honour would be safeguarded —he might grant the duchy of Guelders to the Duke, on such conditions as he and the Queen of Hungary thought fit, and make use of the forces of Guelders and Cleves. That would cut short the designs of Francis for this year at least....
>
> As to Guelders, he said, the thing was not so impossible as he supposed. It was not clear that the Duke of Cleves would be supported in his claims by Germany, considering that his ancestors, paternal and maternal, had not only relinquished all right to it, but promised to assist in its defence when needful, and the Emperor relied on Henry to aid him in the conquest of Guelders, just as Henry's father had assisted King Philip; that the task would be easier now that the Emperor had acquired Groningen and the lands the last Duke of Guelders held in Friesland,[26] besides towns in Utrecht ... Showed that it would be an advantage to England if Guelders was in the Emperor's hands, and that means might be found of detaching the Duke of Cleves from France.

Henry was searching for a *via media*, but unfortunately Wilhelm would prove to be unreasonable and obstinate. The young man had plans of his own.

---

26 In the northwest of Germany, bordering modern-day Netherlands.

8

The Cleves War

The Cleves War, more commonly known as the Third War of Guelderian Succession or the Jülich Feud, was vicious and relatively short. Rumours that Wilhelm and Francis I had formally declared war against Charles V began in July 1542, with the war itself beginning in earnest a few months later. In early July, 'the chief bruits were that war was proclaimed between the Emperor and the Duke of Cleves, and that the French king was upon the borders of Loren, with his army, near a town called Mese. The espial heard of no assembly of men of war, save that captains were warned to be ready.'

Henry did his best to keep England out of harm's way, while Wilhelm and Francis dragged the United Duchies and France right into it.

Maarten van Rossum, the Marshal of Guelders, was seen marching out of Cleves with at least 10,000 foot soldiers and 1,000 horsemen in mid-July, bolstered with artillery. At the end of July, it was clear that Wilhelm intended to attack the Low Countries, whereas Francis was headed to Spain: 'The French king draws towards Spain with a great army. His army has entered Luxembourg, and that of the Duke of Cleves, in his pay, makes war in Brabant and Liège. The Emperor is attacked unawares ... and feels most the opening this war gives to the Turk.' In other words, the Cleves War would be nothing more than an annoyance to Charles V.

It was thought that Wilhelm would advance on Antwerp if he did not divert to join with Francis' troops. Charles V put an army of 14,000 troops in Diest, which is midway between Sittard, in Luxembourg, and Antwerp. Luxembourg was besieged by the Duke of Orléans, the future Henri II. Charles V was still hopeful that things could be resolved peacefully.

Francis sent his wife Eleanor, Charles V's sister, ladies of the court and the princesses to Blois for their safety. He intended to go to Avignon when his supplies and troops were there. The Duke of Orléans was moving to Narbonne. Wilhelm sent for more *Landsknechte* because he received only half the number he anticipated.

The Cleves War

Not far from Barcelona, Charles V had to decide whether to move his troops over the Pyrenees. If not, the other routes out of Spain and toward the Low Countries would bring him within gunshot of Francis I. It was not reported yet whether Charles's brother Ferdinand could send backup from Bohemia and Hungary. This meant that their sister Maria was potentially on her own in the Low Countries if neither Charles nor Ferdinand could come to her aid in time.

By early August 1542, Duke Wilhelm had successfully invaded the Low Countries. He chased the Prince of Orange from Brabant, and secured a foothold in Friesland. He specifically ordered that English merchants remain unmolested, but otherwise his troops could pillage. He then moved his force toward Antwerp, encamping within sight of the city. They 'went to Louvain, sacking and burning on the way, and on the 3rd or 4th [of August] were near Louvain, and by letters from Antwerp of the 5th were expected to make an attack on that city. The Queen [of Hungary, Regent of the Low Countries] meanwhile is doing her utmost for the defence of the country.' Meanwhile, the Duke of Orleans was enjoying his own victories over the Imperial troops.

Charles V pressed Henry VIII for a treaty. Henry was interested, but the terms could not be agreed upon. Henry's ambassadors at the Imperial court were asked about conditions involving Duke Wilhelm of Cleves. They remained vague and gave Charles V no solid answer.

Things fell apart in September 1542, when the Cleves army fractured. According to a message from Maria, Regent of the Low Countries, 'The Clevois, who went to the French service, have mutinied, part of them withdrawing towards Cleves, part remaining with Orleans, and part coming to Vendome.' The portion that mutinied from the French showed that France could not trust Cleves.

Jülich was invaded in October:

14,000 or 15,000 Almains[27] marched into [the Duchy of Jülich], where first [Düren] surrendered and compounded for 70,000 fl. (and, some say, promised to build a castle), and then [the City of Jülich], which held out longer, being fortified, surrendered at discretion on the 10th, and on the 22nd the last town of [the Duchy of Jülich] was gained; the Emperor's army finding no resistance in the field. It is doubted that there will be a little more resistance in Cleves, through the assistance of the Gueldrois, to whom the Duke of Cleves has withdrawn, and the Queen [of Hungary, Regent of the Low Countries] has not gained their favour, as was said, or at least they have not kept neutrality.

With winter approaching, the opportunity for war was closing for the year. This gave Duke Wilhelm the chance to increase his troops and his cache of funds, 'on the side of Guelders the duke of Cleves had 30,000 foot

---

27 Germans

135

and 4,000 horse; he himself was better furnished than last year, especially with money, having a million and a half of francs more than when he commenced the war.' Whatever he was planning, Wilhelm certainly had his resources in hand.

1543

In mid-February 1543, the agreement between Henry VIII of England and Charles V included a clause in the opening statement such that Duke Wilhelm of Cleves could be considered a 'common enemy' of England and the Empire. Whether Wilhelm or Cleves are specifically named in this draft is not known; it requires further research. The treaty was not fully ratified, especially given Charles V's preoccupations with the Germans, French and Turks.

The large army Wilhelm had amassed by the close of 1542 was dissipating by February 1543:

> The Duke of Cleves has this winter retained a number of men of war, with the view of making raids during the frosts into Holland and Brabant to pay his men; but he has been hindered by the great snows and by her frontier garrisons, which she has kept partly at the expense of his subjects, and now his men diminish and retire for want of pay and victuals, of which there is a great scarcity. The men Martin van Rossen brought back from France have dispersed very ill content with him and he has had to fly for his life. The Duke has spread the rumour that their retirement is owing to his refusing to take them into his service, so as not to avow Van Rossen's action; but it is notorious that he did his utmost to retain them, and they refused.

However, Wilhelm was not willing to negotiate with either Maria, Regent of the Low Countries, or Charles V.

Another Imperial diet was held at Nuremburg in February and March 1543, where Ferdinand was one of two princes present. The rest sent representatives if they sent anybody at all. The diet had no impact on the Cleves War.

> The Queen of Hungary's orators implore help against Cleves. The Protestant and other States answer that things at home must first be settled by composing the religious controversy, allowing free course to the Gospel and troubling no one for professing it or separating from the Bishop of Rome. They will then provide against the Turk; but the war of France and Cleves a private matter, not touching the Empire, which, however, they will do what they can to pacify.

It appeared no one else was willing to go to war with Charles V. Even Henry VIII, who had prepared a treaty with Charles, wanted it kept secret for fear of Duke Wilhelm learning of the details.

There were rumours that Charles V was willing to negotiate with Wilhelm. He may have been willing to let Wilhelm keep Guelders for life, with the duchy then going to Charles' family. His sister Maria, however, wanted to pursue a shorter path to resolution. She informed Chapuys, the Imperial ambassador at the English court,

> The deputies of the Electors ... failing to make truce between her and the Duke of Cleves, have retired. Cleves wishes to justify himself by remitting the dispute to the princes and estates of the Empire and other neutral princes, and thinks meanwhile to continue his occupation of Guelders.
>
> He has sent seven ambassadors to Nuremberg to answer her commissioners and complain of the invasion of his country; but she will continue her efforts to force him to come to reason, and is sending towards Maestricht ... 2,500 horse and 10,000 foot, of whom 400 are High Almains, picked men, and some battery pieces; who shall enter the Duke's country within two days. The Duke is determined to give battle. Has levied 3,000 Limburgers to reinforce her army. If the Duke gives battle, he hazards all, and if not his countries receive inestimable damage. Has also levied some men about Münster to enter his countries of Ravensberg and Mark from the other side, and her garrisons on the side of Utrecht and Brabant will not be idle.

Unfortunately, Maria would suffer a serious blow on Easter Sunday.

The Battle of Sittard began after Maria, Regent of the Low Countries sent her representative to assess a city of hers located in Cleves:

> The town of Heinsberg, which she holds in [the Duchy of Jülich], being in want of victuals, she sent the Duke of Aarschot with 2,500 horse and 10,000 foot, of whom 4,000 were High Almains, to revictual it; and he entered [Jülich] on the 20th inst. and on the 21st and 22nd revictualled Heinsberg, and on the 24th camped before Sittard, where the enemy, numbering 3,000 horse and 10,000 foot, offered battle.
>
> The horsemen on both sides met and after a struggle ours put the enemy to flight, but our footmen would not fight, and abandoned the artillery, so that when our horsemen returned from the chase, they found both the enemy's artillery and ours abandoned and the horses taken. As they could not bring it away (nor encamp for want of footmen) the artillery is lost. Two bills herewith show what happened and what the enemy has lost.

Chancellor Johann Ghogreff's brother-in-law died during the Battle of Sittard, but the victory bolstered Wilhelm.

Charles V secretly ratified the treaty with Henry VIII in April 1543, although he remained concerned that Henry was not sincere about Wilhelm being a common enemy. Charles pressed Chapuys to have Henry declare this in a letter or directly to Chapuys. In the background, another Imperial diet was taking place at Nuremberg. A draft treaty was drawn up, meant to be ratified by Duke Wilhelm, Charles V, Henry VIII and Regent Maria. Come early May, it was still not signed. On the contrary, Duke Wilhelm had decided to attack Heinsberg, which is not far from Sittard. In response, Charles V left for the Low Countries with his army.

Duke Wilhelm's army slowly amassed outside Heinsberg, to the north-east of Sittard, beginning in May 1543. By early June, it was reported that a large French army was gathering and that Swiss troops were making their way there to assist Duke Wilhelm. The Prince of Orange, fighting for Regent Maria and Charles V, remained camped within sight of the enemy. Wilhelm finally besieged Heinsberg in mid-June.

Still hoping to keep the accord between himself and Charles V a secret from Duke Wilhelm, Henry VIII married his sixth and final wife on 12 July 1543. By marrying Catherine Parr, Henry was unavailable to marry Anna. This sent the quiet message to both Charles V and Duke Wilhelm that Henry would not support Cleves in any military endeavours.

Having learned that the eastern Imperial border was secure against Turkish invasion for the time being, Charles expected to be in Speyer with his large army by 20 July.

Having since learnt affairs of Germany ... and of the Low Countries by correspondence with his sister, ...he sends to declare that ... his chief aim has been to pass hither as soon as possible, in order to employ his forces, with the King's correspondence, against the common enemy. Since his arrival, has levied 4,000 Italians and 600 light horse, to take with him, together with 3,000 Spaniards besides those sent by Biscaye, which will have arrived in the Low Countries. These are over and above the 2,000 horse and 6,000 foot who await him at [Speyer]. Brings also experienced captains (some without charge, to be employed as shall be requisite) and continues his journey without sojourning anywhere, so as to be at [Speyer] by 20 July, where he will find about 100 pieces of great artillery ready. Thence he will march as may suit his sister's forces in the Low Countries, according as he learns the state of the common enemy and the duke of Cleves, and the intention of the king of England. ...

If the King makes difficulty in the enterprise of France whilst the Emperor is in war against the Duke of Cleves, he is to be reminded that the Duke wrongfully detains Guelders, wickedly caused the enterprise of Martin von Rossen last year, and obstinately continues for war... When the Duke hears of the Emperor's approach he will conform to reason; and if not it will not take long to force him to it.

If the King speaks of the assistance which the Emperor should give him... the likelihood of the King's making war against France this year; having regard always to getting the King to declare openly against France, so as to compel the king of France to divide his forces and keep him and Cleves from aiding each other, and to prevent the King's excusing himself because war is not made against France (for war with Cleves is tantamount to war with France, whom Cleves would otherwise assist, and France has invaded the Low Countries without England's aid being demanded according to the treaty) or because he is not furnished with all he would require.

One must wonder how much Anna or Sybylla knew of their brother's predicament. Sybylla likely had more information than Anna, given that Sybylla's letters with her family were not being read and filtered through the government, unlike Anna's.

The Prince of Orange advanced on Duke Wilhelm the night of 24 June. The Cleves army effectively abandoned Heinsberg without much of a fight, leaving behind all of Duke Wilhelm's artillery. In the meantime, Francis I's French army continued to seize small cities and towns in the Low Countries. He promised to send Wilhelm an additional 10,000 foot soldiers.

Duke Wilhelm moved his troops into Brabant by mid-July. Regent Maria had withdrawn from the area to protect against the French, and he took the opportunity to attack Amersfoort, not far from Utrecht. Despite lacking the all-important artillery, Wilhelm was able to subdue Amersfoort. He wisely did not approach the much larger city of Utrecht just yet, only staying in the area for a couple weeks and taking no further action. At the same time, the French slowly withdrew from Hainault. Charles V was days away from Speyer, bringing with him an army roughly 30,000 strong.

Duke Wilhelm attacked a couple smaller towns in his vicinity, killing everyone within. Regent Maria continued relying on the Prince of Orange to keep Wilhelm from overrunning the eastern portion of the Low Countries. Regent Maria sent additional troops to Maastricht, in case Duke Wilhelm decided to go there. Regent Maria did not want to openly engage with Duke Wilhelm until her brother Charles V came.

Charles V was in Speyer by 25 July 1543, when Wilhelm sent a representative to negotiate with him. 'The Emperor replied that his patience was exhausted since the Duke had seized upon his Duchy [of Guelders], invaded Brabant, and was continuing depredations upon his subjects.' Charles had arrived 'with a great company of Spanish noblemen, and 400 horse besides his bodyguard' and he left on 5 August. 'The day after the Emperor left, 4,000 Spanish arquebusiers arrived and took charge of the ordnance in the ships.' Things did not look promising for Duke Wilhelm.

By early August 1543, Duke Wilhelm was starting to doubt Francis I's desire to continue warring with Charles V. Wilhelm demanded that his wife, Jeanne d'Albret, be delivered to him immediately. By this time they had been married for two years, and Jeanne was fourteen. Although still a little young to live with her husband, she was no longer so young that it would cause a scandal. To that end, Jeanne and her ladies were moved to La Fère, north-east of Paris.

The Cleves army continued burning and pillaging little towns in the Low Countries between Amersfoort and Amsterdam. Additionally, Maarten van Rossum charged some of his *Landsknechte* to preach the Gospel:

Where must needs be a good sight, to see a *Landsknechte*, his cap full of feathers, his doublet and hosen cut and jagged, his sword by his side, an arquebus in his neck, to preach and set forth the Word solemnly, as though it were not Christ's Gospel but Mahumettes Alcorane[28] which may not be taught but if there be a sword there in presence.

Van Rossum, for his part, was 'before Heinsberg where the Clevois lay before. Cannot think that he will besiege it, but rather go up to view the towns of [the Duchy of] Jülich as Düren, Sittard, Jülich, Nideggen, &c., [are] in the Emperor's way.' Wilhelm surely knew that once Charles V arrived the United Duchies could expect a tremendous amount of destruction.

Up until 12 August 1543, Duke Wilhelm could not be bothered to appear with his troops, preferring to rely heavily on Van Rossum's expertise. He blamed his absence on not having proper armour. Once he showed himself on the battlefield, it was already too late. Morale was low among the troops, and there was a real sense of fear over the Emperor's impending arrival.

On 20 August, the Prince of Orange successfully attacked Montjoie, a city in Jülich close to Aachen. The monastery there was plundered and severely damaged. Charles V and his huge host were not far away at this point.

Duke Wilhelm was in Düsseldorf, in the Duchy of Berg, by 24 August. At the same time, Charles V was attacking Düren, the very same city in which Anna of Cleves had her portrait taken by Hans Holbein four years before. The Prince of Orange joined Charles V at Düren, combining tens of thousands of soldiers and more than 100 pieces of artillery. Charles V did not bother listening to ambassadors from Saxony, among other places, in their pleas for mercy upon the United Duchies. Things were too far gone, with Duke Wilhelm's attacks upon Regent Maria being the last straw.

Düren's fortifications had been upgraded in recent years, and the city was considered a stronghold. Charles V arrived on 23 August. He visited a chapel, perhaps the one within the local castle, to pray for God's blessing. He surely thought God was listening on 24 August, when he attacked the city of 3,000 with over 60,000 troops. A large part of Düren was devastated by a fire in tandem with the Imperial attack.

After Düren, Charles V marched south to Niddegen, the ancestral home of the dukes of Jülich. The ancient castle, fortified with thick walls, was built on a high hill and like Düren was thought to be impregnable. Unfortunately, the square shape of the castle with its flat walls could not withstand the artillery of Charles V. It was not properly updated for the modern threat, so easily succumbed to the mortars fired at it by the Imperials from a neighbouring hill. The stronghold there fell, too. It is rumoured that Amalia was inside the castle as it was bombarded. Despite the drama of the attack, Niddegen, and soon after the city of Jülich, capitulated early in the siege.

---

28 Mohammed's Quran

The city of Cleves was not keen on resisting Charles V. Neither were many of the other cities in the duchy, few of which were properly fortified. They handed their keys to Charles V without resistance. That done, Charles V moved toward Guelders. He stopped just outside Venlo.

The destruction of the duchies of Jülich and Berg devastated Dowager Duchess Maria, who was said to have been heartbroken. She died on 29 August 1543, mere days before Wilhelm's total defeat. Her body was entombed at the Carthusian monastery in Wesel, on the island of Grav, but when it was badly damaged in 1590, both Adolf and Maria of Burgundy were moved to Sankt Maria Himmelfahrt in Wesel. It is unclear whether Duchess Maria was moved to the same church, or if she was buried beside her husband in Cleves.

Henry VIII's ambassador Wotton reported, 'The old lady Duchess of Cleves is departed this world raging and, in a manner, out of her wits (as it is reported) for spite and anger of the loss of her country.' After Duchess Maria's funeral and burial, Duke Wilhelm 'fell out with certain of his Council and would have slain one or two of them'. Wilhelm, overwhelmed with grief, attacked Francis' ambassador. Surely if Francis had come to Wilhelm's aid he would not have suffered so many losses.

Wilhelm Capitulates

After Wilhelm's sound defeat in Jülich-Berg, he chose to capitulate to Charles V. On 7 September 1543, Henry VIII's ambassador Edmund Bonner reported from Cologne:

Word came that the Duke of Cleves had come, with the Duke of Brunswick, from Düsseldorf and submitted to the Emperor, and thereupon the Emperor's camp before Venlo ceased operations, while the Emperor's Council and the Duke's meet at Gladbach monastery, between Roermond and Venlo, to draw articles of peace. The Emperor is to enjoy wholly [the Duchy of] Guelders and [the County of] Zutphen, and the Duke his hereditary lands of Cleves, Berg and Mark, and a conditional investiture of Jülich from the Emperor. The Emperor first spoke with the Lady Regent [Maria] at Horn near Roermond. Most of the Court here tarry the Emperor's further pleasure; some saying he will go with the Duke of Cleves into Guelders to receive their oath, some that he will go to Flanders to order the war against France, some that he will settle things hereabouts and return to the Diet at Speyer, or hither, where his jewels and most of his ordnance remain.

To memorialise the capitulation, Charles V drew up the Treaty of Venlo with Duke Wilhelm. Among the terms was the following:

That the said Duke shall conserve his subjects in the Catholic Faith and reform error. That henceforth he will be loyal and obedient to the Emperor

[Charles V] and [Charles's brother Ferdinand,] the King of the Romans, renouncing all leagues against them with the French king, Duke of [Holstein], or other princes. That he renounces all title to Guelders and Zutphen and transfers to the Emperor any right that he could pretend thereto. He will at once dismiss his soldiers out of Guelders and Zutphen, and render Aremberg castle to the lord Aremberg and Amersfoort to the Emperor. And other articles providing for his delivery of other places, restoration to him of the Duchy of Jülich, &c., pardon of partisans and release of prisoners.

Because Wilhelm could no longer be in league with Francis I of France, he would have to give up his French wife.

Duke Wilhelm's foolishness had many negative results. His reputation with the other German princes was tarnished. He was trapped in a marriage that had borne no fruit and his ally was now useless to him. Several of his major cities were badly damaged. Surely, none of his sisters were happy with him. On top of that, their mother died because of the stress from the war. Adding insult to injury, the lands for which he fought were lost.

The remainder of the 1540s were not very promising for Wilhelm as he adjusted to his new restrictions. He had to remain a Catholic, as did the United Duchies. Emperor Charles V was now far more in control of Wilhelm's decisions and the future of the United Duchies. Whatever autonomy he had enjoyed previously as a ruler was greatly curtailed, if not lost.

Wilhelm went on to claw back as much as he could from Charles V. Ferdinand, King of the Germans and Charles' brother, was still willing to be friendly toward him. Within a few short years, the two families would grow closer. The affinity between the Von der Marks and the Habsburgs would blossom into a mutually beneficial relationship by the 1560s, even if it was difficult to envisage that day in September 1543 at the camp outside Venlo.

9

Changing Imperial–Cleves Politics

After the Third War of Guelderian Succession, Duke Wilhelm and Charles V went back and forth on the final terms of the Treaty of Venlo. The Emperor, for his part, was busy plotting against the French. The major cities within the United Duchies were notified of the Treaty of Venlo's contents by the end of October 1543.

Charles V removed to Brussels. Duke Wilhelm, wanting further assurances, sent an envoy after him to further negotiate. Chancellor Ghogreff and Vice Chancellor Olisleger were part of the official delegation[29] to Brussels in late 1543. The Brussels Alliance was concluded on 2 January 1544. Two different documents were drawn up, one of amity between Wilhelm and Charles, the other a mutual defence treaty.

As part of the two treaties, Wilhelm and Charles solidified who was giving up what in a series of fourteen articles. This finally resolved the Guelders dispute once and for all. For his trouble, Wilhelm received a £10,000 annual stipend and a new wife. Wilhelm was set to marry one of Charles V's nieces, either Anna or Maria of Austria. Both candidates were daughters of Ferdinand, King of the Germans, and Anne of Bohemia and Hungary.

Wilhelm received his first £10,000 stipend in April 1544. A month later, in May, the documents of amity and protection were fully ratified. He received a further 20,000 guilders from Charles V in August of that year, in recognition of the Brussels Alliance.

---

29 The rest of the Cleves delegation included Georg von Boenen from Berg, Chamber Master Nikolaus von Harff, and two jurists, Johannes van Essen and Johann Faltermeyer. Van Essen is sometimes called 'Pottgiesser'.

Ghogreff, after the Colloquy of Regensburg, was still interested in seeing reform take hold in the United Duchies. With Duke Wilhelm, Court Preacher Arnold Bongard and Heresbach he worked to draft a document calling for actual reform of churches within Jülich-Cleves-Berg, not just church visits.

End of the Navarrese Marriage

Wilhelm needed a new wife, and preferably one related to Charles V. Christina of Denmark, whom he considered as a bride in the late 1530s, had married Anna of Cleves' former fiancé Francis of Lorraine in 1541. Fortunately, Charles V's brother Ferdinand had four daughters who were of age. Unfortunately, by March 1545, Wilhelm was still married to Jeanne d'Albret and Ferdinand's daughters were betrothed elsewhere:

> Nothing of the marriage of the Duke of Cleves and the King of Romans' daughter has been treated at Brussels, as the writer was assured last night, at supper, by [Olisleger], the Duke's chancellor, and [Karl Harst], formerly ambassador in England; and this Olderstain confirms, saying that none of Ferdinand's daughters was ever promised or even proposed, the four eldest of them being engaged, viz., Anna to the Duke of Orleans, [Maria] to the son of Duke William of Bavaria, Elizabeth to the duke of Mantua, and Margaret ... to the Duke of Savoy's son, and the rest too young ...

This particular report is slightly incorrect. Elisabeth, the eldest, was already married to a Polish prince.[30] However, the results are the same. It appeared that the only eligible Habsburg girls were unavailable. Given the recent warring between Charles V and Francis I of France, it was no surprise that the engagement between Charles's niece Anna and Francis's son did not come to pass.

Duke Wilhelm did not want Jeanne d'Albret, or for that matter Francis I, to slip away so easily. Despite Jeanne protesting the marriage back in 1541, even going so far as to create a written document and sign it, Wilhelm wanted her to make a more formal protest. One had been required as part of a peace treaty, too, but that was not good enough for Wilhelm. She was sixteen now, and old enough to be his wife. Besides that, one can imagine that Wilhelm was petty enough to enjoy making both Jeanne and Francis I uncomfortable. There was also the concern of avoiding any impediments to Wilhelm's future marriage, or the legitimacy of any children he might have during another marriage. Wilhelm wanted ecclesiastical officials to hear Jeanne's protest:

> The authentic protest made by the Princess d'Albret in accordance with the treaty of peace, does not satisfy the Duke of Cleves, who, in the Emperor's

---

30 The poor thing was never well received by her husband and mother-in-law, and suffered from epilepsy and frail health. Her seizures increased during early 1545, and she died from complications of her epilepsy in June 1545.

name, insists that she should make her declaration in presence of some cardinals; and to this the King [of France] has now consented ... As to the Cleves affair, the Emperor says that the Princess's protest before a bishop will be sufficient, and she is now summoned to this Court, from Alencon, to make it.

Jeanne completed her renunciation of Duke Wilhelm in early May 1545. The pair were still man and wife until the Pope officially declared their marriage annulled.

The bonds of marriage between Duke Wilhelm and Jeanne d'Albret were severed via a letter from the Pope in October 1545. The marriage was officially annulled, and both were free to marry others. Jeanne was sixteen years old, and Wilhelm was twenty-nine.

Before the Cleves match, Charles V sought a match between Jeanne and his son Philip. Upon the death of the King of Navarre, Philip would then become King of Navarre *jure uxoris*, gaining even more territory on the Iberian Peninsula. In the meantime, Philip had married his cousin Maria Manuela of Portugal, but she had died a few days after the birth of her only child, Carlos, in July 1545. With the annulment of the Cleves marriage, Jeanne was available to wed either Philip or Carlos. In the end, she married Antoine de Bourbon in 1548.

Charles V Arrives in Regensburg

The Emperor came to Regensburg on 10 April 1546, two months before the official start of the Imperial diet. He had hopes of discussing issues facing the Empire with the other princes already in Regensburg. Unfortunately, there were not really any there yet. This aggravated Charles, particularly because he was still hoping to resolve religious differences. By doing so, he hoped to make a smoother path toward pacifying the rebellious members of the Schmalkaldic League. The differences between the Lutherans, who were anti-Empire, and the pro-Empire Catholics had grown too great over the interceding decades between the 1521 Diet of Worms and the 1546 Diet of Regensburg.

Things had grown tense between Charles V and his younger brother Ferdinand over the interceding years. Ferdinand repeatedly stood in for Charles at Imperial diets as the Emperor was frequently busy trying to maintain the security of his borders, defending against outside enemies like the Turks and internal rebels like Duke Wilhelm. When Ferdinand represented Charles at the diets, he had a habit of pursuing a middle ground when it came to religion.

When it came to Duke Wilhelm's assertion that he had the true right to possess Guelders, Ferdinand tried to mediate between Charles and Wilhelm. During his time as the King of the Romans-Germans, starting with his elevation in 1530, Ferdinand overall seemed to take a more even approach to the changing political and religious temperature in central Europe. Charles, on the other hand, always demanded absolute loyalty and adherence to the traditional way of doing things.

Ferdinand handled Wilhelm gently in hopes of forging a stronger relationship with the powerful young duke. He had many daughters who would one day need husbands, and bringing Duke Wilhelm and the United Duchies of Jülich-Cleves-Berg into the Habsburg fold could only be advantageous. Of course, not all Habsburg political marriages bore fruit in anywise. Charles and Ferdinand's eldest sibling, Eleanor, had been Queen Consort of France since 1530, yet not only did she remain childless but her presence failed to prevent Francis attacking the Holy Roman Empire. Hopefully things would be a little less strained with Wilhelm.

By May 1546, it was widely rumoured that there would be a triple Habsburg marriage. Specifically, Anna, Maria and Magdalena, all in their teens, would be wed to the dukes of Bavaria, Cleves and Piedmont. Magdalena chose never to marry, becoming a nun in 1564.

Unfortunately, the Von der Mark family was not out of the woods yet. Despite Wilhelm's defeat, Charles V still had his eye on another enemy within the Empire. Wilhelm's sister Sybylla and her husband Elector Johann Friedrich of Saxony would be the next branch of the family to war with Charles. Preparations for the Schmalkaldic War were underway at the Diet of Regensburg.

A Habsburg Wedding for Wilhelm

Maria von Habsburg, Hereditary Archduchess of Austria, arrived with her older sister Anna and their mother Anne Jagiellon of Bohemia and Hungary in Regensburg in mid-June 1546. There were complaints that Duke Wilhelm had not bothered to show up in Regensburg yet, which delayed things. Presumably, Duke Albert of Bavaria was already there and finalising his marital negotiations.

To Wilhelm's credit, he had a band of 200 horsemen prepared to ride with him to Regensburg. Just before leaving, there was an incursion into his lands which had to be put down. Wilhelm arrived in Regensburg by early July 1546.

Duke Wilhelm's sister Anna sent Wilhelm a present, possibly a wedding gift, in late June 1546. Anna sent 'two ambling horses and two brace of greyhounds' to her brother. The ambling horses, which would have been trained to provide a smooth riding experience, would be a lovely gift for Wilhelm and his new bride. Hopefully the newest spouse welcomed into the Von der Mark family enjoyed hunting and would make good use of the greyhounds with Wilhelm.

The negotiations for Wilhelm's marriage to Maria of Austria were completed in July 1546 as part of the Diet of Regensburg. Wilhelm brought his new chancellor Olisleger of Cleves-Mark and chancellor Ghogreff of Jülich-Berg and other members of court with him to Regensburg. Wilhelm originally hoped to marry Anna of Austria, who was almost eighteen, but Duke Albrecht V of Bavaria married Anna instead.

It was rumoured that the Landgrave of Hesse tried convincing Wilhelm not to marry a Habsburg. Wilhelm was originally intended to marry the older daughter, Anna:

> The Duke of Cleves was going to the Emperor to marry one of the daughters of the King of the Romans when dissuaded by the Landgrave [of Hesse] and others, who thought to gain him over to their faction, and the Emperor, thereupon, married the said daughter to the Duke of Bavaria's son, and is thought to have concluded the marriage of another of the King's daughters with the son of the Duke of Savoy...

It seems there was little truth to this rumour.

Wilhelm received a description of Maria from Ghogreff and Olisleger, among others in his council. She was 'almost intelligent', which is certainly a curious descriptor. Maria had excellent manners, understood German, Italian and Latin, and was attractive. She was small for her fifteen years, especially when compared to her elder sister Anna. Her face was characteristic of the Habsburgs, being long and narrow with a prominent lower jaw. What potentially was most attractive about Maria was that she came from a very fertile family, with Maria being one of fifteen children born to her parents.

The double Imperial marriage of the two Habsburg brides to their princely husbands was quite the event for the people of Regensburg. The weddings occurred about a week apart, which ensured a prolonged display of Habsburg power and wealth within the city. Such a display would not be seen again until Duke Wilhelm's son Johann Wilhelm finally wed in 1585.

Charles was reported to have said at the wedding, 'We do not appear here as a [Holy] Roman Emperor, but as a brother and supporter, [and] therefore pay tribute to our loved ones as the bride's father [would].' The weddings would have the intended effect of binding Bavaria and the United Duchies to the Imperial family.

Wilhelm was days away from his thirtieth birthday when his engagement and marriage to Maria of Austria took place between 16 and 18 July 1546. The marriage contract was ratified on 17 July 1546 during the Imperial diet then taking place in Regensburg. The marriage was a spectacular affair. It took place on Sunday, 18 July 1546, in Regensburg. Charles V, Ferdinand, Ferdinand's sons and Anne of Bohemia were all present, as were some of the Electors. The wedding was magnificent, and fitting for the marital unification of one of the most powerful dukes in the Holy Roman Empire with the niece of the current Holy Roman Emperor.

Maria was of course an important political bride due to her uncle Charles, and then her father Ferdinand, being the Holy Roman Emperor. Ideally, the marriage between Wilhelm and Maria would ensure Wilhelm's good behaviour. Maria's mother, Anne Jagiellon of Bohemia and Hungary, was roughly three months pregnant with her daughter Joanna, whose birth killed Anne in early 1547.

Maria was considered moody, or having noticeable mood swings, apparently given to occasional descents into some kind of madness. As a granddaughter of Juana of Castile, known as 'the Mad', it was assumed that Maria inherited her slight mental instability from Juana. Maria's suffering became more prominent later in her life. She began exhibiting disorganised thoughts, and her mental state markedly deteriorated before her death.

As part of the marriage agreements, Wilhelm and Maria's children enjoyed special privileges. Any daughters they had would be allowed to claim title to the United Duchies in their own right if there were no sons. This ensured that the United Duchies would stay within the clutches of the Habsburg family.

A few days after Wilhelm and Maria were wed, an article was passed against Johann Friedrich of Saxony and Landgrave Philip of Hesse of the Schmalkaldic League.

Return to Cleves

After the marriage, the newlyweds left for the United Duchies on 24 July. The couple journeyed west from Regensburg to Miltenberg, a distance of roughly 150 miles. After arriving in Miltenberg, they travelled by boat up the Main River to where it converges with the Rhine by Wiesbaden. They overnighted in Siegburg, just south-east of Cologne, on 9 August. Continuing their journey to Maria's new home, they finally landed in Düsseldorf on 15 August.

The new couple intended to visit Regent Maria in Brussels or thereabouts. They made plans to arrive at the Imperial court in October 1546. Regent Maria likely seldom or never met her namesake, who was the new Duchess Consort of Jülich-Cleves-Berg. Regent Maria would be able to gauge Duke Wilhelm's behaviour toward her niece, and to have a private word with the new duchess about how her marriage was going.

Changes in the United Duchies

Shortly after his marriage to Maria, Wilhelm began shifting some of Ghogreff's responsibilities to Olisleger. By 1547, Ghogreff was Chancellor of Jülich-Berg, whereas Olisleger was Chancellor of Cleves-Mark. The pair travelled together to a diet in the Archbishopric of Cologne, where they advocated for allowing Protestantism to take hold where it was found. This was a clever way to try and bolster Protestantism; the chancellors did not ask that Protestantism be officially supported, but rather that it not be stamped out where it already existed. A month later, Archbishop Hermann V von Wied stepped down from his position.

In May 1547, a serious fire broke out in the city of Jülich, destroying the medieval portion of the town. At this point in 1547, almost four years after the Cleves War, the local castle was still in disrepair. Duke Wilhelm took this event as an opportunity to update the buildings and architecture within the United Duchies. He invited a famed Italian architect, Alessandro Pasqualini, to help rebuild and expand the city.

Pasqualini was already known and residing in Guelders. Wilhelm had originally asked for him to come to the United Duchies back in April 1546, but after the fire in Jülich it was all the more necessary. Pasqualini was in the employ of Maximilian of Egmond, a relative of the deceased Duke Karl of Guelders. Wilhelm had to wait for Maximilian's death in 1548 before sending for Pasqualini.

Religious reform within the United Duchies continued slowly gaining ground in the late 1540s. This had mixed results, forcing Catholic churches to allow for Protestant portions in their services and vice versa. In around August 1548, Ghogreff urged the pastors within Cleves-Mark to allow parishioners to observe the Last Supper in both Catholic and Protestant fashion. However, later that year, the starkly Protestant city of Soest was forced to accommodate both Catholic and Protestant beliefs during church sermons.

Possible Husbands for Anna and Amalia

Also in 1548, Wilhelm attempted to secure husbands for both Amalia and Anna. He first looked to the Margrave Ernst I of Baden-Durlach's family, who pursued a middle ground between Catholicism and Protestantism, like the United Duchies. Wilhelm wanted an alliance between his family and theirs. The historical territory of Baden was close to Hesse, as well. Wilhelm wanted the margrave's son and Amalia to marry in support of the alliance. The margrave's two eligible sons were Bernhard, who was rejected by his family due to his raucous and immoral behaviour, and Karl, born in 1529 and twelve years younger than Amalia. Karl was the product of a morganatic marriage, making his legitimacy dubious. Wilhelm refused to marry Amalia to either a man who had led such a dissolute life, like Bernhard, or a mere child, like Karl.

Anna would not wed either candidate for similar reasons, although a marriage for Anna was sought elsewhere. Anna's situation was much more complicated, given her known prior marriage to Henry VIII of England. She was still in England at this point too, and there was the matter of bringing her back to Germany and who would foot the bill. After the death of Henry VIII in 1547, Anna's quality of life plummeted under the boy-king Edward VI. Wilhelm's hope of wedding her to a German prince, aside from providing the obvious political benefit, was likely an attempt to help maintain her dignity and lifestyle.

1549

The year 1549 was symbolic of the changes Duke Wilhelm and the Von der Marks experienced during the decade. The ambitions and fortunes of the Von der Mark family rose, fell and rose again rather swiftly throughout the decade. In early 1540, they were allied with the kings of England and France, plus the Electorate of Saxony. Wilhelm's ambitious goal of keeping Guelders looked as if it might come to pass. But all his alliances had failed by

1543, between the annulment of Anna's marriage, Sybylla's husband having his own struggles with the Emperor, and Wilhelm's French alliance proving useless in his time of need. One can imagine Amalia was fairly fed up with her brother by this point.

Wilhelm found a good match through his marriage to Maria von Habsburg. Although his wings were clipped and he would never again fly as high as he had a few short years before, the United Duchies' fortunes were now secure. Or at least, the United Duchies would be harder to undo because of the Habsburg connection. Unfortunately, this connection subjected the United Duchies' citizenry to additional burdens, even if they would remain safe.

In May 1549, the Turkish threat to the Holy Roman Empire was still pressing. To secure border towns, the Emperor requested a rise in taxes from the German princes, which Wilhelm's councillors assisted in confirming and collecting. Realistically, Wilhelm could do very little to resist Charles V or the Habsburg family at this point.

The Ottoman Empire, referred to in the sixteenth century as the 'Turks', was led by Suleiman the Magnificent from September 1520 to September 1566. It was Suleiman's army that had killed Regent Maria's husband at the Battle of Mohacs in 1526. Through his leadership, other Hungarian territories fell. Suleiman was very successful in expanding his empire on land and his supremacy at sea.

Aside from that, the Turks were a threat to everyone. A few years earlier, Wilhelm's father-in-law Ferdinand had to capitulate to Suleiman in 1544 by effectively agreeing to allow him title to a section of conquered Hungarian lands, though Ferdinand would pay a tax on the lands and continue to rule them. To add insult to injury, Charles was called simply the 'King of Spain' in the 1544 peace treaty with Suleiman.

For his part, Duke Wilhelm was preoccupied with a more pressing matter: his brother-in-law Johann Friedrich of Saxony was imprisoned by Emperor Charles V in 1547. Wilhelm was in a difficult position. He tried to help his sister Sybylla and act as intermediary between the Emperor and Johann Friedrich. He tried speaking with the Emperor's son Philip II of Spain, as well, to little effect. Wilhelm continued to delicately press for Johann Friedrich's release throughout 1548, finally giving up the suit in early 1549. Again, one can imagine that Sybylla, Anna and Amalia were none too impressed with Wilhelm.

10

Saxony Asserts Itself in the 1540s

Charles V Turns His Bellicose Gaze to Saxony

Sybylla von der Mark had her own serious changes to deal with in the 1540s. Her husband Johann Friedrich and his family had been bothering Holy Roman Emperor Charles V for decades. Her father-in-law John the Steadfast famously and notoriously disobeyed Charles V and showed deference to him only when necessary. There was the Schmalkaldic League, which Johann Friedrich founded with his close friend Philip, Landgrave of Hesse, back in 1531 and extended in 1536.

The Schmalkaldic League did not directly provoke the Holy Roman Emperor. Instead, its members would take Church lands in their respective territories, or otherwise make it difficult for Catholicism to remain rooted in each member's respective territory. For his part, Charles V largely ignored the league because he was too busy fending off the Turks and dealing with Cleves and later, France. After the Cleves War ended in 1543, Charles V warred with France until the Treaty of Crépy was signed in 1544. Finally, Charles V was able to turn his attention fully to Germany.

Moritz of Albertine Saxony

Moritz of Saxony became Duke of Albertine Saxony in August 1541, after the death of his father Duke Heinrich the Pious. His uncle George the Bearded took him under his wing back in 1532, mentoring him to be a strong Catholic leader of Albertine Saxony. Of George's ten children, half were boys, all of whom were dead by February 1539. Only his daughter Christina, the beleaguered wife of Philip of Hesse, survived him. George himself died in April 1539.

Moritz's father Heinrich converted to Protestantism in 1536. As a result, the rearing of Moritz was reassumed by his mother and father. Thereafter, Moritz was raised in the Protestant faith. Next, Moritz was transferred to the care of

Johann Friedrich. Johann Friedrich likely recognised the threat Moritz posed to Johann Friedrich's sons with Sybylla of Cleves, so did not do much in support of furthering Moritz's education. Moritz was on good terms with Philip of Hesse, however. Moritz married Philip's daughter, Agnes of Hesse, in January 1541.

After becoming Duke of Albertine Saxony, Moritz was advised to remain on good terms with Charles V and Ferdinand. He instead pursued his own course, dissolving monasteries, seizing property and wealth belonging to the Catholic Church while nonetheless helping the Holy Roman Empire fight off the Turks. In his own way, the young Moritz pursued his own middle ground, quelling Catholicism in ducal Albertine Saxony, but showing up to fight for the Empire when asked.

Moritz avoided joining the Schmalkaldic League out of distaste for Johann Friedrich. Not even Moritz's father-in-law, Philip of Hesse, could convince him to join. His refusal to become a member of the Schmalkaldic League eventually led to greater successes as he managed to remain on Charles V's good side.

Part of Moritz's hatred of Johann Friedrich stemmed from the latter's occupation of his territory. Wurzen Abbey and the Wurzener Land were held jointly by both the Ernestine and Albertine branches of the House of Wettin. Johann Friedrich demanded that the people of Wurzen pay taxes to raise troops for the effort against the Turks. Wurzen Abbey would not do it. In response, Johann Friedrich sent an armed band of over 100 men from Torgau to Wurzen in March 1542, to force the payment of taxes. Moritz, who wanted full control of Wurzen, reacted by threatening to attack Johann Friedrich. The amusing part about all this is that both Johann Friedrich and Moritz wished to push the Reformation within Wurzen, but the two despised each other so much that they could not simply discuss a mutual plan for their joint territory.

Martin Luther intervened in April 1542, writing a letter to the two princes. At the same time, Philip of Hesse met with each prince to try and settle the matter. Everything was settled by 12 April 1542 or so, and no blood was shed. Known officially as the Wurzener Feud, it is sometimes colloquially called the Flatbread War because the troops returning home in time for Easter were given a type of flatbread commonly eaten in Saxony around Easter.

The Wurzen Feud illustrates the dynamic between Johann Friedrich and Moritz. They wanted the same things, but their mutual antipathy prevented them from making any progress. Had these two gotten along, the Reformation may have taken a greater hold in Germany.

Electoral Saxony Agitates the Empire

Over the summer of 1542, the Schmalkaldic League, aided by troops from the Imperial Free City of Goslar and the City of Brunswick, took over the pro-Catholic Duchy of Brunswick-Wolfenbüttel. It was the last Catholic territory in northern Germany. Duke Henry II, known as the Younger, was captured and carted off to Hesse for the next several years, a prisoner of the Schmalkaldic League. The Reformation quickly swept through Brunswick-Wolfenbüttel, much to Charles V's dismay.

Adding insult to injury, the mint at Goslar began circulating German taler bearing the likeness of Johann Friedrich on one side and Philip of Hesse on the other. This currency, used in Saxon federal territories, was a form of propaganda for the Protestant princes. A later coin, featuring Moritz of Saxony, was minted in 1545 to celebrate his capture of Duke Henry the Younger.

Things appeared to be looking up for the Schmalkaldic League at the Diet of Worms in spring 1545. Charles V had promised to discuss reforms or at least tolerance of Protestantism, if only the Protestant leaders would come to the Council of Trent. In reality, Charles was quietly garnering support for the pro-Catholic, pro-Imperial cause at the diet. The glimmer of hope Charles received at the diet combined with the Pope's promise of troops made Charles believe he could finally overthrow the Schmalkaldic League.

Martin Luther, the great reformer who was based in Saxony, died on 18 February 1546.

Tensions over religion, loyalty and rebellion came to a head at the Diet of Regensburg in June 1546, the very same diet where Duke Wilhelm of Jülich-Cleves-Berg negotiated his marriage to Maria von Habsburg, Hereditary Archduchess of Austria. On 7 June 1546, Charles signed treaties with both the Duke of Bavaria and the Pope, who provided supplies and troops, respectively, for Charles's cause. The Duke of Bavaria was promised that one of his sons could marry one of Ferdinand's daughters. This arrangement was nothing new, given that Ferdinand's third child and second daughter, Anna von Habsburg, was previously betrothed to the Duke of Bavaria's eldest son. Sadly, he died young. Anna was briefly betrothed to Duke Wilhelm of Cleves, but instead married Albrecht of Bavaria.

A Treaty between Moritz of Saxony and Holy Roman Emperor Charles V

Moritz of Saxony, still quite proud over capturing Henry of Brunswick, even wrote a book about it. He brought the book with him to the Diet of Regensburg in June 1546. Charles V found Moritz to be trustworthy, and a loyal vassal to the Empire.

On 19 June 1546, Charles V and Moritz of Saxony entered into a treaty that would set the stage for Moritz to express his bitter hatred of Johann Friedrich. Charles V wished for his help in a battle involving the Landgrave of Hesse, Moritz's father-in-law, and Moritz stated that he 'will not take arms against his own kin, but will aid the Emperor with victuals and other things'. Moritz was approached by the Schmalkaldic League, too. He promised to be neutral, although that did not last long.

Charles was openly frustrated with Johann Friedrich of Saxony and Philip of Hesse. After many years,

All [Charles's] efforts to tranquillize Germany вeing frustrated by the opposition of the Duke of Saxony and Landgrave [of Hesse], who keep prisoners Duke Henry of Brunswick and his son and occupy their territories, and refuse to attend the Diet, he is raising horse and foot to reduce these two princes to obedience. The Emperor will shortly send information of this … As many people try to make out that this enterprise against the Duke and Landgrave is really undertaken on religious grounds … the Emperor does not intend to meddle with the religious question.

Now that he had the time, Charles wanted to put down the rebellion of Saxony and Hesse once and for all. The impending war was 'of great moment, another manner of matter than the war out of which we are lately delivered [between England, France, and the Empire]'. Charles was ready to use every bit of his might to put down Johann Friedrich.

On 25 June 1546, it was well known at the diet that Charles V intended to attack Saxony, Hesse and possibly Brandenburg. There were other rebellious areas within Germany which he considered attacking; he wanted to put down the Protestants once and for all. Upon Charles V being directly asked whether he planned to use his army against the Germans, his reply was to the effect 'that he was not so unnatural, but if he did attempt anything it should be against such as were disobedient and would not consent to reasonable devices for the peace of Germany, whom he must correct'. Despite the subtle threat, some of the individuals present at the diet 'knew not how the Emperor would expound disobedience'. Others, however, knew better than to think Charles would speak the way he was without wishing to use force. 'These men seem appalled; and yet the Emperor is not ready, for the 8,000 Spaniards from Naples, Sicily, Italy and Vienna cannot be soon here. He … will probably make decrees in the absence of the Protestants from the diet, and declare them [contumacious], being roused by their absenting themselves and recalling their learned men…'

Either way, all at the Diet of Speyer agreed that they

… shall shortly know the quarrel that the Emperor will have against these men … but if they had not this obstinately refused, to come to him upon his often calling … assuredly he would not so soon been moved against them in respect only of him; and so think also a great many sober men of their own sort.

All Charles had to do was wait for his forces to amass.

A terrifying report from 29 June detailed just how large Charles V's army would be:

The Emperor will himself set upon the [Swabian circle] and the Landgrave, that is to say upon the Protestants, and has with him Maximilian, King Ferdinand's eldest son. The Bishop of Rome sends 22,000 Italians and Spaniards and 4,000 light horse called 'Husserner horses,' with whom come … lords of Italy, and their mustering place is [Sonthofen] in Algau,[31] the

---

31 A mountainous area in Bavaria

Duke of Bavaria refusing to have it in his country. The Duke of Bavaria has prepared 1,800 horsemen only to prohibit musters in his country. Besides these the Emperor and Ferdinando bring 86 ensigns of footmen and 8,000 great horse armed in [German] fashion, and musters are appointed... The lord Great Master ... shall bring 1,800 horsemen to serve the Emperor. Moreover, out of the Low Countries against the bishopric of Cologne and land of Saxony goes ... 4,000 horsemen, besides the garrisons, and 40,000 footmen, making up that number of '[Landsknechte]'... The bishop of Rome has bound himself to help the Emperor with seven millions of gold; upon which he sends the 22,000 footmen and 4,000 horsemen. The bishops ...also help the Emperor with money, who, besides, brings up a great sum and spares no interest to set it by exchange where he wishes.

It seems that Charles was not wishing to take any chances. He united as much of Catholic Christendom as possible against Saxony and the other Protestant territories. Many of these troops would have to pass right through Jülich-Cleves-Berg to reach Algau.

A couple of weeks later, on 4 July 1546, Johann Friedrich and Philip of Hesse met to discuss how best to preserve the Schmalkaldic League in the face of what surely would be the bellicose actions of the Emperor. Realising that the Emperor had superior resources but that the Schmalkaldic League's troops could organise rapidly, they decided the best action would be to attack the Emperor Charles V first, in hopes of preventing a larger conflict. Their thought was that the Schmalkaldic League could make Charles uncomfortable, and more likely to negotiate. That is not at all what happened.

The Schmalkaldic War

The Schmalkaldic War turned out to be a series of poor decisions. Hindsight is always twenty-twenty. Johann Friedrich and Philip of Hesse effectively did not let their appointed military leader do his job. Several strategic missteps early into the war influenced the eventual failure of the Schmalkaldic forces in spring 1547.

The Schmalkaldic League began raising forces in the north, with Sebastian Schertlin von Burtenbach appointed as the leader of the Protestant Schmalkaldic forces. By mid-July, the Schmalkaldic troops numbered about 5,000 cavalry and 30,000 infantry. The Schmalkaldic forces were split into a smaller northern group and a larger southern one. Schertlin wanted to use the southern forces to stop the movement of Charles V's troops. To do this, the southern Schmalkaldic army invaded the city of Füssen, close to the modern-day border of Bavaria, Germany and Austria. Charles V and his army stayed in Regensburg, north-east of Füssen, waiting for troops to come from Hungary, the Low Countries and Italy. Finding both the Emperor's and the Schmalkaldic League's troops in Bavaria, the Duke of Bavaria once more declared himself neutral. Despite this declaration, he was still a Catholic, which caused anxiety for the Schmalkaldic League that Bavaria might join with the Emperor.

Schertlin, who was instructed not to pursue the Emperor's troops into Bavarian territory, chose to move further south in hopes of cutting off Imperial reinforcements coming up through Tyrol. Unfortunately, the Schmalkaldic League did not like the idea of having the southern contingent tied up so far away. Additionally, by moving their troops that close to the Hungarian border, provocation of Charles' brother Ferdinand was a distinct possibility. Ferdinand had declared himself neutral as well, and there was no sense in testing his fraternal feelings.

On 19 July 1546, Charles V, unhappy with the increasing expansion of the Schmalkaldic League, imposed the Imperial ban on Johann Friedrich and Philip of Hesse. The ban was based on the theory that Johann Friedrich and Philip illegally authorised the seizure by Schmalkaldic troops of Duke Henry of Brunswick back in 1545. When someone was put under the Imperial ban, they were declared a public enemy and ceased to exist in a legal sense. The person's property could be taken from them without legal process. More threateningly, the subject of the ban could be killed on sight, by anyone, at any time, without repercussions.

The size of the Schmalkaldic force grew throughout July. By the end of the month, there were more than 45,000 infantry and about 7,000 calvary, compared to the Imperial force of about 30,000 infantry and 5,000 calvary. The Schmalkaldic troops met at Donauwörth, to the north of Füssen and west of Regensburg. In late August, Imperial troops moved to Ingolstadt, to the east of Donauwörth and halfway to Regensburg.

The fortress of Ingolstadt was built between 1538 and 1545 by the Duke of Bavaria. Ingolstadt's strategic location had become obvious to the duke by 1537. One can imagine he did not know how soon the fortress would be put to use.

Charles V approached his brother Ferdinand and Moritz of Saxony, asking them to assist him in enforcing the Imperial ban against Johann Friedrich. It is not known exactly when Charles approached them, but it is thought he first asked for their help in late summer 1546.

At Antwerp, per a dispatch to Henry VIII of England, a Schmalkaldic victory was predicted. On 1 August 1546, Stephen Vaughn, an English merchant based primarily out of Antwerp, reported,

> I am told this evening that the Landgrave of Hesse and Duke of Württemberg are departed towards the Emperor with 50,000 men (though I write to my lords but 40,000). In truth, the wisest here think that the Emperor can never match them this year, and may chance to run into great danger.

If this was the same intelligence that Johann Friedrich had, one can see why he would have pressed on with the war.

In late August, Charles V and his army had left Regensburg and arrived at Landshut in Bavaria, close to Johann Friedrich of Saxony and Philip of Hesse.

[Charles V] with his army is fortnight past in camp and marched as far as the town of Landshut in the country of Bavaria ... 7 leagues from the Landgrave [Philip of Hesse]'s army, who is, together with the Dukes of Saxony and Wittenberg, beside Munich, likewise pertaining to the Duke of Bavaria. The Emperor has of Bavaria, Tyrol, Austria, Bohemia and thereabouts 45 ensigns of footmen. Also he has 16,000 Italians, 12,000 Spaniards, and 400 men of arms from Naples ...

Here [in Brussels] the Emperor is reckoned to have half won, having his full army, and the Landgrave and Dukes of Saxony and Wittenberg, at 'short words' about the defraying of their charges. The said Landgrave and Dukes have 50,000 men, and the Emperor will give them battle without tarrying... Wise men think it too great a venture, for the Landgrave's men are counted best for the battle only. They of Augsburg have not rendered to the Emperor. They intercepted two cartloads of gold coining out of Italy, but the Emperor's army rescued it. The Landgrave, who was marching towards the Emperor, stopped when he heard that the Italians and Spaniards were arrived. The Emperor will come through Germany hither maugre all his adversaries; which will be a marvelous pestering for this country if his army come too. The King of Romans [Ferdinand] is returned to Vienna, with his second son, the eldest remaining with the Emperor. The Duke of Cleves is returned home to Cleves with his wife.

Johann Friedrich of Saxony and Philip of Hesse were still banking on Charles V being weak because he had a smaller army.

With the Emperor so close and at a numerical disadvantage, Johann Friedrich and Philip tried to engage him in battle. Charles V simply shut himself and his forces inside the fortress. Mixed reports bruited that Ingolstadt was overtaken by the Schmalkaldic League, although this did not meaningfully shake the Imperialists.

Henry VIII Is Finally Invited to Join the Schmalkaldic League

In the meantime, Johann Friedrich and Philip sent ambassadors to England in hopes of convincing Henry VIII to join the Schmalkaldic League, sometimes called the 'Protestant League' in England. Henry, having lost some of his zeal for Charles V's friendship, was willing to at least feign interest. On 30 August 1546, in response to Johann Friedrich's request, he laid out his conditions for joining:

1. Thanks for the Landgrave's offer to serve him alone and take no other pension, to furnish him with soldiers when required, and to hinder their passing to any other prince against him. Upon that promise he accepts the Landgrave as his friend, servant and councillor, and gives him a pension of 12,000 fl.
2. If the Protestant League sends hither with diligence commissioners fully instructed, with the names of all its members and the aid at which each is rated or to be rated, he will enter league defensive with them against

all men and for all causes; provided that he may have the chief place in the league, which shall thenceforth be called the League Christian, and that no other may afterwards enter it without his consent. He will be bound to give the aid at which he shall be rated only in cases when all give aid; and as he supposes that they will look for a greater aid from him than from the rest, he will expect in all assemblies to have three voices for two of any other member. As sundry of the members can conveniently act by sea, regard should be had in rating them to have their rates proportioned to be set forth by sea for the aid of confederates who shall have most need of the same.

3. His Majesty thanks the Landgrave, Duke of Saxony, and the rest for their good opinion of his zeal for their sincere union in one opinion of religion, and readiness to follow his advice upon conference between their learned men and his in his presence, in accordance with Holy Scripture or the General Councils before 500 or 600 years. He trusts that they will send men who are both learned and unprejudiced, and requires them, when they send commissioners to conclude the League, to send also the names of ten or twelve learned men, that he may choose 4, 5, or 6, to be sent hither as soon as convenient, to debate points of religion wherein at present he and they differ.

4. He heartily thanks the Duke of Saxony for gentle offers and request of amity made ... on the duke's behalf.

Remember that this was the very same league which Cromwell wanted England to join way back in 1539, when the marriage between Anna of Cleves and Henry was negotiated. Unfortunately, entry to the Schmalkaldic League was controlled by Sybylla of Cleves' husband Johann Friedrich of Saxony, and not by Duke Wilhelm. Johann Friedrich, who was not greatly in favour of the match between Anna and Henry, put in place a rule that banned entry of new members for a couple of years.

Henry's inability to enter the Schmalkaldic League no doubt made the marriage to Anna, coupled with everything Duke Wilhelm was doing, even less of a good choice for the security of England. Had Henry been allowed into the Schmalkaldic League in 1539 or 1540, England would have had greater protection from Charles V's whims. Anna of Cleves might have been Henry's fourth and final wife. That did not happen, and Henry had interesting ideas about joining the League now.

Having heard of Charles V being holed up inside Ingolstadt, and his inferior number of troops, Henry was willing to be friendly toward Philip and Johann Friedrich. Henry's promised pension to Philip that is listed in the first paragraph was a good diplomatic way of showing just enough support without fully committing himself. Whether the pension made it to Germany, or if it would be enough to aid against the Emperor, was an entirely different matter.

In the second paragraph, Henry, or his counsellors, want to ensure that each member of the Schmalkaldic League is willing to participate in any war which any other member faces. Henry wanted to be the head of the League, and change its name. The first part of his request, that all members must participate in each other's wars, would be difficult to enforce at that or any other moment and could quickly change if the Emperor gained ground. The second part of the request, that Henry be made the head of the League and have a controlling vote, was unlikely to pass.

The third paragraph was not practical for Johann Friedrich or Philip while they were attacking Charles V. The fourth was a nice platitude. Henry's response was a tactful way of dodging an alliance with the Schmalkaldic League at that point.

A week later, Henry was discouraged from communing with the Germans:

> With good words and protestation of the goodness the King has shown him and the Emperor's devotion to his Majesty, he wished we might not be seduced by these mean men of Germany; for so noble a prince as the King, who was meet to be arbitrator between the great princes of Christendom, should be ill matched to be treated with by the princes of Germany, who had brought themselves into bondage with the people and the displeasure of their sovereign.

It now made no political sense for Henry to ally himself with Saxony and the Schmalkaldic League now that they were warring with Charles V, instead of simply wishing to follow whatever form of religion the local ruler thought best.

Back in Bavaria

Pro-Imperial reinforcements arrived in the middle of September, levelling the playing field. Charles V moved further north, and the Schmalkaldic League followed him. On 4 October, the League again tried to attack Imperial forces. They intercepted the Emperor at Noerdlingen, west of Ingolstadt. It was hoped that the Emperor could be forced to make concessions to the Protestant princes, but that hope began to fade.

A glimmer of hope for the Protestants came in October, when Imperial troops were weakened by illnesses spreading around their camps. The Schmalkaldic League's only hope for victory, or at least to avoid defeat, was to force the Emperor into negotiating with them before he could amass enough troops. Unfortunately, this strategy and the Schmalkaldic leader's choices to ignore Schertlin's advice proved to be foolish. They were already low on money, and winter privations were coming.

Charles V chose to reserve his personal troops at this point, especially since winter was on the way:

> No battle is fought. The Landgrave retires and the Emperor follows. Now it is said here that some princes labour to the Emperor for the Duke of Saxony and the Landgrave, but the Emperor insists on their yielding themselves into his hands, as the Duke of Cleves did. Hears that the

Emperor will not join battle but keep his army together all winter, and so wear out the adversary part; for most of his charges are borne by the churches of Italy and Spain and other countries where he and the Bishop of Rome have to do. Here [in Brussels] is a saying that the said Emperor and Bishop will deprive the Duke of Saxony and his posterity of the electorship and put another in his place.

Charles did not wait long to make his move.

Landgrave Philip of Hesse's troops began deserting him in early October 1546, despite monies sent to Philip from Francis I of France with which Philip could pay them. Charles V went to the trouble of having a book printed in the Low Countries, explaining why he was justified in attacking Johann Friedrich and Philip. For his part, Duke Wilhelm and his new wife were on their way to Brussels to visit Regent Maria. This might have been a clever way for Wilhelm to avoid any pleas from Sybylla or her husband to help them.

In the middle of October, Electoral Saxony, virtually unguarded, was invaded by Moritz of Saxony and Ferdinand, Emperor Charles V's brother. Charles V had already promised the electoral dignity to Moritz, who was finally ready to attack his cousin. Johann Friedrich and Philip of Hesse argued over whether it was prudent for Johann Friedrich to return his troops to Electoral Saxony. He finally decided to send them back in mid-November 1546.

Unfortunately, Duke Moritz of Saxony had successfully invaded Saxony in November. It was too late for Johann Friedrich to recover his lands, a large portion of which were handed over to his cousin Moritz, who was recognised as the Elector of Saxony. He invaded Johann Friedrich's territory of his own volition:

[Moritz], Duke of Saxony remained quiet and the Bohemians refused to go outside their own kingdom. [Moritz] has since broken the league between the Elector of Saxony and him handed down by their ancestors, and, at the bidding of the Emperor and King of Romans, has seized the cities and lands where the silver and copper mines are which were common between him and the Elector, and proceeds to the capture of places belonging to the other, feigning that he is compelled to this by the Emperor...

All the Protestants wrote to him to desist at this most troubled time from his enterprise; but he goes from bad to worse, for he is young and rather hasty than wise, and his chief councillors more eager for the rewards of the Emperor and King of Romans than for the public good... The Bohemians also invaded the Elector's province adjoining Bohemia, where the Hussars ... who formed the majority of the Bohemian army, killed over 200 horse and 2,000 foot, and then retired. Many believe that this was done to give [Moritz] a pretext for invading the Elector's territory, which is

The 'Rosenbach portrait' of Anna of Cleves, *c.* 1538–1539. (Courtesy of Rosenbach Museum)

Above: 'Charles V Enthroned among his enemies' by Simonzio Lupi, c. 1556–1575. Left to right it shows Suleiman the Magnificent, Pope Clement VII, Francis I, Duke Wilhelm V of Cleves, Elector Johann Friedrich of Saxony, and Landgrave Philip of Hesse. (Courtesy of the British Library)

Left: The left wing of the Reformation Altarpiece at St Mary's in Wittenberg from the workshop of Lucas Cranach the Elder and the Younger. Sybylla of Cleves is shown at the bottom left, looking at the viewer. Some historians believe she might also be the woman depicted at the top left, participating in the baptism. Other persons at the top of the piece are, left to right, possibly Lucas Cranach the Elder, Philipus Melanchthon (holding the baby), and the preacher Caspar Aquila (holding the Bible).

Sybylla of Cleves, *c.* 1531, by Lucas Cranach the Elder.

Left: Sybylla of Cleves, 1526, by Lucas Cranach the Elder. This portrait was created with a companion portrait of Johann Friedrich of Saxony to commemorate their engagement.

Below: Nineteenth-century image showing Sybylla of Cleves pleading with Holy Roman Emperor Charles V for the release of her husband Johann Friedrich of Saxony.

A court hunt at Hartenfels Castle by Lucas Cranach the Elder, *c.* 1540. Sybylla of Cleves is shown in the right-middle, holding a crossbow. It was customary for a woman to take a ceremonial first shot during a court hunt. Her husband Johann Friedrich is in the bottom left, wearing green. (Cleveland Museum of Art)

'Youth, Marriage, and Accession to Government of Johann Friedrich I of Saxony', early 1600s. The marriage of Sybylla of Cleves, in white, and Johann Friedrich, is depicted in the upper middle. (Deutsches Historisches Museum)

Engagement portrait of Johann Friedrich of Saxony, by Lucas Cranach the Elder, 1526, held by Schloss Weimar.

Johann Friedrich of Saxony as duke, *c.* 1550. It is a very flattering portrait of Johann Friedrich at this stage in his life. If you look closely at his left cheek, you can see a hint of the scar from his lip to his eye that he received at the Battle of Mühlberg in 1547.

Weimar Castle Chapel altarpiece by Lucas Cranach the Elder and Younger, completed 1555. On the left is a posthumous portrait of Sybylla and Johann Friedrich. To the right are depicted their sons, John Frederick II, John William, and John Fredrick III (the younger). (Courtesy of GFreihalter under Creative Commons 2.0)

Johann Friedrich of Saxony playing chess with a Spaniard, 1548, by Antonis Mor. Sybylla of Cleves was known to play chess with her husband. (Courtesy of Friedenstein Castle)

Above: 'The Battle of Mühlberg 1547', early 1600s. Sybylla of Cleves can be seen pleading with Charles V in the middle. (Deutsches Historisches Museum)

Below: 'Life of Johann Friedrich of Saxony: His Return and Last Years'. Sybylla of Cleves can be seen greeting Johann Friedrich to the bottom left, and her death is depicted at the top left. His own death is depicted in the top right. (Deutsches Historisches Museum)

Jakoba of Baden, Johann Wilhelm's first wife, by Crispin de Passe, 1592.

Antoinette of Lorraine, Johann Wilhelm's second wife, late sixteenth century. (Courtesy of the Alte Pinakothek München under Creative Commons 4.0)

Left: Anne of Jülich-Cleves-Berg, Wilhelm V's daughter, by the Master of the AC Monogram, *c.* 1576. (Courtesy of the Alte Pinakothek München under Creative Commons 4.0)

Below: Page 47 from *Códice de trajes*, created *c.* 1540, held by the National Library of Spain. The book shows clothing styles across Germany and other places. In the page for the fashion of nobles in Jülich, two young women and a man are depicted. This could be a nod to Anna, Wilhelm, and Amalia. In any case, it is a contemporary recording of how the three younger children of Cleves would have dressed. (Courtesy of the Biblioteca Nacional de España under Creative Commons 4.0)

Johann Wilhelm,
c. 1600, by
Dominicus Custos.
(Courtesy of the
Rijksmuseum)

Magdalena,
Wilhelm V's
daughter, 1610, by
Cripijn van de Passe
the Elder. (Courtesy
of the Rijksmuseum)

Wilhelm, Duke of Jülich-Cleves-Berg, in his prime. (Courtesy of the National Museum, Stockholm)

Maria von Habsburg, Wilhelm's second wife, *c.* 1560, by Hieronymus Cock. (Courtesy of the Rijksmuseum)

Rosenkrantz Triptych, 1528. It depicts Wilhelm (approx. 12 years old) and Johann III on the left wing (see enlargement below left), and Maria, Anna (probably in red, approx. 13 years old), and Amalia (in gold, approx. 11 years old) on the right wing (see below right).

Left: Posthumous portrait of Johann III from the left wing of an altarpiece. It is thought that the right wing included Maria of Jülich-Berg. Created *c.* 1540, possibly from the workshop of Jan van Scorel, and held by St Maria Himmelfahrt in Cleves.

Below: Depiction of the 1547 Battle of Mühlberg, 1550, by Luis de Avila y Zuniga. Johann Friedrich of Saxony's capture is depicted in the top right corner.

Right: Family tree of the dukes of Jülich-Cleves-Berg, beginning at the bottom with Johann III of Cleves-Mark and Maria of Jülich-Berg, and ending with Johann Wilhelm and his four surviving sisters. *c.* 1610. (Courtesy of the Zitadelle Jülich)

Below: The death of Karl Friedrich, 1575, by Dominicus Custos. (Courtesy of Museum Kurhaus Kleve)

The six dukes of Cleves, *c.* 1605s. Left to right: Adolph I, John I, John II, Johann III, Wilhelm V, and Johann Wilhelm I. Cleves and the Swan Castle are in the background. (Courtesy of Museum Kurhaus Kleve)

Above left: Johann Wilhelm, created 1610 (posthumous), in the style of Johan Malthain. (Courtesy of the Rijksmuseum)

Above right: Wilhelm V, painted in 1591 by Johan Malthain, months before Wilhelm died. (Courtesy of Museum Kurhaus Kleve)

now destitute of soldiery as he took almost all the nobility and men of war with him against the Emperor.

This defection of [Moritz] is the work of one by whose promises and artifices many nobles in Germany are deceived; for if all those who embrace and profess the [Protestant] Religion aided their allies it would be impossible for the Emperor to overcome it... The armies of both Emperor and Protestants are still in camp less than a German mile apart. There are daily skirmishes but nothing memorable...

Despite a promising start to the war for Johann Friedrich and the Schmalkaldic League, Moritz's betrayal was a decided turning point. A few weeks later, Johann Friedrich and Philip had run out of money to pay their troops, and the force was disbanded.

Moritz attacked Wittenberg in December. By Christmas, Johann Friedrich had successfully pushed back Moritz's invasion and secured the city once more. Moritz was not making any friends for himself with his exploits, either. Specifically,

[Johann Friedrich] Duke of Saxony, Elector, has again conquered the regions of Thuringia, both his own and that of his kinsman duke [Moritz], and on St. John's Day [27 December] ... led his whole army to Heldrungen ... and he at once gained it, for the defenders were terrified.

The Elector now proceeds against Duke [Moritz's] town of Leipzig, so that a battle between their armies is to be feared. Many gentlemen, both horse and foot, of Duke [Moritz's] army have been captured and have sworn obedience to the Elector. Duke [Moritz] lately sent his soldiers ... into the Duke's country of Anhalt, who committed outrages, such as cutting off the breasts of women and the arms of children, and devastation which it is impossible, but that God will avenge.

Not a good way to make friends, Moritz.

Between the withdrawal of Saxon forces, ongoing lack of funds and the promise of winter struggles, the rest of the Schmalkaldic forces in the south disbanded. The plan to force Charles V to capitulate fell apart completely. There was a glimmer of hope provided by Elector Friedrich of the Palatinate[32] and the Duke Württemberg, who brought reinforcements, but they chose to recognise Charles V's supremacy as Emperor and did not attack. This was secured through a treaty signed around Christmas 1546.

Charles V won the autumn skirmishes by barely raising a finger.

---

32 Elector Friedrich of the Palatinate was the husband of Dorothea of Denmark and Norway. Dorothea was Charles V's niece. Dorothea's younger sister Christina, once a possible bride for Wilhelm of Cleves, is famous for allegedly saying, 'If I had two heads, one would be for the King of England.'

1547

In January 1547, Johann Friedrich pushed out the enemy forces he found in Saxony. He had managed to retain Wittenberg and Gotha throughout the invasion by Moritz. Sybylla and two of her sons were installed at the fortress in Wittenberg, and she did her best to keep Wittenberg loyal to her husband.

On 6 January, the Schmalkaldic League attacked Leipzig, which was held by Moritz and his army of *Landsknechte*. Moritz ordered that silverware and other metals be taken from the religious houses within Leipzig so he could mint money to pay the *Landsknechte*.

Johann Friedrich's army was divided, with a portion remaining with him to the south-east of Leipzig and the other portion going with Colonel Wilhelm von Thumshirn to Chumotov,[33] part of the Bohemian Empire. It was hoped that the Schmalkaldic League would find further support among Bohemian Reformers. Chumotov is roughly halfway between Leipzig, the city by which Johann Friedrich remained, and Prague, where Charles V's brother Ferdinand waited. Unsure of how to perceive the presence of von Thumshirn, Ferdinand rallied his troops.

Over in Bohemia, King Ferdinand of the Romans-Germans lost his wife, Anne of Bohemia and Hungary. She died on 27 January at the age of forty-three. The couple had been married for almost twenty-six years, and had fifteen children together. The birth of their youngest, Joanna, on 24 January in Prague, led to Anne's death. Like his older brother Charles V, Ferdinand never remarried.

Duke Moritz of Saxony's troops in Leipzig were barely able to hold back those of Johann Friedrich. Margrave Albrecht Alcibiades of Brandenburg-Kulmbach brought his army to aid Duke Moritz. Johann Friedrich and his Saxon army left Leipzig on 27 January.

The Margrave was captured on 25 February and imprisoned for the rest of the war. The continued weakening of Moritz's forces and the failure of the Margrave made it possible for Johann Friedrich to march into Bohemia and join his other troops at Chumotov. In what was surely another blunder, Johann Friedrich decided to maintain his position.

The Bohemian armies rebelled against King Ferdinand, refusing to help in Charles V's enterprise against the Schmalkaldic League. This rebellion, called the Estates Revolt, continued into July. Ferdinand eventually regained control, severely hamstringing the Bohemian nobles and military leaders.

The Battle of Mühlberg

Charles V had held off from personally engaging in battle during the winter of 1546/47. Johann Friedrich managed to regain some of his Saxon electoral lands, likely to the relief of Sybylla of Cleves. Aside from her beloved husband, she had three sons to worry about. If Johann Friedrich

---

33 Chumotov, or Komotau, is in the modern-day Czech Republic.

were defeated, there was an excellent chance that things would go very badly for Sybylla and her sons. Since the beginning of the First Schmalkaldic War, Sybylla was appointed the Lady Keeper of Wittenberg by Johann Friedrich.

With their own difficulties to manage, both King Ferdinand of the Romans-Germans and Moritz of Saxony thought it would be best for Charles V to come to the battlefield with his army. Charles prevaricated for about a month. By this time, he was in his mid-forties and suffering from gout at times. He decided in early March to enter the Saxon theatre of war.

Charles left Nuremberg on 28 March, heading toward Saxony. Johann Friedrich was camped at Meissen by the Elbe River. Strategically, Johann Friedrich could easily flee Charles V and destroy any bridges crossing the Elbe. That would give him time to regroup before Charles and his host could ford the river.

On 23 April, Johann Friedrich and his army went across the Elbe and destroyed the nearest bridges. He had a mere 7,000 troops in his army, whereas Charles V had an army of 27,000. Johann Friedrich decided to set up his camp just outside Mühlberg, on the north-eastern bank of the Elbe. Judging by the events that followed, Johann Friedrich seemed to have poor intelligence and did not realise the close proximity of Charles V's army.

Charles V's force attacked on the morning of 24 April. At the time of the assault, Johann Friedrich's army was striking camp and getting ready to move out. Charles V's Imperial soldiers had found a place to ford the Elbe. A portion of the Imperial soldiers swam across, while the rest availed themselves of the ford. Caught unawares, the few soldiers who were ready did their best to fend off the Imperial army. Johann Friedrich gave the order to withdraw.

The Imperial army chased and battled the small Saxon army, who fought valiantly. If Johann Friedrich could have reached Torgau or Wittenberg, both fortified cities, he would have been safe. Unfortunately, both were much too far away. Johann Friedrich's soldiers slowly splintered away and fell around him. Johann Friedrich made it as far as Falkenberg.[34]

Johann Friedrich was surrounded by Charles V's horsemen. He tried to fight them off, receiving a huge slash on his left cheek that extended from the corner of his left eye all the way down toward his mouth. He was then captured and brought to Charles V. Sybylla and Johann Friedrich's eldest son, John Frederick the Middle, was also captured at the Battle of Mühlberg.

In all his portraits after the Battle of Mühlberg, one can see Johann Friedrich's scar. It was untypical for a person of the sixteenth century to show any imperfections in portraiture, whether it be from a birthmark, mole or scar.

Sybylla was likely beside herself when she heard of Johann Friedrich's capture. Given his injuries, he very easily could have died. As the Lady Keeper of Wittenberg, she had to prepare her city, and her sons, for the worst. Now was not the time to lament the capture or death of her husband.

---

34 Modern-day Falkenberg/Elster.

The Siege of Wittenberg

Charles V turned his attention to Wittenberg, arriving there by early May. The countryside was deserted, with all the inhabitants hiding inside the walled city. Sybylla, John William and John Frederick the Younger took shelter inside the castle with the rest of the Saxon court.

Charles's army plundered and burned the countryside. Sybylla's army was rather small, with only 3,000 defenders. Hopefully, Wittenberg's walls would hold and the moat and swamp around the city would protect everyone inside.

The castle was built not only to withstand a siege but to counter-attack. The two great towers of the castle were mounted with cannons to repel the Imperial army. Its bridge was destroyed before the Imperialist army arrived. Multiple earthworks were built up as well, providing more protection for Wittenberg and difficulty for Charles V.

Unfortunately for the city, Charles V came prepared. Aside from the sheer size of his army, he had multiple long guns that would have no problem reaching and heavily damaging Wittenberg. He expected reinforcement from Moritz, who was trailing up the Elbe toward Wittenberg.

The Siege of Wittenberg began on 4 May 1547. Charles's artillery included 60-, 80- and 100-pound guns. The weapons were new to the Imperial army, which was nevertheless able to utilise them to great effect. Sybylla, Lady Keeper of Wittenberg, bravely defended her city.

News of the mortal danger in which Sybylla, John William and John Frederick the Younger found themselves broke Johann Friedrich's spirit. Already a prisoner of Charles V, he merely had to await whatever horrendous fate was coming for him and his family. Johann Friedrich's sentence, passed on 10 May, was death. Hoping to save himself and his family, he surrendered his control of Electoral Saxony.

Sybylla continued to hold the city when Johann Friedrich entered into the Capitulation of Wittenberg on 19 May 1547. Sybylla had no idea that her husband was still alive, and may have been surprised when Charles V ceased the attack on Wittenberg. Spanish troops continued to pillage the area. The Siege of Wittenberg and its aftermath were heinously gory, with bodies strewn about the area and everything seemingly spattered with blood.

Sybylla threw open the gates of Wittenberg on 23 May 1547. With this, Charles V had won a huge victory over the Schmalkaldic League.

Within a day or two, Sybylla and her *Frauenzimmer* went to Charles V's camp. She was dressed as a widow, not knowing if her husband or eldest son, John Frederick the Middle, were still alive. In tears, she fell to her knees in front of Charles V, begging for news of Johann Friedrich. She offered to exchange high-ranking Imperial prisoners for his return. Sybylla learned that both Johann Friedrich and John Frederick the Middle were alive. Lifting Sybylla to her feet, Charles gave her whatever polite words he could under the circumstances. After some assurances, she returned to Wittenberg.

Sybylla welcomed Charles V into Wittenberg, where they continued to bargain over the fate of the city. Johann Friedrich was allowed to stay with Sybylla and their sons in Wittenberg between 28 May and 3 June. After that, he was imprisoned by Charles V and exiled to Worms. The former Electoral couple were allowed to write letters to each other throughout Johann Friedrich's imprisonment.

Aftermath

Duke Henry the Younger of Brunswick-Wolfenbüttel was released after Johann Friedrich's defeat at the Battle of Mühlberg. He was eventually recaptured, and held captive by the Schmalkaldic League for several years. After his release, Duke Henry fervently desired to reinstate Catholicism in his territory. The Schmalkaldic Wars did nothing to stop disputes over religion within Germany.

During his imprisonment in the late 1540s, Johann Friedrich was very busy with his pen. He and Sybylla exchanged a large volume of letters during his imprisonment, and he kept in contact with Charles V. He presumably wrote to his sons John Frederick the Middle and John William, who were eighteen and seventeen, respectively, to give them advice on how to administer the Ernestine lands.

John Frederick the Middle and John William briefly tried to rebel against Charles V again. That did not go anywhere. Instead, Charles V agreed to give them 50,000 guilders per year in exchange for control of some of the Ernestine lands. Needing the money, John Frederick the Middle and John William agreed.

Johann Friedrich did his best to collect intelligence about the Albertine Moritz of Saxony, now the Elector of Saxony. Anything he could use against Moritz, he wrote about it to Charles V. In the end, Moritz would not remain Elector of Saxony for every long. However, the title remained with his descendants until the Electorate of Saxony was extinguished in 1806.

Sybylla remained as the Lady Keeper of Wittenberg throughout Johann Friedrich's imprisonment. She and her sister-in-law Maria von Habsburg, Duchess Consort of Jülich-Cleves-Berg, petitioned Edward VI of England in November 1547 to help Johann Friedrich. Edward VI was an openly Protestant King of England, and it was hoped by Sybylla that he would be inclined to help. Unfortunately, neither Edward VI nor his council were successful in helping Sybylla.

[Sybylla] the Duchess of Saxony, the wife of John Frederick, and her children had begged the King [Edward VI], as also had the Duchess of Cleves [Maria von Habsburg], to be good enough to intercede with us for the deliverance of the said John Frederick of Saxony. The King of England, being desirous of complying with the request of the Duchess, and also because he likewise desired the liberation of John Frederick, had instructed his ambassador here to submit the request to [Charles V] very earnestly, in the hope that, out of consideration for the King of England [Charles V] would display clemency towards the person in question. He (the King of England) felt quite certain that [Charles V] would willingly do more for him ... the King of England was extremely desirous of obtaining the favour he craved, and he prayed ... sincerely that [Charles V] would please him in this.

Charles V had no intention of releasing Johann Friedrich:

[Charles] replied to this, first praising very highly the action taken by the King of England in this matter. Being a young prince as he was, it was quite right and proper that he should incline to clemency, and should be easily persuaded to accede to the prayers and requisitions of other princes and princesses to gain and preserve their friendship. But ... the imprisonment of John Frederick of Saxony was of such grave importance and concern for the public welfare of the whole of Germany that at present [Charles was] unable to decide touching the disposal of the person of John Frederick. Nevertheless ... the King of England might rest assured that the affection [Charles] felt towards him was such that if the matter was in such a position that [Charles] could decide to liberate John Frederick [Charles] would rather do it on the intercession of the King than of anyone else.

Bottom line, Johann Friedrich was not getting out captivity anytime soon.

Sisterly Disaffection

No doubt Wilhelm's sisters were unimpressed by their brother. After becoming Duke of the United Duchies of Jülich-Cleves-Berg, he entered two failed marital alliances, namely the one between Anna and Henry VIII of England, and one between Wilhelm and Jeanne d'Albret. One could see how Anna might blame her brother for going behind Henry VIII's back, and almost roping England into the Cleves War all so that Wilhelm could keep a piece of land, costing Anna her marriage. He completely ignored the advice of their father Johann III, who warned against tangling with Emperor Charles V over Guelders.

The war cost Wilhelm his French alliance, too, and his chance at becoming King of Navarre instead of a mere German duke. Along those lines, Wilhelm could have become King of Denmark if he gave up Guelders and married Charles V's niece Christina of Denmark. Instead, he alienated his allies across Europe, had his wings clipped by the Holy Roman Emperor Charles V, and became utterly useless to his sisters. Anna was trapped in England for the first several years of the 1540s, Amalia was never able to wed because of his focus on keeping Guelders, and he could not even help Sybylla free her husband after his capture. Even if he wound up being a successful duke, Wilhelm was not a useful brother.

11

Changes for the Von der Mark Siblings

Changes in the Wind

The 1550s were a mixed bag for the Von der Marks. Anna, still in England, continued to flirt with poverty. Edward VI and his counsellors did not care one whit about this foreign woman, his former stepmother, even if his father had adopted her as his sister. She was no family to him. Sybylla continued to do her best to secure the release of her beloved husband Johann Friedrich, while trying to assist their sons in navigating the family's reduced status. Amalia, well into her thirties, was still unmarried and living at Wilhelm's court, which was primarily based in Düsseldorf. Wilhelm seemed to be the only one of the siblings experiencing a modicum of good luck, or at least no misfortune.

Wilhelm Welcomes His First Child

The first six of Wilhelm and Maria's seven children were born in the 1550s. Amalia had a hand in raising Wilhelm's daughters, who grew up in the *Frauenzimmer*. The first child, Maria Eleonore, was born 16 June 1550 in Cleves. The little girl may have been named after her Habsburg great-aunts Maria and Eleonore. Conveniently, 'Maria' was also the name of Wilhelm's mother. Maria Eleonore proved to be very headstrong, and had Lutheran sympathies that were no doubt encouraged by her paternal aunt Amalia. Wilhelm, a Reformed Catholic, did not approve and was concerned that Maria Eleonore would influence her younger sisters.

The State of Things in Germany

Beginning in 1550, Wilhelm's father-in-law Ferdinand was at odds with Holy Roman Emperor Charles V. Ferdinand, the younger brother of Charles, had been elected King of the Romans-Germans in 1531. This meant that he was the Emperor Elect, and the likeliest candidate for the position of Holy Roman Emperor should he outlive his older brother. Charles' son and heir to his hereditary possessions, Philip of Spain, was born in 1527. By 1550, Charles was looking toward the future. As part of this, he decided he wanted Philip to become King of the Romans-Germans in place of Ferdinand.

Should Philip become the King of Romans-Germans, attempts at the Lutheran Reformation would almost certainly be violently quashed if Philip were then confirmed as Emperor. Wilhelm, despite remaining Catholic his whole life, exhibited sympathy toward reform of the Catholic Church at least and the Lutheran cause at most. His father-in-law Ferdinand, meanwhile, was much less opposed to religious reform than either Charles or Philip.

There was a great deal of pushback against Charles' plan to install Philip, especially in Germany. Charles hoped that Philip could be a sort of coadjutor with Ferdinand, whereas Ferdinand wished for his own son Maximilian to be coadjutor. Charles and Ferdinand were clearly thinking about their advancing years, and each wanted to ensure stability for the Holy Roman Empire. Debates and discussions over what to do with Philip and Maximilian continued throughout 1550 and 1551.

Wilhelm Tries to Help Anna

Wilhelm sent Herman Crüser to England around 30 March 1551 in hopes of helping the beleaguered Anna. Anna was not important to either Edward VI or his uncles, and so little attention was paid to her other than taking away her properties and not paying her income. There was a moment when Anna was considered as a possible bride for Thomas Seymour, but naught came of it. Crüser arrived in late May, when Edward sent word back to Wilhelm about how he wished to treat Anna. Clearly, it was unlikely that she would live as well under Edward VI as she had under Henry VIII.

1552

Duke Moritz of Saxony, whose father-in-law Philip of Hesse had been taken into custody alongside Johann Friedrich, was increasingly disillusioned with Charles V. The Emperor had ordered Moritz to attack the city of Magdeburg, in present-day Saxon-Anhalt, in 1550. The city had refused the interim decree from the Augsburg Diet in 1548 and continued supporting Protestantism. Charles wanted to put down the rebellious citizens. The attack on Magdeburg was part of the greater Schmalkaldic Wars, the same conflict that saw the capture of Sybylla of Cleves' husband Johann Friedrich of Saxony.

The war in Magdeburg dragged on into 1551, before Moritz took drastic measures the following year. On 15 January 1552, with a couple of other Protestant German princes, Moritz agreed to the Treaty of Chambord with Henri II of France. The parties agreed that Moritz, who identifies himself in the treaty as being the 'Duke of Saxony, Arch Marshall and Elector of the Holy Roman Empire', was nominated the General Colonel of the allies against Charles V. In exchange, Henri would receive the Archbishopric of Metz in Lorraine.

Over in England, Anna was still unhappy in January 1552. Yet another property, Bisham Abbey in Berkshire, was taken from her and sold to the Hoby family. The abbey, which was dissolved in June 1538, was sold to Sir Philip Hoby, a diplomat under both Henry VIII and Edward VI. Hoby was one of the agents sent by Henry to France to find a fourth bride for him in 1538, and was later entrusted to negotiate for a marriage between Edward VI and Elizabeth of France in 1551. Before that, he was the ambassador to the Imperial court. One can assume that Edward VI, or at least his uncle the Lord Protector, did not have much use for Anna and had no problem further impoverishing her to reward loyal courtiers. Philip Hoby took possession of Bisham Abbey in March 1552. After that, presumably, Anna lost the income from the property.

Duke Wilhelm and Maria anticipated the birth of their second child, who would hopefully be a boy. The ducal couple welcomed their second daughter on 1 March 1552 in Cleves. They named her Anne of Jülich-Cleves-Berg, presumably after her paternal aunt, the former queen consort of England. The infant girl had a Habsburg aunt named Anna, as well. Anne was influenced by her paternal aunt Amalia, and grew to have Lutheran leanings. She had the long Habsburg face, but otherwise appeared to have her Habsburg features balanced by the Von der Mark side.

In late summer 1552, representatives from the Holy Roman Empire went to Passau to try and negotiate peace between Moritz of Saxony and Charles V. Duke Wilhelm dutifully sent his own representatives, and Charles sent his brother Ferdinand. The Peace of Passau was signed by Ferdinand and Moritz on 2 August 1552. Charles V, who was not present, did not agree to all the terms of the original document but signed an amended version on 15 August 1552. The Peace of Passau had several positive results for the German princes generally, and Sybylla of Cleves in particular. Moritz secured the release of his father-in-law, Landgrave Philip of Hesse. Moreover, some joy came to the Von der Marks when Johann Friedrich, Sybylla's husband, was finally released from captivity on 1 September 1552 after five long years.

The Siege of Metz took place in autumn 1552, roughly six months after Henri II's arrival there. He was not warmly welcomed. Charles V half-heartedly attacked, but not much came of it and he left Metz to Henri. To this day, Metz retains a heavy Germanic influence despite being part of France for almost 500 years.

Another Daughter for Cleves

By early 1553, it was rumoured that Wilhelm would never have any sons. Philipus Melanchthon was under the impression that various astrologers at the Saxon court had predicted Wilhelm and Maria would only have girls. If that were the case, it was believed in Saxony that Jülich-Cleves-Berg would go to Sybylla's sons. Never mind the agreement that Emperor Charles V had made for Wilhelm and Maria's daughters.

Magdalena, the third child and third daughter of Wilhelm of Cleves and Maria von Habsburg, was born on 2 November 1553. It is not known whether the news of her birth brought much joy for Anna or Sybylla, given that England was still not the kindest of places for Anna and that Sybylla was growing rather ill in Saxony. Amalia could have looked upon the birth of another girl as a failure by her Catholic sister-in-law.

Weeks later, Maria von Habsburg, apparently sufficiently recovered from Magdalena's birth, was expected in the Low Countries for the baptism of the Prince of Orange's son. She planned to attend the baptism with her aunt, the Regent Maria, in Breda, Netherlands. Surely this would not have been an easy journey for Maria von Habsburg.

Sybylla's Last Months

In Saxony, Sybylla maintaining her possession of and command over Wittenberg, had moved to Weimar and administered Wittenberg from there. Despite Johann Friedrich's freedom, he was still rather busy trying to secure what remained of his lands. He engaged in skirmishes with Moritz of Saxony. The ongoing battles agitated Sybylla, who was reminded of the outcome of the Schmalkaldic Wars. Her bitterness over the years of separation, compounded by his continued absence enforcing his rights, were evident in letters she wrote throughout summer 1553 to her husband. She wished to be released from what she saw as an evil, cursed existence so that she could enter eternal happiness.

Sybylla, whose body was breaking down, was in low spirits on 28 June 1553 when she received the sacrament and last rites.

Johann Friedrich wrote to Sybylla in October 1553, telling her she was perfectly safe in Weimar and that there was no need for her to worry herself about the city being overrun. However, it was necessary that Sybylla not disclose the content of their letters relating to what was happening on the battlefield, or Johann Friedrich's plans.

On 4 November, Sybylla of Cleves seems to have had a brief burst of good health. She planned a hunting trip with Johann Friedrich and their sons. She set off, only to write to her husband on 12 November to tell him that her illness would not permit her to go.

That same month, Johann Friedrich travelled to Coburg to resolve outstanding issues from the death of his half-brother, Johann Ernst. Dominion over the territory of Coburg had to be resolved between his sons. He asked Sybylla to meet him with her *Frauenzimmer* in Coburg, a three- or four-day journey from Weimar. He suggested that she travel in a litter, and assured her that her every comfort would attend her. Unfortunately, Sybylla was too poor in health on 14 November to make the journey. She complained of her legs and heart not being strong enough. Her lung disease had returned, accompanied by vomiting. On top of that, she complained of having her period, which was unusually heavy. Sybylla knew she would be dead before long, likely during the winter.

After being ill for a couple weeks, Sybylla grew emaciated by 26 November. She desperately wished to join Johann Friedrich at Coburg but simply didn't have the strength. She had difficulty walking, and was unable to scale the stairs at the palace in Weimar.

A week later, Sybylla of Cleves sent her husband Johann Friedrich the last of her known letters. On 3 December 1553, she told her husband that winter had coldly grasped Weimar, and she was not able to venture out. On 4 December 1553, she gifted Johann Friedrich six pomegranates, hoping that they would restore him to health. It was a present for St Nikolaus Day, the common day in German lands for winter gifts to be exchanged. Sybylla mentioned that she received all her husband's most recent letters that same day, and hoped that she could respond to them with her own hand. She never did write to Johann Friedrich again.

The Deaths of Sybylla and Johann Friedrich

After receiving her letters, Johann Friedrich decided to move his court to Weimar so he could be nearer the deathly ill Sybylla. Her condition dramatically worsened in early February 1554, after which time Johann Friedrich would not part with her. Only he, their sons and a couple of servants had access to her chamber at this time. Sybylla died in Weimar on 21 February 1554 at around nine o'clock in the morning.

Sybylla held an important position for the early Lutheran Church, the Saxon court, and for her husband. She was not just a Duchess Consort of Saxony, nor simply a Princess of Cleves. Sybylla was the 'Church Mother', and a mirror to Johann Friedrich's own religious beliefs. She never lost her faith, despite the trials and tribulations of the Schmalkaldic Wars, her husband's imprisonment, and her own physical illness. Sybylla was indeed the devout Mother of the Lutheran Church in those early days in Saxony.

Johann Friedrich survived Sybylla by ten days. Upon his death, the Lutheran Church bestowed upon Johann Friedrich a new title:

Johann Friedrich by God's grace, Awakened Witness and Martyr of Jesus Christ, Prince of the Afflicted, Duke of the Righteous, Confessor of Faith, Count of Truth, rich in the Holy Cross, an example and image of patience and persistence, inheritor of eternal life, has in Christ blissfully fallen asleep, and parted from this miserable life to the heavenly fatherland, at Weimar, on the 3rd day of March in the year 1554.

With that, the Electoral couple, staunch supporters of Martin Luther and the Lutheran reform, passed into history.

Death of Edward VI and Rise of the Tudor Queens Regnant

Edward VI of England was gravely ill by June 1553, though he was just fifteen. During his reign of six and a half years, Edward VI and his councillors did their best to establish Protestantism in England and stamp out Catholicism.

Edward's childlessness meant that there was a very real danger that Henry VIII's eldest, Catholic daughter Mary, could become queen.

An Act of Parliament from 1544 declared Edward the lawful heir of Henry, legitimately begotten. By this, known as the Third Act of Succession, Henry left the crown to the 'heirs of his body lawfully begotten, that is to say, to the first son of his body between His Highness and his then lawful wife Queen Jane, now deceased, begotten, and to the heirs of the body of the same first son lawfully begotten'. If Edward died without his own lawfully begotten children, then the crown was left to Mary and her children, then to Elizabeth and her children. It is worth noting that neither Mary nor Elizabeth were referred to as Henry's lawfully begotten, and therefore legitimate, daughters.

Henry drafted his will on 30 December 1546. In it he reinforced the Third Act of Succession:

> As to the succession of the Crown, it shall go to Prince Edward and the heirs of his body... In default, to his daughter Mary and the heirs of her body, upon condition that she shall not marry without the written and sealed consent of a majority of the surviving members of the Privy Council appointed by him to his son Prince Edward. In default, to his daughter Elizabeth upon like condition. In default, to the heirs of the body of Lady Frances, eldest daughter of his late sister the French Queen. In default, to those of Lady Elyanore, second daughter of the said French Queen. And in default, to his right heirs. Either Mary or Elizabeth, failing to observe the conditions aforesaid, shall forfeit all right to the succession.

Edward VI eventually succumbed that summer of 1553, possibly to pneumonia or tuberculosis. Knowing that death was near, he drew up his will along with a document known as the Devise for the Succession. The Devise, a draft document in Edward's hand, was written in April or May 1553. There is ongoing debate as to whether Edward created the document himself or merely transcribed what his councillors suggested, and equally as to whether he left out both Mary and Elizabeth because he saw them as illegitimate, or because he feared Mary's vehement dedication to Catholicism.

The young Edward's Devise was turned into Letters Patent on 21 June 1553. Edward left the throne to Lady Frances Brandon and her heirs male. After Lady Frances, the succession went to her daughter Lady Jane Grey and Lady Jane's heirs male. Thereafter, the succession would go to Lady Jane's sisters and their heirs male.

Lady Frances was not quite thirty-six when Edward VI died, and presumably still capable of bearing children. However, Edward left the caveat that Lady Frances' heirs male had to be born before Edward's death. She was not pregnant that summer, and without a son the succession would fall to her daughter Lady Jane Grey. Edward died on 6 July 1553.

On 10 July 1553, Lady Jane Grey was declared Queen of England and Ireland by Edward's Privy Council. This declaration was circumspect, and swiftly led to Jane's overthrow. Jane, for her part, was only fifteen years old. Though a reportedly bright if melancholy and anxious teenager, Jane was essentially under the control of the men around her. Unfortunately for her, in their rush to exclude Mary and Elizabeth they overlooked various legal impediments to Jane's accession. Haste makes waste, as it is said, and to this day there is strenuous debate over whether the Nine Days' Queen truly was a queen regnant.

Also on 10 July 1553, Mary's letter declaring her new status as Queen of England was received by the council. Mary would not sit idly by and let her father's will – and more importantly, her destiny – pass her by. Thirty-six-year-old Mary was ready to become queen, even if that meant using military force. She gathered an army and headed toward London.

Mary met with very little resistance and was declared queen on 19 July 1553. She officially entered London on 3 August. By the end of that month, the singing of Mass was restored in England. Anna of Cleves and Elizabeth had not shown themselves in church: 'Mass is sung habitually at Court; not one Mass only, but six or seven every day, and the Councillors assist. My Ladies of [Cleves] and Elizabeth have not been present yet.' Mary was unimpressed.

On 30 September 1553, Mary I enjoyed her traditional progress from the Tower of London to Westminster Abbey. Anna and Elizabeth rode together behind Mary for the event:

> The Queen of England was led from the Tower of London to Westminster with the wonted ceremonies, in an adorned open litter, with the small crown on her head. She was followed by two coaches in one of which rode the Lady Elizabeth and [Anna], and several ladies of the Court in the other. [Anna stood behind Elizabeth in] a chariot having canopy all of one covering, with cloth of silver all white, and six horses betrapped with the same ... and therein sat at the end, with her face forward, the Lady Elizabeth, and at the other end, the Lady Anne of Cleves.

Elizabeth and Anna wore red velvet dresses for the occasion. Anna and Elizabeth sat together at Mary I's coronation banquet, too. Once Mary arrived at Westminster on 1 October 1553 for her coronation,

> There her Grace heard mass, and was crowned upon a high stage, and after she was anointed Queen, the first day of October. When all was done, her Grace came to Westminster Hall ... and there the duke of Norfolk rode up and down the hall ... and there was [great melody] ... and at the end of the table dined my Lady Elizabeth and my Lady Anne of Cleves; and so it was candlelight ere her Grace or she had dined, and so [anon] her Grace took barge.

Things seemed to be improving for Anna.

Anna, Queen Dowager of England?

After the death of Henry's widow Catherine Parr in September 1548, the position of Queen Dowager of England was vacant. Promptly after Mary I's coronation in 1553, Anna did what she could to undo her annulment from Henry VIII, making herself Henry's only surviving lawful wife:

> My Lady ... of Cleves is taking steps to get her marriage to the late King Henry VIII declared legitimate, so that she may enjoy the dowry, treatment and prerogatives of a Queen Dowager of England, and also continue to enjoy her dowry even if absent from England ... the case will be adjourned till later; when more urgent and important affairs have been settled and decided.

If Anna were successful in claiming the status of Queen Dowager of England this would ensure her financial stability, something which she did not have during the reign of Edward VI.

As Queen Dowager of England, she would have her own steady source of income and would certainly improve her standard of living. She would even have the means to return to the United Duchies if she wanted. In England Anna was a wealthy landowner, but in the United Duchies custom dictated that she would be entirely reliant on her brother Wilhelm. If she remarried, she would become dependent upon her husband. Given that she was thirty-eight years old by the time Mary became queen, Anna was past the age of marrying. It might not have made sense for her to return to Jülich-Cleves-Berg anymore.

Anna was never recognised as Queen Dowager, so her ultimate intention remains a mystery.

Anna at Mary I's Court

Anna von der Mark was mere months older than Mary Tudor, now Mary I of England. It was no secret that Mary longed for a husband, and the more devoutly Catholic the better. Anna had just the candidate for Mary, and it would increase the familial bond between the Von der Marks and the Tudors.

Wilhelm's wife Maria von Habsburg had an elder brother named Ferdinand. This Ferdinand, son of Charles V's brother Ferdinand, was an Archduke of Austria and born in 1529. He was thirteen years Mary's junior, and culturally Germanic. The young man was known for speaking multiple foreign languages and admiring the arts.

Anna suggested the younger Ferdinand to Mary in mid-October 1553. Such a match had the potential to strengthen Anna's standing with Mary and firm up an alliance between the United Duchies and England through the mutual Imperial Habsburg marriages. Following up on Anna's suggestion, Ferdinand, King of the Romans, sent ambassadors in November 1553 to discuss the match with Mary. In the end, Mary wed Philip II of Spain, son of Emperor Charles V. Philip was slightly older than the Archduke Ferdinand, being only eleven years younger than Mary. Importantly for Mary, Philip was Spanish, and Mary heavily identified with her Spanish descent from her mother Katharine of Aragon. An official announcement of Mary's impending marriage with Philip II of Spain was given on 15 January 1554.

Wyatt's Rebellion

For any number of reasons, which are still debated by historians, Sir Thomas Wyatt the Younger, Sir Edward Courtenay and their friends were not in favour of Mary's Spanish marriage. Their rebellion began shortly after the marriage announcement in January and fell apart within weeks. Unfortunately for Anna, she was implicated in the rebellion. Simon Renard wrote to the sickly Emperor Charles V:

Sire: To-day [9 February 1554], ... this present dispatch will partly serve as an answer to the ... intrigues which have now been discovered. Most of the conspirators [of Wyatt's Rebellion] are prisoners, and it only remains to come to a decision as to the arrest of Courtenay and the Lady Elizabeth. That would be the way to deal with them, now that God has permitted the conspiracies to come to light sooner than their authors had intended, and the Queen has had the victory... I assure you that there never was seen a more steadfast lady than the Queen, nor one more devoted to you... I expect to see the King of France make war on England ... because he does not wish the Queen well ... [and] because he has promised the Duke [Wilhelm] of Cleves, at the Lady Elizabeth's request, thus to revenge himself for Henry VIII's repudiation of his sister [Anna], and in order to give the German princes an opportunity of turning their forces against your Majesty's dominions.

A few days later, Mary investigated. Renard wrote to Charles V on 12 February:

Sire: The Queen of England summoned me this morning and informed me that the Council had issued orders for Courtenay's arrest and imprisonment in the Tower, because Wyatt, without having been tortured, accused him ... of being of the conspiracy... The Queen, moreover, told me that the Lady [Anna] of Cleves was of the plot and intrigued with the Duke of Cleves to obtain help for Elizabeth: matters in which the King of France was the prime mover... The Queen ... is now absolutely determined to have strict justice done and make herself strong against further eventualities.

Whatever part Anna may or may not have played in Wyatt's Rebellion, Mary believed, at least outwardly, that Anna was a danger. This might explain why Anna's suit to become Queen Dowager of England never gained traction.

Charles V, who had such trouble with Duke Wilhelm ten years before, wrote to Renard on 18 February:

We have received your letters of the 5th and 8th instant, together with the enclosed papers, and learnt details of the success God was pleased to bestow on the Queen by delivering into her hands the leaders of the rebellion who are still alive... We will only add that we wish you to leave nothing undone to obtain information on a point mentioned in your last letters: the promise made by the King of France to the Duke of Cleves, at his sister's request—she who was abandoned by the late King Henry—and by the intermediary of the Lady Elizabeth. Thus we may use the information acquired in deciding what we had better do, and we have no doubt that the Queen will realise how important it is to us, and afford you all the help you need to get to the bottom of it.

Neither Anna nor Wilhelm were ever reprimanded because of the accusation.

The blows kept coming for Anna, who learned in mid-March 1554 of the deaths of her sister Sybylla and Sybylla's husband Johann Friedrich of Saxony. Wilhelm sent a personal message to Mary I:

William Duke of Cleves to Queen Mary. Thanks her Majesty for the great kindness shown to his sister the Lady Anne, and to his Councillor Dr. Herman Crüser on his recent visit to England. Crüser now returns to convey to Lady Anne the melancholy intelligence of the death of their sister Sybil Duchess of Saxony, and will wait upon her Majesty to offer his Grace's congratulations on her comparatively bloodless victory over some of her traitorous subjects.

Crüser arrived in England in early April, tasked with consoling Anna over Sybylla's death:

A servant of the Duke of Cleves ... broached no matter except to congratulate the Queen [Mary I of England] on her victory and marriage with his Highness [Philip II of Spain] on behalf of the Duke [Wilhelm] and Duchess [Maria von Habsburg] of Cleves. He thanked the Queen for her favourable treatment of the Duke's sister [Anna], and asked leave to go and console her for the loss she has sustained by the death of her brother-in-law and sister John Frederick of Saxony and his wife. He obtained leave, and said he would not be away more than six or eight days.

It seems from this interaction between Mary I and Hermann Crüser that either Mary did not believe the allegations against Anna or Wilhelm. Unfortunately, Anna would remain mostly away from court for the rest of her life.

12

Growth and Changes for the United Duchies

Karl Friedrich, Heir to the United Duchies

Finally, on 28 April 1555, the long-awaited heir was born at four o'clock in the morning at the Swan Castle in Cleves. The birth of Karl Friedrich secured the succession of Julich-Cleves-Berg, which no doubt brought much relief to Wilhelm and Maria. Before his birth, the United Duchies was in danger of falling into either Saxon or Imperial hands, requiring a war to settle the matter. Saxon rights were guaranteed in 1526 via the marriage of Sybylla of Cleves with Elector Johann Friedrich, and Imperial rights secured more recently in 1546 through the marriage of Wilhelm and Maria.

Karl Friedrich spent his early years in the *Frauenzimmer* with his older sisters Maria Eleonore, Anne and Magdalena, under the careful watch of their paternal aunt Amalia. The little boy was regarded as intelligent and vivacious, showing great promise of being a strong Duke of Julich-Cleves-Berg. Karl Friedrich's features heavily favoured his Habsburg mother, with a long face and prominent jaw. He received the best education Wilhelm could secure. He was the perfect heir, and, as his parents hoped, would lead the United Duchies to continued prominence and prosperity.

When Karl Friedrich was seven years old, his princely education began. He was taught about the arts, instructed in virtue and told to fear God. He learned to write and speak in Latin, and by the age of twelve he had memorised passages from Virgil. Before long he could speak French, Spanish and Italian as well.

Attention was paid to strengthening Karl Friedrich's body and physical abilities from a young age. Given his youth, hunting was the best introductory sport. He began instruction in the use of various weaponry when he was slightly older.

Children of the House of Cleves

Another Daughter Is Born to Wilhelm and Maria

A fifth child, Elisabeth, was born in 1556 but did not survive past childhood. Elisabeth may have been named after her maternal great-aunt Isabella, whose name was changed to Elisabeth when she became Queen Consort of Denmark. Another, less remote possibility was that Elisabeth was named after her illegitimate aunt of the same name. The illegitimate Elisabeth of Cleves, closely related to Duke Wilhelm, was the grandmother of Olisleger's second wife, Gottfrieda von Bemmel. The illegitimate Elisabeth died in Xanten on 15 July 1554, shortly before Elisabeth of Jülich-Cleves-Berg was born. Wilhelm's daughter Elisabeth drops out of records in the early 1560s, and appears to have died of illness in around 1561.

Anna's Last Months and Death

Anna and Mary I were friendly with each other during Christmastide 1556 and New Year 1557, with Anna present at court and meeting with Mary at least once. Mary gave Anna several presents for New Year's 1557, including a covered bowl, a gilt cup and a gilt cross. Anna personally presented to Mary a gift of £20, delivered in half-sovereigns.

Anna's health declined in early 1557. Her illness was obvious by April, when she complained of an abdominal ailment which could have been a form of cancer. The other possible culprit was a strain of influenza that tore through England during 1557 and 1558. This seems to have been the killer of a multitude in Tudor England, including Mary I and Cardinal Reginald Pole. Whatever her affliction, Anna moved to her manor at Chelsea that spring. She never recovered.

Anna had her last will and testament prepared in mid-July 1557. She is identified as the daughter of Johann, lately the Duke of Cleves, and sister of the distinguished current prince, Duke Wilhelm of Cleves, Jülich and Berg. Anna is described as having a sickly body but all her mental faculties intact at the time her testament was written. She asked that Mary I intercede on her behalf and that all her creditors be satisfied. Anna expressed hope that the executors and Mary could complete the settlement of any debts by the Feast of St Michael, or 29 September 1557. She wished that her servants and household receive their due payment.

Anna left money to several of her servants explicitly, and asked Mary to distribute alms in the amount of £4 to each village in the areas of Hever, Bletchingley, Dartford and Richmond. She left her best jewels to those whom she loved in England and Cleves.

To her younger brother Wilhelm, Duke of the United Duchies of Jülich-Cleves-Berg, Anna left a ring that had several diamonds in the shape of a heart, and engraved wings. To her sister-in-law, Duchess Consort Maria, Anna left a golden ring with a large, dark ruby. She gave Amalia a golden ring with a pyramid-shaped diamond. To Catherine Willoughby, Duchess of Suffolk and a woman with whom Anna maintained a relationship from her very first days in England, she gave another gold ring with a square-shaped diamond. To her cousin Waldeck she gave a necklace adorned with a ruby. She left her best jewel to Mary I, and her second-best jewel to Lady Elizabeth Tudor.

Anna wished to be buried 'according to the Queen's will and pleasure and that we may have the suffrages of the Holy Church according to the Catholic faith wherein we end our life in this transitory world'.

Anna von der Mark, Hereditary Duchess of Jülich-Cleves-Berg, 'Beloved Sister' to Henry VIII of England, briefly Queen Consort of England and later the Daughter of Cleves, died quietly on 16 July 1557, surrounded by her household. Her body was quickly cered, or wrapped in a wax cloth to preserve it, and placed in a lead casket. The fact that it was cered and wrapped so quickly could be an indicator that Anna died from an infectious disease and not a type of cancer.

Anna asked that Mary I choose where her body was to be interred and requested that her burial be performed according to the rites of Rome. At Richmond on 27 July 1557, the Privy Council learned that Mary had sent a letter to the Lord Treasurer

> ... that where it hath pleased Almighty God to call to His mercy the Lady Anne of Cleves, the Queen's Majesty, being careful that she should be honourably buried according to the degree of such an estate, have referred the consideration of the order thereof to [the Lord Treasurer], praying him ... to draw a plat [plot] of the same as he shall think convenient, and send the same hither.

Mary chose to bury Anna in Westminster Abbey, on 4 August 1557, on the south side of the High Altar. Anna's testament was submitted to probate on 2 September 1557 in front of William Cook, a Doctor of Laws. Cardinal Reginald Pole notarised the soundness of her testament.

Anna's Funeral and Burial

Anna's funeral was a grand affair. The diarist Henry Manchyn provides a full description of the solemnities for Anna, noting that she died on 16 July and was a queen of Henry's but had never been crowned. On 29 July 'began the hearse at Westminster for my Lady Anne of Cleves, with carpenters work of 15 principals, as goodly a hearse as...' The diary trails off here, having been damaged over time. Manchyn continues that on 3 August,

> My Lady Anne of Cleves, sometime wife unto King Henry the VIII came from Chelsea to be [buried] unto Westminster, with all the children of Westminster and [many] priests and clerks, [including] ... the monks of Westminster, and my Lord Bishop of London and my Lord Abbott of Westminster [who] rode together next the monks, and then the 2 secretaries Sir Edmond Peckham and Sir (Robert) Freston, Cofferer to the Queen of England; and then my Lord Admiral, my Lord Darcy of Essex, and many knights and gentlemen ... afore her servants, and after her banner of arms;

and then her gentlemen and her head officers; and then her chariot with 8 banners of arms of diverse arms, and 4 banners of images of white taffeta, wrought with fine gold and her arms.[35]

This lengthy train of mourners went by Saint James's Palace,[36]

> ...and so to Charring Cross, with a hundred torches burning, and her servants bearing them, and the 12 bed-men of Westminster had new black gowns; and they had 12 torches burning, and IV white branches with arms.

After this large retinue of men came 'ladies and gentlewomen all in black, and horses, and 8 heralds of arms in black, and their horses, and arms said about the hearse behind and before; and 4 heralds bearing the 4 white banners'. Once at Westminster Abbey,

> All did alight and there did received the good Lady my Lord of London and my Lord Abbott in their miters and copes, censing her [with incense], and there men did bear her with a canopy of black velvet, with IV black staffs, and so brought into the hearse and there tarried ... and so there all night with light burning.

Banners of saints were held aloft around Anna's coffin as it was brought into Westminster. All the men took off their hoods before entering the church. A Mass was given there for Anna:

> The IV day of August was the mass of requiem for my Lady Princess of Cleves, and daughter to [Johann III of Cleves and sister to Wilhelm] Duke of Cleves; and there my Lord Abbott of Westminster made a godly sermon as ever was made, and [then] ... the Bishop of London sang mass in his miter; [and after] mass my Lord Bishop and my Lord Abbott mitered did cense the corpse; and afterward she was carried to her tomb, [where] she lies with a hearse-cloth of gold, the which lies [over her]; and there all her head officers broke their staffs, [and all] her ushers broke their rods, and all they cast them into her tomb; the which was covered her corpse with black, and all the lords and ladies and knights and gentlemen and gentlewomen did offer, and after mass a great [dinner] at my Lord Abbott's; and my Lady of Winchester was the chief mourner, and my Lord Admiral and my Lord Darcy of either side of my Lady of Winchester, and so they went in order to dinner.

---

35 A seventeenth-century depiction of Anna's funeral train is printed on the half-title and title pages of this book.

36 St. James's Palace may have originally been intended as a residence for Anna when she was Queen Consort. Cromwell employed an artist, most likely Holbein the Younger, to decorate or design the decoration of the ceiling of the Chapel Royal with Anna's and Henry's coats of arms, with references to the United Duchies.

Despite any falling out that Anna and Mary had early in Mary's reign, Mary gave Anna an extravagant funeral. Her property was later distributed as per her will, including jewels sent to her still-living brother Duke Wilhelm V and younger sister Amalia in the United Duchies. Shortly after Anna's death, her youngest niece was born.

The Last Daughter of Jülich-Cleves-Berg Is Born

Sibylle entered the world on 26 August 1557 in Cleves. No doubt named after her aunt Sybylla, Duchess Consort of Saxony, Sibylle was the last of her siblings to marry and was extremely influential at court in the 1590s. No stranger to intrigue, she is believed to have been heavily involved in the curious fate of one of her sisters-in-law, as will be seen later.

Death of Charles V and a Change in Religious Influence

Charles V abdicated the throne of Holy Roman Emperor in favour of his brother Ferdinand in August 1556. For Wilhelm, having his father-in-law as the most powerful person in Christendom after the Pope was a welcome change from Charles V. Ferdinand was less harsh in enforcing Catholicism throughout the Holy Roman Empire, which allowed Protestantism to quietly wax throughout Germany.

In the United Duchies, Wilhelm appointed Protestant court preachers including Gerhard Veltius, from the Netherlands, and Nicolaus Rollius. Protestant preachers remained present at the court of the United Duchies from 1558 to roughly 1566, and did take part in teaching Wilhelm's children. This Protestant influence, combined with Amalia's own impact, had a lasting effect on Wilhelm's daughters.

Wilhelm gave the appearance of at least not wishing to persecute those who practised Protestantism. Beginning in Easter 1558, Wilhelm took Holy Communion in both the Catholic and Protestant forms. The last time he had done this was in 1541, when he was openly antagonising Charles V over the Duchy of Guelders.

Wilhelm took both forms of communion over the next several years, but never formally declared himself a Protestant. It could be that he was curious about Protestant teachings, or partially supported some of them. However, as part of the Treaty of Venlo from 1543 and subsequent involvement with Charles V, Wilhelm was prohibited from being anything other than Catholic.

Despite not being openly against Protestantism, Wilhelm reviled some of the sects that splintered off from the main body of Protestant thought. The Anabaptists, against whom Wilhelm's family fought in the 1530s, were still around. The Calvinists, viewed as another group of religious extremists, were slowly gaining ground within the United Duchies. Neither sect ever became a serious issue in the territory, however.

The False Anna

In late 1558 to early 1559, a woman claiming to be Anna, Daughter of Cleves appeared at the court of Duke John Frederick the Middle in Weimar. The woman's likeness to a portrait of Anna in John Frederick's possession was unmistakable, possibly including the scar on Anna's forehead from Sybylla throwing scissors at her when they were children. The woman had an interesting tale for John Frederick.

In December 1558, John Frederick received a letter from a woman styling herself as the Duchess of Aybelen. The woman asked that he send a discreet, trustworthy person to where she was staying in Eckartsberga, roughly 15 miles from Weimar. The woman had news about Anna of Cleves and her real fate, but she dared not put it in a letter where the information could be intercepted. Intrigued, John Frederick sent a couple of horsemen on 20 December 1558 to meet with the Duchess of Aybelen.

Seeing that she had piqued John Frederick's interest, the Duchess of Aybelen demanded to speak with him in person. John Frederick declined, but sent his personal secretary instead. The Duchess of Aybelen agreed to give her information to the secretary so that it could be relayed to John Frederick.

The Duchess of Aybelen claimed to have been imprisoned in England for an undisclosed reason at an undisclosed place, but managed to escape in early 1558 by climbing down a rope she dangled out the window and then making for the next boat out of England. The one upon which she managed to gain passage was sailing to Danzig. It just so happened that Anna of Cleves, who herself had recently escaped a nunnery in England, was on the same ship. Both women were granted passage to Danzig by the King of Poland. However, the Duchess of Aybelen was burgled while staying overnight somewhere around Warsaw, losing roughly 8 tons of gold. Several of the woman's servants either perished or were brutally injured in the burglary. She herself escaped in her shift, and sought refuge in Krakow for three months.

The woman then relayed that she decided to seek out John Frederick's court. She told of how she had to pawn some of her belongings in Wittenberg. The Duchess of Aybelen then told of how Anna was in Germany, and that she brought an awesome load of English treasure with her. Aside from the crown and sceptre of England, Anna brought with her costly jewels, garments, necklaces, chains, caps, girdles and so on, amounting to roughly 35,000–40,000 gold crowns in value.

The Duchess of Aybelen continued that Anna once saved a merchant, who was now ferrying Anna's treasures for her. This merchant was known to facilitate business between the Kingdom of England and the Fuggers, a powerful banking family from Augsburg. The Duchess of Aybelen was supposed to retrieve the treasure, which Anna had willed to her nephews by her sister Sybylla. Anna herself was tied up in France trying to negotiate a marriage between a French princess and John Frederick, oblivious that

John Frederick had just married. The duchess showed Anna's gold signet ring, as well.

After telling her tale, she retired to a lodging in Rossla. John Frederick's secretary returned to court and gave the entire story to John Frederick.

John Frederick immediately accepted the woman's story, and sent fine food and wine to her. His chancellor went to the pawnbroker in Wittenberg to retrieve the Duchess of Aybelen's things. John Frederick decided to meet the duchess in person. A short time later, he held an interview with her.

At this interview, the woman declared that she was truly Anna von der Mark, Queen of England. John Frederick was overjoyed. He sent word to his younger brother, John William, who was serving in the French army along with John Frederick the Younger, to tell him about the woman. She did bear a striking resemblance to Anna of Cleves.

Days later, John Frederick received a letter from Leipzig. The letter talked about a woman in Rossla known to have tricked several other German nobles, including the Elector of Brandenburg. John Frederick assumed it was sent from England to dissuade him from assisting his aunt. He paid the information no mind, especially because this Anna promised John Frederick the kingly sum of 5 tons of gold. She was the Queen of England, after all. Somehow, Anna's wealth grew from 5 tons to 20 tons of gold in a very short time.

On 15 January 1559, two days before John Frederick's thirtieth birthday, he sent Anna a ring, accompanied by a letter from John Frederick's new wife, Elisabeth von der Pfalz. He further gave to Anna her own court, and the castle of Grimmenstein. Grimmenstein was later replaced by the baroque palace of Friedenstein, which still stands today.

The supposed Queen Anna borrowed money from any courtier who would let her, and used the signet ring in her possession to seal her official documents. Particularly, Anna used it to seal the papers leaving all her money and jewels to John Frederick the Middle and John William, but practically left out John Frederick the Younger. She left to him the comparably paltry sum of 500,000 crowns out of the 20 tons she was leaving her older nephews.

This Queen Anna, so bountiful was her largesse, invited Amalia von der Mark, the youngest of the Cleves siblings, to join her at Grimmenstein. Amalia was still, at the age of forty-two, unmarried. On top of that, Amalia stood to inherit gold from this Anna, 2 tons' worth.

Queen Anna's next move was to tell John Frederick about all the powerful people who owed her money. John Frederick, whose coffers were not as full as he would have liked, was entranced by Queen Anna's wealth. He was happy to help her call in her various debtors, as he had grown eager to see physical evidence of Anna's wealth. She claimed that the City of Nuremberg owed her a ton of gold. John Frederick sent a member of his court to call in the debt, and the man was laughed right out of the city. At that point, John Frederick finally became suspicious.

John Frederick continued to send Anna cordial, familiar letters. He made sure eyes were kept on this woman claiming to be his aunt.

By the time late June 1559 came around, John Frederick had word from John William. The latter was in Paris and had looked into the matter of the Duchess of Aybelen. He was able to learn that, at most, this woman was a lady-in-waiting to their beloved aunt. Challenged, Queen Anna responded by insisting that she dash off a letter to the King of France, endorsing the match between John Frederick and the king's daughter. John Frederick declined, though he was surely grateful for the gesture.

Duke Wilhelm of Jülich-Cleves-Berg, brother and living sibling of the true Anna, decided he'd had enough. He sent an ambassador to John Frederick's court to put an end to things. The woman claiming to be Queen Anna was examined by three jurists. Initially, she continued to state that she was who she said she was. No one believed her. She was moved to Tannenberg Castle, which was more of a fortress. The additional pressure forced the woman to change her story. She was not truly Anna von der Mark, but a Countess of Friesland. Duke Wilhelm was told the new tale, which he still did not believe.

Her next tale included an element wherein she was brought to England and introduced to Anna. She joined Anna's court there. Wilhelm remained unimpressed. The executioner of Jena was brought in to continue questioning the woman, who claimed she was visited by the devil and given hallucinations by him.

The woman's lies became even more extravagant, to the point where she claimed to be an illegitimate sister of the Von der Mark siblings. She stated that their father, Johann III, arranged for her to have an honourable marriage and granted money for her dower. After the death of her husband, she went to England, where she was introduced to Anna and joined her court. Anna, upon seeing the woman with her own eyes and being assured of the woman's breeding by a peculiarity of the big toe, was certain that the woman was her half-sister. The woman's big toe curled under the neighbouring toe, as did Anna's, Sybylla's and Johann III's, according to the woman. The real Anna allegedly saw a similarity in their features, too. She very well could have been one of Anna's illegitimate cousins who joined Anna in England, and about whom Harst complained. This was sufficient proof for Anna to embrace the woman and invite her into service in England.

Another desperate lie was that the woman was the incestuous product of a union between Anna's father Johann and sister Sybylla.

Wilhelm was unmoved. He acknowledged that Johann, their father, had two illegitimate daughters, but by 1559 one was dead and the other in a nunnery. Mentioned above, Elisabeth of Cleves, grandmother-in-law of Olisleger, passed away in 1554. Additionally, Wilhelm cross-checked the woman's claim that Johann provided a dowry for her. No such expenditure was recorded in Johann's accounts. The woman was put to the rack.

By 10 October 1559, Wilhelm still refused to acknowledge the imposter as an illegitimate half-sister. The woman was kept at Tannenberg Castle, presumably until her death. It is possible that she was an illegitimate sibling of the Von der Marks. It was even more plausible that she attended Anna in England. She did possess Anna's signet ring, or a very good likeness. The ultimate fate, and identity, of the False Anna is unknown.

The Von der Marks at the End of the 1550s

The Von der Mark dynasty experienced loss throughout the 1550s, in some ways changing the trajectory of the family. At first, the joy over Johann Friedrich's release was a wonderful balm for Sybylla's heart. Unfortunately, she had been ill for some time and was not going to get better. Her death in 1554, swiftly followed by Johann Friedrich's, lessened whatever connection Anna, Wilhelm and Amalia had with Saxony. True, Wilhelm maintained contact with his Saxon nephews, but that is not the same as having the ear of his sister.

Anna's last few years in England saw her continue to stay away from court. She was implicated in a very serious uprising, although later forgiven. She enjoyed the friendship of Mary I, to whom she was vaguely related because of Wilhelm's Habsburg marriage. Reflecting Anna's status as a Princess of Cleves and, as Henry VIII's adopted sister, an honorary Princess of England, Mary gave Anna a funeral worthy of her status.

Amalia must have been slightly relieved, if not outright happy, that Wilhelm welcomed Protestant preachers to court. She was likely even more delighted that her brother was taking both forms of communion, which would have allowed Amalia to observe Protestantism and take communion how she wished. She might have even had a sliver of hope that Wilhelm would eschew his agreements with the departed Charles V and heartily embrace Protestantism.

Wilhelm was in much better standing with the reigning Holy Roman Emperor at the end of the 1550s than at the beginning. Of course, it helped that his father-in-law was the new Emperor. Wilhelm had a son, his health and a reasonably bright future.

13

The United Duchies and the Holy Roman Empire in the 1560s

Wilhelm's Religious Sympathies

Wilhelm expressed respect for the articles of the Augsburg Confession, which later became the foundational documents for the Lutheran religion. He also had an interest in continuing to reform religion within the United Duchies. He was quite cautious, however, to avoid creating – or giving the appearance of creating – a religious sect. Wilhelm was treading the line between Catholicism and Protestantism as gently as he could during the first part of the 1560s. He wanted to reform Catholicism, and was interested in what the Protestant leaders at his court had to say. This is in line with his father Johann III's *via media* approach from forty years earlier.

Death, Doubt and Birth

Sadly, Duke Wilhelm and his wife Maria lost one of their children while she was still very young. Little Elisabeth of Jülich-Cleves-Berg died in 1561. She was roughly five years old, and it is thought she died from disease as opposed to accident. Elisabeth was the only child born to Wilhelm and Maria who did not survive to adulthood.

Duke Wilhelm and Maria did not have any other children after the birth of Sibylle in 1557 until the 1560s. Maria had given birth to six children between June 1550 and August 1557, no doubt leaving her feeling exhausted. She grew more melancholy after Sibylle's birth, and by the early 1560s openly doubted the validity of her marriage to Wilhelm. This caused a great deal of consternation and concern for Wilhelm, who might have called to mind his former brother-in-law Henry VIII of England's struggle with the validity of his marriage to Katharine of Aragon.

Maria fixated on the idea that Wilhelm's first marriage to Jeanne d'Albret was never properly annulled. Whether Maria came upon this idea from her own ruminations or whether it was put to her by someone else, it became a serious concern of hers for a period during 1560 and 1561. There was some basis to her concern, given that the Pope merely sent a letter announcing the annulment between Wilhelm and Jeanne rather than a Papal Bull or any other more official document. However, Maria was a Habsburg, and would be the niece, daughter, sister and aunt of the Holy Roman Emperor, through Charles V, Ferdinand I, Maximilian II and Rudolf II respectively. It was highly unlikely that anyone was going to put Maria or her children in a bad position, let alone make any offspring of a Habsburg illegitimate. There was the additional issue of the United Duchies slipping out of the Habsburg family's grasp, which simply was not going to be allowed. Aside from possible political issues for the Habsburgs, Wilhelm felt there was no impediment to his marriage with Maria and believed their children to be legitimate.

Whatever Maria's misgivings, she was pregnant again by late 1561. Wilhelm was somewhat sickly around the time when the child was conceived, and Maria was still in the throes of melancholy. Otherwise, her pregnancy and the birth of her child was unremarkable. On 29 May 1562, Wilhelm and Maria welcomed their last child into the world. They named their little boy Johann Wilhelm, possibly after his Von der Mark grandfather Johann III and Jülich grandfather William. The little boy, as the second son, was destined for a life dedicated to the Church. He, too, would be brought up adhering strictly to Catholicism, as was part of the agreement made between Duke Wilhelm and Charles V well before Johann Wilhelm's birth.

Death of Ferdinand I

Holy Roman Emperor Ferdinand I, Duke Wilhelm's father-in-law, died in Vienna on 25 July 1564. He served as Holy Roman Emperor for almost eight years, having succeeded his brother Charles V. A couple of years before his death, Ferdinand fought to have his son and Wilhelm's brother-in-law Maximilian made King of the Romans-Germans. Maximilian was successfully elected King of the Romans-Germans, and thus Emperor Elect, in November 1562. He promised to uphold Catholicism but was willing to fully recognise the Augsburg Confession as legitimate. This was a degree of radicalism that went farther than any of the three prior Reformation emperors. When Ferdinand died, Maximilian became Holy Roman Emperor Maximilian II.

Hambach Castle

Wilhelm renovated and repaired Hambach Castle between 1558 and 1565. It was badly damaged decades before, in 1512. A fire had started in the castle's *Schneiderzimmer*, or tailor's room. The castle had a defective chimney. The room in which firewood for the castle was stored was right underneath the

Schneiderzimmer. When the chimney plate in the *Schneiderzimmer* failed, sparks fell into the room below and directly onto the firewood. The stored firewood caught fire, as could be expected. The large fire then made its way to a store of gunpowder, worsening things considerably. Eighteen people died because the castle was not laid out very well in terms of escape routes. The building sustained tremendous damage, and its initial restoration was not completed until 1537.

Wilhelm's renovation, finished in 1565, was Renaissance in style. It was one of the many projects for which he hired the architect Alessandro Pasqualini. Upon completion, Wilhelm commonly used the castle as his hunting lodge.

A Note on Amalia of Cleves

Amalia of Cleves, probably born on 17 October 1517, is the most elusive of the Von der Mark siblings. She may have been born as late as 14 November 1517, according to the chronicler Gert van der Schuren, but was definitely born at some point between mid-October and mid-November. Either date is realistic when one considers that her elder brother was born 28 July 1516. Unlike their elder sister Anna of Cleves, whose birthday was erroneously held to be 21 or 22 September 1515 until a chronicle by Johann Wassenberch revealed her true date of birth as 28 June 1515, their mother Maria's obstetric history would allow for Amalia to be a full-term healthy baby regardless of whether she was born in October or November 1517. Wassenberch recorded the dates of birth for Sybylla, Anna and Wilhelm, but stopped recording shortly before Amalia's birth. It is thought that the chronicler died from plague, which was infecting Duisburg in autumn 1517.

Very little is directly recorded about Amalia, with whatever letters she may have written lost. Her behaviour and personality are mostly reflected in what is noted about her interactions with Duke Wilhelm and his family. She was perceived late in the reign of Henry VIII of England and early in the reign of his son Edward VI as being too Lutheran to marry, and indeed she never did. Whether her strong faith was the true reason for Amalia never having a husband, or if it was because of the vacillating politics of the United Duchies, is unclear. She appears to have spent her later years at the Swan Castle in Cleves for the most part, away from the hustle and bustle of Düsseldorf unless she was needed.

Fortunately, there is a small book owned by a courtier that still survives and shows Amalia's interests. It might even give some insight into why she never married, although that mystery will likely never be completely solved. The Staatsbibilothek in Berlin possesses a collection of poetry, written in at least five different hands. The book contains five spiritual songs, all dedicated to the Virgin Mary. There are twenty-seven love songs, interspersed with short poems or rhymes. One of the poems, in Amalia's handwriting, is about longing for a beloved. Amalia of Cleves' signature can be seen after this poem. The book itself was broken up in the nineteenth century but was mostly reassembled in the twentieth century. The bulk of the book is held in Berlin, with a few leaves in Frankfurt.

The aforementioned courtier, Katharina von Hatzfeld, wrote in the book as well. In the front, she wrote, 'Kathryn van Hatzfeld owns this book, God give her honour and goodness, and give her what she desires because she deserves every possibility.' Katharina's husband was the godfather of little Elisabeth of Jülich-Cleves-Berg, who died young. Katharina was the original owner of the book before it passed into Amalia's ownership. As a matter of historical curiosity, Katharina wrote down her laundry list in the back of the notebook. It is a rare glimpse into the more mundane aspects of day-to-day early modern life.

It seems obvious from the presence of both women's handwriting in the leather-bound book that they were close. It has been assumed, or at least has not been discounted, that Amalia had romantic feelings for Katharina. Amalia remained unmarried her whole life, and there was the poetic content of this book which might have reflected Amalia's feelings for another woman. The poem 'Song about Longing', written in Amalia's hand, reads,

> My heart, courage and mind are troubled
> Probably now for this new year.
> My hope still carries me
> And mustn't reveal it
> That I am so upset
> Hidden in secret love.
>
> That I must avoid you dear girl
> brings me secret pain
> is a heavy repentance to my heart
> and hurts me from the heart,
> So, I live in hope
> That my grief will turn.
>
> I wait for the time to go on
> My heart with all bitterness,
> And heal my wounded heart,
> Help us both.
> To you, my esteemed, good-bye and good night,
> I have to part with you now.

The poem is signed 'Ammellya, Hereditary Duchess of Cleves, Jülich, and Berg'. While the poem overtly expresses feelings for a woman and is written in Amalia's handwriting, that does not mean she is the author of the poem. It could be that, like at the English court, it was fashionable for women to record poetry heard there. Mary Howard, Duchess of Richmond kept such a book, which is now in the possession of the British Library. Mary

Howard's book contains poetry by no fewer than nine people, and is a major source for the poetry of Sir Thomas Wyatt. It is possible that Amalia merely wrote down a poem that was popular at the Cleves court. On the other hand, Amalia's eldest sister Sybylla and their brother Wilhelm were known to write poems, so it is certainly possible that the poem in Amalia's hand came from her.

Perhaps Amalia did have genuine romantic feelings for Katharina. Katharina's life is much more obscure than Amalia's, but it is certain that she was roughly twenty years younger than Amalia. The two women were cousins, and spent much of their time together in the *Frauenzimmer*. Although more research is needed, it is rumoured that at one point the behaviour between the two women was considered inappropriate. The precise nature of this behaviour is not recorded, but it resulted in Katharina moving away from court. The extent of the relationship between the two, and any possible romantic feelings, will never be known. Thankfully, the two women were some of a handful of people at court in the United Duchies who recorded poetry that was popular or created there.

Another poem, wherein a woman complains about her husband, can be found in the book. It is unknown if the poem was in the book before or after it was given to Amalia. It is called 'A Wife's Complaint':

> I complain very much, do I, poor woman,
> scratching my proud body.
> The fleas bite me,
> I'm tearing my robe.
> If only I knew a friend
> who could drive that away from me.
>
> I would give everything for that!
> My husband lies like a stump
> does not help me crush the fleas,
> lies in his shoes at night
> just like a dirty pig,
> himself done from wine.
>
> Oh god, how am I going to take it at home?
> My husband, who lives in awe,
> he comes crawling home at midnight.
> He stinks of wine,
> He also stinks from his maw,
> In bed, he's lazy.
>
> I don't enjoy him
> because he drinks so much
> to his breaking point.

If I lay on a pinnacle
and fall into the Rhine
that would be a great pleasure for me.

When he dies in pain
I would make up my mind
to put after a boy,
that made me amuse myself with displeasure,
who drove my fleas away,
I would stay with him.

It is certainly a remarkable insight into a woman's thoughts on marriage in the sixteenth century!

Amalia's favourite book was the Bible. The Von der Mark girls read a version of the Bible that was translated into German. Amalia lived most of her life at the Swan Castle in Cleves and less so at the Ducal Palace in Düsseldorf. She died there on 1 March 1586 at the age of sixty-eight. Amalia converted to Lutheranism, and the Pope referred to her as *miserabilis Lutherana*, miserable Lutheran woman. She raised her four surviving nieces – Maria Eleonore, Magdalena, Anne and Sibylle – to be Lutherans. Maria Eleonore and Anne married Lutherans, after which Duke Wilhelm hoped he could convert his sister and remaining two unwed daughters to at least participate in Mass, if not fully to Catholicism. To that end, Amalia was a thorn in Wilhelm's side. Regardless of his true feelings about the faith, and though he himself flirted with Lutheranism, he was to remain Catholic, and his sons were Catholic.

Amalia herself observed the Lutheran faith and was unwilling to allow her nieces to adhere to Catholicism. Her dedication to Lutheranism so enraged Wilhelm at one point that he drew his sword and went after her. But for the quick thinking of a servant who shut the door in Wilhelm's face, things could have turned grim for Amalia quite quickly.

Wilhelm's Great Illness

The summer after Hambach Castle was restored, another Imperial diet was called at Augsburg. On his way to the diet, Duke Wilhelm experienced his first stroke or seizure. He recovered quickly, with little difficulty. Wilhelm, whose birthday was in late July, was roughly fifty years old.

Unfortunately, Wilhelm would go on to have another dozen strokes or seizures. His second stroke was on 30 September 1566. He was en route from Bensberg via Benrath, on his return trip to Düsseldorf. This one was much worse than the first, paralysing his tongue and right hand.

The exact cause of the strokes or seizures is unknown. It is possible that they were brought on by high fevers. Wilhelm was very ill around the time that Johann Wilhelm was conceived, suffering from fevers. It is anyone's guess as to the exact nature of what caused Wilhelm's fevers in the early 1560s, or whether those led to Wilhelm having either seizures or a series of strokes. Whatever the cause, Wilhelm suffered from these attacks mostly during the late 1560s and throughout the 1570s.

As a result of the attacks, Wilhelm experienced occasional mental and physical paralysis. Eventually, he became paralysed on the left side and his speech was permanently slurred. He would randomly fall asleep at inappropriate times, too. No regency was ever officially established, so it seems that Wilhelm still retained his mental acuity for the most part. However, during the last few years that Wilhelm was alive he ruled with great difficulty and was very paranoid about his heir overthrowing him.

The severity of Wilhelm's debilitation is reflected in a portrait by Johan Malthain completed in 1591. It shows Wilhelm, by then roughly seventy-five years old, in Spanish dress. His head is cocked severely to his right side, his mouth almost in a grimace. A large cape covers his upper body, making it difficult to tell what else was impacted by his episodes. Given that portraits of the time were meant to be flattering, one can imagine that Wilhelm's appearance was much ghastlier than what is seen in the 1591 portrait.

Wilhelm's crypt was opened in 1954, and an examination of his body performed by Dr Heinz Schweitzer. Schweitzer discovered that Wilhelm's spine was impacted by an osteoporotic collapse. This, combined with compression of his spine, would have made sitting and standing quite painful.

The United Duchies and the Dutch Revolt

The Dutch Revolt began in the same year in which Duke Wilhelm was stricken with episodes of illness. In 1566, the revolt began with acts of iconoclasm in the Westkwartier in modern-day Groningen, Netherlands. Calvinism grew deep roots in the area, and the people were tired of the very Catholic Philip II of Spain forcing his religion on them. The iconoclasm, or destruction of religious images, was a violent demonstration of anti-Catholic and anti-Philip II sentiment.

Philip II and his father Charles V had very much been in the habit of hunting down and destroying heretics. By the 1560s, a large group of lesser nobles was able to convince, or gently coerce, Margaret of Parma, Philip II's Regent of the Netherlands,[37] to capitulate to the Dutch nobles' desire for peace and freedom from persecution, which resulted in Margaret suspending heresy laws. Dutch governmental leaders experienced the violent, radical Anabaptist insurgency of 1534–35, and saw a distinction between the violent Anabaptists and those simply disagreeing with Catholicism. Many of the

---

37 Margaret of Parma was the illegitimate daughter of Charles V and Johanna Maria von der Gheynst. She was acknowledged in 1529, at the age of seven years, as Charles V's daughter and became known as Margaret of Austria. She grew up in Italy at the Medici court. She married Alessandro de' Medici when she was thirteen. She was left a widow at the age fifteen, and married Ottavio Farnese, Duke of Parma and the Pope's nephew, in 1538. She was sixteen and he was fourteen. Afterward, she became known as Margaret of Parma.

dissenters were members of the lesser nobility. On top of that, enforcement of anti-heresy laws in the Netherlands had more or less dropped off by the end of the 1550s. Many of the iconoclasts who acted in August 1566 believed they were acting on behalf of the local nobility. For a time after the August iconoclasm, the idea of religious peace spread throughout most of the Netherlandish provinces. Unfortunately, the peace was not to last, and Philip II took action to oust the heretics.

The iconoclastic riots started with a man attacking a little chapel by Steenvoorde. The chapel was dedicated to St Lawrence, and was attacked on his feast day of 10 August by a Calvinist preacher and some of his followers. After preaching a sermon, the group entered the church and destroyed whatever paintings and statues of religious figures they could find.

The idea that religious imagery was popish, violative of the second commandment and decidedly pro-Catholic and pro-Spanish was common in anti-Catholic and anti-Spanish Netherlands. Little escaped the iconoclasts' reach, and they destroyed baptismal fonts, vestments, and liturgical books, not just decorative elements.

The iconoclasm of 1566 in the Netherlands was carried out by an organised group of religious rioters following the direction of their preachers. The attacks were coordinated events, not random happenings. Several of the iconoclasts worked in draperies or were artisans –shoemakers, innkeepers, clothmakers and chairmakers, even some civil servants. Jobs related to draperies were swiftly losing their earning capacity due to poor trade agreements between Philip II, hereditary overlord of the Burgundian Circle, and Elizabeth I's England, which produced much of the wool used in the Netherlands.

Further iconoclasm endured through 1572 and 1573, when rebel armies killed priests in the provinces of Zeeland and Holland. Convents were plundered and Church property was continuously seized. In 1573, Catholicism was banned. Book burnings led by Calvinists regularly took place from 1577 to 1585 in major cities. The Catholics still in the Netherlands passively stood by as this happened.

Religious Formalities in the United Duchies

On 7 January 1567, a great delegation of officials met to finalise the concept of a *via media* religious reform within the United Duchies that was first put forward back in 1532. William of Ketteler, Bishop of Münster was the driving force, along with Konrad Heresbach and Olisleger, for finishing what Johann III had started. The leaders were all heavily influenced by Erasmus. The delegation included the aforementioned dignitaries, plus members of the clergy, noblemen, knights, scholars, the Duchy of Jülich's full council, Wilhelm's paternal cousin Franz von Waldeck, and William of Orange-Nassau's brother Johann.

Two weeks later, the group completed its deliberations. They agreed upon a reformed Catholicism, and created a new catechism to be adopted by the churches within the United Duchies. The *via media* was complete. Unfortunately, the new reformed religion did not please everyone at court. The Lutherans, like Amalia of Cleves, who adhered to the tenants of the Augsburg Confession, were not interested in going back to any form of religion that smacked of popery. The staunch Catholics were unimpressed, and did not wish to reform their religion at all. Several of the important courtiers of the United Duchies, like Werner von Gymnich, the tutor of Wilhelm's son and heir Karl Friedrich, and William von Orsbeck, Chancellor of Jülich, were themselves Roman Catholic and did not support the proposed changes.

After the changes, Wilhelm sent envoys to Brussels to speak with Margaret of Parma. They were to plead for leniency toward the Protestant rebels. In general, Philip brought back the Inquisition of the Netherlands with a vengeance. The Inquisition of the Netherlands was different from the Spanish Inquisition in that it was led by a single person and not a group, and was not active for anywhere near as long a period as the Spanish Inquisition. However, the Inquisition of the Netherlands was still brutal and merciless. Margaret, who herself adopted a *via media*, was powerless to insist on some mercy for the rebels. Her half-brother Philip II of Spain was unimpressed with how she was governing the Low Countries.

On 19 May 1567, the procession of Corpus Christi was banned in the Duchy of Jülich by the Protestants. This officially pulled Jülich into the Dutch Revolt. In response, the influence of the pro-Catholic faction at court grew. The United Duchies was at a crossroads: join with the Protestant Dutch and throw off the varying degrees of Habsburg influence, or remain in line with the 1543 Treaty of Venlo and subsequent treaties, keeping Jülich-Cleves-Berg safe.

Overall, this was not the right time for Duke Wilhelm to officially tamper with religion. Aside from the brewing Dutch Revolt, Wilhelm's health and mental acuity were constantly under threat resulting from his episodes of stroke or seizure over the last several years. With the Spanish on their doorstep, it was feared by Wilhelm's advisors that his surviving four daughters and two sons could be taken away by Philip II of Spain or Emperor Maximilian II. On top of that, the ferocious Duke of Alba, Fernando Álvarez de Toledo y Pimentel, was coming to replace Margaret of Parma as Regent of the Netherlands.

For the United Duchies, the Dutch Revolt meant the infusion of Spanish troops in their backyard. Fernando Álvarez de Toledo y Pimentel, 3rd Duke of Alba, was just the general for the job. The Duke of Alba enjoyed a very long military career, including serving Charles V at the Battle of Mühlberg. In Philip II's mind, his half-sister Margaret of Parma was not able to control the rebellious Protestant element in the Netherlands. Philip installed the Duke of Alba as Regent of the Low Countries in 1567. The Duke of Alba and his huge army arrived in August 1567, and ousted Margaret of Parma in September 1567.

The councils of Jülich-Berg and Cleves-Mark met in October 1567 to discuss the situation brewing at their doorstep. It was decided that no further changes in support of the Church orders from 1532 would be made. Calvinists, who were seen as the main aggressors in the Netherlands, would be expelled from the United Duchies.

William of Orange-Nassau

William of Orange-Nassau fled the Netherlands after the Duke of Alba arrived in autumn 1567. He did not agree with Philip II's immediate, violent persecution of the Protestants in the Netherlands, and so went to his castle in Dillenburg, south-east of the United Duchies and part of modern-day Germany. His castle in Breda was confiscated by the Duke of Alba under the pretence that he was a traitor.

In April 1568, a Dutch delegation visited William of Orange at Dillenburg. Other nobles who were seen by Philip II as traitors had already been executed in the hopes that this would put down the Dutch rebellion. Unfortunately, it only added fuel to the fire. It was hoped that William would help the rebels and resist Spain.

On 20 April 1568, William of Orange sent roughly 3,000 troops to storm the city of Roermond. Part of Guelders, Roermond had been officially under Habsburg control since the 1543 Treaty of Venlo. It was a strategically important city. Orange's troops were intercepted by the Duke of Alba's in the German city of Rheindahlen, which was west of Düsseldorf.

Rheindahlen in the Duchy of Jülich became the first theatre for the Dutch Eighty Years War. Orange's rebel army crossed into Jülich on 20 April 1568. The Duke of Alba's Spanish troops intercepted them on 25 April 1568, leading to the Battle of Dahlen. The rebels were comprehensively crushed by the Spanish troops. Unfortunately for Duke Wilhelm, the Spanish troops did not care that he had declared Jülich-Cleves-Berg neutral. Rheindahlen's hinterland was looted by the Spanish, their troops were billeted in the homes there and horses were taken from the citizenry.

At the same time, the council for the Duchy of Jülich declared on 28 April 1568 that no further action would be taken toward reforming religion for the time being. Once proceedings over religious reform were suspended in Jülich, the most powerful of the United Duchies, further reform was effectively abandoned for the rest of Duke Wilhelm's long reign. He himself turned strongly back toward Roman Catholicism, and his heir Karl Friedrich continued under the tutelage of Werner von Gymnich.

Unfortunately, none of his efforts saved Jülich from destruction. The damage done to Rheindahlen was expensive, and Duke Wilhelm was stuck with the cost. Wilhelm sanctioned the clipping of his coins for several years so as to make the treasury's money stretch further, temporarily debasing his currency. Neither Philip II nor the Duke of Alba had any particular sympathy for Wilhelm, and they were more concerned with stopping the Dutch from continuing their rebellion. For the rest of the sixteenth century, Duke Wilhelm and his heir contested with the rapacious Spanish soldiers in the hinterlands of Jülich-Cleves-Berg.

14

Karl Friedrich, the Pride of the United Duchies

By 1570, Duke Wilhelm was firmly Catholic again. Both of his sons Karl Friedrich and Johann Wilhelm regularly attended Mass with him. However, his four surviving daughters, who spent much of their time with their aunt Amalia, were evangelicals at least or out-and-out Lutherans. Only the youngest, Sibylle, was recorded as a Catholic much later in her life.

In 1571, at the tender age of nine, Johann Wilhelm was sent to St Viktor's in Xanten to begin his religious career. This was a very common fate for spare sons, not only in the Holy Roman Empire but across western Europe. Johann Wilhelm was eventually destined for the Bishopric of Münster, where his paternal cousins lived.

Duke Wilhelm's elder son, Karl Friedrich, turned fifteen and was full of promise. Karl Friedrich needed a new tutor, having been under the instruction of the very Catholic Werner von Gymnich. Stephanus Winandus Pighius was mentioned as a possibility to Duke Wilhelm. Steven Winand Pigge, who later latinized his name to Stephanus Pighius, was born in the Netherlands in roughly 1520. His maternal uncle was the famous theologian Albertus Pighius. Stephanus likely wanted to take advantage of his relative's renown when he latinized his own name.

Stephanus Pighius's Life before the United Duchies

Pighius began his studies in Utrecht before moving to Loewen in 1540. He obtained his doctorate at Loewen in 1543. By 1548, Pighius was working as a secretary for the Vatican in Rome. Specifically, he was the secretary for Cardinal Marcello Cervini, who was elected Pope in April 1555 with the regnal name Marcellus II. Pope Marcellus II served for only three weeks before he died, leaving Pighius without employment. He promptly left Rome and returned home.

After returning home, Pighius was able to secure a position with Cardinal Antoine Perronet von Granvelle, Bishop of Arras, in Brussels. Granvelle had been instrumental in negotiating the marriage between Karl Friedrich's cousins Mary I of England and Philip II of Spain, moving to Italy in 1566 at the behest of Philip II to rule as Viceroy of Naples and leaving Pighius in Brussels. Pighius worked for Granvelle from around 1556 to 1570. He frequently complained of not being paid enough or in a timely fashion. However, his experience in Rome and his connections to the Imperial-endorsed Granvelle made Pighius an attractive candidate for Karl Friedrich's tutor.

Pighius first came to Duke Wilhelm's attention in the autumn of 1570. He was finally summoned by Wilhelm in August the following year. Shortly after he arrived at court in 1571, preparations were made for Karl Friedrich to go on a tour to Vienna and Rome. Maria hoped that such a journey would strengthen family ties with her Habsburg relatives at the Imperial court. There was the added benefit of further refining Karl Friedrich, and giving him an opportunity to practise his linguistic abilities.

Karl Friedrich and Pighius Leave for Vienna

Pighius' main responsibility outside of being Karl Friedrich's tutor was to escort the Von der Mark heir to the Viennese Imperial court, and then on to Rome. Roughly two months after Pighius's arrival, in mid-October 1571 a respectable train led by the Cleves Marshal Werner von Gymnich headed out for Vienna. Gerhard Mercator, the renowned cartographer from Duisburg, created an atlas specifically for the journey. Duke Wilhelm was part of the farewell party, with everyone setting off from Düsseldorf for Bensberg, about 27 miles south-east of Düsseldorf, across the Rhine from Cologne.

Duke Wilhelm, Karl Friedrich and their host left via ship from Bensberg on 20 October 1571. Their destination was Mainz, and it took six days to get there. Once arrived, the group from Jülich-Cleves-Berg was greeted on behalf of Archbishop Daniel Brendel, who was also the Elector of Mainz. The group spent the night at the Kürfurstlichen Schloss, or Elector's Palace, which was updated by Brendel.

The next morning, Duke Wilhelm, Karl Friedrich and company went to the city hall to enjoy breakfast. Afterwards, it was time for Duke Wilhelm to head back to the United Duchies. Duke Wilhelm bade a fond farewell to his favourite son, the shining beacon of the United Duchies' future. Both father and son shed tears during their parting. Wilhelm did not know it was the last time he would ever see his beloved Karl Friedrich.

Several Stops Along the Way

The group headed due east to Aschaffenburg, roughly 43 miles away. After a brief rest, they went south-east to Wertheim. Next was Würzburg, where they crossed the massive bridge over the Main River. They were greeted by the church elders and city magistrate.

In Würzburg, the group partook of a cask of Franconian wine, and were invited to stay in a local guesthouse. Hearing that they were nearby, the bishop invited them to stay at his palace, the Fortress of Marienberg.[38] The elderly bishop took them down to the 'Grotto of Father Bacchus',[39] which presumably could only be reached by descending a set of stairs by torchlight. It housed anywhere between 63,000 and 78,750 litres of the oldest and finest wines, and Karl Friedrich was welcome to select the wines he wished to have at his formal daytime reception. Everyone whiled away the hours with chatting, drinking, eating and generally enjoying the bishop's fine hospitality.

After Würzburg, Karl Friedrich journeyed to Nuremberg, an Imperial Free City. Nuremberg served an administrative purpose within the Holy Roman Empire, and was considered a cultural hub in the fifteenth and sixteenth centuries. Nuremberg lies about 60 miles south-east of Würzburg, and marked the halfway point for the journey to Vienna.

The plan was to stay in Nuremberg for two days. Given the city's wealth and importance to the Holy Roman Empire, there were many sites for the young Karl Friedrich and his entourage to see. For example, the Deep Well, which was hundreds of years old, was considered one of the wonders of the Imperial Castle. There were remarkable gardens, the late twelfth-century chapel and the overall magnificent architecture of the palace. The city leaders of Nuremberg greeted Karl Friedrich with yet more wine, which the sixteen-year-old surely enjoyed. Two members of the city council were chosen to show Karl Friedrich around the city and the extensive palace grounds. Karl Friedrich was also shown the city hall.

By 11 November, Karl Friedrich was welcomed into Regensburg with much fanfare and the blowing of trumpets. Regensburg was another Imperial Free City, but with the added curiosity of its city leadership being comprised of Lutherans. Importantly, Regensburg was on the Danube River, which Karl Friedrich would sail down to reach Vienna. Karl Friedrich wrote to Duke Wilhelm from Regensburg of his adventures so far, including the sites he visited. The stay lasted for three days.

The entourage from Jülich-Cleves-Berg left Regensburg on 14 November 1571. The large ship Karl Friedrich was set to use was impressive, but not as impressive as the ship his father Duke Wilhelm used for the journey to Mainz. Two smaller ships were used to transport the party's provisions, armour and horses.

Karl Friedrich made two stops along the way to Vienna. The first was in Passau, seat of the Bishopric of Passau, so he could see St Stephen's

---

38 One can still see the Marienberg Fortress and the Old Bridge which crosses the Main River.

39 Bacchus being the Roman god of wine and freedom.

Cathedral. The cathedral, originally founded in the eighth century, was in the process of a roughly 200-year update and renovation plan. When Karl Friedrich arrived, the cathedral was about three-quarters of the way done. The second layover, in Linz, was so that the party could rest.

Cleves Marshal Werner von Gymnich cut short his stay in Linz. He wanted to arrive in Vienna before Karl Friedrich so that he could warn the Imperial court of the boy's imminent arrival. A lot of preparations needed to be made, and Gymnich wanted things to go smoothly for both Karl Friedrich and his cousin Archduke Rudolf, Governor of Lower Austria. Rudolf was the son of Holy Roman Emperor Maximilian II and Maximilian's first cousin Maria of Spain. Rudolf eventually followed his father in becoming Holy Roman Emperor.

Karl Friedrich in Vienna

Karl Friedrich, Stephanus Pighius and the rest of the illustrious group from the United Duchies arrived at Vienna on 24 November 1571. They disembarked from the ship at about three o'clock in the afternoon, arranging themselves for the formal entry into Vienna. Once assembled, Karl Friedrich and his parade of 200 horsemen rode across a bridge spanning the Donau River, and into Vienna proper. Again, the heir to the United Duchies was met with much fanfare and the playing of trumpets. They rode all the way to the Hofburg, where the party stayed during their time in Vienna.

Pighius took advantage of the stable palace life by instituting a curriculum for Karl Friedrich: history in the morning, ancient texts in the afternoons. Karl Friedrich was not terribly pleased to be studying once more, with his mind seemingly emptied of new learning as quickly as it was filled.

The entourage from the United Duchies settled into life in Vienna. They spent Christmas there, and the New Year. Spring came, as did Karl Friedrich's seventeenth birthday. He continued learning the skills he would need as the next Duke of Jülich-Cleves-Berg. In Vienna, he had many opportunities to meet and hold discourse with his maternal cousins. Archduke Rudolf was a mere three years older than Karl Friedrich, which hopefully made it easier for the two to get along. Bonding with his powerful Habsburg cousins would only help Karl Friedrich's future success as a leader.

Karl Friedrich enjoyed two major spectacles in Vienna during the year of 1572. The first, a mock sea battle on the Danube, was held on 29 June that year. Called a naumachia, these typically used to-scale war ships, mock armies, pyrotechnics and other combinations of theatrical devices. This naumachia was part of grander celebrations for the feast day of Saints Peter and Paul.

The second event was the crowning of Archduke Rudolf as King of Hungary in Pressburg on 27 September 1572. Pressburg is now known as Bratislava, in modern-day Slovakia. Rudolf, perceived as more of a

Spaniard than anything else, made his new subjects suspicious. His paternal and maternal great-grandparents were Juana of Castile and Philip von Habsburg.[40] Most alienating was that Rudolf spent 1563 to 1571 at the conservative Catholic court in Spain, returning to Austria in mid-1571. The Austrian court was more liberal, and tolerant of divergent religious views. However the Hungarians felt about their new king, the celebrations for his coronation were grand.

Karl Friedrich had a special position in one of the pageants performed for Rudolf's coronation, performing as the masked individual named 'Julius Clivimontius', with 'Julius' sounding similar to Jülich, and 'Clivimontius' being a combination of the Latin names for Cleves and Berg. Specifically, he was the Prince of Youth, embodying all the ideal virtues for a young prince.

Karl Friedrich's Hungarian Adventure
On 27 October 1572, Karl Friedrich decided he would visit the Hungarian front with the Turks. He surely would have heard about the Battle of Lepanto, a great sea battle which took place in 1571. Ever since 1568, the Turks remained mostly peaceful on the Hungarian front. Karl Friedrich wanted to see the Turkish threat for himself. He certainly was gallant, if also a bit foolish. Accompanied by eight military wagons and a small band of presumably armed and trained followers, he ventured forth to the border.

Karl Friedrich toured the border city of Raab, which is now Gyor in modern Hungary, roughly 75 miles south-east of Vienna. Pighius recorded this part of Karl Friedrich's journey in detail:

Ferries lay on the banks of the Danube, on which Prince Karl crossed the Danube with his companion and the entourage. In front of the gates were Garrison soldiers under arms, the city commanders and the military commanders as well as the magistrate and the nobility, who met the newcomers and welcomed them.

Due to the natural situation, the city is very solid, surrounded by swamps, Raab and Danube. The old remains of the castle, tombstones with sculptures and robed statues embedded in the cathedral wall, proved the age of the city and the former existence of a Roman winter camp at this location. In our century, the emperors Ferdinand and Maximilian fortified the city in such a way that it now seems impregnable. Hungarian cavalry and German infantry are ready as strong protection troops to fend off attacks by the Turks with constant vigilance.

---

40 By the mid-sixteenth century, the practice of wedding a Habsburg cousin, niece, nephew, etc. to another Habsburg cousin, uncle, aunt, etc., was in full swing. By the end of the sixteenth century, the family trees of the Spanish Habsburgs and Austrian Habsburgs were immensely intertwined.

In order not to lose the rest of the day – they had arrived late in the afternoon – Karl asked to start inspecting the fortifications presently.

His wish was readily granted, and horses were immediately fetched on which he and his companions could ride if desired. He began to pace the walls and ramparts and to inspect the moats and extensive bulwarks.

He looked at the guns and came into the vaulted passageways under the walls from which the ditches could be defended. He then left the gates, intent on exploring the structure of the bulwarks and walls, the width and depth of the ditches, the meaning and purpose of all the complexes.

The sun set over the city and the night was already dawning when he was escorted into the palace to the prepared accommodation, where he was received magnificently at the expense of the Count of Salm. There was a feast, which was just as brilliant in the variety and abundance of the dishes as the choice of gesture proved to be worthy of the prince.

The next morning he saw the armory and the magazines. He climbed a high tower from where he could see the location of the city, the course of the Danube and the surrounding area with its cities. Then he had breakfast and began his journey back to Vienna.

Karl Friedrich showed a great interest in architecture and engineering, whether for day-to-day or military purposes, throughout his young life. After his return from Raab, he had to return to Vienna. The journey back took three days.

Meanwhile in the United Duchies

Maria Eleonore was the first of Duke Wilhelm's children to marry. Born in 1550, she was twenty-three years old and at a more than suitable age for marriage in the sixteenth century. Duke Wilhelm wished to rid his court of his eldest daughter for fear that her passionate interest in Lutheranism would infect the other Von der Mark girls. Amalia was likely delighted that her niece shared her strong convictions.

Duke Wilhelm naturally wished to find someone who was of proper status, but they also had to be far enough from Düsseldorf that Maria Eleonore would effectively keep her thoughts to herself. One advantage that Duke Wilhelm's daughters had dated back to the Imperial privilege given in 1546 by Holy Roman Emperor Charles V, whereby Wilhelm and Maria's daughters could assert inheritance rights to the United Duchies should Wilhelm either not have sons or the sons die without issue. Duke Wilhelm settled upon Albrecht Friedrich of Prussia, who was born in 1553. The twenty-year-old Duke of Prussia married Maria Eleonore on 14 October 1573 in the city of Königsberg, the main seat of power for the dukes of Prussia.

Unfortunately, the marriage was tense. Maria Eleonore's first child, a daughter, was born in 1576. By 1577, Maria Eleonore's husband was showing signs of madness. Not long after, a regency council took over.

Maria Eleonore had seven known children, five girls and two boys. All the girls survived to adulthood and wed, whereas both baby boys tragically died in infancy.

Moving Maria Eleonore out of the United Duchies helped Duke Wilhelm give his court a more Catholic flavour. Wilhelm himself was more closely observing Catholicism thanks to Gymnich's efforts before he left to escort Karl Friedrich to Rome. Unfortunately, Wilhelm's sister Amalia and his three unmarried daughters completely refused to attend Mass and had given up any pretence of attending by 1575.

The goal for Duke Wilhelm was to find appropriate placement of his younger son, Johann Wilhelm, within the Church. The youngest child, Johann Wilhelm turned eleven on 29 May 1574. As the second son, he was destined for a religious life unless his elder brother died. He was already a fervent Catholic despite his tender age, and strange, too. No matter; he would do just fine as a bishop. To that end, Johann Wilhelm was the youngest person ever to be elected Bishop of Münster, with no little help from Olisleger. On 5 April 1574, Johann Wilhelm was chosen for the position, and the rest of his life was plotted for him. That same year, a sort of inquisition like the infamous Spanish sort was introduced at the Imperial diet, although it never gained momentum.

During the summer of 1574, final negotiations were sorted for Duke Wilhelm's second child, Anne, to marry. Anne, born in 1552, married Philip Ludwig, Count Palatine of Zweibrücken on 27 September 1574. Philip Ludwig was roughly five years older than Anne. Their marriage was a long and happy one, despite early concern that Anne was in fact a Catholic. She was not, and got on with her Protestant husband well. The couple had eight children together, four girls and four boys. Two children, a girl and a boy, did not survive infancy.

Back in Vienna

Karl Friedrich remained at court in Vienna throughout 1573 and into 1574. He was originally intended to be gone from the United Duchies for two years, but was either enjoying himself too much at the Imperial court or was not allowed to take his leave, so he stayed on. Only a letter from Pope Gregory XIII, inviting Karl Friedrich to Rome to celebrate the upcoming holy year, was enough to force Rudolf and others at court to let Karl Friedrich leave.

By July 1574, Karl Friedrich, Werner von Gymnich, Stephanus Pighius and the rest of the group from Jülich-Cleves-Berg were ready to leave for Italy. On 7 September, they left the court in Vienna. Karl Friedrich's Habsburg cousins escorted him for about three hours before they had to part ways.

Almost two weeks later, on 20 September 1574, Karl Friedrich and his entourage reached Ambras Castle in Innsbruck. The castle lies roughly 300 miles west of Vienna, and is not far north of the Italian border. Before reaching Ambras, they had briefly stopped in Salzburg where they enjoyed the hospitality of the archbishop.

Ambras Castle had recently been completed by King Rudolf's uncle, Archduke Ferdinand II. This iteration of the castle replaced a tenth-century structure. A labour of love, Ferdinand II had it built as a wedding present for his morganatic wife, Philippine Wesler. Children born to Ferdinand and Philippine were excluded from the Habsburg succession, although they were welcomed into the family and provided for. Philippine had two sons who survived to adulthood, Andreas and Karl. She also had twins, Philip and Maria, who died at the age of five months. Maria survived her brother by sixteen days. The younger boy, Karl, was almost fourteen years old when his cousin Karl Friedrich came to visit Ambras. Some twenty-seven years later, he would marry Karl Friedrich's youngest sister Sibylle.

The lower portion of Ambras housed Ferdinand's extensive art collection, which is still open to the public. By the time of Karl Friedrich's arrival, the castle's famous gardens had been completed. Pighius described the fantastic contents of the gardens. There were grapevines, trees of all sorts, and fruits. Parts were terraced. Pighius further described Karl Friedrich's stroll through the gardens:

> They went over to carefully tended gardens and saw paradises ... labyrinths and various grottoes dedicated to the nymphs, watered by ornate little fountains. [The fountains'] water comes out abundantly in different places; wild torrents bring it in from the nearby mountains in underground pipes. People liked the seats and dining tables in the open air, which were surrounded by beautifully cut hedgerows, but especially the rotunda at the foot of the neighbouring mountain, in the middle of which there was a round table made of maple wood, which sometimes slowly, sometimes by means of wheels driven by water, could be spun around quickly together with the dining guests and so – if desired – made the guests dizzy from the vortex.
>
> Thereupon [the visitors] were led into the sanctuary of Father Bacchus, a huge, spacious and dark rock cave, into which several steps cut out of the stone led down. The strangers admired the large capacity wine vats.

Bacchus seems to have been a popular figure throughout young Karl Friedrich's travels.

After the stop in Ambras, the group set out for the Brenner Pass around 29 September 1574. Their first stop, not far down the road, was at the Wilten Monastery. While there, the monks showed Karl Friedrich the tongue of a dragon, which was bony and long. He was also shown the blade-like bill of a swordfish, the very same one that is in the monastery's museum today.

On 30 September, the party came upon the Brenner Pass, a way through the Alps that today forms the border between Austria and Italy. During the journey to the pass they hunted chamois, a type of mountain goat. Once through, Karl Friedrich and his entourage made several stops on their way to Venice, the next major destination on their journey. They were met by a small Venetian delegation, which stayed with Karl Friedrich the rest of the way.

Most importantly, the Venetian delegation warned Karl Friedrich to avoid Trento, which was ravaged by plague. Having opted to cross the Adige River before Trento, one of their luggage wagons became stuck in the river, so all its contents had to be removed and dried by a fire. Next, it rained. And rained, and rained. It rained so much that the Avisio, a tributary of the Adige, burst its banks and was too treacherous to cross. This was surely the most miserable part of the trip, given that they could not house themselves within Trento and simply had to endure the bad weather. Pighius, who never saw an opportunity to instruct Karl Friedrich that he did not take, made use of the time by helping the young duke brush up on his Latin and Italian. After all, the ultimate destination in Italy was the Vatican.

Venice

Karl Friedrich finally set foot in Venetian territory on 18 October 1574. He crossed the famous Palladio Bridge, designed by the Italian architect Andrea Palladio. The group made their way to Magera, crossing a dam there. Upon reaching Mestre, just to the west of the islands which make up Venice, Karl Friedrich was met by two Venetian procurators who guided him and his train to gondolas. The horses were left behind in Mestre.

Once in the gondolas, they crossed to San Secondo Island, a very small piece of land just north-west of Venice. Karl Friedrich was greeted there by sixteen Venetian senators. After he gave thanks for his safe arrival at the church on the island, they returned to the gondolas and entered Venice by way of the Grand Canal from the west. Upon arrival at the Palazzo Ducale just off Saint Mark's Square, Karl Friedrich was greeted by two young linguists who had excellent manners. Karl Friedrich spent his stay in Venice in the Palazzo Ducale.

The next morning, a rested and refreshed Karl Friedrich was taken by the two young linguists to see the beauty of Venice. He viewed the wonders, including several artifacts from ancient Aquileia. His intellect was certainly stimulated throughout this trip.

On Sunday, 24 October, Karl Friedrich met the Doge of Venice, Alvise Mocenigo. It was a busy year for Mocenigo, who had welcomed Henri III of France in July of the same year. Mocenigo was also part of the negotiations with the Turks after the Battle of Lepanto.[41] During his time with Mocenigo, Karl Friedrich discussed politics, then was given a tour of the palace. A portion of the palace was augmented by the architect Andrea Palladio. Karl

---

41 Sadly, Mocenigo grew increasingly depressed in his later years and hanged himself in 1577. He was still buried in the traditional place for deceased doges.

Friedrich, usually rather interested in architecture, was instead quite taken with the collection of weapons in the Palazzo Ducale.

After the Palazzo Ducale, Karl Friedrich went to St Mark's Cathedral. Presumably he saw the relics and other precious items held by the Church. Next, he climbed the belltower across the way and took in the panorama.

The day after his meeting, Karl Friedrich was taken to Murano to see the famed glassblowers. He was positively taken with the many decorative figures made by the glassblowers. To thank Karl Friedrich for his visit, and no doubt raise their renown, the glassblowers sent him a set of glassware fit for a king. Before leaving Murano he strolled through the gardens, which were well known at the time.

After Murano, Karl Friedrich continued his tour of Venice. He encountered a representative of the Pope, who possibly sent a dispatch back to Gregory XIII about the progress of Karl Friedrich's travel to Rome. The day before leaving Venice, Karl Friedrich was shown the impressive Venetian Arsenal, and the Turkish ships captured during the Battle of Lepanto.

Milan, Rimini and Everywhere in Between

Karl Friedrich left Venice for Padua on 27 October 1574, travelling by boat. The large ship was towed down the Brenta Canal by horses. After arriving in Padua, they waited outside the city gates before being invited in by the local bishop. Spending only a night or two in Padua, they set out for Vicenza.

Travelling over land this time, Karl Friedrich's train included twelve wagons. He received a fabulous reception, and was given quarters within the Thien Palace. Vicenza boasted the magnificent architecture of Andrea Palladio, the very same architect of the bridge Karl Friedrich crossed on his way to Venice. They did not stay long in Vicenza before heading to Verona.

After arriving in Verona, Karl Friedrich was treated to a two-hour concert. He stayed at the count's palace there, touring the expansive gardens. Although they were not so great as those at Ambras Castle in Innsbruck, they were still quite something. The palace boasted an impressive collection of art and statues, too. Karl Friedrich was shown the ruins from antiquity, such as the amphitheatre that still stands today.

What was meant to be a quick stopover in Verona dragged on, much to the distress of Gymnich. After sufficient encouragement and pressure, the group left Verona for their planned lodgings in Villafranca, just south-west of Verona. Having made it there, Karl Friedrich fell ill and once more stayed on longer than he intended.

A request for an audience with Karl Friedrich was sent by the Duke of Mantua on Sunday, 31 October 1574. Karl Friedrich was asked to travel to Marmirolo, just outside of Mantua. His twelve-year-old cousin Vincenzo was sent to provide an escort. Karl Friedrich was again taken to see the sights, this time in Marmirolo, which boasted decorative fishponds, fountains, orchards and wineries. He then went with Vincenzo to Mantua, where his relatives awaited. Of course, Karl Friedrich could not resist enjoying a hunting party while on the way.

Karl Friedrich was received in Mantua by his maternal aunt Eleonore of Austria, who had married the Duke of Mantua in 1561 before having a son and two daughters in quick succession. He stayed at the duke's palace in Mantua, and attended Mass on 1 November in the palace's recently completed chapel. On 2 November, the stay at Mantua began with Karl Friedrich enjoying breakfast with Eleonore in the new palace. That afternoon he was shown the Te Palace, famous for its gorgeous frescoes. One of the more famous pieces shows the Roman gods supporting the giants. It covers an entire wall and is painted as an optical illusion. In the evening, the group visited a theatre in Mantua to take in a play.

Karl Friedrich awoke the next day, 3 November, hoping to leave Mantua. However, his aunt wished him to stay on for another day. He agreed, and enjoyed a rabbit hunt that day. In the evening, he saw another comedic play before retiring for the evening.

On the morning of 4 November, Karl Friedrich's aunt and uncle gifted him a beautiful horse with elaborate bridle worthy of Karl Friedrich's station. After saying goodbye to his relatives, the grateful prince set off for Milan.

Karl Friedrich spent a handful days travelling from Mantua to Milan, making short stops along the way. On this leg of the journey he received gifts of pastries, good wine and gold. He finally reached Milan rather late in the evening, presumably arriving after darkness had fallen.

Milan was held by Karl Friedrich's cousin Philip II of Spain. A series of battles known as either the Italian Wars or the Habsburg–Valois Wars had been fought over Milan, with the dispute finally settled in 1559 when Philip II of Spain and Henri II of France signed the Peace of Cateau-Cambrésis, by which treaty Milan went to Habsburg Spain.

During his stay in Milan, Karl Friedrich witnessed a military parade and a tourney in his honour. Later that evening, after dinner, an intricate Spanish dance was performed by two young sisters. The girls were blonde and wore elaborate, colourful clothing, including gold nets in their hair. Guitars provided the music. None of the Germans had seen the dance before, and they were charmed.

After the stay in Spanish-held Milan, Karl Friedrich left for Parma. On the way, he came across the castle of San Giovanni, another Spanish possession. It was midday, and the governor rode out from the fortification with twenty men on horseback, all carrying torches. Karl Friedrich was escorted to Parma, where he saw the newly constructed castle and churches made at Philip II's behest.

Once formally in Parma, Karl Friedrich was greeted by more of his Habsburg cousins in the ducal Farnese family. Duke Alessandro's mother was Margaret of Parma, a recognised illegitimate daughter of Charles V.

Margaret of Parma and Karl Friedrich's mother were first cousins. The young men enjoyed a spectacular feast together, accompanied by music.

The next day, Karl Friedrich was shown the sites in Parma. One must wonder if the young man ever tired of the almost constant stream of travel, feast, tour, with the occasional hunt thrown in. After the obligatory tour of Parma, Karl Friedrich enjoyed watching a series of dances performed by the women and young ladies at court.

On 16 November 1574, Karl Friedrich left Parma. He stopped in Reggio first, then Modena. Next, Karl Friedrich arrived in Bologna, where he saw a leaning tower. The tower began to lean after the combined issues of possible poor planning by the architect and soft ground beneath the structure.

Next came a stop in Ferrara. Karl Friedrich was met by yet another relative, Duke Alfonso II d'Este, a few miles outside the city. Alfonso was Karl Friedrich's uncle by his marriage to Barbara of Austria, a younger sister of Karl Friedrich's mother. Karl Friedrich stayed in Castello Estense for the three days he was in Ferrara.

Much ado was made over Karl Friedrich by the citizenry of Ferrara. It culminated in a huge attendance at Mass on 21 November, with many of the people there simply curious about the German prince. One can imagine that he enjoyed the attention, or at least appeared to enjoy it.

On the evening of 22 November, Karl Friedrich was treated to yet another banquet in his honour and entertainments including dancing. The next morning, he readied himself to travel to Ravenna via the River Po. Wishing for his nephew to travel in style, Duke Alfonso lent Karl Friedrich his gilded gondola, which the young man took all the way to Ravenna. There, he visited Dante Alighieri's tomb. After Ravenna, he went to Rimini.

Once in Rimini, Karl Friedrich was delighted to find that Guidobaldo II della Rovere, Duke of Urbino, put the utmost care and effort into preparing comfortable lodgings. Karl Friedrich and his entourage had been travelling for more than four months by now, and surely were exhausted.

Karl Friedrich left Rimini around noon the next day. In Pesaro, he met the Duke of Urbino and the duke's wife Vittoria. They and the court were dressed in mourning; the duke's father had died a couple months before.

Karl Friedrich next headed down the Adriatic coast to Senigallia, where he was forced to stay for a couple of days due to poor weather. The surrounding rivers were flooded and the ground too soggy for wagons and horses. The men sent by the Duke of Urbino to accompany Karl Friedrich did their best to entertain him with card games and excursions to the harbour.

Finally, on 1 December 1574, the weather cleared and Karl Friedrich headed across the Italian peninsula. He stopped in Ancona, then on 5 December left for Loreto, where he observed Mass. On 6 December they made for Macerata, Spoleto and Otricoli. After Otricoli, and several months on the road, Karl Friedrich finally arrived in Rome.

The year 1574 was a triumphant one for Duke Wilhelm and Maria.[42] Their eldest daughters were securely married, and the daughters' religious influence was safely removed from the United Duchies. Johann Wilhelm, the younger son, was now Bishop of Münster and out of the direct public eye. His behaviour and development could be monitored within the church. Finally, and surely most proudly, their eldest son, Karl Friedrich, was a success at the Imperial court, and was popular at the many courts he visited in Italy. He would surely make an excellent impression on Pope Gregory XIII, too.

42 In the Art Institute of Chicago is a stoneware jug from 1574 bearing a likeness of Wilhelm and his wife Maria. Stoneware was mass produced within the United Duchies, and there are many examples of it in various museums. It is possible the jug now in Chicago was created as either a part of one of the Von der Mark family's many celebrations in 1574 or simply to commemorate this as a golden year for them.

15

Karl Friedrich in Rome

Rome

On 15 December 1574, Karl Friedrich and his train quietly entered Rome. He sent a messenger ahead to the Vatican to notify Gregory XIII of his arrival. Because of the impending Holy Year or Year of Jubilee beginning on 24 December, upwards of 300,000 people were expected to flock to Rome for the celebration.

During Holy Year, indulgences are granted and people go on pilgrimage to the four Holy Doors within Rome. The Pope opens the door in St Peter's, and then the Holy Doors are opened at the other three major basilicas in Rome: St John Lateran, St Maria Maggiore and St Paul Outside the Walls.

Karl Friedrich chose to stay in more private, modest accommodation for his first night in Rome. His quarters were near the Milvian Bridge, about 3 miles from the Vatican. The next morning, the Pope sent his head chamberlain to greet Karl Friedrich and escort him to the Vatican.

The chamberlain, named Coroliano, conducted Karl Friedrich discreetly. Rather than going directly through the city, they skirted around the outside. After traipsing through various fields, Karl Friedrich was greeted warmly at the Vatican Palace by Gregory XIII. He asked about the youth's journey, and inquired after the young man's family and Imperial relations. He also fished for details about the state of religion in Jülich-Cleves-Berg, which was at the heart of the Counter-Reformation in Germany.

The hope of Gregory XIII and those interested in the ongoing religious turmoil in Germany was that Karl Friedrich would start his own Counter-Reformation once he became Duke of Cleves. The Pope had good reason to think this was possible: between Karl Friedrich's strong Catholic inclinations and his brother Johann Wilhelm's elevation to Bishop of Münster in 1574, it seemed feasible that the United Duchies could become fully Catholic again.

After their meeting, Karl Friedrich was shown to the Belvedere Court, a fabulous structure finished during the sixteenth century. Karl Friedrich stayed there for seventeen days, recuperating after his arduous trek. While lodging at the Belvedere Court, Karl Friedrich was able to take advantage of the tranquil settings. He strolled around the gardens and the beautiful building itself, and generally restored his health in the crisp Roman air. He was visited by bishops, cardinals and other prelates.

Now fully rested, Karl Friedrich was ready to look at the ruins. In the sixteenth century, the ground of the famous Forum Romanum was overgrown and had become good grazing for livestock. Pighius described the visit:

> Then the ancient monuments ... were also visited, works of truly gigantic proportions, when you see the huge clusters of vaults and arches, the huge ruins of towers and walls in the thermal baths, temples, amphitheaters, circuses, Aqueducts, theatres and many other public buildings. The not uneducated visitor is amazed and cannot get enough of it, like Prince Karl and some of his companions when they came to the amphitheatre of Titus Vespasian (Coliseum), which is raised in a wonderful epigram by the poet Martial about the seven wonders of the world, to the pantheon of Agrippa, (completely preserved as the church of S. Maria ad Martyres), and reached the baths of Caracallas, Constantine and Diocletian. The latter extend over wide areas and are surrounded by very high towers and walls in the manner of large cities.
>
> They admired a large number of marble triumphal arches and columns of honour, which with their images chiselled from life depict military expeditions. They marvelled at the stone masses of the (Cestius) pyramid and the huge needles of the obelisks, for whose transport ships had been built, so that the yokes of the mountains could be brought over the angry waves, so to speak. What should I call the gigantic monolithic colossi ... and the stored bodies of the huge river gods (on the Capitol), also the many statues made of bronze and precious, rare marble, ornately carved, the huge columns, vases, basins, fountain bowls and huge bathtubs. These were once used in thermal baths and public baths ...

Karl Friedrich saw countless statues, including the still-famous *Laocoön and His Sons*. Karl Friedrich would have had the chance to see the works of Raphael and Michelangelo, including the Sistine Chapel. All of this must have left quite the impression on the nineteen-year-old prince, much as it does anyone who visits the Vatican today.

The Start of the Holy Year

The Holy Year officially began on 24 December 1575. A large throng of people gathered at a still-standing portion of Old St Peter's Basilica, outside

Constantine's Gallery. The dome of the new St Peter's was still under construction. The Pope sat on a throne in the gallery, facing the pilgrims, while various cardinals and bishops sat to his right. To begin the Holy Year, the Pope unlocked the Holy Door named Santa Porta. He would then travel to the other three Holy Doors and unlock those.

When the Pope unlocked and walked through Santa Porta, Karl Friedrich walked through the gate immediately behind him. Later that evening, he received communion directly from the Pope. Both events were great honours.

Duke Wilhelm's eldest son Karl Friedrich was by all accounts a talented, vivacious young man, abounding in princely qualities. Karl Friedrich had very much impressed Pope Gregory XIII, who invited him as a guest of honour to the Holy Year celebration held in St Peter's Basilica on Christmas Day 1574. Karl Friedrich's piety and dedication to the Catholic Church would make him a valuable ally in the centre of the Holy Roman Empire, in the Church's pursuit of the Counter-Reformation.

On 28 December 1574, Karl Friedrich participated in the pilgrimage around Rome. This involved visiting the churches of San Giovanni in Laterno, Santa Croce, Saint Peter, Saint Paul, Santa Maria Maggiore, San Sebastiano and San Lorenzo. Of Karl Friedrich's pilgrimage, Pighius wrote,

> When Karl visited the seven famous churches of the city, which were sanctified and venerable ... the Pope sent his valet and priests ahead and had all the sanctuaries opened and everything unlocked and displayed, such things which are otherwise rarely shown: the most sacred Veronica's handkerchief with the image of Christ our Saviour; Captain Longinus' lance, which opened the side of the dead man on the cross; a nail with which He was nailed to the cross; a Rhodian coin from the thirty pieces of silver for which He was sold out by the traitor Judas. [The Pope] had innumerable relics of saints, rare gifts and other treasures shown to the prince in [their full glory].

Karl Friedrich continued to receive honours from the Pope in recognition of his commitment to Catholicism.

On New Year's Day 1575, he was granted the Golden, or Blessed, Sword and Hat by Gregory XIII. The ornate ceremonial sword, scabbard and light-blue velvet ducal hat were typically blessed by the Pope on Christmas Eve and bestowed upon secular rulers in recognition of their service and piety during the same ceremony. Presumably, the ceremony was pushed back to 1 January due to the start of the Holy Year on 24 December. Karl Friedrich was charged by the Pope with protecting and following the faith, given the title *Fidei Defensor*. His receipt of the honour was extraordinary. The title was typically only given to kings, such as Karl Friedrich's former uncle Henry VIII of England.

A celebration was held at the Belvedere Court after Karl Friedrich's blessing. There was much music and feasting. To commemorate the event, a relief was created. It depicts Karl Friedrich receiving the sword from Gregory XIII, and shows Werner von Gymnich kneeling in the foreground. The relief can still be seen at the church of Santa Maria dell'Anima in Rome.

After the Ceremonies

Karl Friedrich set out for a multi-week excursion to Naples, Tivoli and other places on 3 January 1575. As with his trip to Rome, Karl Friedrich was fêted at every stop he made along the Via Latina. At his last stop, in Capua, he took in a local festival. Once in Naples, he observed the Spanish triumphal arch and the tomb of Virgil. He also visited the crypt, which is now usually closed to the public.

After exploring Naples, Karl Friedrich and his small band of followers went to Tivoli. Once there, he visited the fabulous gardens at the Villa d'Este. Three main gardens make up the overall composition, and to this day they are extraordinary in their variety of decoration, layout and display of horticulture. Pighius had begun memorising the layout of the massive gardens as early as 1573 from a woodcut. He wrote in detail about the gardens in his work *Hercules Prodicius*, the best source for Karl Friedrich's life from his departure of the United Duchies court and throughout his time in Italy. Pighius describes the gardens:

> After his arrival, Prince Karl spent the rest of the day wandering the elaborate gardens that Cardinal Ippolito of Este-Ferrara had laid out on a mountain slope together with a magnificent palace... To the right of the palace is the so-called secret garden, in which 16 marble fountain bowls dispense clear water. In the middle there is a raised four-sided arch with also four fountains, which have mirror-image ornaments. On the left side of the palace there is a ball court and other lavish playgrounds. Various marble statues and ancient sculptures adorn the front [of the palace] and also the vestibule, which has a double stone staircase.
>
> In the square in front of the hall there is a very beautiful fountain with a picture of Leda. From there the hill falls in a gentle slope... [The square] includes four charming, spacious gardens in front of the palace. You can descend to them on three neat stone double stairs on both sides and in the middle. From step to step, jets of water as wide as a finger accompany the stairs and do not form pools. The individual gardens are very nicely divided and with their semicircles, you can enjoy a wonderful sight when you walk from one part to the other through arcades and paths that are covered by evergreen ivy. Fragrant blooming flowers and herbs in beds and borders captivate everyone's eyes with their colourful splendour and invite you to linger. The visitor cannot get enough of the countless wonderful statues and fountains...

Beyond this introductory description, Pighius talks about each of the three main gardens in detail.

On the afternoon of 23 January, Karl Friedrich and his company left Tivoli for Rome. Along the way, they visited the ruins of the Villa Hadriana. Most of the ruins were overgrown with plants, and otherwise exposed to the elements. It was evening before the group had finished exploring.

Karl Friedrich's Last Days in Rome

After entering Rome, Karl Friedrich passed by the Diocletian Baths. Waiting there for him was a great showing of Roman nobility. The Roman nobles escorted Karl Friedrich to the Vatican with much flair and flash. It was finally the nobility's turn to show their welcome to Karl Friedrich, and they wanted to make an impression.

Once back at his lodgings in the Vatican, Karl Friedrich made it known that he hoped to leave for Düsseldorf before the end of the month. Gregory XIII preferred that Karl Friedrich stay until Candlemas, 2 February, and Karl Friedrich could do naught but acquiesce. In hindsight, much of the length of Karl Friedrich's journey could be attributed to his hosts asking him to stay just a little longer.

On the night of 24/25 January, Karl Friedrich was not feeling well. According to Pighius, he suffered from 'headache, fever, and shivers' beginning at around five o'clock in the evening. Alexander Petronius, a medical historian, recorded the course of Karl Friedrich's illness and treatment in his 1581 publication. The report, which appears to have been created by Petronius with Michael Mercatus, provides a fascinating look at sixteenth-century medicine and a ghastly insight into common diseases before modern treatments. Pighius included the medical report in the 1609 publication of *Hercules Prodigious*.

Karl Friedrich could not get any sleep because of pain in his chest. The doctor prescribed wine boiled with cinnamon and barley water, and for Karl Friedrich to eat a porridge made of meat and barley. A record of his bodily fluids began on 25 January.

By Wednesday, 26 January, it was becoming obvious that this was a serious illness. Per the report, Karl Friedrich emptied his bowels five times on Tuesday, and the contents did not look like those of a healthy young man.[43] More prescriptions were given by the Roman doctor, including a broth made from figs, citrus and other fruits. By five o'clock in the evening, Karl Friedrich's fever returned, and red bumps were spread all over his body save his face. He was ill with smallpox, a heinous, often fatal disease.

---

43 Urine, blood and phlegm are mentioned often in the report because early modern doctors based their diagnoses off the appearance, smell, substance, etc., of bodily fluids.

It was at around this time that Werner von Gymnich wrote to Duke Wilhelm to inform him of Karl Friedrich's illness. Smallpox was common in the sixteenth century, and it was possible to survive it. Karl Friedrich's aunt Anna of Cleves was known to have slight scarring on her face from her bought of smallpox when she was a child. On the other hand, it is possible that Karl Friedrich's little sister Elisabeth of Jülich-Cleves-Berg, who died at around six years old, could have been felled by the disease. There was really no way of knowing what the next few days held in store for Karl Friedrich and the Von der Mark dynasty.

Karl Friedrich's Battle with Smallpox

On Thursday, 27 January, Karl Friedrich's face was swollen, and his bottom lip unusually dark. He was prescribed more barley water boiled with cinnamon, but no wine. A broth made with citrus fruits was prepared. Karl Friedrich was urged to try the various concoctions in hopes that a sense of hunger would return. If he were hungry enough to eat, then there was hope that he would regain his strength.

There was serious debate as to whether Karl Friedrich was well enough to be bled. It was thought that the sooner he was bled the more likely the treatment would have a positive effect. On the other hand, he had barely eaten and was weak. If he was bled at a low ebb, his condition might worsen.

Karl Friedrich was bled three times on 27 January, in small amounts each time. His hands became cold after the last bleeding. It was hoped that this treatment would prevent the bad, diseased blood from entering his lungs. It was believed that through this method the fever would be drawn out of Karl Friedrich's arteries even if left in the veins. Karl Friedrich's rash persisted, and it was recommended that an attempt be made to clear away the pustules.

His rash worsened on the Thursday. Karl Friedrich slept very little, and still had a fever. He finally had some rest just before daybreak the next day.

On Friday, 28 January, the smallpox rash became severe. It was all over his body and face, including on his tongue and the palate of his mouth. The pox on his forehead looked like millet seeds instead of the large, lumpy pustules everywhere else on his body. His eyes poured out a constant stream of tears. His lower lip had turned blackish. He sneezed a lot. The tears and sneezing were evidence that the smallpox was in his eyes and nose. His urine was reddish in colour, which was believed to be due to the medical treatments.

The disease was expected to run its usual course, meaning that it would be at its worst by the ninth day, improving over the subsequent nine days. Effectively, this meant that Karl Friedrich could begin to recover by 4 February. The rash would abate by then, and the fever by 6 February.

There was more discussion about bleeding Karl Friedrich again, for the second day in a row. Sometimes, copious amounts of blood could be let out of a person to draw out the infection. Given the extent of Karl Friedrich's illness, however, bleeding him again so soon would kill him. Providing proper nutrition and letting nature run its course was likely the better option.

It was a difficult day for Karl Friedrich. He drank a little bit of the water concoction but could not take in a proper meal. That evening his 'urine was slightly thicker, content similar, pulse quieter, warmth milder, thirst not slight, supper almost nothing'. He felt weak the entire day, which was thought be in part due to his youth. He was a teenager still, nineteen years old, and accustomed to taking in a lot of food at mealtimes. Now he spat out anything he tried to eat due to the smallpox in his throat making it painful to swallow.

Karl Friedrich had a phlegmy cough the entire day. He was wheezing. It was suspected that the smallpox had made it into his lungs. Petronius believed that either the pus from the pox or the physical presence of the pox were taking up too much space, making it difficult for Karl Friedrich to breathe. At this point the ailing prince got out of bed a few times so he could sit up and breathe more easily.

That night, he was delirious and restless. He did try to eat something, although not enough to comprise a proper meal. He finally fell asleep at around six o'clock the next morning, but only for two hours.

By Saturday morning, 29 January, Karl Friedrich's entire face was tremendously puffy and swollen. He could not see well because of the swelling, and had a mild fever. His urine was still reddish. He was given diamoron, a liquid medicine made from honey and mulberries, to gargle. He was fed a soup of dates, lentils, figs and citrus fruits boiled in barley water. His fecal matter was examined, as nothing had come out of him in a while. Blood came out with everything else, although not much.

Karl Friedrich began confronting his own mortality that day. He realised that, unless he could properly eat and drink, he would not survive. He began begging for wine, which he had not been allowed after the first couple days of his illness. He remained delirious, and his throat was in an awful state from the smallpox rash. The doctors and advisors would not let him have any wine, but he argued that he was accustomed to it and that the major changes to his diet since the beginning of his illness were making things worse.

Finally, it was settled that Karl Friedrich could have wine. It was within the ancient teachings of Hippocrates, after all. Unfortunately, the wine recommended by Hippocrates was greatly watered down. Karl Friedrich's wine was therefore diluted. The wine kept its red colour, and was boiled with cinnamon. He attempted to dip bread in the wine and eat it. Sitting in bed, he was able to consume a small amount of bread this way. It was still not a full meal, but it was much more food than he had eaten in a while. He fell asleep after dinner. While he was asleep, a plaster was applied to his eyes that was made in part with saffron and rosewater.

The physicians tried to make another porridge for Karl Friedrich, this time with pomegranates, barley, figs, shellfish, fennel and leafy greens. Some of it was then boiled to make a broth, while the rest was reserved for him to eat properly. He was to take the broth an hour before breakfast and dinner, and a small portion at lunchtime. It was hoped that the medicine would escape the food and soothe any pox in his throat. The doctors did not want him to take too much medicine so close to mealtime in case the effects made him sick to his stomach. By Saturday night, he was swallowing with a little less difficulty, and was expelling a thick mucus with the remnants of pustules from his nose. As disgusting as all this sounds, it suggested he was on the road to recovery.

Karl Friedrich slept a total of four hours going into Sunday, 30 January. His fitful sleep was full of nightmares, and at times that night he was delirious. Despite his poor sleep, the fever was almost gone on Sunday morning. He did not have any trouble with his bowels. However, the colour of his urine was still too red. His eyes, full of pox, were runny. Overall, the rash on his body was worse than the day before. Nonetheless, he did manage to drink watered wine throughout the day.

After his evening meal, Karl Friedrich's condition worsened. He fell asleep for a couple hours, but then awakened from feeling too hot. He tried to drink, but could not swallow. The fever came back with a vengeance, and the smallpox rash became even worse. He coughed a lot. Karl Friedrich's cheeks, nose, lips and eyes were completely swollen. His lips were still black. He tried to drink sweetened pomegranate juice.

The form of the pox was worrisome. In the experience of his doctors, the less dangerous manifestation of smallpox caused well-defined pustules that were white in the middle. Karl Friedrich's were indeed white, but they had less defined edges and had an indentation in the middle. This was believed to represent the more deadly form of smallpox. The report could have been describing what is now known as malignant smallpox, which occurred most often in adults and was almost always fatal.

Karl Friedrich tried to sleep that night, but was kept awake by his inability to breathe.

The hope from the day before continued into Monday, 31 January. However, his body was beginning to show signs of losing its battle. In his urine, still too red for comfort, there were three or four dark, solid bits. Blackish blood had erupted from a few of the pustules on his back. Those on his chin were better, but elsewhere on his face and body they were white and had a foul smell. His fever was not as bad, and the swelling around his left eye had lessened enough for him to open the eye. He could not really swallow that morning, though.

By Monday evening, Karl Friedrich was able to eat a light meal and sleep off and on. His lips were still completely black, pointing to him suffering from the haemorrhagic form of smallpox. Whichever form he had, it was obvious to his observers that his survival would be a miracle.

Karl Friedrich looked even more ghastly the morning of 1 February 1575. Dead skin had fallen off his upper lip, leaving it quite raw. His urine, red as ever, was of a thicker consistency. The pustules on his extremities were larger and whiter, still without defined edges. His spittle contained blood, and his nostrils were swollen shut. His head hurt, and the fever was still there.

Karl Friedrich was extremely thirsty, so the doctors administered white wine mixed with water and cinnamon, which he was able to drink for the most part. He did not eat much that evening, but his fever lessened. The pox appeared to be coming to a head, taking on an ashen colour common to malignant smallpox. His face was still swollen, especially the left cheek. He breathed well enough at times, and terribly at others.

Karl Friedrich was determined to get out of bed. He wanted to sit up in a chair, despite his minders being against it. During one of his attempts to stand up, he started to faint. There was concern that if he moved around too much, the fluid or pox in his lungs would become agitated and make matters worse. He coughed up a lot of thick, brownish-red phlegm. The pressure from lying on his back in bed did not help matters.

His throat felt better by the evening, so he ate a regular meal. However, he could barely sleep that night. His throat was once again swollen, to the point that he stopped breathing twice or thrice.

On Wednesday, 2 February, Karl Friedrich had a slight fever and a sluggish pulse. His cheek area on both sides was deformed from the illness, and his nose swollen shut. Despite the state of his nose and his breathing the night before, he breathed more easily on Wednesday. His throat was the same as it had been. The pustules covering his body had turned itchy, and were white.

Karl Friedrich showed more interest in food on Wednesday. He ate something for breakfast and lunch, and asked for his dinner a little earlier than usual. His urine was unremarkable, as were the contents of his bowel movements. Best of all, there was no blood. He drank a lot of barley water that day, and was able to doze periodically. During one of these dozing sessions, Karl Friedrich rubbed his right hand on his face, which came away bloody. The spot where he rubbed his face turned black. When he retired for the evening, his insomnia returned.

The next day, 3 February, Karl Friedrich seemed to show some improvement. He had an easier time eating, and coughed up less phlegm. His face was slightly swollen. On the other hand, his voice was weak. He tried to sleep during the day, but was roused at around eight o'clock that night complaining of the stench in his chamber. He almost fainted when he leapt out of bed. Once placed back in his bed, Karl Friedrich raised his arms over his head, then lowered them. His head rolled back on the pillow. His pulse was weak. His mouth was relaxed into an unnatural position. Showing agitation, he pulled off his blanket. By this point, his heart was beating so hard that it seemed like a fist was trying to punch through his chest from the inside. He was delirious again, and would go from lying still in bed to being animated. He felt a dull pain in his head and chest. Dark patches of skin began peeling off his face.

Meanwhile, Karl Friedrich's attendants were afraid of his behaviour and the condition of his body. The stench might have been attributable to the breakdown of his body, the peeling pustules, infected skin, fluids trapped in the bedlinen or any combination of these. There was fear that the smell was coming from his lungs.

Karl Friedrich kept throwing off his covers as though they were a huge weight pressing on him. He grasped at his chest as if he was trying to push off whatever was making it feel so heavy. At this point he became anxious, tossing and turning. His pulse was rapid one moment and sluggish the next.

It was clear by now that Karl Friedrich's lungs were severely damaged from smallpox. They were likely full of fluid, too. He had such difficulty breathing that he stood up and began forcefully hitting his own chest. Seemingly giving way to his force of will, his lungs spasmed briefly and he felt better. He crawled back into bed, and his pulse stabilised.

Karl Friedrich's voice remained soft because he was not pulling in enough air to support his speech. He drank some watered wine before bed but did not meaningfully sleep. He was awakened by nightmares at around four o'clock in the morning on Friday. His fever was high again, and the pox on his body stank. He ripped the blankets off and tried pacing around the room. He eventually went back to bed, and slept for fifteen or twenty minutes at a time until about nine o'clock in the morning.

Around this time, an owl kept appearing in Cleves. It perched on the Swan Castle around midday for several consecutive days. The owl would not leave, and could not be chased off. It was taken as a bad omen that someone was going to die. In Xanten, meanwhile, Johann Wilhelm had a disturbing dream of a funeral. Whether he thought it was the funeral of his father, brother or someone else is not certain. It was an alarming enough dream to spur the child to voice his concern.

Later on Friday, Karl Friedrich began spitting up a red liquid. He was able to eat a little, but overall was incredibly weak. He managed to eat again around dinner time, and was still terribly thirsty. He vomited a little. By that night, the right side of Karl Friedrich's face was swollen, but the left side was better. His heart was likely moving the blood through his left side, helping the swelling to subside.

Although some of the swelling was better, Karl Friedrich's face was in a horrifying state. Patches of brownish-red skin peeled from his cheeks, revealing blackened skin underneath. His nose and lips were peeled and sore. He ate more, but there were no genuine improvements in his condition.

By 5 February, Karl Friedrich's appearance was ghastly, and he continued to complain of agonising pain in his chest. The report at this point remarks that Karl Friedrich's lungs were so badly damaged that he would die prematurely. Whether this meant that he would generally live a shorter life or would die within the coming days is unclear.

Despite the pounding of his heart, the prince's pulse was weak. He continued drinking watered wine to sustain himself. His urine was red, with a grainy substance in it, like sand. He gurgled between coughs when he tried to breathe. The skin on most of his face was black. Medicine was prepared to treat his suspected heart failure. He took a spoonful of the medicine, and shortly afterward coughed up a black clot of blood. He still felt a lot of pain in his chest, particularly around his sternum and in his throat. He slept for a couple of hours going into 6 February. He had no appetite.

On Sunday, 6 February, Karl Friedrich began coughing up a lot of bloody spittle. His heart and pulse seemed improved, although this could have been because his body was no longer fighting. That afternoon, he tried his best to eat oranges but mostly rolled around the segments in his mouth. He was offered orange juice throughout the rest of the day, although he was producing so much spittle that he could not really drink the juice.

That night, he could not sleep because his nose was still swollen shut. Karl Friedrich convulsed a couple times. When he tried to sleep that night, he continued to suffer from terrifying nightmares. He himself was making horrible noises in his effort to breathe. He tried to sleep on his left side, and attempted to drink a broth that was prepared for him, dipping bread in the broth to eat. He drank diluted wine. He urinated in his bed at least twice overnight, and did not seem to notice.

The next day was no better. He was coughing up black blood clots with more regularity, and producing so much spit that he was choking. His tongue was not terribly swollen. He still felt short of breath, although his nose was starting to clear. He ate and drank a little, which helped with the spitting. He began having a dry cough, which produced speckles of bright red blood.

Karl Friedrich still looked ghastly. Portions of his face remained darkened, and were peeling. He had black blisters, not pustules, in a couple of spots on his body.

That night, his breath was so shallow that it was difficult for Karl Friedrich to spit out the extra fluid in his mouth. On the other hand, his pulse seemed stronger. He regained more of his sight, presumably because the swelling in his face had gone down enough. His sleep continued to be fitful and full of terrors.

When Karl Friedrich awoke on 8 February, he did not know it would be his last full day alive. He was feverish and thirsty the entire day. He could not breathe well, and ordered his attendants to shift his body this way and that in hopes of easing the burden on his lungs. His pulse was faint, his hands twitched with tremors. He continued to cough up dark material, along with some fresh blood.

Karl Friedrich had absolutely no sleep that night. He tried to speak, but barely could. He stayed positioned on his back, his breath tremulous and laboured. He rejected all food and wine. His refusal to drink wine was of particular concern because that was the one thing he consistently drank throughout his illness.

When morning dawned on 9 February, Karl Friedrich could barely breathe, and was neither eating nor drinking. Early in the afternoon, blood flowed out of his mouth for a moment. He seemed to rally after that. He breathed more easily, and his pulse strengthened a little. Despite this seeming improvement, Karl Friedrich von der Mark, heir to the United Duchies of Jülich-Cleves-Berg, died two hours later. He was nineteen years old, and had not seen his parents or his home in more than three years.

16

Mass Flux in the United Duchies, 1575–1579

Karl Friedrich's Autopsy

Karl Friedrich was autopsied the day after he died, on 10 February 1575. His muscles were deteriorated, and his body very thin. His abdomen had no fat and was distended, another possible sign of malignant smallpox. The pustules and dead skin fell away from his face. Karl Friedrich's lungs were said to be completely detached from his chest wall. It is thought that the blood which came out of Karl Friedrich's mouth shortly before his death was because of this.

Karl Friedrich's other organs were in bad shape, too. It appears his spleen was ruptured, or at least in very poor condition. There were pieces as big as a thumb which had separated from the main organ. A black liquid was found in his shrivelled heart. His stomach was red on the outside, and had depressions in it. The inside was white. The intestines were empty and swollen. There was a collection of black blood inside his abdomen, behind his kidneys. His neck and head were not examined for fear of accidentally decapitating him.

The two doctors mentioned earlier, Michael Mercatus and Alexander Petronius, signed off on the report. It is difficult to discern if they had accompanied Karl Friedrich from Germany or if they were Roman.

Karl Friedrich's Funeral

After the autopsy, Karl Friedrich's body was quickly prepared for his funeral. It began that very afternoon at St Peter's, in the vestibule. His coffin was covered in black fabric, his pox-ridden face was hidden under a piece of white silk. The coffin was carried on a bier by eight men from his entourage, all dressed in black. The procession crossed the Tiber River to the east, ending about a mile away at Santa Maria dell'Anima, then the main church in Rome for individuals from the Holy Roman Empire.

So great were the masses of people gathering to pay their respects that the funeral train did not actually leave St Peter's until two hours after the official beginning of the funeral. The train began with representatives from different brotherhoods. Eighteen groups attended in all, with a total of roughly 1,000 representatives between them. All of them masked their faces.

Roman monks wearing white came after the members of the various brotherhoods. The orphans of San Spirito followed, carrying torches and wearing white and blue. Forty more men carrying long torches walked behind the orphans.

In front of Karl Friedrich's coffin walked nobles, ambassadors, cardinals and princes. Sixteen more men who had joined Karl Friedrich on his journey to Rome came behind the coffin, occasionally switching places with a pallbearer if one of them became tired.

Behind the men who went with Karl Friedrich to Rome came the various members of the curia, and other religious figures. They were organised behind the coffin as though it were the funeral of a cardinal. The bishops, masters of the keys and other notables wore purple. There were roughly fifty chamberlains, all wearing red. The citizens of Rome came after, with a multitude entering the church to pay their respects to the German prince.

On 2 March 1575, obsequies were given for Karl Friedrich in the black-cloaked church. All the decorative paintings were covered to allow those who attended to contemplate death and the brevity of life. In the middle of the church, a platform was built to hold Karl Friedrich's coffin. It, too, was covered in black fabric. The various arms for the United Duchies were displayed, as was the motto *amor optima custodia*, or 'Love is the best protection'. It is not specified whether this was Karl Friedrich's personal motto, although it is certainly a possibility.

Duke Wilhelm's Reaction

Wilhelm soon knew that Karl Friedrich had died. The Pope sent a letter to him on 10 February, and Wilhelm wrote his response almost a month later, on 7 March 1575. He and Maria were devastated. He was writing from his 'castle in Cleves', meaning the Swan Castle. He told Pope Gregory XIII that the news 'cast me into the greatest sorrow of sorrows'. Wilhelm had high hopes for his eldest son, writing that his confidence in Karl Friedrich had eased his fear of old age.

A priest had been sent by Gregory XIII to comfort the grieving parents. Wilhelm welcomed the priest's consolation and messages, but Maria was less receptive. Already prone to melancholy, the news of Karl Friedrich's death surely did not help her disposition. Wilhelm was happy to hear how warmly Karl Friedrich had been received by the Roman nobles and at the Vatican. Despite his tremendous sorrow, he expressed his gratitude to the Pope for providing his own doctors to help Karl Friedrich. The Pope had ordered prayers to be said for Karl Friedrich during his illness, too. Wilhelm pledged to uphold the Catholic faith, and signed the letter as a 'most obedient son'.

Come early April, Karl Friedrich remained unburied in Santa Maria dell'Anima. Pope Gregory XIII was waiting for permission to bury him in Rome. If Duke Wilhelm was not in agreement, then he was willing to facilitate Karl Friedrich's burial elsewhere. The young man's lead coffin was encased within a wooden one, still laid out in the church as it had been for the past month. Eventually, Duke Wilhelm gave his permission for the burial.

John of Cleves, who could have been a relative of Karl Friedrich, wrote the eulogy. The late prince was buried in a grand tomb opposite Pope Hadrian VI, of Dutch origin, who died in 1523. The style of Karl Friedrich's tomb clearly echoes that of Hadrian. The inscription under Karl Friedrich's carved figure reads:

God, the best and greatest. Karl Friedrich, Duke of Jülich-Cleves-Berg, Count of the Mark and Ravensberg, Lord of Ravenstein, possessed experience and knowledge of different languages, and was famous through his unique knowledge of languages and ability and beyond his age, and fear of God; he was honoured at the court of his uncle Emperor Maximilian II, and in other places with various honours; he came [to Rome] out of zeal for faith and thirst for knowledge when Pope Gregory XIII called the peoples of the Christian world together for the Jubilee Year. Here he was brilliantly received by the Pope and after the opening of the Holy Door, he was honoured in a festive service with sword and hat in the old-fashioned way.

When he fulfilled all the duties of Christian piety and thought of returning [home], he was seized with a serious illness and left the earth to rejoice in Heaven; his funeral was thanks to the same benevolent kindness with which the Pope gave him and he had received since his arrival; and [the Pope] visited him at his sickbed, [gave him] splendid exequies and great escort, with a huge crowd of people from all classes, colleges and brotherhoods mixed together, [and he was] celebrated with deep sadness and unbelievable sympathy from the whole city. Duke Wilhelm had the monument erected for his older, dearly beloved son.

Karl Friedrich still rests in the same tomb today.

Pighius, who arrived back in Cleves in April 1575, was understandably afraid to speak with the grieving parents about Karl Friedrich's demise. Thankfully, Wilhelm had time to collect himself between learning of his eldest son's death and Pighius' arrival at court. Wilhelm bestowed the office of canon on Pighius in September 1575, who was then installed in Xanten. Pighius died in 1604.

Things Fall Apart
A mere six days after Karl Friedrich's death, he was followed by Heinrich Barr, better known as Chancellor Olisleger. It is unknown exactly when

Olisleger was born, although it was likely not later than 1500. He came from a family of the lesser nobility based in Wesel. He was known to have studied both theology and the law, in Cologne and in Italy. He was rewarded with a Doctorate of Laws in his youth. Olisleger was religiously moderate, and very much in favour of the *via media* proposed at the Augsburg Diet in the 1550s. He was a true humanist, and respected in the administrative centres of Cleves and Düsseldorf.

Olisleger first came to the attention of Johann III of Cleves in 1532, and was elevated to Vice Chancellor of Cleves in 1534, keeping his position after Wilhelm became the ruling duke in 1539. He was instrumental in the shifting politics and intrigues at the United Duchies court of the 1530s. Considered the top man in Cleves politics, he helped Wilhelm negotiate the marriage between Anna of Cleves and Henry VIII of England. He was part of the delegation that escorted Anna to England, and provided the insightful report to the Cleves court as to Anna's first days in England with Henry. In 1541, he stayed on at court in Navarre during the early years of Wilhelm's marriage to Jeanne d'Albret.

The death of Olisleger on 15 February 1575 could not have been easy for Wilhelm. He had faithfully served the dukes of Cleves for over forty years, and he may have been a father figure to Wilhelm as well. Olisleger was buried in the family chapel in Wesel. One can imagine that Wilhelm was already sorrowful over the death of Olisleger when news of Karl Friedrich's passing reached him.

Gerhard von Jülich, who served Duke Wilhelm as personal secretary, died in February 1576. He might have been Wilhelm's cousin through the latter's illegitimate maternal uncle, John of Jülich. The important people surrounding Wilhelm were dropping like flies.

Konrad Heresbach, another advisor present at court since at least 1534, died in October 1576. Sometime in the 1560s, Heresbach had retired to an island in the Rhine with his second wife. He built a lovely country house there, and lived quietly. Despite his retirement, Heresbach's advice was still periodically requested for important matters. Born 2 August 1496, the elderly Heresbach was another who may have been a father figure to Wilhelm.

The backdrop to these losses in the United Duchies was the early stages of the Dutch Revolt. Across the Rhine in the Habsburg Netherlands, William of Orange began rebelling against the Duke of Alba in 1568. Two years earlier, in 1566, iconoclasm had swept through the Netherlands in response to professions swiftly losing their earning capacity due to poor trade agreements between the Spanish king, Philip II, who was the hereditary overlord of the Burgundian Circle, and England, who produced much of the wool used in the Netherlands.

William of Orange's initial attempts to defeat the Spanish were unsuccessful, partly because he could not secure support from the French Huguenots, Elizabeth I of England or German Lutherans. Between 1572 and 1573, an outburst of violence swept through the Netherlands. Commoners murdered priests, took Church property and destroy convents. By 1574, Catholicism was completely outlawed in certain parts of the Netherlands, with Calvinist leaders outlawing Catholicism in major cities like Ghent, Bruges, Antwerp and Brussels by 1577. Bearing in mind that being anti-Catholic also meant being anti-Habsburg and anti-Spanish, Philip II was in danger of losing dominion over the Habsburg Netherlands. He had to find somewhere to lodge his troops so that he could regain control.

Conveniently, as mentioned before, the United Duchies bordered the Netherlands. Furthermore, Philip II's father Charles V had dominated and subjugated Duke Wilhelm thirty years earlier, and Wilhelm's wife was a Habsburg. To that end, Philip II could place his Spanish troops in the United Duchies, and there was not much that Duke Wilhelm could do about it. Unfortunately for them, Philip II had a nasty habit of underpaying or not paying his *Landsknechte* and Spanish troops. This resulted in mass looting and destruction starting in 1576. The Spanish Habsburg's forces remained within the United Duchies throughout the rest of the sixteenth century, a looming spectre of violence enforcing Catholicism at court.

There was sufficient pushback against Catholic dominance within the United Duchies, with Berg and Mark remaining strongly Protestant in the 1570s and beyond. In 1574, a Spanish-influenced Inquisition of Faith was ordered at the Imperial diet but was later defeated at a local diet in 1577 because of the obstinance of Berg and Mark.

After the deaths of Olisleger and Heresbach, who were moderate in their approach to religious reform, traditional Catholicism came sweeping back into court in the United Duchies. The area remained mostly tolerant of Protestantism, but it was clear that the United Duchies was once more firmly dedicated to Catholicism. Johann Wilhelm, Duke Wilhelm's new heir, participated in his First Communion at Christmas 1578. It was conducted completely in the Catholic fashion.

A Positive End to the 1570s

Duke Wilhelm's third daughter and third child, Magdalena, married in 1579. She was matched with John I, Count Palatine of Zweibrücken. Magdalena was roughly twenty-six years old and her groom was twenty-nine. John I was known as John the Limping due to a physical handicap he had suffered since childhood, if not birth. The couple had eleven children between 1579 and 1593, five girls and six boys. Five died in infancy, and one before she was ten. The surviving two daughters and three sons went on to make good matches.

17

1580–1584

A Bride for Johann Wilhelm: Preliminary Search

In mid-1581, Duke Wilhelm began searching for a bride for his nineteen-year-old son and heir. Jakoba of Baden,[44] a Jesuit raised at the Bavarian court of her uncle, came to Duke Wilhelm's attention. Her cousin, Ernst of Bavaria, was on friendly terms with Duke Wilhelm. Ernst was a candidate for the position of Archbishop-Elector of Cologne. A union between the margravate family of Baden and ducal family of Jülich-Cleves-Berg was first considered in 1548, with Wilhelm hoping to wed at least Amalia, if not Amalia and Anna, to members of Baden's influential families. In 1571, Wilhelm's youngest daughter Sibylle was briefly considered as a potential bride for the young Margrave of Baden. Sibylle was marginally Catholic, and strengthening Catholic alliances for the United Duchies would serve to further the aims of the Counter-Reformation. This plan was never pursued because in 1578, when Sibylle was twenty-one, she declared that she wished to marry Count Karl von Arenberg. When Emperor Rudolf II rejected her request, Sibylle declared that she would rather spend the rest of her days in a cloister than wed anyone else. Negotiations for her marriage came to a standstill.

In 1579, the Catholic faction at the ducal court sought a Catholic bride for Johann Wilhelm in earnest. There were very few Catholic families who had young ladies of marriageable age, narrowing the choice to a bride from Lorraine or from Baden. Lorraine was not a palatable union at court due to the family's connection with the French royal family, the very same family

---

44 The German name Jakoba is similar to French/English Jackie. Loosely, it is pronounced YA-ko-ba. The true spelling in German is 'Jakobe', but the name has been anglicized slightly for ease of the reader. Her grandmother was named Jakobäa, which is the German form of 'Jacqueline'. Presumably, Jakoba was named after her grandmother.

who betrayed Duke Wilhelm during the Cleves War in 1543. A Bavarian bride was the best choice.

The main pro-Catholic officers at court were the Jülich Steward Johann von Ossenbroch, the Jülich *Landdrost*[45] Werner von Gymnich and Chamber Secretary Paul Langer. Gymnich had served in Karl Friedrich's household until the young man's death in 1575, going on to serve Johann Wilhelm until 1578. A staunch Catholic, he started out at the Imperial court. Gymnich was viewed as the leader of the pro-Catholic faction at the court of the United Duchies. Paul Langer and Gymnich enjoyed a reasonably good working relationship and provided stability to the administration of Jülich. Paul Langer died in November 1581 after a fall from his horse.

The ducal courts in Bavaria and the United Duchies exchanged wards from time to time, so a connection already existed. Ossenbroch sent his only son, John, to serve at the Bavarian court. When John left for Bavaria, Duke Wilhelm sent a horse as a gift to Duke William V of Bavaria, telling him that John had served Wilhelm's wife Maria well. Duke William V of Bavaria's mother was Anna of Austria, sister of Maria, Duchess of Jülich-Cleves-Berg. Wilhelm's daughters kept up some correspondence with their maternal cousins as well.

Duke Wilhelm was not terribly keen to see his son and heir marry just yet. Now in his early sixties, Wilhelm's speech and thought process showed the effects of his numerous strokes which had begun in 1566. He held on fiercely to his old ideas and modes of thinking, and was terribly afraid that once his son married he would try to oust his father. Wilhelm's fears for his own rule and the succession continued to grow, especially since he considered his surviving son Johann Wilhelm to be 'soft-headed'. Wilhelm was only too happy for the young man to be far away in Münster.

Sadly, the death of Wilhelm's wife Maria, by now mentally ill, temporarily stopped the search for a bride for Johann Wilhelm.

Death and Funeral of Maria

Maria von Habsburg of Austria, Duchess Consort of Jülich-Cleves-Berg, died on 12 December 1581, a little after midnight. The fifty-one-year-old had fallen ill on 4 December at Hambach Castle in the Duchy of Jülich. Maria and Wilhelm's daughter Sibylle was present, as were the court chaplain and various court officials. Her death was formally announced to the councillors of Cleves two days later, on 14 December. Johann Wilhelm, then in Münster, was notified last. Wilhelm asked him to abandon his ecclesiastical work in Münster and prepare to lead Cleves.

---

45 This word does not have an English equivalent, but appears similar to the French position of seneschal. The *Landdrost* is appointed, and governs with the assistance of an advisory commission; in addition, the *Landdrost* would oversee the administration of justice.

Preparations were made for Maria's funeral, which began on 21 December 1581. The citizens of the United Duchies were ordered to pray for Maria's soul, and mourning bells tolled throughout Jülich-Cleves-Berg for two days. The entire court wore mourning clothes. Wilhelm, Sibylle and their train prepared to accompany the coffin to Cleves.

A week later, on 28 December 1581, the funeral procession left Hambach Castle for the Ducal Palace in Düsseldorf, arriving there on New Year's Eve. As the mourning courtiers wound their way through the city, all the Düsseldorf officials, and many citizens and young scholars, joined the procession. The people fell away shortly before Maria's body reached the palace, where she was placed in the chapel. As part of the procession to Cleves, a dozen of the local nobles and their servants carried torches in front of the coffin, which was then led into the local church, likely St Lambertus. Maria was prayed over at each overnight stop by local clergy before being moved again. The cortège was accompanied by knights, and bells rang wherever it passed.

The usual New Year's festivities were held, despite what was surely a difficult time for Wilhelm, Sibylle and Johann Wilhelm.

On 3 January 1582, the court went to the fortified city of Orsoy, now part of the City of Rheinberg. The new fortress at Orsoy, ordered by Wilhelm in 1565, had just been completed by the architect Johann Pasqualini the Elder, son of the aforementioned Alessandro. On 4 January they continued their journey to Cleves, with Maria's coffin stopping in Xanten before finally arriving on the outskirts of Cleves on the 5th. Prayers were said over the casket on 7 January.

The Rhine was threatening to burst its banks by this time, so the funeral was pushed back by a couple days to allow for more people travelling to Cleves for the event to safely arrive by boat. Resuming their journey to the Swan Castle in Cleves, the party left on 9 January and finally arrived in Cleves on 11 January, a Thursday.

Maria's body was taken to the Swan Castle and placed in a chamber. The funeral was delayed until Monday 15 January because Wilhelm was not in good health over the weekend, presumably experiencing complications from his strokes. Maria was moved to Sankt Maria Himmelfahrt in Cleves for the funeral service, which was attended by Wilhelm and his daughter Sibylle. Johann Wilhelm missed it, sending his representative Dietrich von der Horst instead.

Amalia, Wilhelm's younger sister and Maria's sister-in-law, did not attend. She was residing at the Swan Castle, so easily could have, but refused because she was a staunch Lutheran and would not have been able to bring herself to attend Catholic Mass. Wilhelm, slighted by Amalia's behaviour, would get his revenge for the snub a few years later.

Written condolences came flooding in, including from the Imperial court. Pope Gregory XIII sent his condolences as well. Despite her melancholy nature and early reservations over the marriage, Maria and Wilhelm enjoyed a caring, fruitful marriage. Maria fulfilled her duty as Duchess Consort of the United Duchies perfectly. Her death was surely a great loss to Duke Wilhelm and their people.

Will Wilhelm Wed Again?

Wilhelm saw the death of Maria as an opportunity for him to remarry and produce more male heirs. Should he wed again and have more sons, Wilhelm could leave Johann Wilhelm in Münster, where he could continue in his position as Bishop of Münster. That would have made both Duke Wilhelm and Johann Wilhelm happy.

Wilhelm entertained the idea of marrying a woman from the ducal house in Bavaria, so long as she was at least seventeen years old. The best possible candidate from Bavaria was the Hereditary Duchess Maximiliana Maria of Bavaria, born in 1552. However, she was committed to staying at the court of her brother William V and focusing on her musical pursuits. Emperor Rudolf II, meanwhile, thought it more important for Johann Wilhelm to wed than for the physically impaired and elderly Wilhelm to do so in hopes of begetting more sons.

Aside from that, Rudolf II had other fires to put out. In the Archbishopric-Electorate of Cologne, neighbouring the United Duchies, the current leadership was becoming heavily Protestant. Trifling with Duke Wilhelm taking a youthful bride to produce a new heir, which could potentially disrupt stability in the area even further, did not seem to be a banner idea.

The Cologne War, 1583–1588

The Truchsessischer War, as it is known in Germany, or Cologne War, took place in the Archbishopric-Electorate of Cologne during the 1580s. Jülich-Cleves-Berg was drawn into the war owing to the United Duchies' proximity to Cologne, and because of the close relationship with the Imperial court.

The Cologne War was caused by the Archbishop-Elector Gebhard von Waldburg-Trauchburg, who wished to turn the Archbishopric-Electorate of Cologne into Protestant territory, take a wife and make the electoral seat hereditary. Holy Roman Emperor Rudolf II did not like that idea. Gebhard pushed forward, eventually meeting defeat. The Cologne War simmered in the background of the United Duchies' politics during the mid-1580s.

The Cologne War did not have a huge impact on the United Duchies, but Gebhard's actions during the war make it interesting. Born in 1547, he was elected to the position of Archbishop-Elector in December 1577, with the help of the counts of Neuenahr-Moers. The counts were very much in favour of the Reformation and anti-Catholic.

In March 1578, Gebhard became an ordained priest. This was not required for him to be the Archbishop-Elector of Cologne; the prior four archbishops had themselves renounced the priesthood. Gebhard was finally confirmed as the newly elected Archbishop-Elector by Emperor Rudolf in 1580. At this time Emperor Rudolf seemed to appreciate that Gebhard had won the election.

In the meantime, beginning in 1579 and two years after his elevation to Archbishop-Elector of Cologne, Gebhard found that he was in love with

Agnes von Mansfeld-Eisleben. Nicknamed *die schöne Mansfelderin* or the Beautiful Woman from Mansfeld, Agnes was born in around 1550, and had brown hair and dark brown eyes. She became the Canoness of Gerresheim, a Protestant establishment. Today, Gerresheim is part of Düsseldorf.

The counts of Moers owned the castle in Moers, which today is north of Düsseldorf on the west bank of the Rhine, across the river from Duisburg – in other words, firmly within the United Duchies. Given that Agnes was Protestant, and the counts of Moers were Protestant, they wished to pursue the relationship with Gebhard. Multiple secret meetings were arranged at Moers Castle to nurture the couple's budding romance.

Gebhard initially wanted to live with Agnes without marrying her. Agnes's family would not agree, especially because she was a Hereditary Countess of Mansfeld-Eisleben. However, if Gebhard gave up his post he might be able to marry her. Unfortunately, Gebhard was already an ordained priest, and could not cast off his spiritual duties so easily. This was the main distinction between Gebhard and others who gave up their offices to enter into Catholic marriages: he was a priest, and he could not give that up.

Instead, Gebhard decided to eschew the procedures set up in the Augsburg Religious Peace, become a Protestant, wed Agnes, establish a hereditary archbishopric and flagrantly break Imperial law. If successful, his actions would have a direct impact on the monasteries in Essen, Paderborn and, most importantly to Duke Wilhelm, Münster. On top of that, creating yet another Protestant Electorate meant that the next Holy Roman Emperor could potentially be a Protestant, which was anathema to Emperor Rudolf II.

In 1582 Gebhard attempted to pull Sybylla of Cleves' surviving sons to his side, along with the princes in the Palatinate, Brandenburg and Hesse. However, those princes were Lutherans, whereas Gebhard was leaning toward Calvinism. He found no support.

Rumours of Gebhard's plans eventually reached Pope Gregory XIII. Of course, the Pope was not enthusiastic about Gebhard's plot. He wrote to Gebhard, urging him to return to the fold. He also wrote separate letters to the Catholic officials within Cologne, telling them to resist Gebhard's ideas. If Gebhard were successful in turning Cologne into a Protestant territory, it was possible that the entirety of north-western Germany would follow suit. That would make way for a Protestant Holy Roman Emperor, spelling the end of Catholicism within the Empire.

To stop Gebhard, the choir bishop Friedrich of Saxon-Lauenburg seized the customary monies paid to the cathedral chapter and refused to give Gebhard access to them. Incensed, Gebhard raised troops in November 1582 and headed toward Bonn. He seized the city, plus a couple castles and towns in the surrounding area. Things were escalating quickly.

Negotiations began. Unfortunately for Gebhard, none of the important powers within Cologne agreed with him. Growing increasingly frustrated with the stalemate, Gebhard officially renounced Catholicism in December 1582. Now publicly Protestant, he also stated that he would not give up his position as Archbishop-Elector. Two months later, on Candlemas, 2 February 1583, Agnes and Gebhard were wed in Bonn.

Later, another Imperial diet was held in Cologne. Wishing to take a passive approach, Rudolf II asked Gebhard to step down. Gebhard dug his heels in further. In response, Pope Gregory XIII excommunicated Gebhard on 1 April 1583.

The Habsburg web of connections swiftly moved against Gebhard. In May 1583, Ernst of Bavaria was elected Archbishop-Elector of Cologne. His mother, Anna, was the daughter of Holy Roman Emperor Ferdinand I. Duke Wilhelm of Cleves' wife Maria was Anna's sister. Holy Roman Emperor Rudolf II was Anna and Maria's nephew through their brother Maximilian II. This also meant that Ernst of Bavaria and Emperor Rudolf II were cousins of Philip II of Spain, who sent in his Spanish forces to assist in securing Cologne. Ernst's brother William V of Bavaria sent in troops as well.

Support for Gebhard proved weak. By the end of 1583, the area around Bonn was recaptured and Gebhard fled to the Netherlands. With the assistance of William of Orange and his Dutch troops, he seized Bonn and its hinterland once more in 1587. The war effectively ended when Gebhard gave up in 1589 and moved to Strasbourg. He had been written out of his father's will back in 1583, and inherited nothing when his father died. He himself passed away in 1601, and was given a funeral worthy of his station.

Agnes Mansfeld-Eisleben

Agnes was the sixth of thirteen children born to her parents. As mentioned above, it is thought that she was born in 1550. Her parents were dedicated Lutherans. Agnes's maternal line came from Western Germany, not far from Cologne. Her paternal uncle was a canon in Cologne.

Agnes and Gebhard met in 1579 during an event held in Cologne celebrating the peace between Spain and the Netherlands. Accounts differ as to whether it was love at first sight for Gebhard or if Agnes seduced him, or some combination of the two.

On 16 December 1579, Agnes and her family were in Brühl, south-west of Cologne, to see off her sister and brother-in-law. Hearing that they were in the area, Gebhard invited Agnes and her parents to dine with him. They stayed the night, which wound up turning into a three-year affair between Agnes and Gebhard. They maintained separate residences during their relationship.

After the couple's Protestant marriage ceremony on 2 February 1583, they enjoyed a wedding feast at an inn in Bonn. They then packed up their valuables and headed north-west, visiting various noble houses during February and early March 1583 in hopes of winning more people to their cause. They were largely unsuccessful. The couple finally arrived in Cologne in mid-March.

Reports of the couple's behaviour after their arrival in Cologne vary. Those in favour of the couple wrote that they attended multiple church services together. Less favourable reports have it that Gebhard comforted himself with drinking all day and dancing with Agnes all night.

While Gebhard was off fighting, Agnes lived alone. In January 1584, Gebhard sent Agnes to the Netherlands in hopes of keeping her safe. They were reunited in April when Gebhard fled to the Netherlands himself. The couple stayed in Delft and then Utrecht, finally moving to Strasbourg in 1589.

Agnes and Gebhard always hoped to have children, although none ever came. They remained married until Gebhard's death in 1601. Agnes remained in Strasbourg for a couple months before fleeing, having been accused of leasing out rooms in her home to unsavoury persons. She then lived in Metz for roughly three years.

It is unclear where Agnes lived out her last year, and what year that was. One thought is that she spent the last few years of her life in the Palatinate, specifically in Grumbach Castle. Her sister was married to a noble who lived there. Some say Agnes died in 1615, in her sixties; others that she lived in Württemberg and died in 1637, well into her eighties.

The United Duchies' Involvement in the Cologne War

Spanish troops occupied portions of the United Duchies during the Cologne War, swiftly wearing out their welcome. Part of the issue was that the Spanish troops were Catholic while Jülich-Cleves-Berg continued to wax Protestant. Duke Wilhelm's council was mostly Catholic, and thus his advisors did not see a problem. The Protestant faction at court, and the Protestant subjects living within the United Duchies, wanted the Spanish troops ousted. There was serious concern that outsiders from either the Imperial or Spanish court would gain a foothold in the local government the longer Spanish troops remained on the United Duchies' doorstep.

Johann Wilhelm, who was twenty years old when the Cologne War started, desperately wished to join the war. Hopes for him were high within the Imperial court as he was a fanatical Catholic. In addition, his maternal cousin was Archbishop-Elector Ernst of Bavaria, upon whom he wished to make a good impression. Johann Wilhelm still held his office within the Bishopric of Münster, too, creating a sense of anxiety over the fate of Münster if the Protestant Gebhard were to succeed. However, Duke Wilhelm could not risk the death of his remaining son, and so forbade Johann Wilhelm from participating directly. This angered his son, causing a rift between the two men.

Marital Negotiations for the Von der Mark Dukes

Beginning in around 1581, it was recognised that Johann Wilhelm needed to wed. His cousins Philip II of Spain and Emperor Rudolf II, along with Pope Gregory XIII, all wanted Johann Wilhelm to marry a woman from a Catholic family. If he did so, the United Duchies would be more likely to continue having Catholic rulers. A Catholic marriage, combined with offspring raised as Catholics, would provide a strong counterbalance to the Protestant princes in Germany.

A Habsburg cousin would make an ideal bride for Johann Wilhelm. To that end, cousins from Mantua, Florence and Lorraine were all possibilities. Eleonora of Austria, younger sister of Johann Wilhelm's mother, was wed to Guglielmo Gonzaga, Duke of Mantua. Anna Juliana Gonzaga, born in 1566 and three years younger than Johann Wilhelm, was an initial candidate. Unfortunately, the untimely death of Archduke Ferdinand II's wife necessitated his remarrying and begetting heirs quickly, and so Anna Juliana wed Archduke Ferdinand II, a mutual cousin of Johann Wilhelm and Anna Juliana, in May 1582.

Another possibility came through Johann Wilhelm's Habsburg aunt Joanna, the youngest child of Holy Roman Emperor Ferdinand I and Anne of Bohemia. In the early 1580s, two of Joanna's three then-living daughters were eligible for marriage: Eleonora de' Medici, born in 1567, and Anna de' Medici, born in 1569. The youngest daughter, Maria de' Medici, was born in 1575 and was too young at the time Johann Wilhelm was seeking a wife. She went on to wed Henri IV of France in March 1600. One of the most enticing aspects of Johann Wilhelm marrying a Habsburg-Medici cousin was the amount of money that would accompany his bride. Sadly, Anna de' Medici died in February 1584, and Eleonora was married in spring 1584. That left only a bride from the Habsburg–Lorraine branch of the family.

The line of Christina of Denmark and Francis I of Lorraine proved very fruitful. Christina, niece of Holy Roman Emperors Charles V and Ferdinand I through their sister Isabella, had a son and two daughters with Duke Francis of Lorraine. Duke Francis was originally intended for Anna of Cleves. Charles III, Duke of Lorraine, married Henri II of France's daughter Claudia of Valois. Together they had nine children, seven of whom lived to adulthood. At the time that Johann Wilhelm came calling, their two oldest surviving daughters were possible brides.

The first Habsburg–Lorraine cousin, Christine, was born in 1565. She eventually wed into the Medici family in 1588. The other cousin, Antoinette, was born in 1568. She was not meaningfully considered as a bride for Johann Wilhelm, although her fortunes would change several years later.

Finally, the orphaned Jakoba von Baden was considered as a candidate for Duchess Consort of the United Duchies. Born 16 January 1558 to the Protestant Margrave Philibert of Baden and the Catholic Mechthild of Bavaria, Jakoba was the eldest of four children. Her only brother, Philip II, was born a year later and her sisters, Anna Maria and Maria Salome, were born in the early 1560s. Anna Maria was married in 1578, leaving Maria Salome as another candidate.

Sadly, the Baden children lost both their parents in the 1560s. Mechthild of Bavaria died on 2 November 1565, two days after the stillbirth of a boy. Their father, Philibert of Baden, died on 3 October 1569 at the Battle of Moncontour during the Third Huguenot War.

Jakoba and her siblings were sent to the court of their maternal uncle, Albrecht V of Bavaria. Albrecht was married to Johann Wilhelm's maternal

Habsburg aunt Anna. He was a committed Catholic and followed Jesuit teachings. Jakoba herself preferred Jesuit teachings as well.

A vivacious young woman, Jakoba was very popular at the Bavarian court. Albrecht was an art collector, and his daughter Maximiliana Maria was renowned for her musical talents. As Jakoba came of age, she had many suitors pressing for her hand.

In summer 1582, Johann Wilhelm decided he preferred Antoinette of Lorraine, who was six years younger than him and only about fourteen years old. His preference delighted the Protestant faction at court because Antoinette's aunt was married to the very Protestant Duke of Brunswick. Johann Wilhelm requested that a portrait of Antoinette be sent to him that July. He began making it known that he much preferred her, and that he was not at all keen to marry Jakoba of Baden.

Wilhelm, realistically favouring neither marriage, was against Johann Wilhelm marrying the very young Antoinette of Lorraine. Perhaps it brought to mind the shortcomings of his first marriage, to Jeanne d'Albret, remembering that she was only twelve years old when they wed. Given how desperate Wilhelm was to have a competent heir to the United Duchies, it's reasonable to think he wished his son to start producing heirs as soon as possible after his marriage.

Negotiations Begin

The 1582 Diet of Augsburg was attended by Duke William V of Bavaria and his sons, plus a delegation from Jülich-Cleves-Berg. The Imperial Commission arrived in early August, along with Jakoba's cousin Ernst, Archbishop-Elector of Cologne. It was decided that Ernst would pay a visit to Johann Wilhelm in hopes of persuading him to marry Jakoba of Baden. Given that the Imperial government was now involved, Johann Wilhelm might find that he had little genuine choice in the matter.

In late September 1582, Ernst ventured into Jülich-Cleves-Berg, staying at Castle Bensberg to the east of Cologne. Duke Wilhelm was also there, so the two men almost certainly had a chance to chat. Ernst left for Münster around 11 October to speak with Johann Wilhelm. That done, he returned to speak with Duke Wilhelm again. In the interim, Duke Wilhelm moved to Hambach Castle in Jülich. He dismissed the idea of Johann Wilhelm marrying at this point, temporarily delaying any type of negotiations. A portrait of Jakoba was requested by Ossenbroch, the last Catholic stalwart still alive at court. Gymnich had died at the end of September 1582, while Ernst was trying to convince Wilhelm that Jakoba was an excellent choice for the heir to the United Duchies.

The portrait of Jakoba did not arrive by January 1583, but small presents for Wilhelm did. Another portrait of Jakoba, specifically for Johann Wilhelm, was requested from the Bavarian court. This portrait arrived around February, but Johann Wilhelm's reaction is not recorded.

Ernst of Bavaria visited the United Duchies again in March 1583. He was intent to stay there a little longer, in part to convince Johann Wilhelm that leaving the Church and marrying Jakoba was the better choice. Discussions intensified in late April, and it was decided that Johann Wilhelm would wed Jakoba.

In early May, Antoinette of Lorraine's aunt Dorothea, Duchess Consort of Brunswick, arrived in Düsseldorf to convince Duke Wilhelm that her niece was a better choice. It was too late. However, Antoinette would eventually get another bite at the apple. Also in May, Johann Wilhelm asked the council in Münster to approve the Jesuit presence within the city. This was a nod to the Jesuit Jakoba.

First Meeting
The next step was to arrange a supervised formal meeting between Johann Wilhelm and Jakoba. This meeting, called a *Brautschau*,[46] was arranged for September 1583. The thought was that the new couple could enjoy the hunting season, always popular at the court of the United Duchies. Johann Wilhelm was known to delight in the sport. A small group of court officials went from Münster to Ingolstadt, then Munich in mid-September to meet with Duke William of Bavaria. The group travelled under the pretence of being a sort of delegation from Ernst to go speak with his brother William. Johann Wilhelm and his head of household, Dietrich von der Horst the Elder, were part of the delegation.

The delegation left Münster on 16 September 1583 and made a detour to Dachau, arriving on 25 September. Conveniently, Jakoba was there. Johann Wilhelm and the rest of the group stayed for a day. Johann Wilhelm was sufficiently impressed with Jakoba, and affectionate feelings for her quickly sprung in his bosom. Jakoba for her part seemed pleased with Johann Wilhelm. It was hoped the match would be successful.

Johann Wilhelm returned to his post in Münster by mid-October 1583, despite his impending nuptials. Marital negotiations carried on, with Duke Wilhelm finally realising that it was time for his son to marry a Catholic princess. Pope Gregory XIII, Philip II of Spain and Emperor Rudolf II all thought that she was a suitable match for the heir of the United Duchies, given her religious leanings. After all, Duke Wilhelm had to keep the Pope, the King of Spain and the Emperor happy or risk interference. Apparently, the potential of meddling from any of the large Catholic powers was more alarming to Wilhelm than being pushed out of the government by his son.

Last Minute Nerves
The papal curia, initially in favour of the match, had doubts by late 1583. Johann Wilhelm was still installed as Bishop of Münster, a position which had to be filled when he left. Additionally, there was still a strong pro-Protestant faction at the ducal court of the United Duchies which unnerved

---

46 Literally, 'bride-showing' or 'see the bride'.

Rome. On top of that, it did not make sense for Johann Wilhelm to carry on in Münster if he were taking a wife. Thus, the Pope demanded that Johann Wilhelm give up his position in Münster and return to the ducal court.

Johann Wilhelm, a zealous Catholic, did not want to give up his position in Münster. Leaving made the young man sad and wayward. His entire life was destined to be led within the confines of the Church. Given his current position in Münster and status as a duke, he could reasonably expect to become the Prince-Bishop of Münster and accrue all the benefits of such a position. By marrying, he would be giving up that path for a life he never intended as Duke of Jülich-Cleves-Berg. A compromise was put forward: Johann Wilhelm could be named Protector of Münster. However, the Pope did not like this half-in, half-out approach. Thus, Johann Wilhelm was forced to fully relinquish his religious life and fulfil his duty as the sole living male heir of Duke Wilhelm.

Emperor Rudolf, after reviewing the situation with the Pope and Duke William of Bavaria, threw his full support behind a Catholic match. While that was not a surprise, he also tacitly agreed that Jakoba was a good candidate for Johann Wilhelm. He decreed that Duke Wilhelm should keep his full power and position as Duke of the United Duchies for his natural life, alleviating some of the elder duke's fears.

Finally, Duke Wilhelm agreed on 6 May 1584 that his son should marry Jakoba in Düsseldorf on 1 July 1584. It is difficult to tell how he felt about his son's marriage. He was embittered for the rest of his life by the untimely death of Karl Friedrich in 1575, and feared for the future of the United Duchies because Johann Wilhelm was not as well suited to the position of duke as one would hope. Wilhelm might have envisioned a sort of retirement or joint reign with Karl Friedrich given his illness in the 1560s. It could be said that his hopes and dreams, even his sense of security, had died along with Karl Friedrich.

Waiting for the Wedding

The final negotiation for Jakoba and Johann Wilhelm was pushed back to later in 1584. It was moved to 12 September because Jakoba's brother Margrave Philip of Baden had some sort of accident from which he had to recover. There was also the issue of how large a dowry Jakoba would bring with her. Duke Wilhelm paid 35,000 guilders for each of his three elder daughters, all hereditary duchesses, and expected Jakoba's dowry to be comparable. Elector Ernst of Cologne, Jakoba's cousin, swiftly corrected Duke Wilhelm and informed him that Jakoba, as a hereditary margravine and thus of lower status than a duchess, would bring with her a dowry of only 10,000 guilders. The dowry and other terms settled, the wedding ceremony was set for 20 January 1585.

Duke Erich II of Brunswick, whose wife Dorothea of Lorraine had gone to Düsseldorf the year before, went himself in early September 1584. He wanted to make a last attempt to convince Duke Wilhelm that it was better to make a match with a Lorraine bride. But things were too far gone. Antoinette was sixteen years old at this point, a year too young for marriage by Duke Wilhelm's standards. The possibility of a Lorraine match was dead in the water.

As it became clearer that preparations would not be completed in time, the wedding was moved to 24 February 1585. Given that this was the wedding of the heir to the powerful United Duchies, a tremendous amount of materials and decorations needed to be ordered or created. It would be the grandest wedding the duchies of Jülich-Cleves-Berg had seen since the 1510 wedding of Johann III of Cleves-Mark and Maria of Jülich-Berg.

By December 1584, it was clear that things wouldn't be ready for the delayed date of 24 February 1585. Johann Wilhelm, anxious to marry Jakoba, was extremely disappointed when his wedding was pushed back again, this time to summer 1585. He railed against his father's council, assuming it was their obstinacy that was delaying things. Pope Gregory XIII was dismayed by the delays as well, and expressed his expectation that the wedding would take place soon.

This second delay provided a glimmer of hope for the Protestant faction at court. While he was in Düsseldorf, Duke Erich II of Brunswick made it broadly known that he had a possible bride for Johann Wilhelm. Duke Erich's cousin Julius had a couple of very young, unwed daughters. Julius was staunchly Protestant, and his proposal never gained any footing in Düsseldorf. The Protestant faction remained disappointed as the wedding date for Johann Wilhelm and Jakoba was rescheduled.

There was one last major step for Johann Wilhelm to take before his nuptials, namely the formal relinquishing of his duties in Münster. On 18 May 1585, Johann Wilhelm resigned his positions as Administrator and Bishop of Münster. Jakoba's cousin Ernst of Bavaria, already Archbishop of Cologne, was elected Bishop of Münster by majority vote.

While Johann Wilhelm was in Münster, Jakoba made her way from Munich to the Margraviate of Baden. She was escorted by her sister Maria Salome and Maria Salome's husband, Landgrave Georg Ludwig of Leuchtenberg. In Baden they met with Jakoba's brother Margrave Philip and their cousin Margrave Jacob, who then escorted Jakoba the rest of the way to Düsseldorf.

18

1585–1589

Jakoba Enters Düsseldorf

On Saturday, 15 June 1585, Jakoba of Baden arrived in Düsseldorf. Her brother Philip allocated as much money as he could to ensure his sister, who would now enjoy an elevated social position as the wife of a duke, would make a respectable first impression. A special parade route was constructed for her entry into the city.

Normally, a parade would enter Düsseldorf from the southern gate and head straight to the palace since it was the shortest and most direct route. For Jakoba's entry, the official path began to the east of Düsseldorf before winding south, then west, curving again to the east and then finally to the north and into the city. This circuitous route into the city allowed Jakoba to take in the view of her new home and for her new subjects to observe her for as long as possible. Soldiers of the United Duchies lined the parade route.

As she came nearer the city, Jakoba and her party were greeted by a salute of guns. She rode in a gorgeous carriage drawn by six horses. Duke Wilhelm's entourage rode out to greet her, accompanied by the joyous sound of many trumpets. A host of knights joined the ducal entourage as they escorted Jakoba and the bridal party the rest of the way into Düsseldorf. As she approached the city, more guns were fired and fireworks exploded to celebrate.

The time came for Jakoba to be greeted by her groom, Johann Wilhelm. He rode to her with ten high-ranking members of court to escort her on the last leg of the trip to Düsseldorf. The bridal and ducal parties then entered the city together. Colourful flags and banners were flown. The meeting was successful, the crowd was delighted.

The next afternoon, the new ducal couple celebrated their wedding ceremony in the chapel at the Ducal Palace. Afterwards, a full eight days of festivities took place.

Wedding Festivities

That evening, the first of many banquets and dances were held. A fabulous collection of coloured woodcuts, along with details of the wedding festivities, was created by Diederich Graminaeus to commemorate the occasion. The book, an original of which is possessed by the City Museum of Düsseldorf, is an excellent example of popular sixteenth-century festival books and gives us an idea of just how spectacular the wedding was.

A massive table was decorated with sweetmeats for the bridal party and nobility to enjoy after their main meal. It was set up in a long hallway outside the Great Hall, and fully laden with sugar works and other subtleties. The table looked as though it were covered in an orchard of trees, each with fruit hanging from the branches by little rings of gold. Surrounding the edible trees and fruits were depictions of rivers, mountains and the like. A major part of the sugary landscape was a fabulous replica of the Ducal Palace complete with flags representing the United Duchies and a figure of Jakoba standing in the main entrance. All manner of exotic animals and birds frolicked through the landscape, pursued by hunters while soldiers and someone riding a camel looked on.

Aside from the gorgeous scenery, various coats of arms were created in sugar work. This included, from left to right, the crowned Imperial eagle atop two lions; a familiar protective symbol, the pelican piercing her breast to feed her young; and the arms of Cleves and the arms of Baden, each held by a lion.

Jakoba, the members of her new *Frauenzimmer*, Johann Wilhelm and their courtiers all ate the delectable works of art created for them. When they were finished, the nobles retired. Afterwards, the palace's servants came and enjoyed what was left.

Ten tapestries were created for the wedding festivities, two of which hung in the Great Hall. They followed the history of the Apostle Paul, from his travels to his eventual beheading on the orders of Nero. Weaving these tapestries was no easy feat. A great deal of work went into designing and properly depicting Paul's trials and tribulations, and innumerable expensive, vibrant threads were used.

The Battle on the Rhine

On the evening of Monday, 17 June 1585, a mock water battle took place on the Rhine just beyond the palace. A heavily decorated ship, with all sails hoisted and flags billowing, sailed up the Rhine and dropped anchor in the harbour right outside the palace. The ship bore munitions and soldiers. A small fleet of three or four boats, carrying the aggressors, followed. These boats were also colourfully decorated. The fleet attacked the main ship, which then symbolically fired back by shooting fireworks towards the bank of the river and the palace.

The fireworks caused a degree of anxiety for the spectators. If they hit the ships that were gathered in the harbour, that would surely lead to disaster. Likewise, if the fireworks hit either the wharf, palace or city buildings, a fire could start and cause tremendous damage. Thankfully, the person who designed the water pageant was savvy enough to make sure the cannons fired far enough overhead, and short enough, that no one was hurt.

Eventually, the little fleet defeated the large ship. A blast of trumpets came from a fifth boat, and sailors from the large ship jumped into the harbour and either swam to the banks of the Rhine or were pulled into the smaller boats. The trumpets grew more intense as the large ship sailed away, then sank in spectacular fashion. The entire pageant could be seen from the Ducal Palace.

Opening of the Celebratory Tourney

On the third day of the marriage festivities, 18 June, the new couple enjoyed a large breakfast before being entertained with a tourney. The arena was a few miles outside the city and was large, with 12-foot wooden walls – after all, the tournament was meant to entertain the royal couple and not the curious public. A decorative arch was placed at the entry to the arena, surmounted by the marital arms of Johann Wilhelm and Jakoba, upon which a figure of Lady Victory was perched. The couple and the *Frauenzimmer* were seated in a three-level, highly decorated gallery across the arena from the judges' box.

Before the tournament began, a masquerade was put on featuring two women on horseback. The women wore their hair down, had attached fish tails and wore garments that made them look nude. The seemingly bare-breasted mermaids were led around the arena, representing either a cautionary tale of the Lorelei[47] and a reminder for Johann Wilhelm to remain faithful to Jakoba, or a reference to Melusine,[48] from whom the Von der Marks and other noble families in Europe claimed descent.

Within the large arena a dramatic piece of scenery was constructed for a kind of tableau vivant or pageant. A mountain, estimated to be roughly 20 feet tall, had an impressive stone gate, representing Thebes, built into the front of it. Music poured forth from inside the mountain. Actors were positioned on the mountain. A man and a woman stood with their male child at the gate, signifying a strong, fruitful marriage. On either side of the mountain were figures of Amphion and Orpheus, musicians from

---

47 This could have been an allusion to the Lorelei, who threw herself into the Rhine after her lover was unfaithful, after which she turned into a siren who lured men to their death on the river.

48 Melusine was a river spirit like a mermaid with either one or two tails, and sometimes wings. She has a penchant for being in holy water, or water at holy sites. The most ubiquitous image of Melusine in modern times is the two-tailed mermaid featured on Starbucks products.

Greek mythology. The music of Orpheus was known to soothe wild beasts. Amphion built the city of Thebes by the power of his music.

The mountain extended behind the gate by about 25 feet. Pan was at the base of the mountain, attempting to control a pair of rams, while other beasts frolicked on the mountainside. The actor playing Pan moved gracefully, like he was dancing.

A series of poems in Latin expressed hopes and dreams for the union between Johann Wilhelm of Jülich-Cleves-Berg and Jakoba of Baden. It was wished that Johann Wilhelm would hew great cities from stone and bring peace to the troubled United Duchies – and, of course, that they would stabilise the United Duchies by producing an heir.

Once the pageant was over, the tournament began. Jousting and running at the rings followed the opening masquerade. Participants in the games wore gay colours and were elaborately costumed. Those taking part in more dangerous aspects of the game wore armour.

The day was capped off with more dancing and a play on a large, purpose-built barge on the Rhine, an interpretation of Seneca's *Hercules Furens*. The five-act play is set, in part, in the city of Thebes. Recall that Thebes was represented in the pageant of the medieval mountain earlier that day. The play made use of fireworks at dramatic intervals, wowing the spectators.

At one point in the play, Hercules goes down to Hades or Hell, with Cerberus depicted at its mouth. Hercules fights a fire-breathing hydra, then enters the mouth of Hell, expelling the Devil through the top. At the end of the play, the hydra, Hell and the Devil were burned on the barge in spectacular fashion as Hercules and Cerberus escaped.

There was much less activity on the fourth day, a Wednesday. The only major event was a display put on by the fencing school in the palace courtyard. Still, due attention was paid to ensuring the pleasure of spectators. The courtyard, surrounded on all four sides by walls, had a dozen or so boxes built for viewing. Jakoba and her new *Frauenzimmer* were able to watch the fencing demonstration from their gallery inside the palace.

The Closing Ceremony

Thursday, 20 June saw more dancing and a flamboyant end to the knightly tournament. The closing events, held at the special arena outside Düsseldorf, were a sight to behold. The tilt yards for the jousting lists were outfitted with a device to shoot off fireworks, and the lists themselves appeared to be on fire. The knights who had participated in the tourney rode by the fire and tossed their broken lances into it. Unfortunately, a stray rocket set alight a portion of the wooden wall behind the judge's box. The sound of gunfire and trumpets marked the official end of the tourney.

Things were more leisurely on Friday, 21 June 1585 as the court and wedding guests toured the gardens of the Ducal Palace.

Another Spectacle on the Rhine

On Saturday there was one final grand spectacle set by the palace, a great battle between a whale and a dragon staged on the Rhine. The effigies of the whale and the dragon were each placed on a floating platform designed and decorated to be almost invisible.

The whale, an allegorical symbol for the biblical beast Leviathan, arrived at the palace first. To gain the attention of the bridal party and beckon them to the spectacle, fireworks were shot off. Fire emanated from within the whale's mouth as well, though it is difficult to tell whether the fire merely glowed inside the whale or if fire came out of its mouth.

Next, the winged dragon, with the Son of Perdition bound in its tail, floated to meet the whale in combat. Fire shot out of the dragon's mouth and eyes. As the fire-breathing dragon approached the whale, it seemed as it would burn it up. At the last moment, two spouts of water shot forth from the whale's back, creating a tremendous amount of black smoke. The whale also breathed fire back at the dragon. Both beasts sprayed fireworks.

Men dressed as sea monsters and soldiers crept out of the beasts and battled each other. The men who came from the dragon tossed the whale's men into the river. The whale was then blown apart from within by fireworks. The dragon's men jumped into the water, giving the appearance that they were chasing the whale's men, who were on their way to the riverbank. The dragon caught on fire because of the whale's proximity. The two models then floated away down the Rhine, burning up on the horizon. It was a truly amazing spectacle.

The Rhine was an ideal place to have fireworks shows because it was at a safe distance from the city, and there was not a proper place within the city to have a full display. The same was true for the tournament arena, built a good distance from Düsseldorf.

Final Amusements for the Celebration

Sunday, 23 June was the final day of festivities. This time, the party was brought to the citizens of Düsseldorf in the marketplace. Overlooking the marketplace stood the gorgeous new city hall, built in the Renaissance style in 1573 and heavily subsidised by Duke Wilhelm. At the time of writing it still stands. A parade from the Ducal Palace to the marketplace began the festivities. Johann Wilhelm participated in this parade, and was the only person on horseback. He was surrounded by knights, the group behind him carrying a massive version of the arms of Jülich-Cleves-Berg. Temporary structures were built for the melee competition, including a box for the judges. A low barrier was constructed in the centre of the square, where the melees took place.

Spectators at the melee enjoyed a fireworks display like the one seen by the nobles days before. On opposite ends of the combat area, perpendicular to the main barrier in the middle, coloured flames seemed to shoot forth from the ground in long lines. One of the judges tossed fireworks into the flames, creating a smaller but still impressive show close to the melee.

Back at the palace that evening, more entertainment awaited the wedding party. A comedic play and horse ballet were the main features. Orators tried their best to amuse the group, too. The play was another extravagant affair taking place in the palace courtyard with a box specially erected for the bridal party, and other spectators looking on from balconies in the courtyard. Bear-baiting might have been part of the entertainment. Two armies battled each other as part of the main show, and then fire-breathing cavalry charged in, leading one side to victory.

The eight-day festival ended that evening with a Mass dedicated to the Virgin Mary.

After the Wedding

Although Johann Wilhelm was pleased enough with his new bride, his father never took a true liking to Jakoba. She enjoyed indulging in parties and other expensive pastimes, which Wilhelm would not continue to provide for his daughter-in-law. Such expenses included keeping fools and actors ready at court to provide amusement, which was typical of the Bavarian court. Wilhelm saw no need.

The relationship between Duke Wilhelm and his son precipitously worsened after the latter's marriage. It got to the point where Duke Wilhelm would leave the room if his son walked in.

On top of this, Jakoba is sometimes blamed for pushing the increasingly ambitious Johann Wilhelm to try and wrest power from his father. Johann Wilhelm's pushiness, combined with his increasing Catholic fanaticism, forced Wilhelm to flee his court for the countryside to make serious decisions without his son's interference. Wilhelm felt contempt for his surviving son, which became increasingly obvious in the later years of the old duke's life. Some of this contempt was transferred to his daughter-in-law.

Johann Wilhelm began to act increasingly strangely in February 1586, but it was apparently nothing too serious. The behaviour was blamed on tensions with his father, or sadness over giving up his position in Münster.

Death of Amalia von der Mark, the Last Daughter of Cleves

Amalia of Cleves died on 1 March 1586 aged sixty-seven. Like her eldest sister Sybylla, she was a dedicated Lutheran. It has been claimed that Amalia was too Lutheran to wed a Catholic, which had been necessary after Duke Wilhelm's capitulation to Charles V in 1543. Amalia and Wilhelm were not always on the best of terms, either. The duke was very uncomfortable with Amalia's presence because of her faith, and as we have seen she refused to participate in the funeral of her sister-in-law because of it. Wilhelm had the last laugh, however, when he buried Amalia in what became a massive tomb dedicated to himself in St Lambertus Church in Düsseldorf. The huge tomb houses Wilhelm, Amalia and several other notable descendants of his.

More Challenges for Duke Wilhelm

As part of his ambitious building project, Duke Wilhelm ordered in 1585 that fortifications be built in Orsoy. The following year, the Spanish invaded the city. Orsoy was completely destroyed, and it took roughly fifteen years to rebuild. The citizens of the United Duchies could not have been pleased.

Johann Wilhelm's behaviour became more and more curious in 1586, including open hostility towards his father. Apart from his abrasiveness, however, he did not begin showing serious signs of mental illness until 1587, when he was about twenty-four. His increasing obsession with Catholicism was worrying to Wilhelm's councillors.

That same year, 1587, Jakoba was awarded the Golden Rose by Pope Sixtus V because of her faithfulness and services to the Catholic Church.

The year 1588 was difficult for Jakoba and Johann Wilhelm. Jakoba's brother Philip II of Baden died without any children. There was a slight struggle over who would inherit the territory, although not for long. Worse for Jakoba and Johann Wilhelm, they were three years into their marriage and Jakoba had failed to become pregnant. The young ducal couple were desperate to conceive a child, so they travelled to Ems in hopes that the waters there would cure their infertility. Despite attempts throughout 1588, nothing happened.

Johann Wilhelm Worsens

In 1589, Johann Wilhelm's paranoia increased. He believed that his father's Protestant officials were trying to poison him and that God's wrath was being visited upon him because of the presence of the very same Protestant officials. He suffered attacks of madness during summer 1589, but completely lost touch with reality in October 1589. Johann Wilhelm was permanently, profoundly melancholy, constantly fearing imminent death.

Wilhelm, for his part, was also profoundly ill from living with the side effects of stroke for over twenty years, and now in his seventies. Surely despairing even further over the loss of Karl Friedrich, Wilhelm was not very engaged with his son's plight. This only fed Johann Wilhelm's paranoid melancholy; surely it was a sign that Wilhelm wished to see him dead. Of course, nothing of the sort was true, but there was no reasoning with the young man.

Johann Wilhelm's mental illness began peaking in October 1589. He refused to take any medications prescribed by the court physicians, which included small doses of opium smuggled into his food. He evaded most attempts at surreptitiously administering medication because of his intense fear of poisoning, simply avoiding eating when he could.

Throughout his initial major spiral, Johann Wilhelm's fanatical obsession with Catholicism and fear of angering God appeared to be the main drivers of his illness. These were first dealt with by Duke Wilhelm's chaplain, Hubertus Fronhoven. The thought was that if Johann Wilhelm's spirit could be reassured of God's love, then he would slowly get better and no longer suffer from debilitating anxiety and fear. Johann Wilhelm was encouraged to pray, ask for the prayerful support of his future subjects, and give alms frequently.

Johann Wilhelm's sister Sibylle, unmarried and living at court, was alarmed by her brother's rapid decline. It did not help things that, like her father, Sibylle was unimpressed with her sister-in-law Jakoba. Still, she did what she could to be supportive of Johann Wilhelm.

Despite the best efforts of Duke Wilhelm, Jakoba, Sibylle and the court's clerics and physicians, Johann Wilhelm did not recover.

19

Descent into Madness

Bad News Spreads

News of Johann Wilhelm's complete descent into madness made its way to the Spanish court in January 1590. Johann Wilhelm was, after all, a cousin of Philip II of Spain. Philip in turn asked that his troops, then resident within the United Duchies and the Low Countries, prepare themselves to intervene in case Johann Wilhelm's Saxon cousins decided to assert a claim to the United Duchies. At this point in 1590, it was well known that Duke Wilhelm was living on borrowed time. Should he die and control go to Johann Wilhelm, the idea of Saxony, Spain or any number of German princes attempting to seize control over the wealthy United Duchies was very real.

Johann Wilhelm, the only legitimate male heir to the United Duchies, fell into an intense rage at the end of January 1590. As with his Spanish cousin Don Carlos,[49] Johann Wilhelm's violent rage resulted in him being confined to his rooms. All weapons were removed from his possession. He stopped bathing, refused to change his clothes, and did not care for his hair or overall appearance. During this onset of symptoms, Jakoba attempted to seize some meaningful influence and control over the United Duchies.

The Nature of Johann Wilhelm's Madness

Johann Wilhelm's illness was specified as melancholia, and one cannot be certain if it was wholly genetic, but unfortunately Johann Wilhelm appeared to have inherited mental illness from both his paternal and maternal sides.

---

49 Carlos, Prince of Asturias, was the first son of Philip II. He lived from 1545 to 1568. Carlos showed signs of instability even as a child, including a strong tendency toward violence. He sustained a head injury in 1562, whereupon his violent tendencies increased. Carlos tried to kill his paternal uncle Don Juan of Austria, and threatened to murder Philip. In January 1568, Philip imprisoned Carlos in his rooms. He died that summer.

On his mother Maria of Austria's side, Johann Wilhelm was a great-grandson of Juana of Castile, known as the Mad. Reports of Juana's madness are dubious, given that the report concerning her carting around her deceased husband's corpse was made by Juana's father to Henry VII of England at a time when the latter wished to marry her. Another report, allegedly signed by Juana, appears to have been forged. However, later in life Juana did appear to fall into deep depression. It would be difficult to discern whether Juana's mental health issues later in her life were caused by her roughly forty-year solitary confinement, enforced by her son Charles V, or an inherent mental condition.

On his father Duke Wilhelm's side, there was mental illness through both Maria of Jülich-Berg and Johann III. Maria's grandfather Duke Gerhard II of Jülich-Berg, Johann Wilhelm's great-great-grandfather, was profoundly mentally ill. He was declared unfit to rule when Maria's father was a young boy. As mentioned before, Johann III was regarded as somewhat simple-minded and Maria as a strong source of support for her husband and the United Duchies' government.

Johann Wilhelm's curious disposition was blamed by Dr Solenander and other court physicians on Maria von Habsburg and Duke Wilhelm. It was determined that Johann Wilhelm was 'by nature melancholy and depressed' and that he inherited his issues from both parents because 'his complexion is inborn, he is this way by nature from his father's seed and his mother's blood.' The doctors blamed Wilhelm's quartan fevers for his part in Johann Wilhelm's disposition but did not specify what it was about Maria of Austria's blood that led to Johann Wilhelm's affliction. The doctors firmly believed that Johann Wilhelm's faults were there at the moment of his conception in 1561.

Recommended Treatments

Johann Wilhelm's rapid and violent decline compelled the court physicians to act. In February 1590, they worked together to create a treatment manual specifically for Johann Wilhelm's recovery. Desperate to cure the future Duke of the United Duchies before the current duke's death, they subjected him to a barrage of treatments during 1590 and 1591. Aside from needing cheerful servants, he was ordered to be kept in rooms neither too hot nor too cold. The lighting must be neither too bright nor too dark. Heavy restrictions were imposed on his diet, and he was not to fall asleep until three hours had passed since his evening meal.

Jakoba and Johann Wilhelm were to enjoy only a moderate amount of sexual activity. It was thought that light activity, including that with Jakoba, was healthy but that anything causing more than a light sweat was too extreme. He was not permitted to fast a great deal, and he had to receive proper spiritual instruction from the United Duchies' official preachers.

A follow-up set of recommendations for Johann Wilhelm was produced in April 1590. Even Jakoba's personal physician contributed to the new instructions. Duke Wilhelm continued to send supportive letters to his son, including gently advising him to wear proper bedclothes, get enough sleep and keep his hair and beard neatly trimmed. A touch of Duke Wilhelm's mortal anxiety was evident in this missive; it wouldn't be long before his son would be duke.

Jakoba did as much as she could to appear as a dutiful wife to Johann Wilhelm. She still wished to conceive a child with him, and so would visit him once or twice a week. As mentioned, she had her own physician attend her ailing husband. She may have felt an odd sense of guilt over his condition, as it seems she was blamed for contributing to his decline by having amorous congress with him too often. That was nonsense, of course, but such were the times in which Jakoba lived.

Sibylle, for her part, wrote encouraging letters to her brother. As the only unwed Von der Mark daughter, she still had a role in assisting her father and brother. One can imagine the strain Sibylle felt in the early 1590s, watching the decline of both her father and brother.

In October 1590, a full year into Johann Wilhelm's madness, it was suggested that he was bewitched. To test this, a sample of Johann Wilhelm's urine was needed. Perhaps he was possessed by an evil spirit and was in need of exorcism. After much spiritual debate at the Jülich-Cleves-Berg court, the matter was referred to a panel of Jesuits in Cologne. They determined that the idea of witchcraft was a bridge too far, but that Johann Wilhelm was distinctly suffering from a combination of a physical inclination toward melancholy and a spiritual affliction.

Johann Wilhelm was deemed too mad for the Psalms to have a curative effect on his mind, and the distribution of alms had no impact. A wild remedy was proposed by a pastor from the countryside who claimed he could cure Johann Wilhelm within a month. The pastor believed that Johann Wilhelm's greatest fear had come to pass, and that the young man had indeed been poisoned. To cure him, the pastor would employ a combination of magical and spiritual remedies. These included special amulets, exorcisms and prayers. The pastor's help was turned down on grounds of superstition – a polite way of saying his remedies were too radically pagan and insufficiently grounded in scripture. More recommendations poured into the court, but most were too fantastical.

Maria Eleonore Returns

In 1591, Maria Eleonore was in a difficult position at the court of her husband, Albrecht Frederick, Duke of Prussia, in Königsberg. His mental health had begun failing in the late 1570s, and so a regency was put in place. The regency turned its eyes toward Maria Eleonore's daughters and their marriages. Maria Eleonore and her husband had seven children together, two boys and five girls, of whom four girls survived childhood and wed. Disagreeing with the regency's plans for her daughters, Maria Eleonore returned to the court of the United Duchies in 1591.

The two eldest daughters, Anna and Marie, were old enough to begin pursuing marriage. Maria Eleonore brought them with her to Jülich-Cleves-Berg in hopes of finding them husbands. The regency wished to marry off the girls to the Polish ruling house, which was very Catholic. Maria Eleonore, a Protestant, could not abide that. While in the United Duchies, she was able to gain control of her daughters' future, resulting in Anna marrying the Elector of Brandenburg in 1594. The rest of her daughters wed in the early 1600s, all to German husbands.

Maria Eleonore could not have been pleased with her Jesuit sister-in-law Jakoba of Baden, nor happy to witness the increasingly extreme mental illness of her brother or the sorry state of her father, who was nearing the end of his life.

Jakoba's First Attempt to Gain the Regency
After Johann Wilhelm went mad, Jakoba saw an opportunity to seize the regency of Jülich-Cleves-Berg. Neither her father-in-law nor her husband could effectively rule the United Duchies. Jakoba allied herself with the Protestant faction, predominantly found among the Cleves-Mark officers. This was mainly because Johann Wilhelm's Imperial cousins wished to take control of the United Duchies should he remain mentally ill. Jakoba, on the other hand, wanted the power for herself. Unfortunately, as a Jesuit, no one at the United Duchies court was very interested in placing her in charge. Jakoba's plan to gain the regency fell by the wayside.

Death of Duke Wilhelm
In December 1591, a regimental order concerning the governance of the United Duchies in the event of Duke Wilhelm's death was created during a recess from the Imperial diet. The Imperial Commissioners completed a draft on 7 December, which was ratified by Duke Wilhelm on 13 December.

Johann Wilhelm's sister Sibylle repeatedly mentioned in 1591 that their father was suffering from declining mental acuity. Wilhelm became increasingly weak by Christmastide 1591, such that he could not leave his bed. His personal physician, Reiner Solenander, reported that he was 'still of sound mind and more cheerful and animated ... [than] any day for the last several years'. Despite this, Wilhelm died on 5 January 1592, having outlived all his sisters, one legitimate son, one legitimate daughter and both of his wives. He was seventy-five years old, and had ruled as Duke of Jülich-Cleves-Berg for more than fifty-two years.

Jakoba's Second Attempt to Gain the Regency
Whatever the cause of Johann Wilhelm's deficiencies, he was mentally so far gone by the time of his father's death that he could not take up the mantle of government. All manner of things were prescribed to revive him, even orders to his servants to always behave cheerfully. Before his passing, Duke Wilhelm, under encouragement from his advisors, wrote caring letters to his

son, encouraging him to live a carefree life of hunting and walking, assured of his father's love. Jakoba offered her support through letters and attention. These efforts temporarily stabilised Johann Wilhelm, but unfortunately his mental illness was too severe.

In the early 1590s, Jakoba began sewing quotes of scripture into her husband's garments after he became Duke of the United Duchies. She was still desperate for an heir, and needed her husband to be well enough to create one with her. She also arranged for unconsecrated hosts to be secretly put in Johann Wilhelm's food. If he ever figured this out, one can only imagine that it exacerbated his mental illness rather than soothed it. After all, he was still terrified of being poisoned. As a last resort, Jakoba set love potions and tokens about Johann Wilhelm's chambers in the hopes of preserving his passions.

After the death of Duke Wilhelm, Jakoba lost no time asserting herself at court. Archbishop Ernst of Bavaria, Elector of Cologne, interceded with Emperor Rudolf II on Jakoba's behalf. He approached their cousin Emperor Rudolf II about granting Jakoba the regency. Emperor Rudolf II granted Jakobe governing powers on 12 May 1592, but she met with resistance. She was not appointed sole regent but rather a joint power with the councillors. She did try to exert power over the governance of Jülich-Cleves-Berg, but her attempts at securing support were often clumsy, vacillating from faction to faction.

With the ongoing support of Archbishop-Elector Ernst of Bavaria, Jakoba petitioned Emperor Rudolf II to give her more power. The ducal councillors were displeased to say the least. In 1593, Jakoba learned that vicious rumours were being spread about her around court. Despite the warning, she ploughed on with her attempts to seize greater powers. Emperor Rudolf II refused her requests.

At the same time, the councillors for Jülich-Cleves-Berg saw right through Jakoba's machinations. She swiftly lost favour with them as well, especially because she had failed to produce the all-important male heir, or any child at all. Jakoba was losing her grip on political power.

Salacious rumours about Jakoba trickled through the court at around this time. One was that she and a ducal councillor had begun an adulterous affair in 1592. This endangered the paternity of any child Jakoba had, and with it the line of succession for the Von der Mark dukes. Even so, she cavorted publicly with Dietrich von Hall zu Uphoven, the ducal councillor, from roughly 1592 through 1595. Her behaviour was flagrant enough that the government chose to involve itself. At the same time, she had physical custody of her mentally ill husband, and maintained herself and Johann Wilhelm in the Ducal Palace in Düsseldorf. It is likely she had liaisons with Dietrich here, as well.

All the while, Duke Johann Wilhelm languished in a state of madness.

Jakoba's Downfall

Jakoba's fall from power was swift and harsh. At the regional Diet of Grevenbroich in 1595, it was decided that Jakoba would no longer care for

Johann Wilhelm. Additionally, control over the Ducal Palace was seized by the government. Jakoba was arrested and held in a tower at the Ducal Palace. Then, finally in a position to oust her awful sister-in-law, Sibylle charged Jakoba with adultery and unlawfully imprisoning Johann Wilhelm. Jakoba's fall from grace was complete when Emperor Rudolf II revoked the powers he had granted her three years before.

Quickly following her imprisonment, members of court were interrogated about Jakoba's behaviour. As result of their testimony, and likely also the acrimony of Sibylle and the ducal councillors, a 100-count indictment was brought against Jakoba. Eventually, she was brought to trial before an Imperial representative. All the allegations were about her immoral, adulterous behaviour. She was found guilty and further imprisoned in autumn 1595. It was hoped that, with Jakoba being found guilty on the Imperial level and not just the local level, her marriage to Johann Wilhelm could be annulled.[50]

Efforts were made by Jakoba's brother-in-law, Landgrave Georg Ludwig of Leuchtenberg. He was married to Jakoba's younger sister Maria Salome, and the only person willing to stand up for her. In his youth Georg Ludwig was a ward of Duke Wilhelm, and lived and worked at the court of the United Duchies in 1580. He had officially escorted Jakoba to her wedding with Johann Wilhelm back in 1585, and the young ducal couple took in Georg Ludwig's son William to raise at court. William was surely named after Duke Wilhelm V.

Georg Ludwig tried to assist Jakoba in convincing the Pope that her case should be heard in Rome, and not Düsseldorf. It was to no avail. Jakoba, who turned thirty-eight in January 1596, was swiftly abandoned and ostracised by her remaining family members. She found herself an orphan of sorts.

Jakoba faced further humiliation when the ducal councillors tried to secure the annulment of her marriage to Johann Wilhelm. The Imperial court was silent on the matter, which had the effect of not supporting or enforcing an annulment. The papal curia was approached between late 1595 and early 1596 to secure an annulment, but the curia would not agree. This was presumably because Jakoba was a Jesuit, meaning that she would uphold Catholicism with any offspring she had with Johann Wilhelm. If the mentally unwell Johann Wilhelm married a Protestant, that could wildly change the religious alignment of the United Duchies.

Jakoba's Mysterious Death

Jakoba remained imprisoned throughout 1596 and well into 1597. Her continued existence posed a problem for the succession of the United Duchies, not to mention an unnecessary expense. Unless Johann Wilhelm,

---

50 Jakoba's swift fall seems reminiscent of what happened to Anne Boleyn sixty years earlier and four hundred miles west, at the Tudor court in England.

now thirty-five, could remarry and produce a male heir, the male line would fail, and the United Duchies would fall into chaos.

In August 1597, Johann Wilhelm signed a document requesting that the thing 'causing him distress be abolished within a few days'. This was all that was needed to remove Jakoba from court. It is not known if Johann Wilhelm comprehended fully what he was signing.

On 2 September 1597, Jakoba von Baden, Duchess Consort of Jülich-Cleves-Berg, was by all accounts quite well. Despite being imprisoned, she was in good health. She was not reported to be ill. The next morning, she was found dead in her bed.

It is unknown how Jakoba died, although strangulation or poisoning were considered likely. Sibylle is often pegged as the mastermind behind Jakoba's death, although there is no proof. This is not surprising because the individuals who would have been involved in a murder plot were also the ones who compiled the official records about the death. Another theory is that Jakoba took her own life. Months before her death, in a letter to Georg Ludwig, Jakoba mentioned that she was so alone and inconsolable that she considered doing something which would not be pleasing to God. Either scenario, a murder or suicide, is possible.

Jakoba's death, though known about court, was not publicly acknowledged. Jakoba was buried hastily and unceremoniously on 10 September 1597 at Kreuzherrenkirche, or Lord of the Cross Church, some 20 miles to the south-west of the Ducal Palace in Düsseldorf. She was not buried in the magnificent crypt created by her father-in-law in the St Lambertus Church, which was just behind the Ducal Palace, and the court did not don mourning garments. There was no marker for Jakoba's final resting place within the church. Her remains were respectfully moved to St Lambertus in 1820, and reburied with appropriate ceremony. A sad end to what was surely a difficult life.

For those interested in the supernatural, it is said that Jakoba haunts the only tower of the Ducal Palace in Düsseldorf still standing. It is now a maritime museum. Jakoba is apparently sometimes seen as a lady in white, silently roaming the tower. Other reports of her ghostly appearance say that she is cloaked in black, with a long train on her dress, which rustles as her headless form slips by.

Johann Wilhelm's Second Wife

Jakoba's death opened the door for Johann Wilhelm, however unstable, to marry again and produce a male heir. Negotiations with the court in Lorraine began almost immediately. Antoinette of Lorraine, a Habsburg cousin of Johann Wilhelm, was a prime candidate. Antoinette was the granddaughter of Francis of Lorraine and Christina of Denmark, and the granddaughter of Henri II of France through her mother, Claudia of Valois. However, the councillors for the United Duchies needed to be certain that Antoinette was fertile. The United Duchies needed an heir, and urgently.

In 1598, a court physician was sent from Düsseldorf to Nancy to determine whether Antoinette was in good enough health to bear Johann Wilhelm's children. She was now almost thirty-one years old, and past her prime for the sixteenth century. She was ten years younger than her predecessor, so at least that was in Antoinette's favour.

The report from the court physician was mostly positive. Antoinette appeared in good health, although her shoulders were noticeably uneven, with one much higher than the other. She had 'a fine face, healthy colour, and … a good nature. She eats, drinks, and converses very well.' Antoinette was finally deemed an acceptable bride for Johann Wilhelm, at least fifteen years after the idea was first broached.

Antoinette and Johann Wilhelm married on 20 June 1599, fourteen years after Jakoba had married Johann Wilhelm. Antoinette, from a very Catholic family and herself staunchly Catholic, strengthened the Catholic faction at court. Johann Wilhelm and Antoinette were both descended from Philip von Habsburg and Juana of Castile. As mentioned, Johann Wilhelm was Juana and Philip's great-grandson, and Antoinette was their great-great-great-granddaughter.

Catholic Antoinette was a more than acceptable bride for Johann Wilhelm in the eyes of the Imperial court. Her blood relation, like Johann Wilhelm's, to Emperor Rudolf II made her seem more trustworthy than her predecessor, who had no such ties. Antoinette succeeded in being appointed by the Imperial authority as co-regent of the United Duchies. Essentially, she succeeded in multiple ways in which Jakoba failed.

After their marriage, Antoinette and Johann Wilhelm toured the countryside of the United Duchies. The couple visited several spas, and sought blessings for their marriage from local priests. Johann Wilhelm, who would never recover from his mental illness, at least seemed relatively pleased and at ease with his new bride. She had a calming effect on him. The new marriage seemed promising.

The Exorcism of Johann Wilhelm

Johann Wilhelm did not remain stable for long. Treatments prescribed by court physicians never really worked. No amount of prayers seemed to help him, either. Antoinette, along with others at court, became convinced that Johann Wilhelm was possessed by the devil himself and needed to be exorcised. To that end, she organised an exorcism in 1599. She sent for a priest from her father's court in Lorraine to lead it. Antoinette was present for the entire event. An unidentified person later wrote an account in 1612 from the recollections of eyewitnesses at the exorcism, documenting how Johann Wilhelm was treated.

The account, written by a 'nobleman and patriot', is undeniably fascinating in that it gives us an understanding of how early modern exorcisms were performed. The fact that a noble was put through this treatment is astounding.

The exorcism, which began around 5 September, was violent, but it started off harmlessly enough. Johann Wilhelm and members of his court were at Hambach Castle, then being used by the duke as a hunting lodge. Foreign priests summoned by Antoinette and their religious retinue awaited Johann Wilhelm and his company as they returned from a hunting excursion. The priests gathered in Hambach Castle's galleries to greet Johann Wilhelm, who was immediately apprehensive when he saw them. According to the report, Johann Wilhelm behaved strangely toward them because 'he was able to think or suspect without a doubt that the priests or monks are not being called for in vain, but are called to the place for the sake of the cause' of exorcising him.

Aside from dispossessing Johann Wilhelm of whatever demon was harassing him, the monks and priests wished to remove any impediment to Johann Wilhelm's congress with Antoinette. The hope was that God would make them fruitful. Johann Wilhelm was keenly aware that the United Duchies needed an heir, especially since his first marriage was childless.

First, the group assembled in Johann Wilhelm's chamber and prayed together. Then, to begin the exorcism, 'according to the old custom, a stool [with] a velvet pillow was placed on the ground in front of [Johann] and his princely Grace kneeled down ... behind him and sitting next to him on both his sides were three spiritual counselors, next to several gentlemen and others ... then the litany was read.' A monk from the Order of St Ambrose, who was likely an Italian, led the reading of the litany with a Jesuit priest.

For the exorcism, the omnipotence of God was emphasised, as was the assertion that God would sanctify all those who asked. Next, everyone present was asked to pray for Johann Wilhelm. In turn, he was exhorted to pray to receive healing. He was told that he was possessed by an evil spirit, and that he needed healing.

After the litany, many benedictions were read by the Venerable Father Zacharias from Lorraine, who led the exorcism. After the benedictions, the exorcism began in earnest. First, a portion of the Gospel of St John was recited. Next, all the religious persons present laid their hands upon Johann Wilhelm to heal him. As they were doing this, Johann Wilhelm made the sign of the cross. He also kissed and blessed a special cross made of black wood (possibly ebony) with gilt silver, used especially for the exorcism.

Father Zacharias prepared his own words for the exorcism, which he screamed and shouted at Johann Wilhelm. The writer of the account quipped that Father Zacharias believed the demon possessing Johann Wilhelm was deaf. Again the word 'attacked' is used to describe the exorcism, but it does not say if there was a strong physical element involved. Johann Wilhelm was a pitiful figure during the exorcism, and several witnesses held back tears over their duke's treatment.

The exorcism next turned to the problems of Johann Wilhelm's marital bed. Namely, it was believed that his demonic possession made Johann Wilhelm impotent. This could be why, having had her own experiences with

Johann Wilhelm, Antoinette thought it so important to have the exorcism. They had to save the succession, or else the United Duchies would very likely face a war fought among Johann Wilhelm's sisters.

Finally, Father Zacharias wanted to identify the malicious spirit possessing Johann Wilhelm. Father Zacharias demanded that whatever possessed Johann Wilhelm place a mark upon his right hand. The purpose was for the priests to identify who or what was responsible. It was feared that Satan was the one possessing Johann Wilhelm, not a lesser demon.

The act of demanding that the spirit show itself by making a mark on Johann Wilhelm is likely where physical violence entered the exorcism. Johann Wilhelm was ordered to produce his right hand for the evil spirit to make its mark. The priests hoped not only to identify the evil spirit from the mark it made, but also to determine if the spirit was inside Johann Wilhelm, animating him, or if it was hovering around him. The assembled group began reciting Ave Maria and Paternoster, genuflecting all the while.

Much to the frustration and despair of the group, 'it was all in vain: none of us could observe a single sign of this or that on the hand.' After considerable effort to force the evil spirit to make itself known, it was decided that the party should leave Johann Wilhelm's chamber and move to the castle chapel. The priests renewed their demands that the evil spirit make an identifying mark on Johann Wilhelm's right hand. It is not stated how physical the exorcism became, but the priests were certainly screaming at Johann Wilhelm for an extended period of time. Still, there was no mark made by a demon on his right hand.

The priests made the exorcism 'too long and too rough for the gentleman ... it finally annoyed him, because they went after the devil so hard to place a sign on [Johann Wilhelm's] hand, that his Princely Grace still at the altar, sat on his knees ... and said in Latin: *ipsi estis Daemones aut à Daemonibus obsessi*; or, They are demons or possessed by demons!' This was taken as the much-desired sign by the priests.

Johann Wilhelm stormed off back through the castle galleries, shouting for his bodyguards. He ordered them to 'attack the traitors and villains' who put on the exorcism. This the bodyguards did not do, even though Johann Wilhelm was in a fearful state.

After his flight to the galleries, Johann Wilhelm was led back to the chapel and made to kneel before the altar again. The priests continued with the exorcism. The evil spirit was once more exhorted to make a sign on Johann Wilhelm's right hand. He was not interested in doing this, so the priests finally gave up on trying to make the evil spirit identify itself.

The priests next began to say Mass, with emphasis on the words of St John the Evangelist. During the consecration of the Eucharist, the priest, presumably Father Zacharias, turned and made the sign of the cross at Johann Wilhelm, then turned back around. When the priest was elevating the Host, he heard a laugh coming from behind him. Assuming it was Johann

Wilhelm, the priest turned back around and 'admonished his Princely Grace and the devil to look at [the Host] properly, and especially ordered the devil, by all the force and power to be moved to be obedient to the priest'. Then Father Zacharias attempted to call out the devil, beginning the closing portion of the exorcism.

Once Father Zacharias finished his part of the exorcism, one of the monks 'began banishing the devil because of his disobedience and … cursing him and banishing him into the Abyss of Hell, and carried on for a good half an hour with terrible curses, at the sound of which one had to be terrified.' Next, an image of the devil was scourged.

After scourging a tall figure of the devil with candle wax and whipping it in front of Johann Wilhelm, an image of the devil made on paper was whipped, burned and ground into powder. The same was done with roughly fifty names of other possible demons, all written on little pieces of paper. Symbolically, the priests and monks burned and stoned Satan and his minions.

All this took quite some time. Johann Wilhelm's courtiers were incensed on their prince's behalf. Johann Wilhelm was openly annoyed, too. It was evident to the priests and monks that those present were quietly mocking them. The religious persons, disheartened by their apparent failure, slackened off toward the end of the exorcism. Johann Wilhelm and the others present were told that, even despite some impediments, St Peter would still welcome into Heaven those who were worthy.

Precautions against Further Possession

After this lengthy and theatrical failure, the clerics repeated the exorcism process two or three more times at Hambach Castle. Although there is not a record of the proceedings, it seems that the subsequent exorcisms were nowhere near as intense or laborious as the first and were limited to the castle chapel. During their entire time at Hambach, they prayed over Johann Wilhelm's meals and sprinkled holy water on his food.

As an ongoing protection against further demonic possession, certain precautions were taken in Johann Wilhelm's bedroom. Although it is unclear from the report, the following precautions and actions were recommended and implemented by the exorcists before they left Hambach:

> … in all 4 corners of all my Grace's Lordship's chambers they had pasted little crosses blessed with holy water, and behind my Grace's Lordships' bed a wooden cross was hung and also one in the middle of his bedroom … they also had his Princely Grace wear a small sachet about his neck full of papers upon which were written prayers against demons, and little crucifixes, which my Grace's Lordship once cut open in the middle of the night and threw [the papers and crucifixes] throughout the room … [bemoaning] all these crimes and superstitions.

A new bed was ordered for Johann Wilhelm as well, with more incantations and crucifixes stuffed into the mattress. At one point, the bed was taken apart for fear that something strange or demonic was in it. Presumably, this fear arose due to Johann Wilhelm's continued erratic behaviour. Nothing out of the ordinary was found, and another bed had to be ordered.

In addition to the steps mentioned above regarding Johann Wilhelm's meals, the parties consumed 'fragrant, round little cakes' in the duke's bedroom. Before bed, consecrated oil was smeared on 'his Princely Grace on his belly just under his navel ... likewise also about the head, about which my Grace's Lordship often complained'. One can guess that the consecrated oil was placed under Johann Wilhelm's navel in hopes of relieving him of his infertility or impotence.

All of Johann Wilhelm's clothes, bedlinen and pillows were burned and replaced, as was the bed itself. The old floor was destroyed and a new one laid in its place, and the plaster walls of the palace were frantically cleaned. Prayers were then said throughout Johann Wilhelm's chambers, and all the food within the palace was blessed as it was delivered. It was as if they were guarding against disease, and not demonic possession.

When it came time for the priests and monks to leave, it was obvious that they had worn out their welcome. They wished to bid Johann Wilhelm goodnight, but he acted as if he did not know them. He did not wish to hear anything else from them, nor to shake their hands. This seems to be more a symptom of Johann Wilhelm's illness than a display of genuine displeasure. The morning after the priests and monks departed, 'when my Grace's Lordship got up, he asked twice whether the monks were going away, to which [the valet] replied: yes; if they would come again, their Princely Grace was told by the valet: no.' Johann Wilhelm was apparently delighted by the news, because a smile broke across his lips.[51]

Lead exorcist Father Zacharias fell ill on the return trip, and stayed over at a palace in Bruges to recover. He was eventually taken back to Lorraine in a horse-drawn litter. Upon his arrival there, he boasted about being transported in the manner of a duke and then 'gave himself up to the Margrave', meaning he reported back to an officer of Antoinette's father, Duke Charles III of Lorraine and Bar.

A New Century, and the End of the United Duchies

Johann Wilhelm fell into a mental stupor as the 1600s began. Rather than suffering from fits of rage, it seemed as though his intelligence was slipping away. While more docile, he was becoming less competent than ever.

---

51 At the end of the recollection, it says, '*Haec sunt, quae de illis et eorum actibus mihi modo occurrunt, sed lecta foras ne efferantur, precor*' – 'These are the things recorded about them and their deeds that occur to me at this moment, but only read the contents, and do not divulge them, I beg you.' Oops.

Sibylle finally left court in 1601 at the age of roughly forty-three. She finally got her wish and married Margrave Karl of Burgau, whose family had hosted Sibylle's brother Karl Friedrich decades before. Cousins through their Habsburg relations, they never had any children. Sibylle was known as a patron of music during her time as Margravine Consort of Burgau.

Johann Wilhelm turned forty years old in 1602. He was still childless. Any hope of him conceiving an heir was virtually gone. Antoinette and the council ran the government, while Johann Wilhelm's sisters and their heirs waited to swoop in and take over as soon as he was dead.

Johann Wilhelm's Death

Johann Wilhelm's physical health noticeably declined in late 1608. His stomach swelled, although at first it was believed that he had overindulged in food and was merely overweight. Until early 1609, despite showing signs of illness, the duke was never bedridden. He was resistant to treatment from his doctors at first, but eventually relented. On the evening of 24 March 1609, Johann Wilhelm's body was seized by a painful swelling. The pain was so bad that he could not sleep, and the normal remedies prescribed by his doctors barely did anything. By the next morning, 25 March 1609, Johann Wilhelm was fading fast. He passed away between seven o'clock and eight o'clock that evening, with his court-appointed priests and chaplains present. His death at the age of forty-six was a shock to the court and his doctors since he had not shown overt signs of illness beyond some swelling.

Prayers and mourning were ordered in Düsseldorf and Cleves for the deceased duke. He was the last of the Von der Mark dukes, and died without any children, either legitimate or illegitimate. There is a claim that he fathered a child with one Anna op den Graeff, named Herman, who was later disinherited; the misattribution comes from the surname 'Op den Graeff', which has been mistakenly translated as 'of the count'. However, the Dutch word for count is Graaf, and the German is Graf, making the words too dissimilar. Additionally, bastard sons born to the dukes of Cleves and Jülich-Berg were typically given a geographical surname instead of something like 'of the count' or 'of the duke'. For example, known bastards in the United Duchies included John of Cleves, John of Jülich and John of Berg. As is evident, they were also usually called John.

Aside from the naming discrepancy, Johann Wilhelm was kept in Münster from his elevation to bishop in 1574 until his marriage to Jakoba von Baden in June 1585. Hermann op den Graeff was born in November 1585, meaning that he had to have been conceived in early 1585. Given his life within the Church and his devout faith, it is highly dubious that Johann Wilhelm would have conceived a child and that there would have been no record of it until the 1800s. Also, given that Johann Wilhelm was deathly afraid of Calvinists and other Protestants, it seems extremely unlikely that he had a morganatic marriage with one. On top of that, surely there would have been gossip at the court of the United Duchies, the Imperial court or that in Bavaria concerning this illegitimate son, especially since there was so much concern over stabilising the United Duchies with an heir.[52]

Johann Wilhelm, last of the Von der Mark dukes, was just shy of forty-seven when he died. Because he had no heir, the United Duchies of Jülich-Cleves-Berg was up for grabs by his nephews. Johann Wilhelm's body was prepared for burial and placed within a lead casket. It lay in the chapel of the Ducal Palace in Düsseldorf for almost twenty years.

When Johann Wilhelm's neglected state was finally recognised, he was given a full state funeral. His body was moved, with full dignity, from the chapel in the Ducal Palace to the magnificent tomb which Duke Wilhelm had built inside St Lambertus. With his belated burial, the line of Von der Mark counts, then dukes, who ruled over Cleves, Mark, Ravenstein, Zutphen and eventually Jülich-Berg, came to an end.

---

52 Although I mentioned Op den Graeff in the epilogue of *Anna, Duchess of Cleves: The King's Beloved Sister*, I found after further research that there is no genuine basis for this connection.

The Thirty Years War

We are now at the end of the Von der Marks' hold on the United Duchies. After Johann Wilhelm's death in 1609, control of Jülich-Cleves-Berg was hotly contested. The dispute between the descendants of Duke Wilhelm V's daughters simmered before erupting in 1618 into the Jülich-Cleves Succession Crisis, which set the stage for the western theatre of the Thirty Years War. This massive conflict was the culmination of multiple issues within the Holy Roman Empire, not to mention other international disputes. It was a time of impossibly complex political divisions. What follows are the broad strokes of the Thirty Years War, including the specifics of the Jülich-Cleves Succession Crisis.

The German Thirty Years War took place from 1618 to 1648. The larger arc of the struggle can be traced back to the 1555 Peace of Augsburg, which allowed for the different principalities in Germany to observe Catholicism or Lutheranism. Thus, the war did have a religious background to begin with, although it turned into a dispute over territory towards the end. There were four main arcs to the war, starting with the Bohemian–Palatinate crisis, then Danish–Lower Saxony, followed by a Swedish element, and finally culminating in a Swedish–French series of battles.

Holy Roman Emperor Rudolf II, grandson of Ferdinand I and grandson and great-nephew of Charles V, never had legitimate children of his own. Additionally, he was exhibiting a high degree of mental instability toward the end of his life. This was perhaps due to his parents being so closely related.

In 1599, Rudolf's younger brother Matthias attempted to persuade Rudolf to leave the Empire to him if he should die without heirs. Rudolf resisted. Seven years later, in 1606, Rudolf was declared mentally unfit by his family, and Matthias replaced him. However, just because the Habsburgs declared Matthias the de facto Holy Roman Emperor did not mean that the various territories under Habsburg rule agreed. As such, gaining control over the eastern portion of the Empire was a struggle for him. Most importantly, religious tensions heightened across the Empire.

Matthias was, in a word, lazy. He was ill with gout and not terribly robust by the time he took the Imperial reins in 1608. After Rudolf's death in 1612, he was formally elected Holy Roman Emperor. Like his brother Rudolf, he did not have any legitimate children. In 1617, the Habsburg territories were divided between the Spanish and Austrian Habsburgs. This still left the question of who would follow Matthias to the Imperial throne. Matthias, although disinterested, saw to it that his and Rudolf's brother Ferdinand was installed as King of Bohemia in 1617. Matthias then called the Diet of Hungary in 1618 to have Ferdinand recognised as his successor as Holy Roman Emperor, among other pressing issues. At the same time, a new palatinate position was established, creating further instability within the Empire.

By the time of Matthias's death in March 1619, the initial rebellion by the Bohemians was underway. With this as a background, the Jülich-Cleves Succession Crisis began.

After Johann Wilhelm's death on 25 March 1609, a rapid series of microaggressions took place in an effort to seize control of Jülich-Cleves-Berg. At first, Johann Wilhelm's widow Antoinette of Lorraine was allowed to administer the territory. Emperor Rudolf II initially required any claimants to the United Duchies to assemble at the Imperial court, but Elector Johann Sigismund of Brandenburg and Duke Philip Ludwig of Pfalz-Neuburg ignored this and laid their own claims to the United Duchies. Johann Sigismund married Anne of Brandenburg, Johann Wilhelm's niece through his oldest sibling Maria Eleonore, and therefore claimed the United Duchies *jure uxoris*. Philip Ludwig of Pfalz-Neuburg was married to Johann Wilhelm's second oldest sibling, Anne, and he, too, claimed the United Duchies *jure uxoris*.

Johann II of Pfalz-Zweibrücken-Veldenz, nephew of Johann Wilhelm through his sister Magdalena, claimed the territory as well. A fourth claimant, the Electors of Saxony, had a much more tenuous connection to the United Duchies. Cleves had been promised to the Electorate of Saxony as part of the marriage negotiations between Sybylla of Cleves and Elector Johann Friedrich I of Saxony in 1526, but the events of 1547 whereby Electoral Saxony had transferred from the Ernestine branch to the Albertine branch could not have been contemplated at that time. The Elector of Saxony laying claim to the United Duchies was from the Albertine branch, not Ernestine and thus was not a descendant of Sybylla of Cleves.

The claims through Johann Wilhelm's sisters stem from the marital agreement concerning the Imperial privilege between Wilhelm V of Jülich-Cleves-Berg and Maria of Austria in 1546.

Fed up with this, Emperor Rudolf II seized Jülich in May 1609. An Imperial officer arrived in the territory and urged the claimants to rule the area together, with Rudolf II overseeing the joint rulership. This did not please the Elector of Brandenburg or the Duke of Pfalz-Neuburg, although they had little choice.

At the Recess of Dortmund that July, it was agreed that Elector Johann Sigismund of Prussia-Brandenburg and Wolfgang Wilhelm, son of Duke Philip Ludwig of Pfalz-Neuburg and Anne of Jülich-Cleves-Berg, would co-administer the United Duchies. Rudolf II did not approve of this plan, and allowed bands of mercenaries under the control of the Austrian archdukes Matthias and Ferdinand to advance on Jülich-Cleves-Berg. The might of Prussia-Brandenburg was magnified in western Germany because Johann Sigismund had control of Cleves-Mark.

In the meantime, in the fortress city of Jülich, Colonel Johann von Reuschenberg zu Overbach, part of Duke Johann Wilhelm's former government, refused to recognise the authority of Wolfgang Wilhelm of Pfalz-Neuburg. Colonel Reuschenberg took over the Jülich citadel in the name of Emperor Rudolf II. The Austrian archdukes joined Colonel Reuschenberg, and they set up a small Imperial government in Jülich. The standoff drew the attention of France, the Netherlands and England. Henri IV of France was willing to provide troops to Elector Johann Sigismund and Wolfgang Wilhelm if the two would provide support for an incursion into the Spanish Netherlands.

In February 1610, Henri IV, Elector Johann Sigismund and Wolfgang Wilhelm entered into a treaty whereby they agreed to defend each other against the Emperor and Spain. The three would besiege Jülich. They managed to muster around 20,000 troops between them. On top of their troops, James I of England and Maurice of Orange mobilised forces to engage in the dispute.

Reuschenberg, and by extension Rudolf II, soon saw that no one was coming to interfere with the succession crisis, and so relented. Nothing came from the Netherlands and France for the time being, because Henri IV of France died on 14 May 1610, temporarily easing the international nature of the brewing conflict. The ensuing peace lasted until 1614.

In 1614, Duke Philip Ludwig of Pfalz-Neuburg died. His son with Anne of Jülich-Cleves-Berg, Wolfgang Wilhelm, then took up the familial claim to the United Duchies. In November 1614, the parties met in Xanten and agreed to the terms of the Treaty of Xanten on the 12th. As part of the treaty, dominion over the Duchy of Cleves and the counties of Mark and Ravensberg was given to Elector Johann Sigismund of Brandenburg and that of the duchies of Jülich and Berg to Duke Wolfgang Wilhelm of Pfalz-Neuburg. However, the peace could not last. The Treaty of Xanten was imperfect, particularly in one major area: a provision stated that the United Duchies were to remain united. Elector Johann Sigismund and Wolfgang Wilhelm did not want that.

The duchies of Jülich and Berg were invaded off and on over the ensuing decades. Finally, in 1651, a preliminary settlement was agreed between Pfalz-Neuburg and Brandenburg. It took a further fifteen years before the Treaty of Cleves was ratified in 1666, handing Jülich-Berg to Duke Wilhelm's great-grandson Philip Wilhelm, Count Palatine of Neuburg, and Cleves-Mark to Duke Wilhelm's great-great-grandson Elector Friedrich Wilhelm of Brandenburg.

The United Duchies of Jülich-Cleves-Berg, united in 1521 under Johann III of Cleves-Mark and Maria of Jülich-Berg, ended with the death of their grandson Johann Wilhelm eighty-eight years later, in 1609. The Duchy of Cleves, led by the Von der Mark dukes, did not last two centuries.

Appendix I

The Great Tudor Die-off

In 1557, an influenza pandemic gripped the known world. The virus was first recorded in Asia, then, following ports of call, emerged in Africa, Europe and finally the Americas. One tell-tale symptom was a person having catarrhal fever, a serious inflammation of the upper respiratory system. The rate of deaths and miscarriages increased during the pandemic, and successive waves of the disease alarmed governments enough to ask physicians to create regulations to control the disease. Economic impacts were palpable.

In England, Wriothesley noted in 1557 that 'this summer reigned in England divers strange and new sicknesses, taking men and women in their heads; as strange agues and fevers, whereof many died.' The disease mercilessly tore through the army of Mary I, making it impossible for her to provide sufficient reinforcements to the Earl of Rutland, then battling with the French at Calais. The Earl of Rutland was doing his best to hold Calais but ran out of men. Mary I lost Calais to the French by January 1558. It was a serious wound to morale for England, which held portions of land in French territory for hundreds of years.

The rate of burials in England escalated between 1557 and 1562, and outpaced the number of christenings. Similar to events leading up to the Black Death in 1347 to 1348, famine preceding the influenza outbreak of 1557 to 1558 weakened the populace. Their weakened constitutions made it more difficult for their bodies to fight off the infection.

The dangerous outbreak continued into the summer and autumn of 1558. In September that year, a couple of months before Mary I died, there were reports of a deadly, highly contagious illness spreading in the port cities of Portsmouth and Southampton, and on the nearby Isle of Wight. A month later, in Dover, people reaching the city by ship were dying in droves. A lot of them had come from Calais. The disease finally reached London around mid-October 1558.

The disease, with fever, body aches, headache and cough, frequently wracked the stomach. Bloodletting was a popular treatment. Unfortunately, bloodletting seems to have increased the likelihood of death.

Several Tudor courtiers and notables died between summer 1557 and late 1558. The list below is not exhaustive, but it provides an idea of the seriousness of the outbreak. For the curious reader, further research is encouraged.

16 July 1557: Anna von der Mark, Hereditary Duchess of Jülich-Kleve-Berg. She was forty-two years old, and complained of a stomach ailment before her death. As noted earlier, Anna's body was cered and placed inside a lead casket quickly after her death. No autopsy was performed.

July 1557: Geoffrey Glynne, Welsh lawyer and graduate of Cambridge. He died in London.

25 August 1557: Mary Fitzalan, Duchess of Norfolk: Daughter of Lady Katherine Grey. She was about thirty-seven years old. She died eight weeks after the birth of her only child. She was buried 1 September 1557.

13 September 1557: John Cheke, English scholar and statesman.

20 October 1557: Mary Fitzalan, Countess of Arundel. During her lifetime, Fitzalan tended to Jane Seymour and Anna of Cleves. She was the stepmother of Mary Fitzalan, Duchess of Norfolk.

25 October 1557: William Cavendish, English knight and courtier. He was fifty-two years old.

7 December 1557: Lady Mary Howard Fitzroy, Duchess of Richmond and Somerset. Mary was the wife of Henry Fitzroy, and only daughter-in-law to Henry VIII. She was roughly thirty-eight when she died.

December 1557: Sebastian Cabot, explorer. He was around seventy-three years old.

31 May 1558: Philip Hoby, English ambassador to the Imperial court. He was about fifty-three years old. Hoby died at his home in Blackfriars, London.

28 June 1558: Thomas Darcy, 1st Baron Darcy of Chiche. Courtier under Edward VI, supporter of Lady Jane Grey. He died at home in the port city of Wivenhoe, Essex. He was fifty-one years old.

29 September 1558: George Brooke, 9th Baron Cobham. English soldier and peer. He was roughly sixty-one.

1 November 1558: Anne Braye Brooke, Baroness Cobham. Part of Anne Boleyn's coronation in 1533, and an accuser of Anne Boleyn in 1536. She wrote her will roughly a month before she died. Anne's husband George predeceased her by roughly a month. She was fifty-seven years old.

17 November 1558: Mary I. She was forty-two years old.

17 November 1558: Cardinal Reginald Pole. He was fifty-eight.

30 November 1558: Lady Elizabeth Stafford, Duchess of Norfolk. She was the second wife of Thomas Howard, 3d Duke of Norfolk. Elizabeth was approximately sixty-one when she died.

November 1558: Hugh Aston, English composer. He was buried on 17 November. Hugh was around sixty-three years old.

16 December 1558: Thomas Cheney, Lord Warden of the Cinque Ports. He was about seventy-three years old.

20 November 1559: Frances Brandon Grey, Duchess of Suffolk. Daughter of Mary Tudor and Charles Brandon; mother of Lady Jane Grey.

Appendix II

Witches and Demons in the United Duchies

Humming along quietly but menacingly in the background, the topic of witches and demons appeared consistently throughout the sixteenth-century history of the United Duchies. The most obvious appearance at the ducal court was during the treatment of Johann Wilhelm, when the council was desperate to heal the duke.

Concerns over diabolical witchcraft were not widespread in German-speaking areas until the early fifteenth century. The first mention of witchcraft is in German-speaking Switzerland at that time. Between 1428 and 1439, more than 200 people were accused of being servants of the devil and executed. By the mid-fifteenth century, witch hunts and witch burnings reached the Rheinland.

During the childhood of Sybylla, Anna, Wilhelm and Amalia, claims of witchcraft and demonic possession abounded throughout the United Duchies. Women were the usual culprits of witchcraft, although at least one man was burned for the offence in the early part of the sixteenth century. Two men from Dortmund were accused of being the devil's servants in 1522, and subsequently burned.

No one was safe from demonic possession, not even nuns.

Weather Witches in Duisburg

The winter of 1513 going into 1514 was uncharacteristically cold. There was very little rainfall during this time, too, meaning the wells and creeks were running dry. On top of that, a large part of the Rhine froze solid, making the movement of goods extremely difficult. Weeks later, a heavy snowfall hit the area and then melted, causing a great flood three days later. The combination of freezing and thawing, drought and flooding, caused extensive damage to homes, docks and ships. Clearly, it was the work of witches, and they needed to be found.

The witches held responsible were discovered between 1513 and beginning of 1514. Two women were executed on a pyre in November 1513, followed by another six soon after. One was burned two weeks later, and another woman was killed in Duisburg on 8 February 1514. Eight days later, another accused witch was executed.

The Demonic Nuns of Xanten

One of the more curious tales about dealings with the devil comes from the area of Xanten, which lies north of the City of Cleves. Within modern Xanten lies the district of Marienbaum, a former hamlet. It was here in 1430 that Maria of Burgundy, wife of Duke Adolf I of Cleves-Mark, established a double monastery of St Mary's Assumption. The new monastery followed the teaching of Birgitta of Sweden.

In the early sixteenth century, a troubling report came in that the nuns at a monastery in Marienbaum had been afflicted by demons for at least ten years. The exact name of the monastery is not specified, but it could have been St Mary's Assumption.

The nuns were horribly vexed by the demons. Their veils were torn from their faces and they were shoved out of their seats while in church. Some of them made terrifying sounds. The nuns' mouths were kept shut so that they could not eat.

A demon appeared to a young woman who was desperately in love with a man whom her parents would not allow her to marry. The demon, who took on the appearance of the young man, directed the young woman to visit the nuns. Once there, she, too, was possessed. Eventually, the young woman managed to escape. She went home to her father, and then was promptly imprisoned in Dinslaken. Over time, all the demonic affectations which the young woman bore disappeared. She eventually recovered.

Years later, two former nuns who were now in their eighties confirmed that they were part of the group who were tortured by demons.

In around 1516, a nun named Ulant Dammarz kept the devil as her lover. She called upon him, and he asked Ulant to be faithful to him. Ulant had to renounce the Virgin Mary and God. Thereafter, the devil and a company of demonic young men and maidens came whenever Ulant wanted. Together, Ulant and the demonic company would spin and dance together, although to onlookers Ulant appeared to be standing still. It was also reported that the demonic company, including Ulant, held amorous congress.

Ulant tried to charm her friends and fellow nuns with various pastries and fruits bewitched by the devil. Her liaison with the devil continued for roughly five years. It got to the point where she could no longer see the Holy Sacrament, and had extreme difficulty performing her duties as a nun. She was convicted of heresy, sorcery and blasphemy, and ultimately burned to death for her crimes.

The United Duchies and Witchcraft

There were many other alleged incidences of witchcraft in the United Duchies. Curiously, witchcraft was never meaningfully legislated against until after the death of Johann Wilhelm.

Bibliography

Primary Sources

31 Hen. 8 c. 8. 1539.

32 Hen. 8 c. 25. 1540. Held by the Newberry Library, Chicago. Case folio KD125 1540.

Bangen, Johann. *Thüringische Chronik oder Geschichtbuch*. Mühlhausen (1599).

Bouterwerk, Karl Wilhelm. 'Exorcizatio, an Herzog Johann Wilhelm geübt'. *Zeitschrift des Bergischen Geschichtsvereins*. Vol. 13.

Brewer, J. S., ed. *Letters and Papers, Foreign and Domestic, Henry VIII, Volume 1, 1509-1514*. London: His Majesty's Stationery Office (1920). Nos. 1071, 1311.

Brewer, J. S., ed. *Letters and Papers, Foreign and Domestic, Henry VIII, Volume 3, 1519-1523*. London (1867). Nos. 274, 1155.

Brewer, J. S., ed. *Letters and Papers, Foreign and Domestic, Henry VIII, Volume 4, 1524-1530*. London: Her Majesty's Stationery Office (1875). No. 6364.

Brewer, J. S., ed. *Letters and Papers, Foreign and Domestic, Henry VIII, Volume 5, 1531-1532*. London: Her Majesty's Stationery Office (1880). No. 707.

Brown, Rawdon, ed. 'Venice: 1503', in *Calendar of State Papers Relating To English Affairs in the Archives of Venice, Volume 1, 1202-1509*. London (1864). No. 830.

Brown, Rawdon, ed. 'Venice: April 1515,' in *Calendar of State Papers Relating To English Affairs in the Archives of Venice, Volume 2, 1509-1519*. London: Her Majesty's Stationery Office (1867). No. 598.

Brown, Rawdon, ed. 'Venice: June 1522, 16-30,' in *Calendar of State Papers Relating To English Affairs in the Archives of Venice, Volume 3, 1520-1526*. London: Her Majesty's Stationery Office (1869). No. 479.

Brown, Rawdon, ed. 'Venice: November 1534,' in *Calendar of State Papers Relating To English Affairs in the Archives of Venice, Volume 5, 1534-1554*. London: Her Majesty's Stationery Office (1873). Nos. 26,

Brüll, Wilhelm. *Chronik der Stadt Düren*. Düren: L. Vetter & Co (c. 1895).

Byrne, Muriel Saint Clare. 1989. *The Lisle Letters: An Abridgement*. Chicago: The University of Chicago Press.

Crecelius, Wilhelm. 'Bekenntnis einer als Hexe angeklagten Nonne aus dem Jahre 1516.' Vol. 9. *Zeitschrift des Bergischen Geschichtsvereins*. Elberfeld (1873).

Gairdner, James, ed. 'Henry VIII: October 1537, 1-5,' *Letters and Papers, Foreign and Domestic, Henry VIII, Volume 12 Part 2, June-December 1537*. London: Her Majesty's Stationery Office (1891). No. 825.

Gairdner, James and R. H. Brodie, eds. *Letters and Papers, Foreign and Domestic, Henry VIII, Volume 14 Part 2, August-December 1539*. London: Her Majesty's Stationery Office (1895). Nos. 200, 223, 248, 274, 286, 328, 347, 388, 389, 469, 493, 675.

Gairdner, James and R. H. Brodie, eds. *Letters and Papers, Foreign and Domestic, Henry VIII, Volume 15, January-August 1540*. London: Her Majesty's Stationery Office (1896). Nos. 14, 68, 76, 161, 169, 171, 242, 243, 267, 304, 309, 315, 334, 344, 356, 368, 389, 401, 482, 483, 800, 801, 843, 845, 850, 860, 861, 872, 873, 881, 991.

Gairdner, James and R. H. Brodie, eds. *Letters and Papers, Foreign and Domestic, Henry VIII, Volume 16, September 1540 – December 1541*. London: Her Majesty's Stationery Office (1898). Nos. 11, 633, 650, 687, 711, 823, 917, 929, 980, 1306, 1328, 1445, 1449.

Gairdner, James and R. H. Brodie, eds. *Letters and Papers, Foreign and Domestic, Henry VIII, Volume 17, 1542*. London: Her Majesty's Stationery Office (1900). Nos. 55, 35, 128, 225, 232, 251, 328, 418, 44, 464, 503, 528, 541, 554, 589, 599, 616, 773, 1014, 1017, 1241.

Gairdner, James and R. H. Brodie, eds. *Letters and Papers, Foreign and Domestic, Henry VIII, Volume 18 Part 1, January – July 1543*. London: Her Majesty's Stationery Office (1901). Nos. 44, 62, 150, 196, 203, 259, 284, 288, 296, 331, 390, 397, 511, 519, 534, 544, 600, 641, 707, 723, 766, 771, 776, 862, 925, 931, 954, 969.

Gairdner, James and R. H. Brodie, eds. *Letters and Papers, Foreign and Domestic, Henry VIII, Volume 18 Part 2, August-December 1543*. London: His Majesty's Stationery Office (1902). Nos. 20, 25, 73, 140, 142.

Gairdner, James and R. H. Brodie, eds. *Letters and Papers, Foreign and Domestic, Henry VIII, Volume 19 Part 1, January – July 1544*. London: His Majesty's Stationery Office (1903). No. 15.

Gairdner, James and R. H. Brodie, eds. *Letters and Papers, Foreign and Domestic, Henry VIII, Volume 20 Part 1, January – July 1545*. London: His Majesty's Stationery Office (1905). Nos. 315, 619, 682.

Gairdner, James and R. H. Brodie, eds. *Letters and Papers, Foreign and Domestic, Henry VIII, Volume 21 Part 1, January – August 1546*. London: His Majesty's Stationery Office (1908). Nos. 479, 931, 998, 1018, 1070, 1112, 1115, 1129, 1155.2, 1165, 1312, 1343, 1392, 1410, 1480, 1526.

Gairdner, James and R. H. Brodie, eds. *Letters and Papers, Foreign and Domestic, Henry VIII, Volume 21 Part 2, September 1546 – January 1547*. London: His Majesty's Stationery Office (1910). Nos. 34, 242, 257, 388, 430, 438, 495, 496, 602, 658.

Grillandari, Giovanni Battista dei. *Repudio della Reina Maria d'Inghilterra*. Bologna: Antonio Giaca (1558).

Graminaeus, Dietrich. *Die Fürstliche Hochzeit*. 1587.

Holinshed, Raphael. 1808. *Holinshed's Chronicles of England, Scotland, and Ireland*. Vols. III and IV. London: Brooke, Paternoster-Row.

Howard, Henry, Earl of Surrey; Sir Thomas Wyatt the Elder; and George Frederick Nott, D. D., F. S. A. 1816. *The Works of Henry Howard Earl of Surrey and of Sir Thomas Wyatt the Elder*. Vol. II. London: T. Bensley, Bolt Court, Fleet Street, for Longamn, Hurst, Rees, Orme, and Brown, Paternoster-Row.

Hume, Martin A. S. and Royall Tyler, eds. 'Spain: November 1547, 1-15,' in *Calendar of State Papers, Spain, Volume 9, 1547-1549*. London: His Majesty's Stationery Office (1912. The Emperor from Augsburg to Van der Delft, 15 November 1547.

Jansen, Jan. 1610. *Des Fürstlichen Geschlechts Und Hauses Gülich/Clef/Berg Und Marck/ u. Stamm Register*. Arnheim.

Kleinsorgen, Gerhard von. *Tagebuch von Gebhard Truchses Kölnischen Erzbischof*. Part III. Münster: Anton Wilhelm Aschendorf (1780).

Kastner, Ruth and Thomas A. Brady, Jr. 1994. *Quellen zur Reformation 1517-1555*. Darmstadt: Wissenschaftliche Buchgesellschaft.

Kohler, J. and Willy Scheel. *Die Peinliche Gerichtsordnung Kaiser Karls V.: Constitutio Criminalis Carolina*. Halle: Verlag der Buchhandlung des Waisenhauses a. S.

Kunde, Anne-Katrin. *Das Stammbuch der Grafen und Herzöge von Kleve*. Kleve: Museum Kurhaus Kleve – Ewald Martaré Sammlung (2017).

Kurfürst Johann Friedrich I. von Sachsen: Korrespondenz aus den Jahren 1549–1551 – Universitätsbibliothek Heidelberg, Cod. Pal. germ. 692 https://katalog.ub.uni-heidelberg.de/titel/67105374.

Lemon, Robert ed. 'Edward VI – Volume 15: November 1552'. *Calendar of State Papers Domestic: Edward VI, Mary and Elizabeth, 1547-80*. London: Her Majesty's Stationery Office (1856). No. 45.

Lossen, Max. 'Drei Briefe an die Gehmahlin des Herzogs Wilhelm von Jülich-Cleve-Berg, Herzogin Maria, Tochter des Roemischen Koenigs Ferdinand (1557 und 1560). Vol. 20. *Zeitschrift des Bergischen Geschichtsvereins*. Bonn: A Marcus (1885).

Luther, Martin and C. A. H. Burkhardt. 1866. *Dr. Martin Luther's Briefwechsel*. Leipzig: Verlag von F. C. W. Vogel.

Luxembourg, John of. *Loraison et remonstrance de haulte et puissante dame Madame Marie (sic) de Cleves, sœur de treshault et puissant seigneur, le duc de Juilliers, de Cleves et de Gueldres, faicte au roy d'Angleterre et a ceulx de son Conseil. Joannes a Luxemburgo III. faciebat*. France (1542). Held by the British Library.

Manchyn, Henry and John Gough Nichols, F.S.A. 1848. *The Diary of Henry Manchyn, Citizen and Merchant-Taylor of London, from A. D. 1550 to A. D. 1563*. New York and London: AMS Press.

Melanchton, Philipp, Christine Mundhenk, Heidi Hein, and Judith Steiniger. 2006. *1648-1979: (1536-1537)*. Stuttgart-Bad Cannstatt: Frommann-Holzboog.

Nichols, John Gough. 1850. *The Chronicle of Queen Jane and of Two Years of Queen Mary*. London: J. B. Nichols and Son, Printers, Parliament Street.

Ryff, Fridolin, Alfred Sterns, and Wilhelm Vischer. 'Die Chronik des Fridolin Ryff 1514-1541'. *Basler Chroniken*. Vol. 1. Leipzig (1872).

Pighius, Stephanus. *Hercules Prodicius seu Principis Juventutis Vita et Perigrinatio*. Cologne: Lazari Zetzneri (1609).

Sloane MS 1047, f. 30Vv. Held by the British Library.

Turck, Johannes and Ferdinand Schroeder. ‚Die Chronik des Johannes Turck'. *Annalen des Historischen Vereins für den Niederrhein, insbesondere das alte Erzbistum Koeln.* Issue 58. (1893/4).

Tyler, Royall, ed. *Calendar of State Papers, Spain, Volume 11, 1553.* London: His Majesty's Stationery Office (1916). Aug. 27. Vienna, Imp. Arch. E.20, Sept. 30. Vienna, Imp. Arch. E. 20, 9. Vienna, Imp. Arch. E. 20, Oct. 15. Vienna, Imp. Arch. E. 20, Nov. 14. Vienna, Imp. Arch. E. 20, Dec. 9. Vienna, Imp. Arch. S.

Tyler, Royall, ed. *Calendar of State Papers, Spain, Volume 12, 1554.* London: His Majesty's Stationery Office (1949). Feb. 8. Vienna, E. 22, Feb. 12 Vienna, E. 22, Feb. 18. Besançon, C.G. 73, April 3. Brussels, R.A. Prov. 13.

Turnbull, William B. *Calendar of State Papers Foreign: Edward VI 1547-1553.* London: Her Majesty's Stationery Office (1861). Nos. 312, 364.

Turnbull, William B. 'Mary: March 1554,' in *Calendar of State Papers Foreign: Mary 1553-1558.* London: Her Majesty's Stationery Office (1861). No. 167.

Van der Schüren, Gert and Dr. Ludwig Tress. *Chronik von Cleve und Mark.* Hamm (1823).

Von Below, Georg. *Landtagsakten Von Jülich-Berg: 1400-1610.* Vol. 1. Düsseldorf: Druck und Verlag von L. Voss & Cie., Kgl. Hofbuchdruckern (1895).

Von der Mark, Sibylla, and Karl August Müller. *Briefe Der Herzogin Sibylla von Jülich-Cleve-Berg an Ihren Gemahl Johann Friedrich Den Grossmüthigen, Churfürsten Von Sachsen – Primary Source Edition.* Dresden and Leipzig: Gerhard Fleischer (1838).

Von Druffel, August. 'Vertrag von Chambord'. *Briefe und Akten zur Geschichte des sechzehnten Jahrhunderts mit besonderer Rücksicht auf Bayerns Fürstenhaus.* Vol. 3. Munich: Commission bei der königlichen Academie der Wissenschaften (1882).

Von Weinsberg, Hermann and Hoehlbaum, Konstantin. *Das Buch Weinsberg, Koelner Denkwürdigkeiten aus dem 16. Jahrhundert.* Leipzig: Verlag von Alphons Dürr (1886).

Wassenberch, Johann, and Arend Mihm. *Die Chronik Des Johann Wassenberch: Aufzeichnungen Eines Duisburger Geistlichen über Lokale Und Weltweite Ereignisse Vor 500 Jahren ; Nach d. Orig.-Hs. Hrsg., Ins Neuhochdt. übertr. u. Kommentiert.* Duisburg: Mercator-Verlag (1981).

Wriothesley, Charles; Lieut.-General Lord Henry H. M. Percy K.C.B., V.C., F.R.G.S.; and William Douglas Hamilton, F.S.A. *A Chronicle of England During the Reigns of the Tudors, from A.D. 1485 to 1559.* Vol. II. Westminster: J. B. Nichols and Sons, 25, Parliament Street (1876).

Add MS 17492. British Library.

Contemporary Transcript of the Will of Henry VIII, Palace of Westminster, 30 December 1546. The National Archives. E315/469.

Das Sächsische Stammbuch. Mscr.Dresd.R.3. https://digital.slub-dresden.de/werkansicht/dlf/56803/13.

Die Vermaehlung des Johann von Jülich, Bastardsohnes des Herzogs Wilhelm von Jülich-Bergmit Maria von Berge genannt Durffendal. AA 0031/Jülich-Berg II AA0031, No. 1931. Held by Landesarchiv Nordrhein-Wetfalen (1526-27).

New Year's Gift Roll of Queen Mary I, 1557, with wedding, christening and other gifts made by the Queen, 8 Feb 1556-10 Feb 1557. Add M.S. 62525, f.1r and f.6v, held by the British Library.

Policeysambt anderen Ordnungen unnd Edicten/des Durchleuchtigen hochgebornen Fürsten unnd Herren/ Herren Wilhelms Herzogen zu Gülich/ Cleue und Berge/Grauen zu der Marck und Rauensperg/ Herren zu Rauenstein etc. Im Jar Tausent/ Fünffhundert unnd Acht unnd Fünffzig aus gegangen. Cologne: Jacob Soter (1558).

Rechts Ordnung des durchleuchtigen hochgebornen Fursten und Herrn Wilhelms Herzogen zu Gulich, Cleve und Berg/Graven zu der Marck und Ravenßberg/Herrn zu Ravenstein/etc. Neben anderen Constitutionen/ Edicten und erklerungen etzlicher selle/wie es derenthalben in beiden irer F. G. Furstenthumben Gulich und Berg gehalten/geurtheilt und erkandt werden soll. Etzo aus gnedigem beuelch/des auch Durchleuchtigen hochgeborenen Fursten und Herrn/Herrn Johans Wilhelm Herzogen zu Gulich/Cleue und Berg Grauen zu der Marck/Rauenßberg und Mörtz/ Herrn zu Rauenstein/ etc. auffs new reuidirt/und mit etzlichen zugesetzten Edicten in truck bracht. Düsseldorf: Bernhardt Buntz (1606).

Römischer Künigklicher Maiestat Krönung zü Ach Geschehen. Author unknown. *Circa* 1520. Held by the Newberry Library, Chicago, Illinois. 'Royal Coronation of Maximilian I.' http://ghdi.ghidc.org/sub_document. cfm?document_id=3756.

Urkundliche Widerlegung Der Von Dem Ehmaligen Adel Der Lande Jülich, Kleve, Berg Und Mark Dem Fürsten Staatskanzler Berreichten Denkschrift. Rhenanien: Rheinpreussen (1819).

Vorzeichnus Sumarien wie sich die frohlickeit der furstlichen heymfahrt unsers gnedigen hernn herzog Johansfriderichen zu Sachsen etcet. zu getragen/ und nach gelegenheit ungeuerlich ergangen ist/Sontags Exaudi Torgaw einkkomen/ Anno domini M. D. XXvij. Wittenberg: Hans Lufft (1527).

Secondary Sources

'A Generous Queen'. *Once a Week: New Series.* Vol. IV, No. 97. London: Thomas Cooper & Co. (1870). Pp. 293-297. Also, Baring-Gould, Sabine. *A Book of the Rhein, from Cleve to Mainz.* London: Methuen & Co. (1906).

Ackermann, Erich. *Sagen des Mittelalters.* Koeln: Anaconda Verlag GmbH (2012).

Alberi, Eugenio, ed. *Relazioni degli ambasciatori veneti al senato.* Series I, Vol. II. Florence (1840).

Anna, Susanna, Frank M. Bischoff, and Heike Preuss. *Heirats Politik.* Stadtmuseum Düsseldorf. Düsseldorf: Droste Verlag GmbH (2015).

Aram, Bethany. *Juana the Mad: Sovereignty and Dynasty in Renaissance Europe.* Baltimore: John Hopkins UP (2005).

Arnade, Peter. *Beggars, Iconoclasts, & Civic Patriots: The Political Culture of the Dutch Revolt.* Ithaca: Cornell University Press (2008).

Bax, E. Belfort. 1894. *German Society at the End of the Middle Ages.* London: W. Swan Sonnenschein & Co. Reprinted in New York: Augustus M. Kelley Publishing (1967).

Bertzen, Nicole Simone (2022). *Mission Impossible? Ambassador Karl Harst, Anne of Cleves and their Struggles to Secure the Strategic Alliance between Cleves and England.* PhD thesis, University of Kent. (doi:10.22024/ UniKent/01.02.95545)

Binz, Carl. 'Solenander, Reiner'. *Allgemeine Deutsche Biographie*. Vol. 34. Historischen Kommission bei der Bayerischen Akademie der Wissenschaften (1892).

Blickle, Peter, Thomas A. Brady, Jr. (Translator) and H. C. Erik Midelfort (Translator). *The Revolution of 1525: The German Peasants' War from a New Perspective*. Baltimore, MD: John Hopkins University Press (1985).

Bouterwerk, Karl Wilhelm and William Crecelius. 1867. 'Anna von Cleve, Gehmahlin Heinrichs VIII.' Part I. Vol. 4. *Zeitschrift des Bergischen Geschichtsvereins*. Elderfeld: Sam Lucas.

Bouterwerk, Karl Wilhelm, 'Anna von Cleve, Gehmahlin Heinrichs VIII., Koenig von England.' Part II. Vol. 6. *Zeitschrift des Bergischen Geschichtsvereins*. Elderfeld: Sam Lucas (1869).

Bouterwerk, Karl Wilhelm and William Crecelius. 1869. 'Anna von Cleve, Gemahlin Heinrichs VIII., Königs von England. Zweiter Theil.' Vol. 6. *Zeitschrift des Bergischen Geschichtsvereins*. Elderfeld: Sam Lucas (1867).

Bouterwerk, Karl Wilhelm and William Crecelius. 1871. 'Sibylla, Kurfürstin von Sachsen.' Vol. 7. *Zeitschrift des Bergischen Geschichtsvereins*. Elberfeld: Sam Lucas.

Brakebusch, Börries, Restaurierungsbericht: Unbek. Maler, 1528, 'Rosenkranztriptychon.' Düsseldorf (2013).

Britannica, T. Editors of Encyclopaedia. 'Year of Jubilee.' *Encyclopedia Britannica*, December 3, 2019. https://www.britannica.com/topic/Year-of-Jubilee.

Bryce, James. *The Holy Roman Empire*. 4th ed. London (1904).

Crecelius, Wilhelm. 1887. 'Der Gelderische Erbfolgestreit Zwischen Kaiser Karl V. und Herzog Wilhelm von Jülich, Berg, und Cleve (1538 -1543).' Vol. 23. *Zeitschrift des Bergischen Geschichtsverein*. Elderfeld: Sam Lucas.

Cooke, Joseph. 1679. *The First Part of the History of the Reformation*. London: Richard Chiswell (1679).

Crowther-Heyck, Kathleen. 'Be Fruitful and Multiply: Genesis and Generation in Reformation Germany.' *Renaissance Quarterly 55*, no. 3 (2002): 904-35.

Darsie, Heather R. *Anna, Duchess of Cleves: The King's 'Beloved Sister'*. Stroud: Amberley Publishing (2019).

De Ruble, Alphonse. *Le Mariage de Jeanne d'Albret*. Paris: Adolphe Labitte (1877).

Die Rheinprovinz der preussischen Monarchie, oder Beschreibung der systematischen Eintheilung in Regierungsbezirke, Kreise, Bürgermeistereien und Honnschaften, so wie der Städte, Flecken, Dörfer, einzelner Etablissements, mit Angabe der Einwohnerzahl, Gewerbe, Merkwürdigkeiten, Anstalten u. s. w.' Ein historisch-geographisch-statistisches Handbuch zum Gebrauch aller Stände. Aus den neuesten Quellen geschöpft und zusammengestellt von mehreren Gelehrten. Vol. I. Düsseldorf (1833).

Diedenhoffen, Wilhelm. *Die Italienreise des Prinzen Karlfriedrich von Jülich-Kleve-Berg 1574/75*. Kleve: Reintjes, Graphischer Betrieb (2008).

Diefendorf, Barbara B. *Beneath the Cross Catholics and Huguenots in Sixteenth-Century Paris*. New York: Oxford University Press (1991).

Eichelmann, Wolfgang. *Gedanken und Betrachtungen zu Münzen und Medaillen des Hauses Brabant*. Münster: Verlagshaus Monsenstein und Vannerdat OHG Münster (2010).

Ennen, Leonhard. 'Heresbach, Konrad'. *Allgemeine Deutsche Biographie.* Vol. 12. Historischen Kommission bei der Bayerischen Akademie der Wissenschaften (1880).

Erdmann, Louis Otto. *The Printed Festival Book: A Study of Northern Continental Festivals in the Late Sixteenth Century.* Columbus: Ohio State University (1967).

Fimpeler-Philippen, Annette and Sonja Schürmann. 1999. *Das Schloss in Düsseldorf.* Düsseldorf: Droste Verlag (1999).

Flathe, Heinrich Theodor. 'Friedrich III. der Weise, Kurfürst von Sachsen'. Vol. 7. Historischen Kommission bei der Bayerischen Akademie der Wissenschaften (1878).

Flathe, Heinrich Theodor. 'Georg, Herzog von Sachsen'. *Allgemeine Deutsche Biographie.* Vol. 8. Historischen Kommission bei der Bayerischen Akademie der Wissenschaften (1878).

Flathe, Heinrich Theodor. 'Heinrich der Fromme, Herzog zu Sachsen'. *Allgemeine Deutsche Biographie.* Vol. 11. Historischen Kommission bei der Bayerischen Akademie der Wissenschaften (1880).

Flathe, Heinrich Theodor. 'Johann der Bestaendige, Kurfürst von Sachsen'. *Allgemeine Deutsche Biographie.* Vol. 14. Historischen Kommission bei der Bayerischen Akademie der Wissenschaften (1881).

Flathe, Heinrich Theodor. 'Johann Friedrich (Kurfürst von Sachsen)'. *Allgemeine Deutsche Biographie.* Vol. 14. Historischen Kommission bei der Bayerischen Akademie der Wissenschaften (1881).

Friedensburg, Walter. 'Philipp I., Landgraf von Hessen'. *Allgemeine Deutsche Biographie.* Vol. 25. Historischen Kommission bei der Bayerischen Akademie der Wissenschaften (1887).

Fuchs, Erwin. *Wilhelm V.: Glück und Unglück des Herzogtums Jülich-Kleve-Berg.* Jülich: Verlag des Jülicher Geschichtsvereins (1993).

Gehrt, Daniel and Vera von der Osten-Sacken. *Fürstinnen und Konfession: Beträge hochadliger Frauen zur Religionspolitik und Bekenntnisbildung.* Göttingen: Vandenhoeck & Ruprecht (2015).

Glezerman, Abraham and Michael Harsgor. *Cleve—ein unerfülltes Schicksal: Aufstieg, Rückzug und Verfall eines Territorialstaates.* Berlin: Duncker & Humboldt (1985).

Hale, J. R. *War and Society in Renaissance Europe 1450–1620.* Guernsey: The Guernsey Press Company Ltd (1985).

Harless, Woldemar. 'Crüser, Hermann'. *Allgemeine Deutsche Biographie.* Vol. 4. Historischen Kommission bei der Bayerischen Akademie der Wissenschaften (1876).

Harless, Woldemar. 'Harst, Karl'. *Allgemeine Deutsche Biographie.* Vol. 10. Historischen Kommission bei der Bayerischen Akademie der Wissenschaften (1879).

Harless, Woldemar. 'Bericht über die Bestattung der Herzogin Maria von Jülich-Cleve-Berg (1582)'. *Zeitschrift des Bergischen Geschichtsverein.* Vol. 33 ½. Elberfeld: B. Hartmann (1897).

Harless, Woldemar. 'Johann II. (Herzog von Kleve-Mark)' *Allgemeine Deutsche Biographie.* Vol. 14. Historischen Kommission bei der Bayerischen Akademie der Wissenschaften (1881).

Harless, Woldemar. 'Johann III. (Herzog von Jülich-Kleve-Berg)'. *Allgemeine Deutsche Biographie.* Vol. 14. Historischen Kommission bei der Bayerischen Akademie der Wissenschaften (1881).

Harless, Woldemar. 'Olisleger, Heinrich Bars genannt'. *Allgemeine Deutsche Biographie.* Vol. 24. Historischen Kommission bei der Bayerischen Akademie der Wissenschaften (1887).

Harless, Woldemar. 'Wilhelm V., Herzog von Jülich'. *Allgemeine Deutsche Biographie.* Vol. 43. Historischen Kommission bei der Bayerischen Akademie der Wissenschaften (1898).

Harless, Woldemar. ,Aktenstünde, betreffend die Bestattung der Herzogin Maria von Jülich-Cleve-Berg in Cleve (1582). Vol. 23. *Zeitschrift des Bergischen Geschichtsvereins.* Elberfeld: B Hartmann (1897).

Hassel, P., Ein Bericht über das 'langen Landtag' zu Düsseldorf. 1591.' Vol. 5. *Zeitschrift des Bergischen Geschichtsvereins.* Elberfeld: Sam Lucas (1868-1870).

Haumann, Heiko and Hans Schadek (Hrsg.): *Geschichte der Stadt Freiburg im Breisgau.* Vol. 1. Stuttgart: Konrad Theiss Verlag GmbH (2001).

Havemann, Wilhelm. *Geschichte der Lande Braunschweig und Lüneburg für Schule und Haus, Bände 1-2.* Vol. 1. Lüneburg: Verlag von Herold und Wahlstab (1837)

Heidrich, Paul. *Beiträge zur deutschen Territorial- u. Stadtgeschichte.* Series I, Book 1: 'Der geldrische Erbfolgestreit 1537-1543.' Kassel: Max Brunneman (1896).

Heidrich, Dr. Paul. *Der Geldrische Erbfolgestreit (1537-1543).* Kassel: Max Brunneman.

Hirzel, Hans Caspar. *Lese-Buch für das Frauenzimmer über die Hebammenkunst.* Zürich: Johann Caspar Füssli (1784).

Hoche, Richard. 'Pighius, Stephan'. *Allgemeine Deutsche Biographie.* Vol. 26. Historischen Kommission bei der Bayerischen Akademie der Wissenschaften (1888).

Hurwich, Judith J. 'Marriage Strategy among the German Nobility, 1400-1699.' *The Journal of Interdisciplinary History* 29, no. 2 (1998): 169-95.

Hurwich, Judith J. 'Inheritance Practices in Early Modern Germany.' *The Journal of Interdisciplinary History* 23, no. 4 (1993): 699-718.

Ives, Eric. *The Reformation Experience: Living through the Turbulent Sixteenth Century.* Lion Books (2012).

Jahn, Johann Gottlieb. *Geschichte des Schmalkaldischen Krieges: eine reformationsgeschichtliche Denkschrift zur Errinerung an das, für die ganze damalige protestantische Kirche verhängnissvolle Jahrzehend von 1537 bis 1547.* Leipzig: Mintzel in Hof (1837).

Küch, Friedrich. 'Die Lande Jülich und Berg waehrend der Belagerung von Bonn 1588.' Vol. 30. *Zeitschrift des Bergischen Geschichtsvereins.* Elberfeld: B. Hartmann (1894).

Kühn Norbert, and Stefanie Schild. *Schloss Burg an Der Wupper.* Köln: Rheinischer Verein für Denkmalpflege und Landschaftsschutz (2015).

Land im Mittelpunkt der Maechte: Die Herzogtümer Jülich-Kleve-Berg. Kleve: Boss-Verlag (1984).

Leppin, Volker, Georg Schmidt, and Sabine Wefers. *Johann Friedrich I. – Der Lutherische Kurfürst.* Gütersloh: Gütersloher Verlagshaus (2006).

Lossen, Max. 'Die Verheiratung der Markgräfin Jakobe von Baden mit Herzog Johann Wilhelm von Jülich-Cleve-Berg.' *Sitzungsberichte der philosophisch-philologischen und der historischen Classe der k. b. Akademie der Wissenschaften zu München.* Munich: Verlag der K. Akademie (1896).

Marquardt, Bernd. 'Imperial Ban'. *Encyclopedia of Early Modern History Online.* (2015) https://referenceworks.brillonline.com/entries/encyclopedia-of-early-modern-history-online/*-SIM_026352.

Maurenbrecher, Wilhelm. 'Ferdinand I., deutscher Kaiser'. *Allgemeine Deutsche Biographie.* Vol. 6. Historischen Kommission bei der Bayerischen Akademie der Wissenschaften (1877).

Maurenbrecher, Wilhelm. 'Karl V., deustcher Kaiser'. *Allgemeine Deutsche Biographie.* Vol. 15. Historischen Kommission bei der Bayerischen Akademie der Wissenschaften (1882).

Maurenbrecher, Wilhelm. 'Moritz, Herzog und Kurfürst von Sachsen'. *Allgemeine Deutsche Biographie.* Vol. 22. Historischen Kommission bei der Bayerischen Akademie der Wissenschaften (1885).

Midelfort, H. C. Erik. *Mad Princes of Renaissance Germany.* Charlottesville: University of Virginia Press (1996).

Moyle, Franny. *The King's Painter: The Life and Times of Hans Holbein.* London: Head of Zeus (2020).

Müller, Albert. *Die Beziehungen zwischen Heinrichs VIII zu Anna von Cleve.* Calw: A. Oelschläger'schenBuchdruckerei (1907).

Münster-Schröer, Erika. *Hexenverfolgung und Kriminalitaet: Jülich-Kleve-Berg in der Frühen Neuzeit.* Essen: Klartext Verlag (2017).

Nichols, John Gough (ed.). *Chronicle of Queen Jane and of Two Years of Queen Mary.* The Camden Society; Marilee Hanson.

Ollman-Kösling, Heinz. *Der Erbfolgstreit um Jülich-Kleve (1609-1610); ein Vorspiel zum Dreißigjährigen Krieg.* Regensburg: Roderer (1996).

Paravicini, Werner, Jan Hirschbiegel, and Jörg Wettlaufer. 'Höfe Und Residenzen Im spätmittelalterlichen Reich. Ein Dynastisch-Topographisches Handbuch.' *Residenzenforschung.* Ostfildern: Jan Thorbecke Verlag (2003).

Paravinci, Werner, Jan Hirschbiegel, and Jörg Wettlaufer. 'Höfe und Residenzen im spätmittelalterlichen Reich. Bilder und Begriffe.' *Residenzforschung 15 II.* Vols. 1 and 2. Ostfildern: Jan Thorbecke Verlag (2005).

Parrott, David. *The Business of War.* Cambridge: University Press (2012).

Pauls, E. 'Zur Geschichte der Krankheit des Herzogs Johann Wilhelm von Jülich-Cleve-Berg (d. 1609). Vol. 23. *Zeitschrift des Bergischen Geschichtsvereins.* Elberfeld: B. Hartmann (1897).

Pleysier, Albert. *Henry VIII and the Anabaptists.* Lanham: University Press of America, Inc (2014).

Pollmann, Judith. 'Countering the Reformation in France and the Netherlands: Clerical Leadership and Catholic Violence 1560-1585.' *Past & Present,* no. 190 (2006).

Reymann, Kristina. *Schloss Jülich: Geschichte und kunstgeschichtliche Beschreibung.* Munich: GRIN Verlag GmbH (2013).

Rexroth, Frank. *Deutsche Geschichte im Mittelalter.* Munich: Verlag C. H. Beck (2005).

Bibliography

Rihartz, Hermann J. *Basilika St. Lambertus Düsseldorf-Altstadt*. Lindenberg: Kunstverl. Fink (2004).

Roelker, Nancy Lyman. 1968. *Queen of Navarre, Jeanne DAlbret: 1528–1572*. Cambridge, Massachusetts: The Belknap Press of Harvard University Press.

Rogge, Bernhard F. W. *Johann Friedrich, Kurfürst von Sachsen, gennant der Grossmütige*. Halle: Verlag von Eugen Strien (1902).

Schmidt, Georg. *Der Dreissigjaehrige Krieg*. Munich: Verlag C. H. Beck, oHG (1995).

Schnütgen, Wiltrud. *Literatur am Klevischen Hof: Vom Hohen Mittelalter bis zur frühen Neuzeit*. Cleves: Boss-Verlag (1990).

Schnütgen, Wiltrud. ‚Von scharfen Degen und frivolen Liedern – die Herzogstochter Amalia von Kleve-Jülich-Berg'. *Lesebuch zur Geschichte der Klever Frauen*. Kleve: Projektgruppe Frauengeschichte der VHS Kleve (2004).

Schumacher, Karl. ‚Amalie von Jülich-Cleve-Berg, die angebliche Liedersammlerin'. *Düsseldorfer Jahrbuch*. Vol.26. Beitraege zur Geschichte des Niederrheins (1914).

Stieve, Felix. 'Johann Wilhelm, Herzog von Jülich-Kleve-Berg'. *Allgemeine Deutsche Biographie*. Vol. 14. Historischen Kommission bei der Bayerischen Akademie der Wissenschaften (1881).

Stollberg-Rilinger, Barbara. *Das Heilige Römische Reich Deutscher Nation: Vom Ende Des Mittelalters Bis 1806*. München: C.H. Beck (2013).

Stöve, Eckehard. 'Via media. Humanistischer Traum oder kirchenpolitische Chance? Zur Religionspolitik der vereinigten Herzogtümer Jülich-Kleve-Berg im 16. Jahrhundert'. *Monatshefte für Evangelische Kirchengeschichte des Rheinlandes*. Vol. 39. (1990)

Taylor, Melanie V. 'A Portrait of Anna, Duchess of Cleves: The King's Beloved Sister'. https://melanievtaylor.co.uk/2021/06/08/a-portrait-of-anna-duchess-of-cleves-the-kings-beloved-sister/

Ulmann, Heinrich. 'Maximilian I., roemischer Koenig und Kaiser'. Vol. 20. Historischen Kommission bei der Bayerischen Akademie der Wissenschaften (1884).

Weigelt, Sylvia. *Sibylle von Kleve: Cranachs schoenes Modell*. Weimar and Eisenach: Wartburg Verlag GmbH (2012).

Wülcker, Ernst. 'Johann Friedrich [der Mittlere], Herzog zu Sachsen'. *Allgemeine Deutsche Biographie*. Vol. 14. Historischen Kommission bei der Bayerischen Akademie der Wissenschaften (1881).

Wülcker, Ernst. 'Johann Wilhelm (Herzog von Sachsen-Weimar)'. *Allgemeine Deutsche Biographie*. Vol. 14. Historischen Kommission bei der Bayerischen Akademie der Wissenschaften (1881).

Wülcker, Ernst. 'Johann Friedrich der Jüngere'. *Allgemeine Deutsche Biographie*. Vol. 14. Historischen Kommission bei der Bayerischen Akademie der Wissenschaften (1881).

Wünsch, Heidemarie. *Agnes von Mansfeld: Erzbischofin in Koeln – Im Jahr 1583*. http://www.frauen-und-reformation.de/?s=bio&id=91.

Index